Shojo Beat

Crimson Hero

Story & Art by
MITSUBA TAKANASHI

7

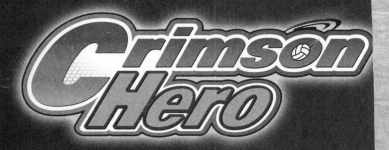

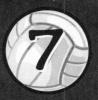

CONTENTS

STORY THUS FAR

Nobara Sumiyoshi is a first-year student in high school who lives for her one passion, volleyball. She's the successor to "Seiryu," the high-class ryotei restaurant her family runs, but she enrolled in Crimson Field High School expressly to play volleyball.

Rebelling against her interfering mother, Nobara begins living and working in Crimson Dorm, the dorm for the boys' volleyball recruits. There she meets Yushin. He provides her with support as she deals with family troubles and quarrels within the girls' volleyball team. Before she knows it, she has fallen in love.

Provoked by newcomer Kanako, a big Yushin fan, Nobara finds herself professing her feelings for Yushin in front of everyone. But Yushin rejects her, and Haibuki, who likes Nobara, starts making advances instead! In the midst of all this, Coach Shima arrives to start training the girls' team. She begins to whip the mentally unprepared girls into shape!! Will they survive her training?

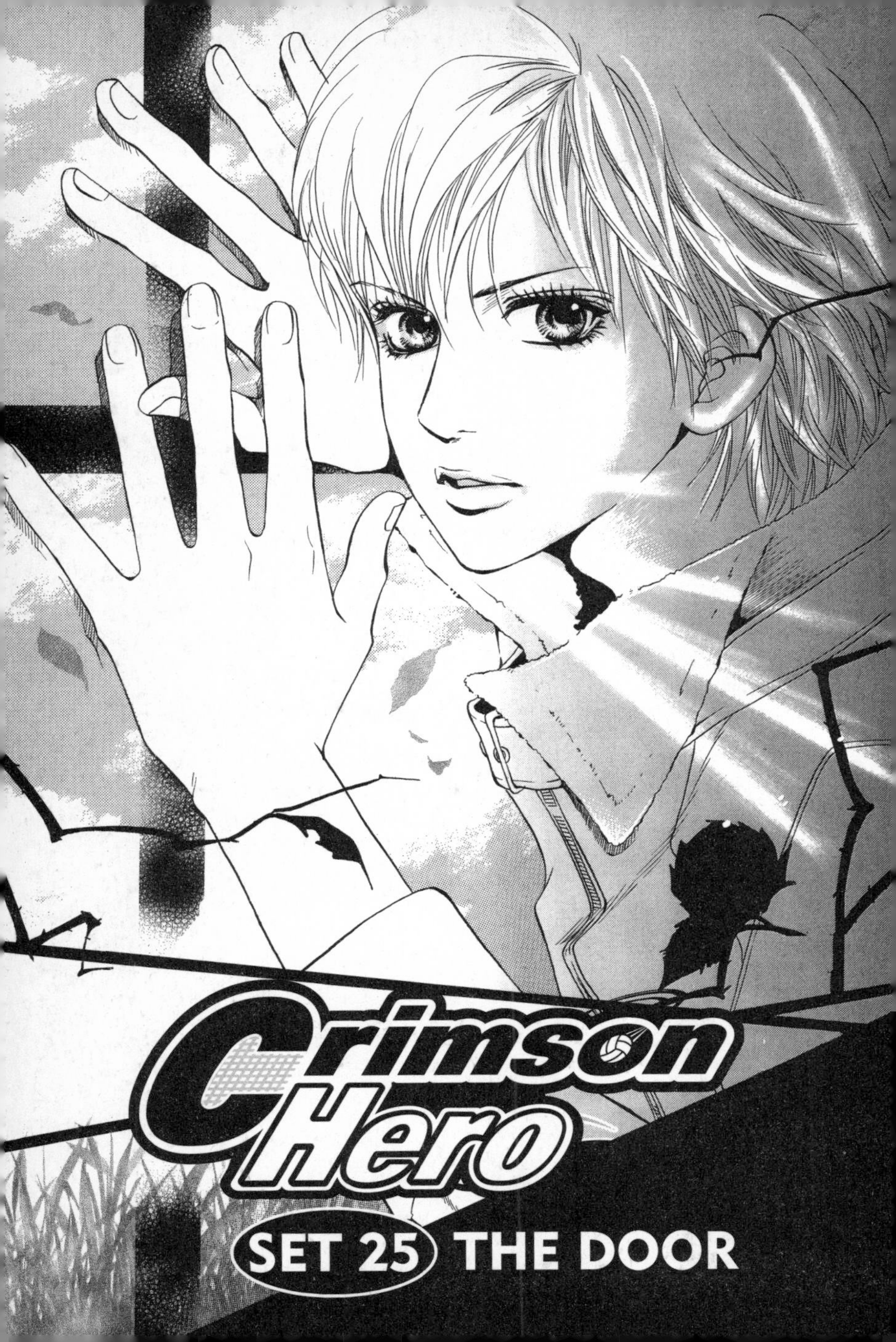
Crimson Hero
SET 25 THE DOOR

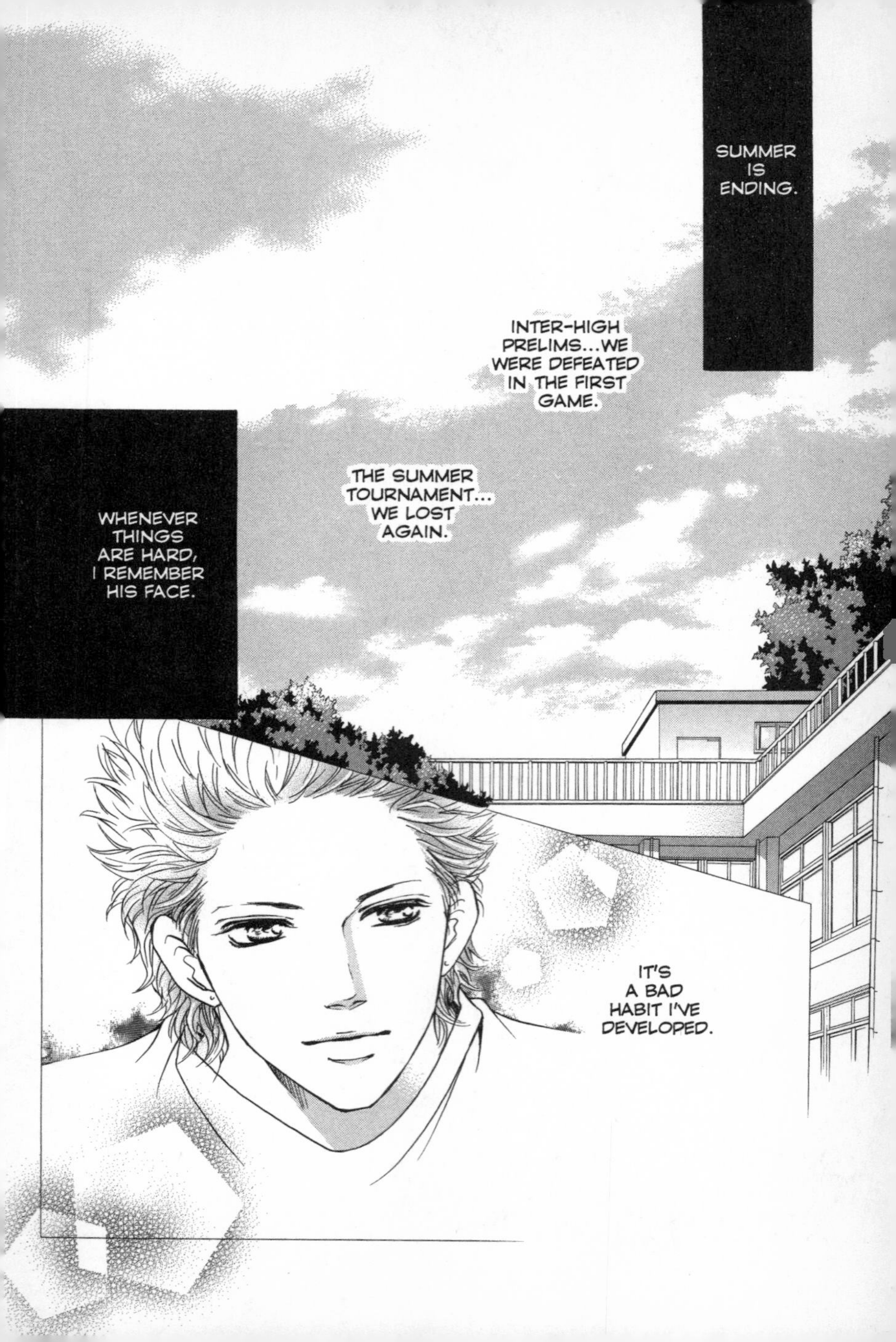
SUMMER IS ENDING.
INTER-HIGH PRELIMS...WE WERE DEFEATED IN THE FIRST GAME.
THE SUMMER TOURNAMENT... WE LOST AGAIN.
WHENEVER THINGS ARE HARD, I REMEMBER HIS FACE.
IT'S A BAD HABIT I'VE DEVELOPED.

GOOD WORK TODAY!

YEAH, YOU TOO!

EMERGENCY EXIT
NOT LEAVE CYCLES BY HIS GATE.

MY, MY. FIGHTING IN THE RANKS AGAIN?

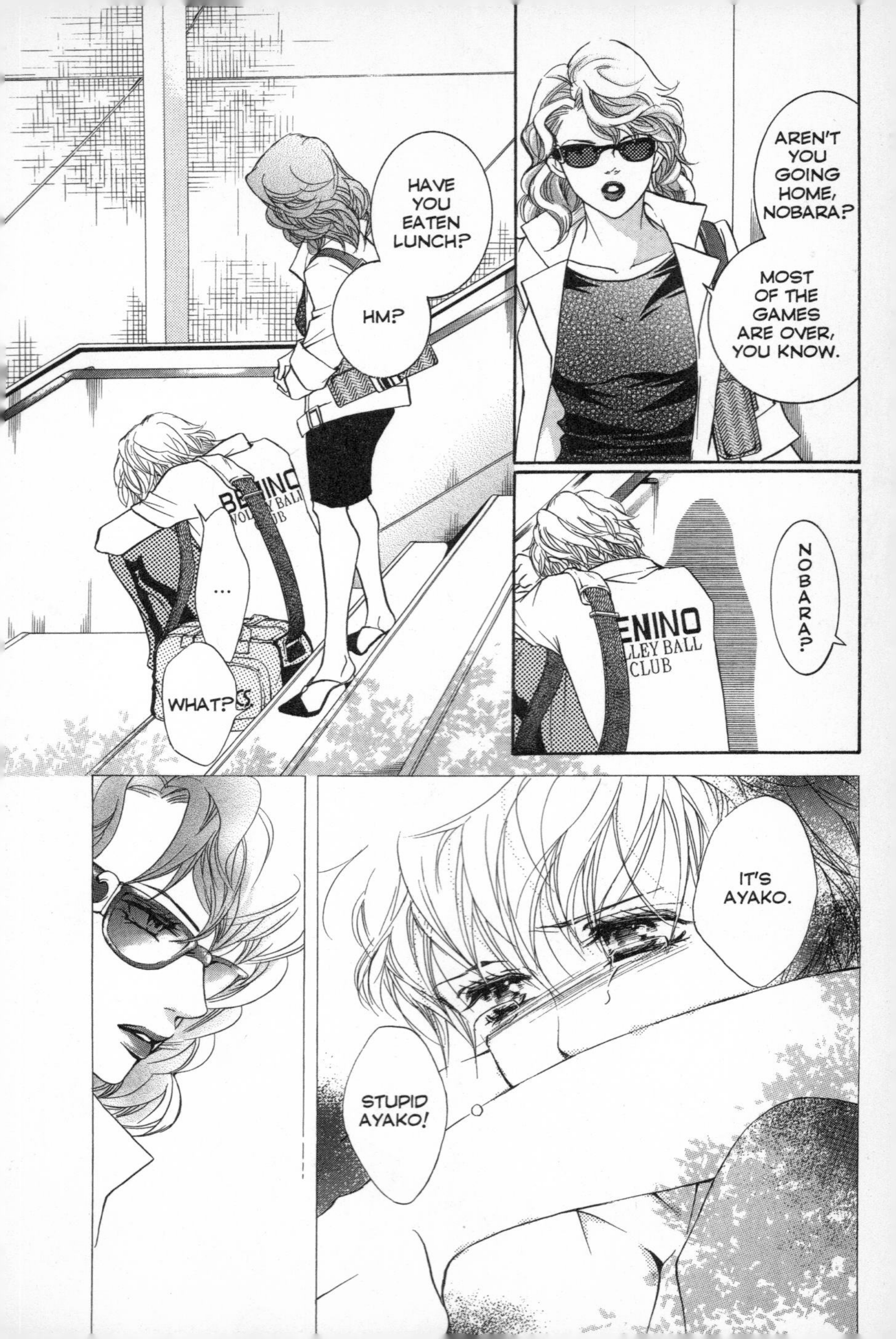
AREN'T YOU GOING HOME, NOBARA?
MOST OF THE GAMES ARE OVER, YOU KNOW.
NOBARA?
HAVE YOU EATEN LUNCH?
HM?
...
WHAT?
BENINO VOLLEY BALL CLUB
IT'S AYAKO.
STUPID AYAKO!

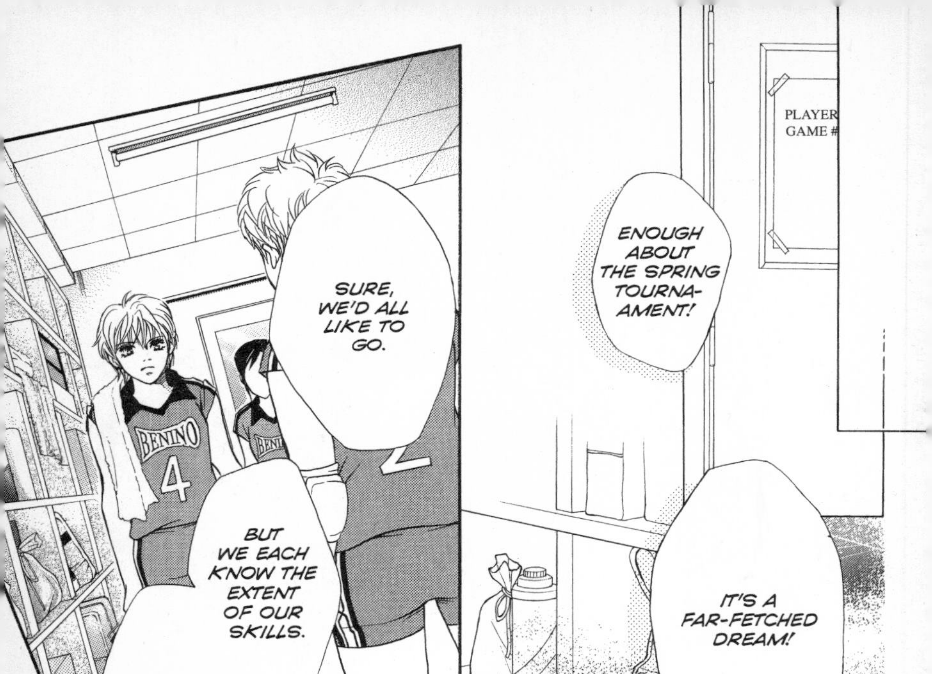
PLAYER
GAME #
ENOUGH ABOUT THE SPRING TOURNAMENT!
IT'S A FAR-FETCHED DREAM!
SURE, WE'D ALL LIKE TO GO.
BUT WE EACH KNOW THE EXTENT OF OUR SKILLS.
WE'RE NOT LIKE YOU, NOBARA.
BENINO 4

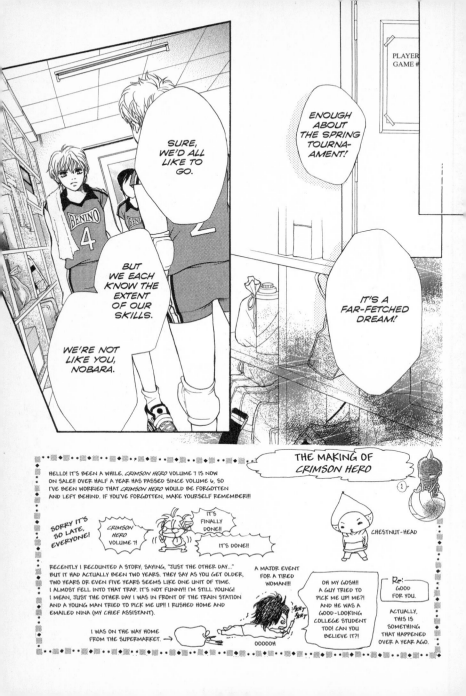

THE MAKING OF CRIMSON HERO

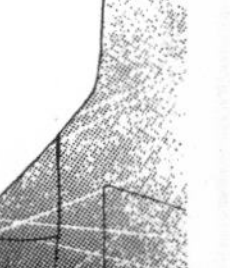
1

HELLO! IT'S BEEN A WHILE. *CRIMSON HERO* VOLUME 7 IS NOW ON SALE!! OVER HALF A YEAR HAS PASSED SINCE VOLUME 6, SO I'VE BEEN WORRIED THAT *CRIMSON HERO* WOULD BE FORGOTTEN AND LEFT BEHIND. IF YOU'VE FORGOTTEN, MAKE YOURSELF REMEMBER!!!

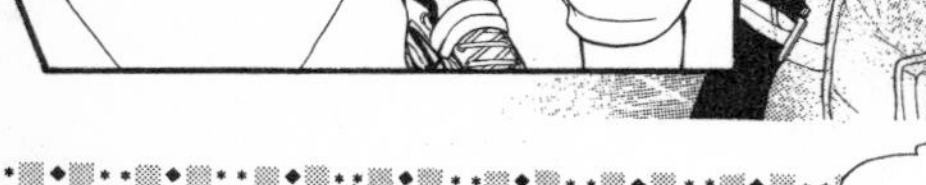
SORRY IT'S SO LATE, EVERYONE!
CRIMSON HERO VOLUME 7!
IT'S FINALLY DONE!!
IT'S DONE!!

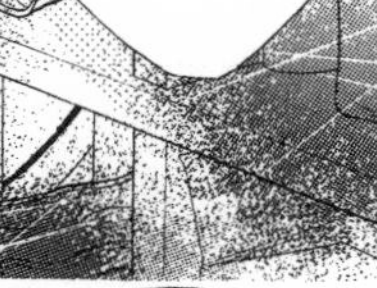
CHESTNUT-HEAD

RECENTLY I RECOUNTED A STORY, SAYING, "JUST THE OTHER DAY..." BUT IT HAD ACTUALLY BEEN TWO YEARS. THEY SAY AS YOU GET OLDER, TWO YEARS OR EVEN FIVE YEARS SEEMS LIKE ONE UNIT OF TIME. I ALMOST FELL INTO THAT TRAP. IT'S NOT FUNNY!! I'M STILL YOUNG! I MEAN, JUST THE OTHER DAY I WAS IN FRONT OF THE TRAIN STATION AND A YOUNG MAN TRIED TO PICK ME UP!! I RUSHED HOME AND EMAILED NINA (MY CHIEF ASSISTANT).

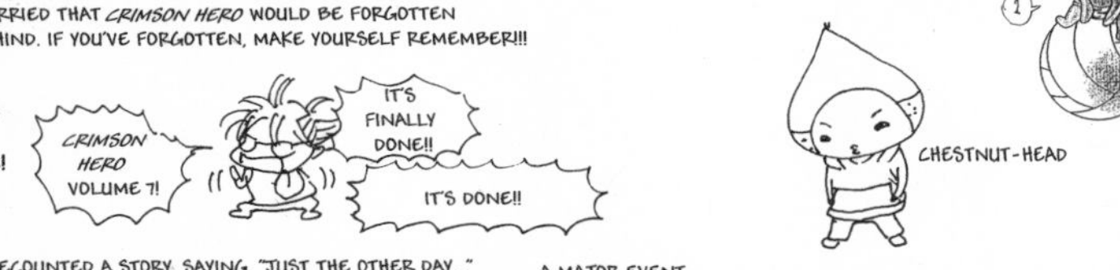
A MAJOR EVENT FOR A TIRED WOMAN!!!
OH MY GOSH!! A GUY TRIED TO PICK ME UP! ME?! AND HE WAS A GOOD-LOOKING COLLEGE STUDENT TOO! CAN YOU BELIEVE IT?!
Re: GOOD FOR YOU.
ACTUALLY, THIS IS SOMETHING THAT HAPPENED OVER A YEAR AGO.
SKRT SKRT
I WAS ON THE WAY HOME FROM THE SUPERMARKET.
OOOOOH

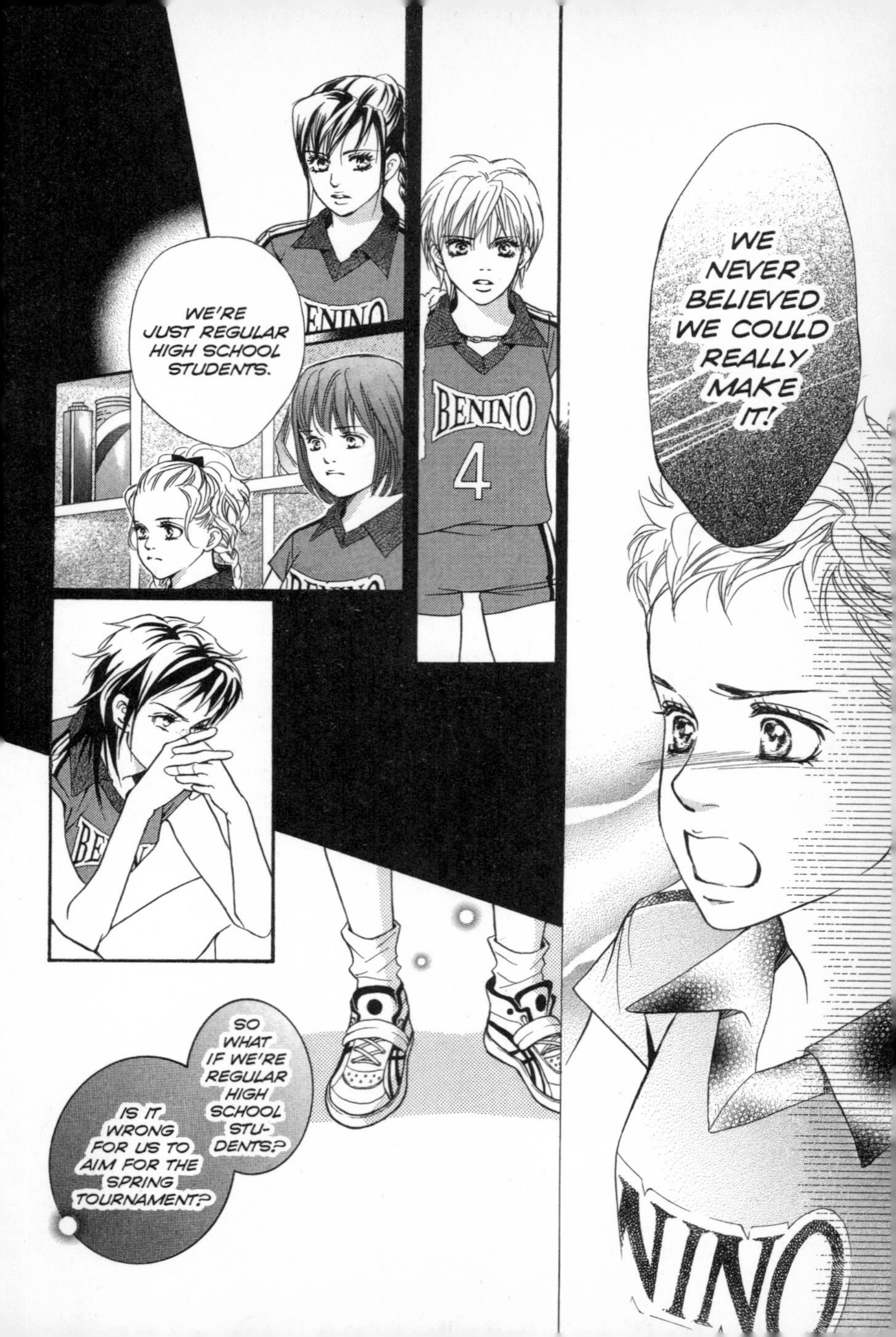
WE NEVER BELIEVED WE COULD REALLY MAKE IT!
WE'RE JUST REGULAR HIGH SCHOOL STUDENTS.
SO WHAT IF WE'RE REGULAR HIGH SCHOOL STU-DENTS?
IS IT WRONG FOR US TO AIM FOR THE SPRING TOURNAMENT?

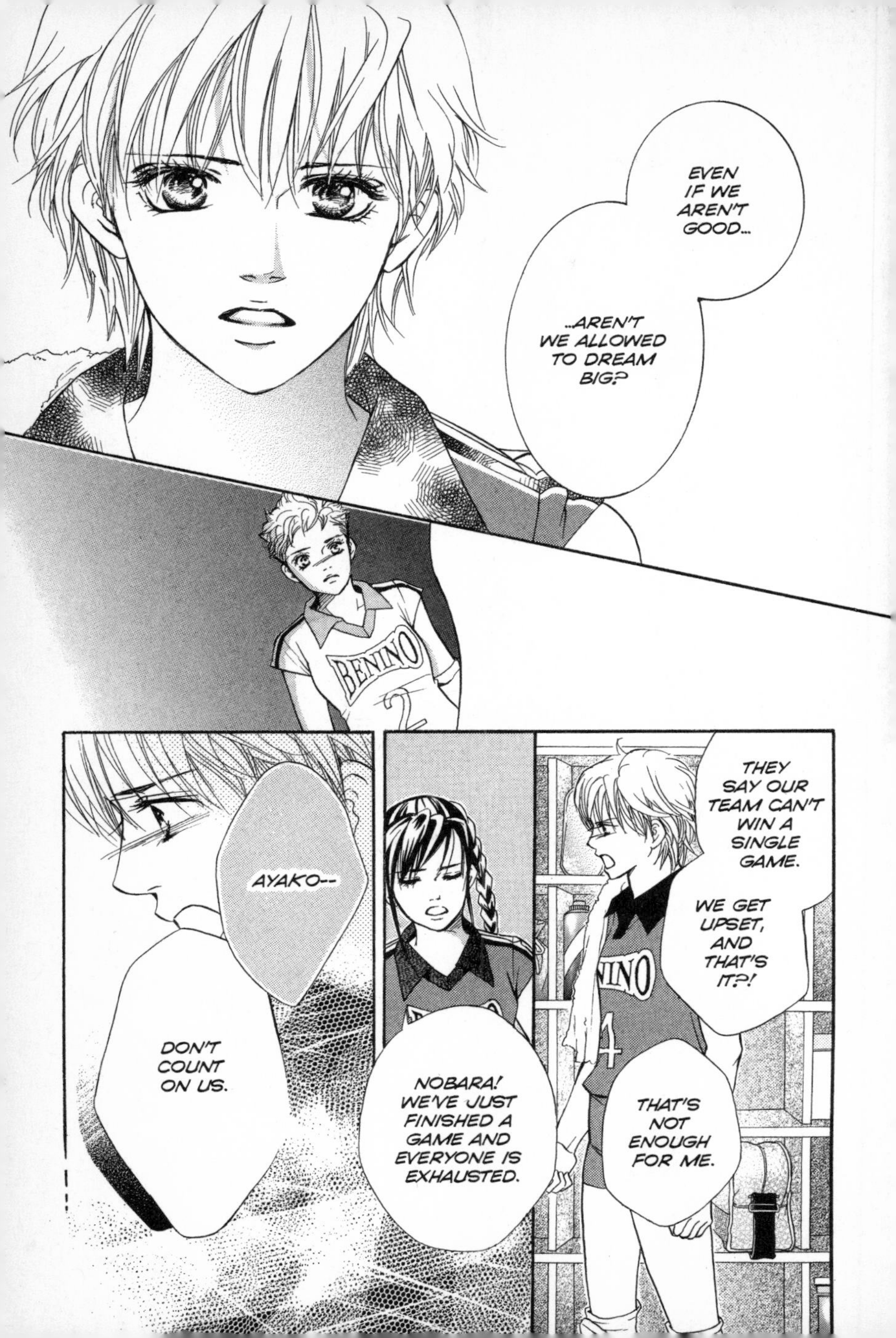
EVEN IF WE AREN'T GOOD...
...AREN'T WE ALLOWED TO DREAM BIG?
BENINO
THEY SAY OUR TEAM CAN'T WIN A SINGLE GAME.
WE GET UPSET, AND THAT'S IT?!
THAT'S NOT ENOUGH FOR ME.
NOBARA! WE'VE JUST FINISHED A GAME AND EVERYONE IS EXHAUSTED.
AYAKO--
DON'T COUNT ON US.

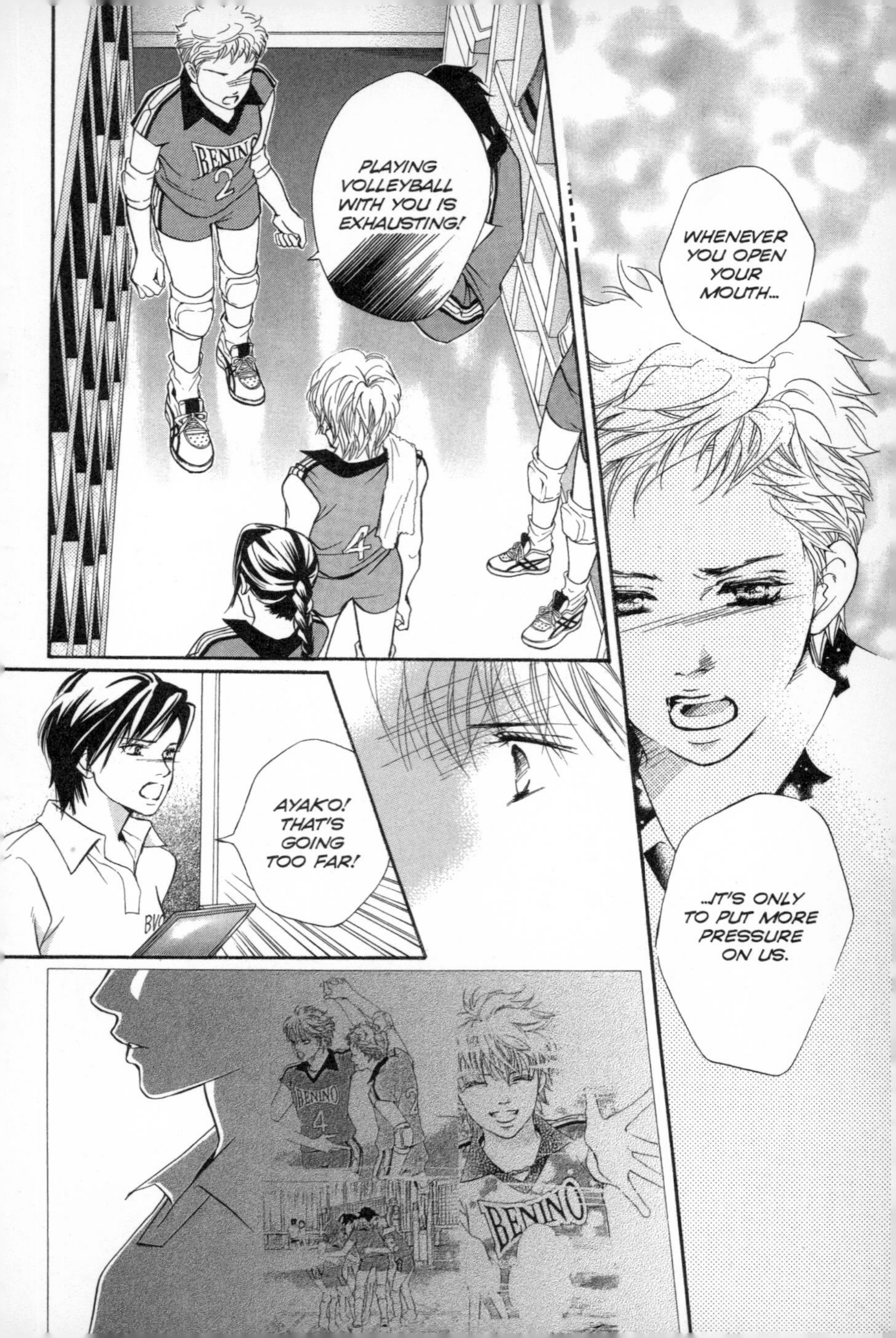
WHENEVER YOU OPEN YOUR MOUTH...
...IT'S ONLY TO PUT MORE PRESSURE ON US.
PLAYING VOLLEYBALL WITH YOU IS EXHAUSTING!
AYAKO! THAT'S GOING TOO FAR!

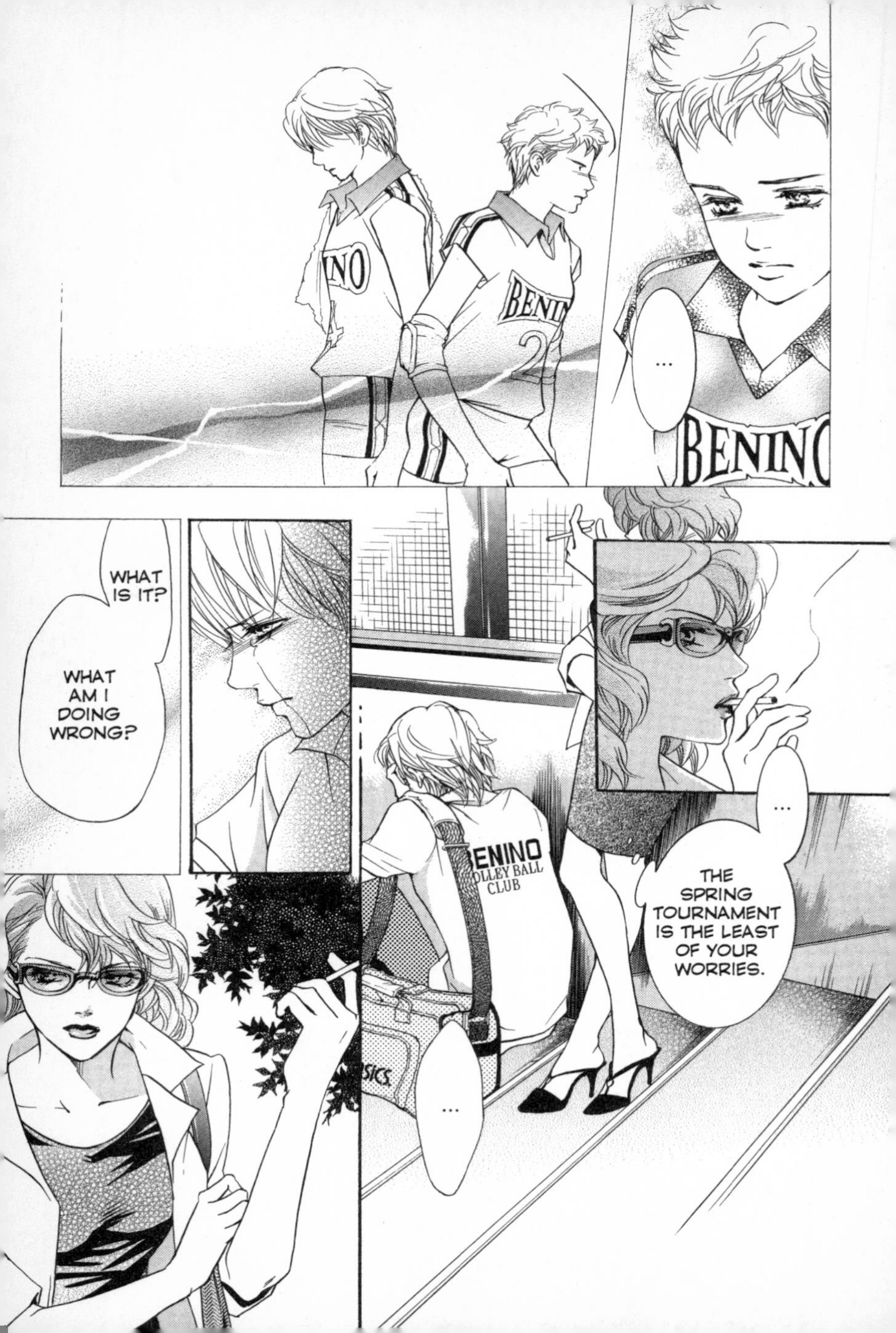
...
...
THE SPRING TOURNAMENT IS THE LEAST OF YOUR WORRIES.
...
WHAT IS IT?
WHAT AM I DOING WRONG?

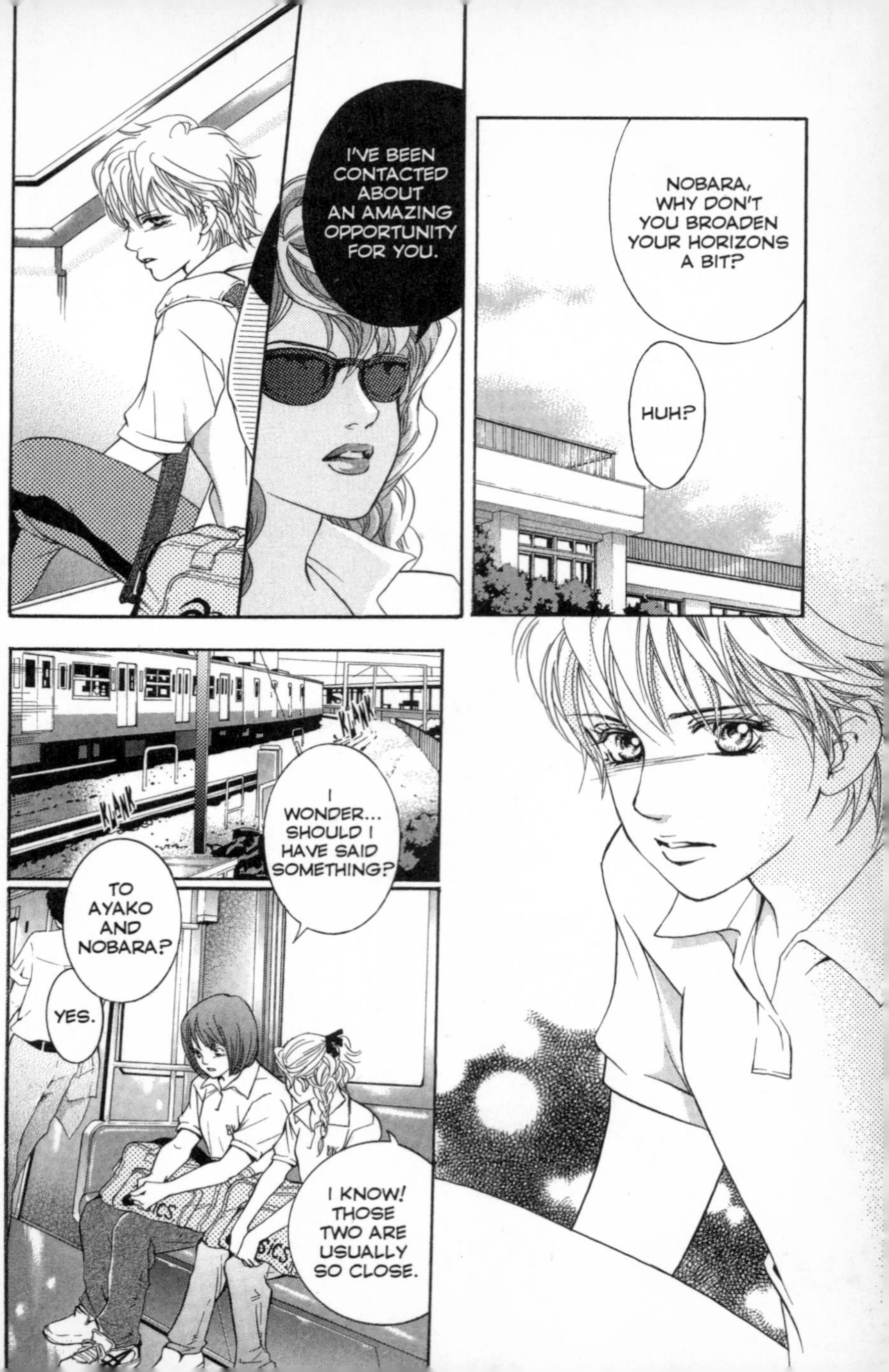
NOBARA, WHY DON'T YOU BROADEN YOUR HORIZONS A BIT?
HUH?
I'VE BEEN CONTACTED ABOUT AN AMAZING OPPORTUNITY FOR YOU.
KLANK
KLANK
I WONDER... SHOULD I HAVE SAID SOMETHING?
TO AYAKO AND NOBARA?
YES.
I KNOW! THOSE TWO ARE USUALLY SO CLOSE.

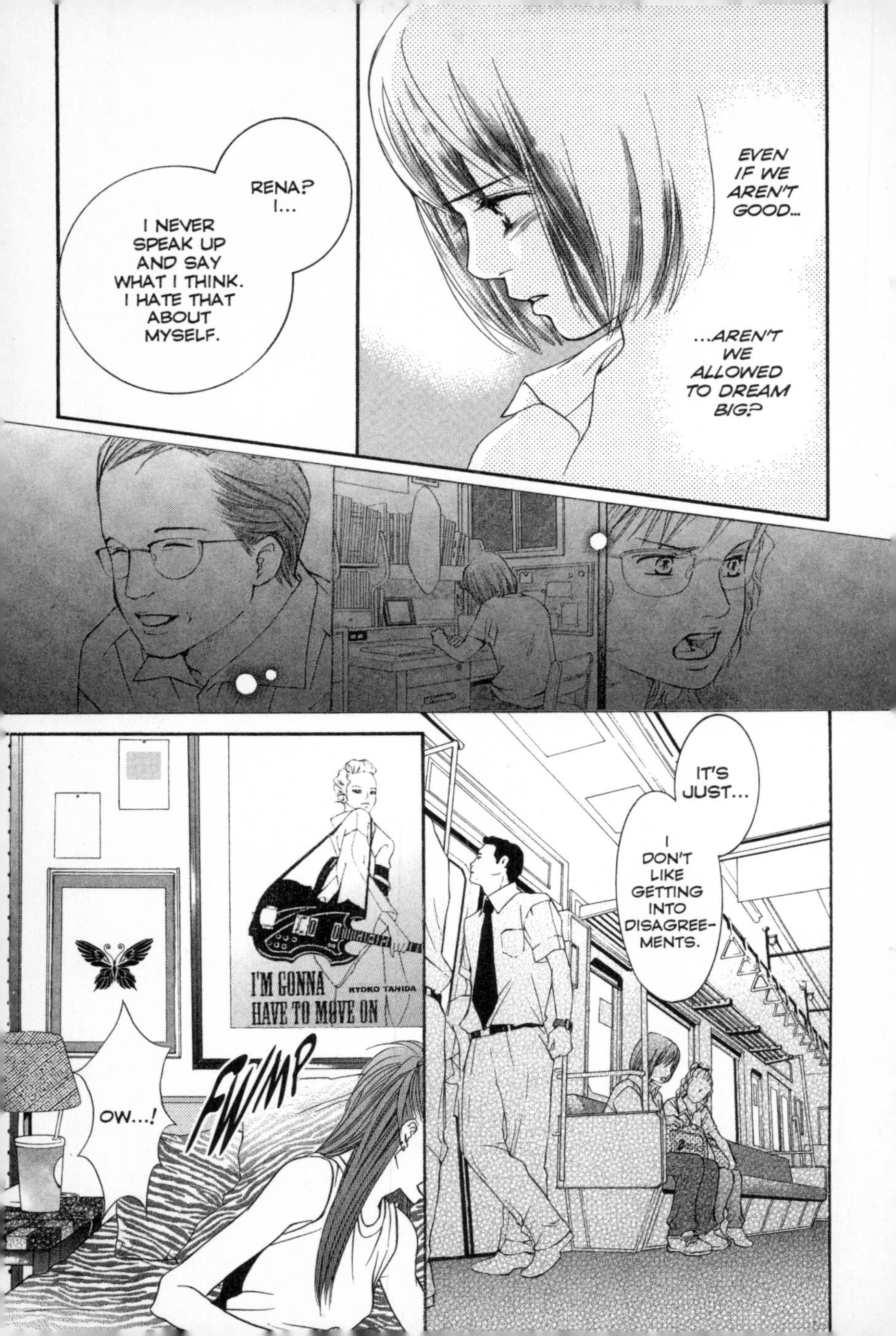
EVEN IF WE AREN'T GOOD...
...AREN'T WE ALLOWED TO DREAM BIG?
RENA? I...
I NEVER SPEAK UP AND SAY WHAT I THINK. I HATE THAT ABOUT MYSELF.
IT'S JUST...
I DON'T LIKE GETTING INTO DISAGREE-MENTS.
I'M GONNA HAVE TO MOVE ON
RYOKO TANIDA
OW...!

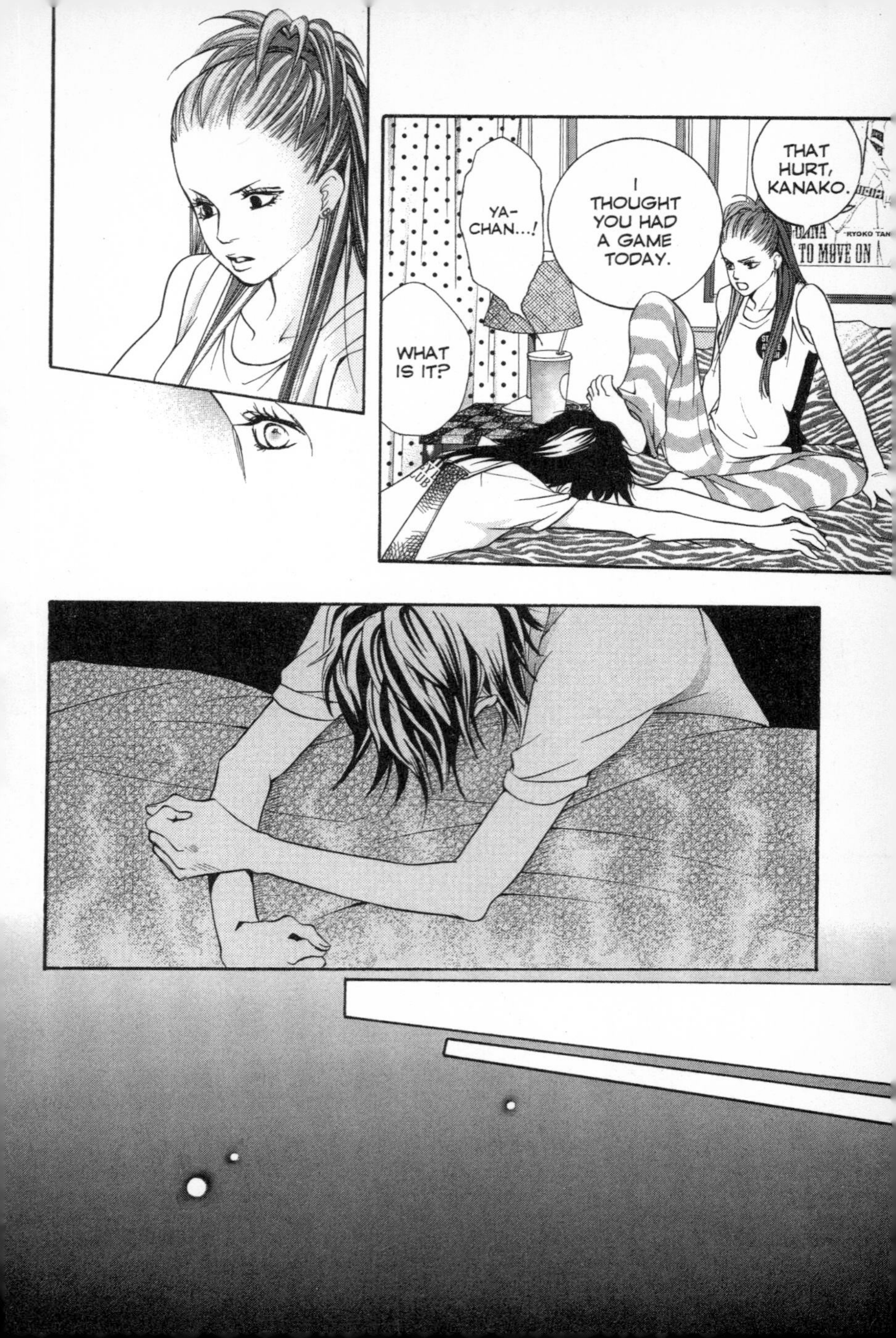
THAT HURT, KANAKO.
I THOUGHT YOU HAD A GAME TODAY.
YA-CHAN...!
WHAT IS IT?

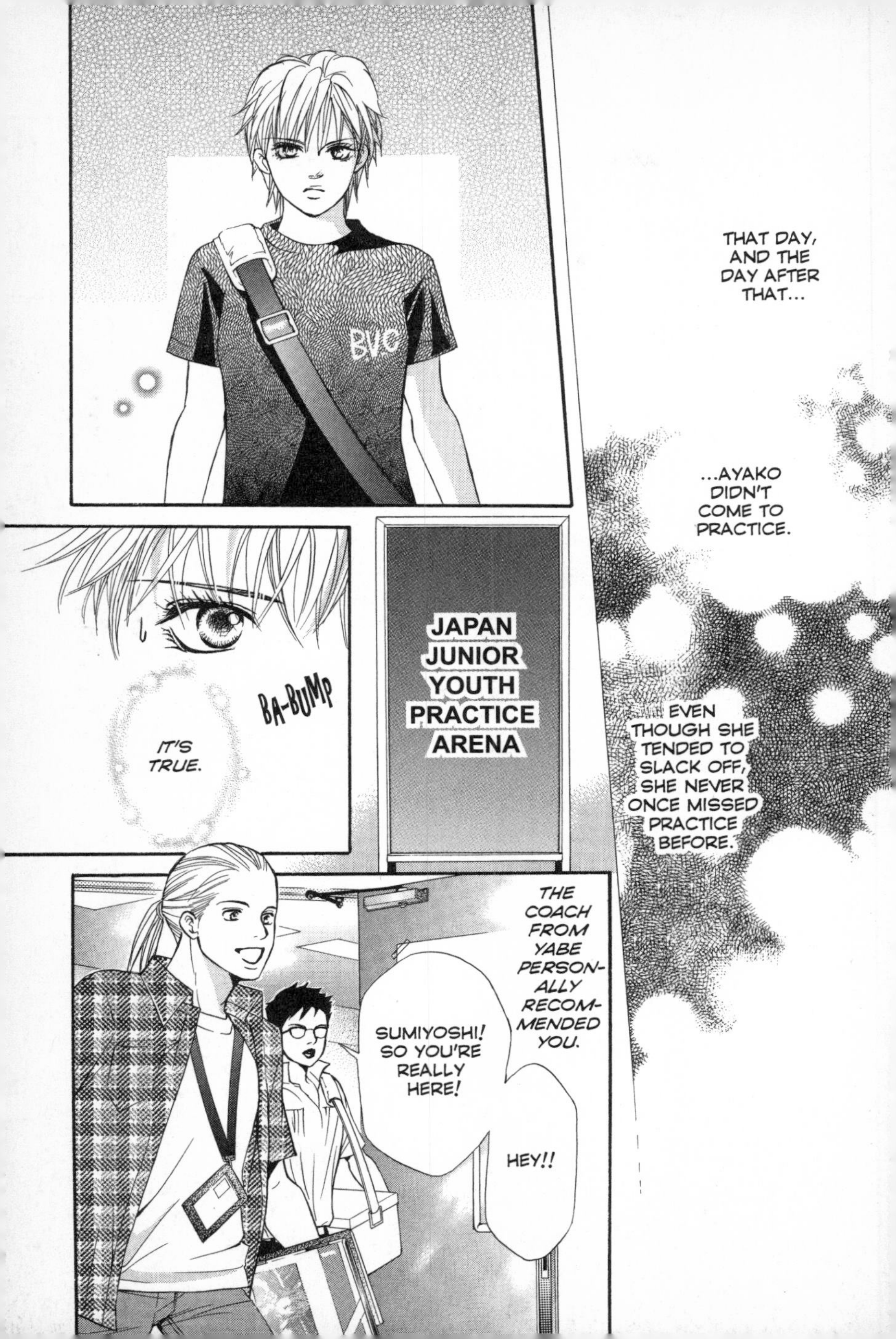
THAT DAY, AND THE DAY AFTER THAT...
...AYAKO DIDN'T COME TO PRACTICE.
EVEN THOUGH SHE TENDED TO SLACK OFF, SHE NEVER ONCE MISSED PRACTICE BEFORE.
JAPAN JUNIOR YOUTH PRACTICE ARENA
BA-BUMP
IT'S TRUE.
THE COACH FROM YABE PERSON-ALLY RECOM-MENDED YOU.
SUMIYOSHI! SO YOU'RE REALLY HERE!
HEY!!

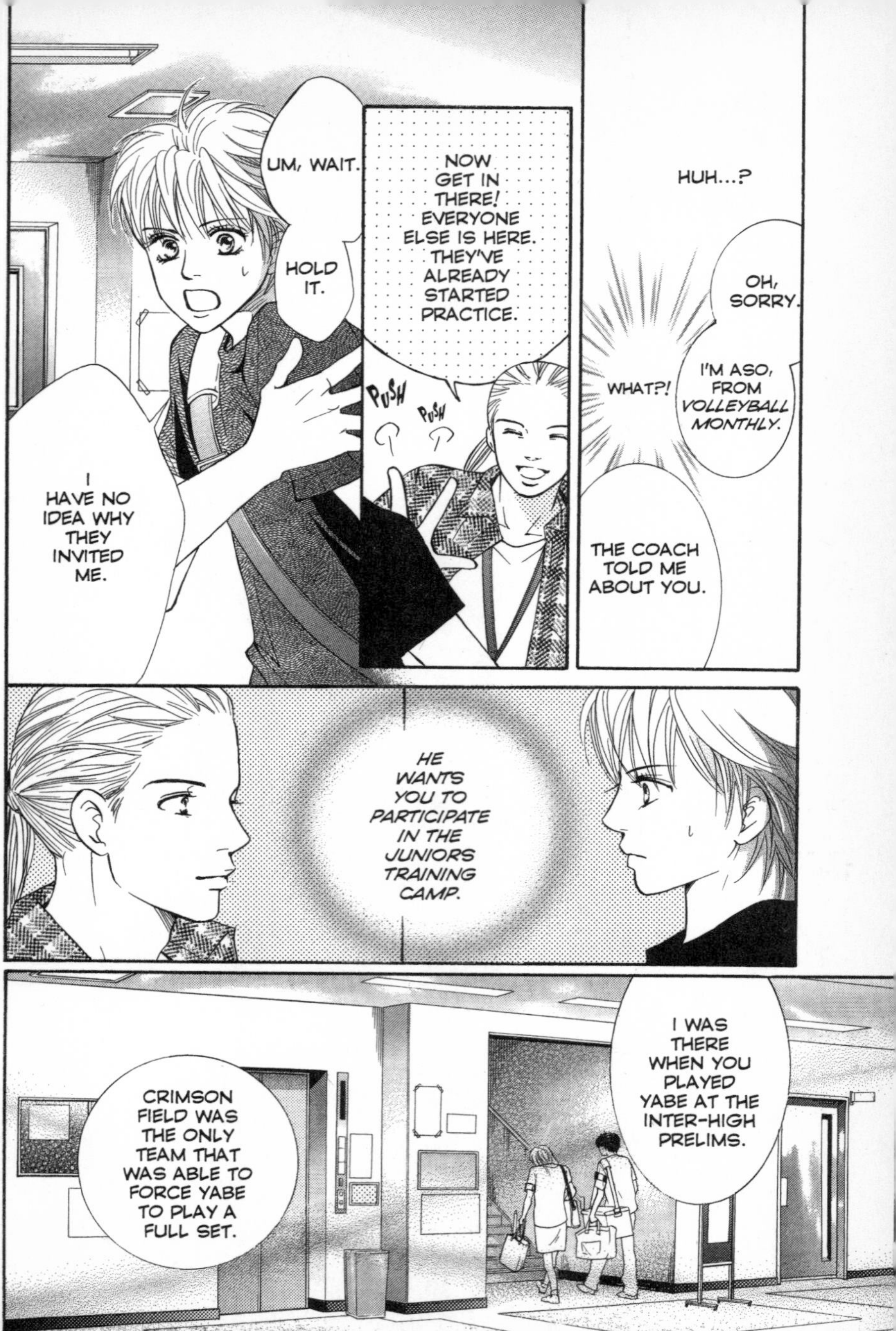
HUH...?
OH, SORRY.
I'M ASO, FROM *VOLLEYBALL MONTHLY.*
WHAT?!
THE COACH TOLD ME ABOUT YOU.
NOW GET IN THERE! EVERYONE ELSE IS HERE. THEY'VE ALREADY STARTED PRACTICE.
PUSH
PUSH
UM, WAIT.
HOLD IT.
I HAVE NO IDEA WHY THEY INVITED ME.
HE WANTS YOU TO PARTICIPATE IN THE JUNIORS TRAINING CAMP.
I WAS THERE WHEN YOU PLAYED YABE AT THE INTER-HIGH PRELIMS.
CRIMSON FIELD WAS THE ONLY TEAM THAT WAS ABLE TO FORCE YABE TO PLAY A FULL SET.

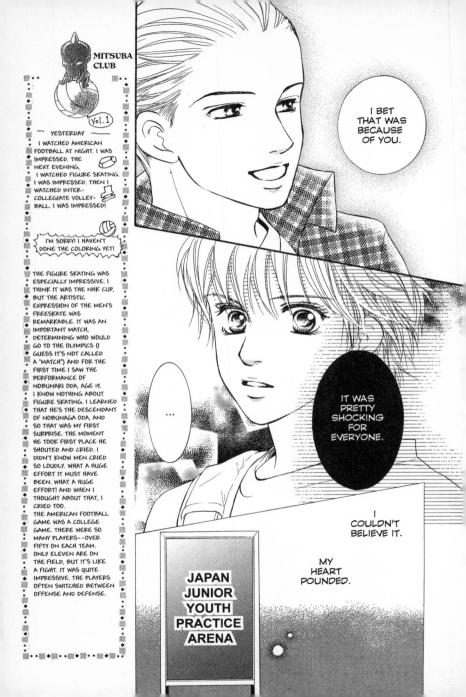

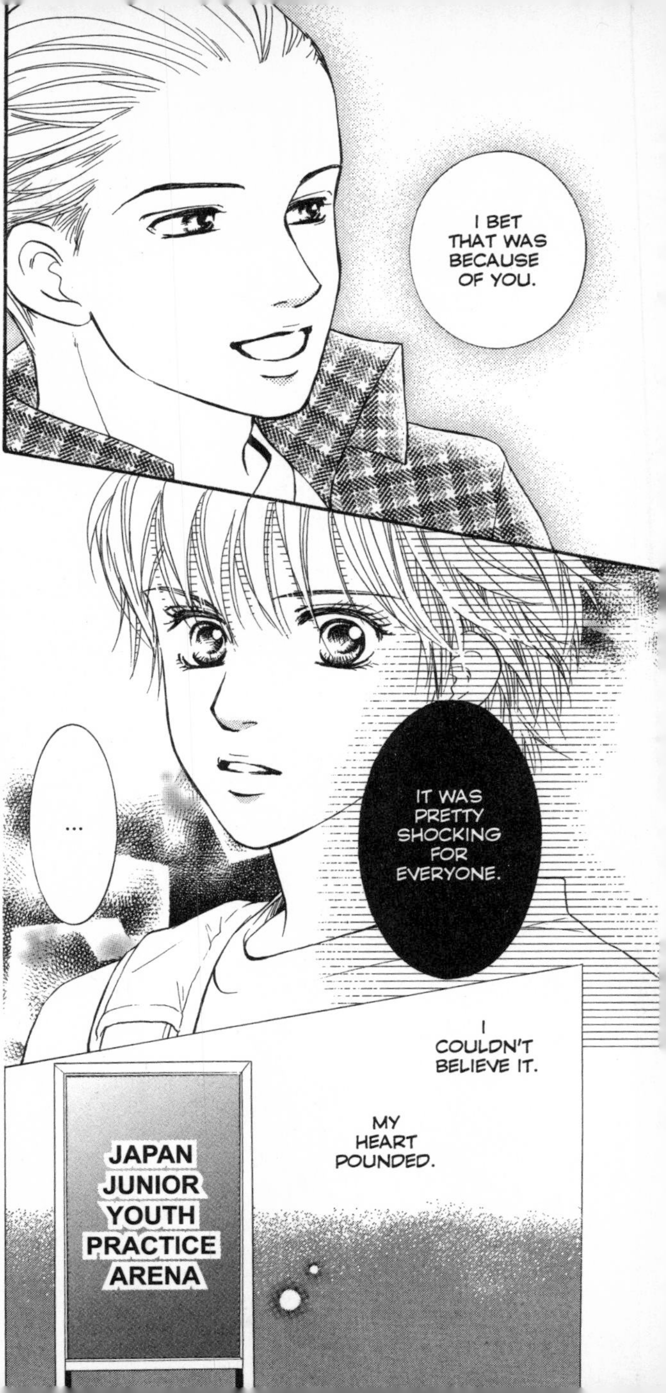
I BET THAT WAS BECAUSE OF YOU.
IT WAS PRETTY SHOCKING FOR EVERYONE.
...
I COULDN'T BELIEVE IT.
MY HEART POUNDED.
JAPAN JUNIOR YOUTH PRACTICE ARENA

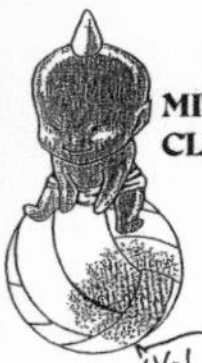

MITSUBA CLUB

Vol. 1

— YESTERDAY —

I WATCHED AMERICAN FOOTBALL AT NIGHT. I WAS IMPRESSED. THE NEXT EVENING, I WATCHED FIGURE SKATING. I WAS IMPRESSED. THEN I WATCHED INTER-COLLEGIATE VOLLEY-BALL. I WAS IMPRESSED!

I'M SORRY! I HAVEN'T DONE THE COLORING YET!

THE FIGURE SKATING WAS ESPECIALLY IMPRESSIVE. I THINK IT WAS THE NHK CUP, BUT THE ARTISTIC EXPRESSION OF THE MEN'S FREESKATE WAS REMARKABLE. IT WAS AN IMPORTANT MATCH, DETERMINING WHO WOULD GO TO THE OLYMPICS (I GUESS IT'S NOT CALLED A "MATCH") AND FOR THE FIRST TIME I SAW THE PERFORMANCE OF NOBUNARI ODA, AGE 19. I KNOW NOTHING ABOUT FIGURE SKATING. I LEARNED THAT HE'S THE DESCENDANT OF NOBUNAGA ODA, AND SO THAT WAS MY FIRST SURPRISE. THE MOMENT HE TOOK FIRST PLACE HE SHOUTED AND CRIED. I DIDN'T KNOW MEN CRIED SO LOUDLY. WHAT A HUGE EFFORT IT MUST HAVE BEEN. WHAT A HUGE EFFORT! AND WHEN I THOUGHT ABOUT THAT, I CRIED TOO.
THE AMERICAN FOOTBALL GAME WAS A COLLEGE GAME. THERE WERE SO MANY PLAYERS--OVER FIFTY ON EACH TEAM. ONLY ELEVEN ARE ON THE FIELD, BUT IT'S LIKE A FIGHT. IT WAS QUITE IMPRESSIVE. THE PLAYERS OFTEN SWITCHED BETWEEN OFFENSE AND DEFENSE.

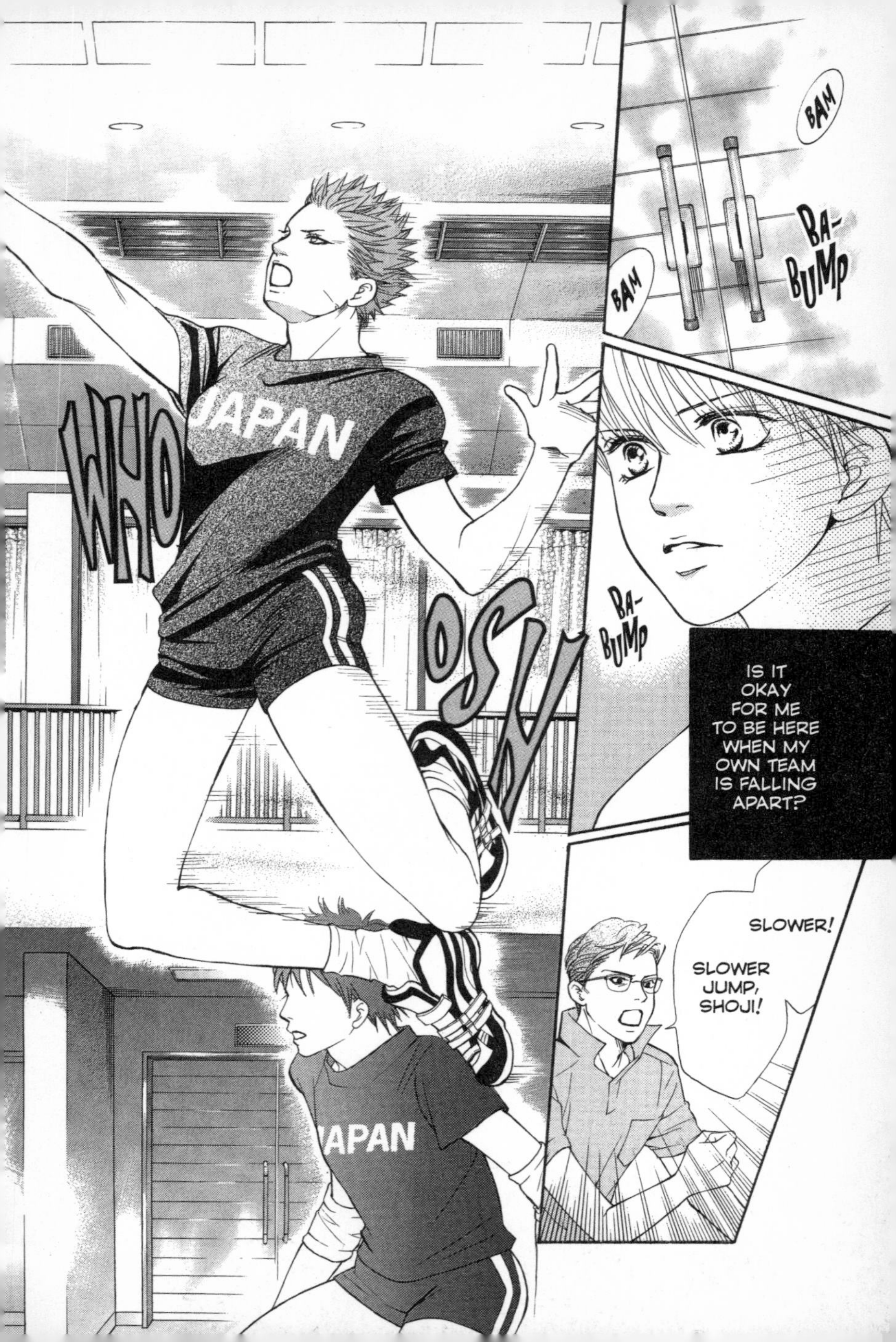
BAM
BA-BUMP
BAM
BA-BUMP
IS IT OKAY FOR ME TO BE HERE WHEN MY OWN TEAM IS FALLING APART?
SLOWER!
SLOWER JUMP, SHOJI!
WHOOSH
JAPAN
JAPAN

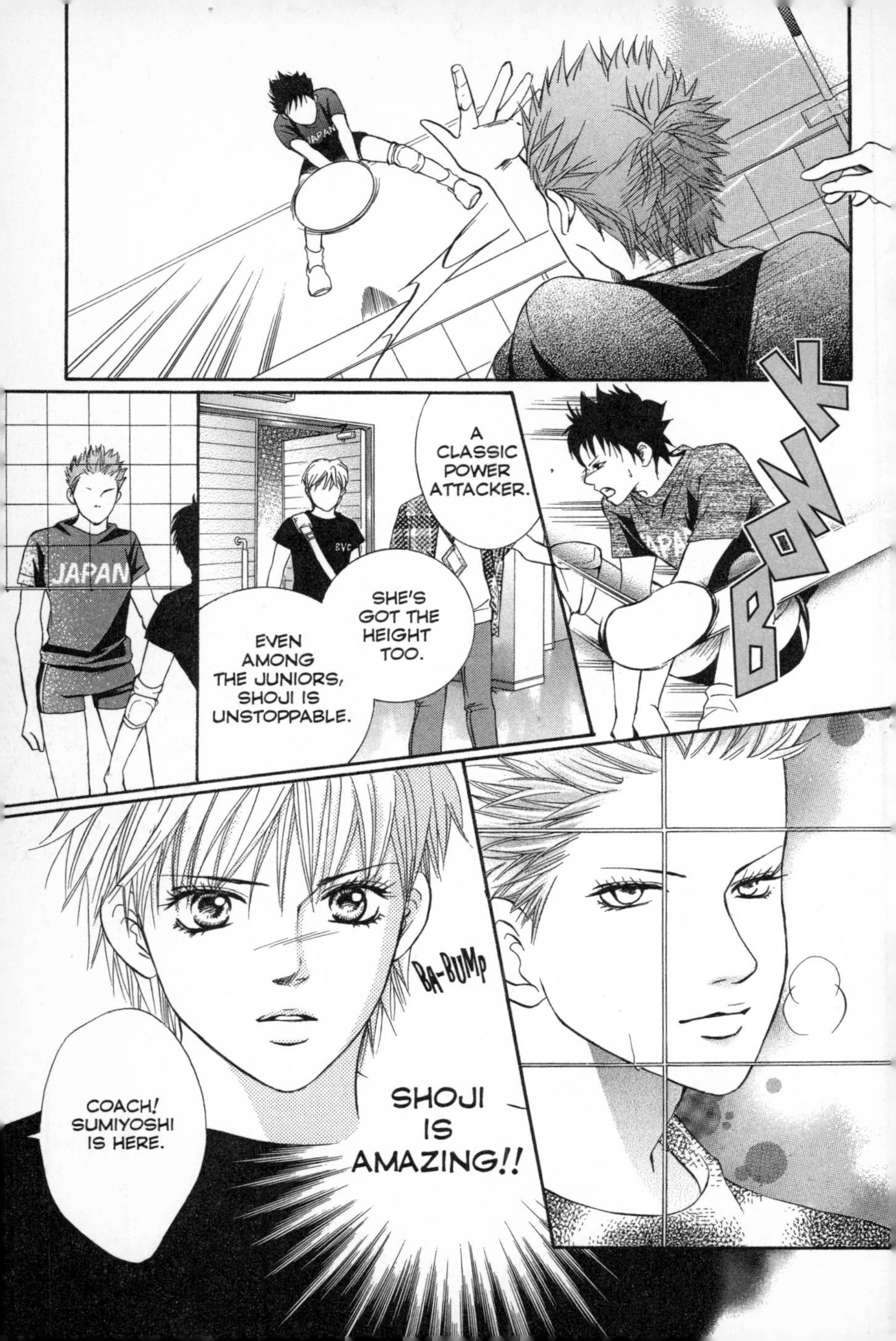
BONK
A CLASSIC POWER ATTACKER.
SHE'S GOT THE HEIGHT TOO.
EVEN AMONG THE JUNIORS, SHOJI IS UNSTOPPABLE.
BA-BUMP
SHOJI IS AMAZING!!
COACH! SUMIYOSHI IS HERE.

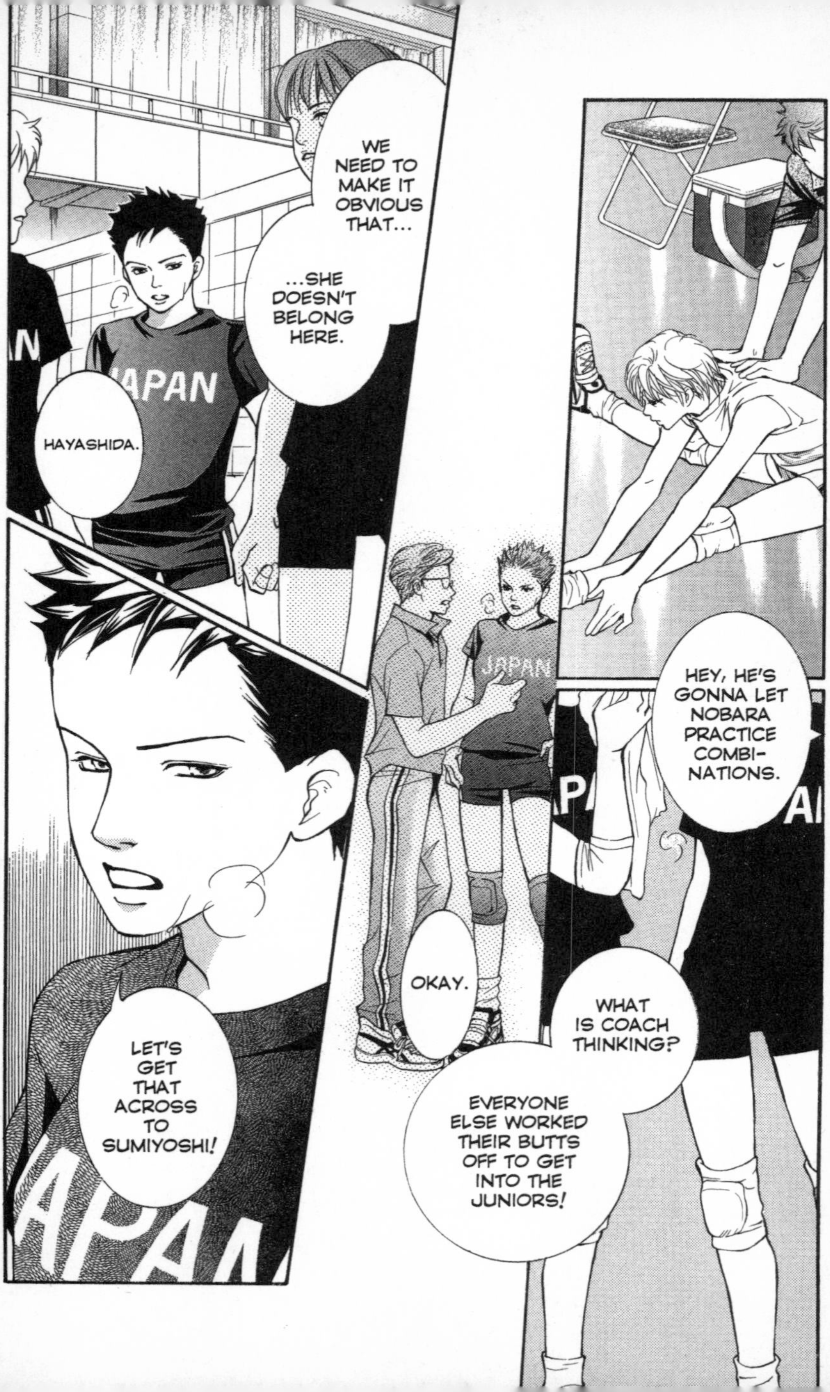
HEY, HE'S GONNA LET NOBARA PRACTICE COMBI-NATIONS.
OKAY.
WHAT IS COACH THINKING?
EVERYONE ELSE WORKED THEIR BUTTS OFF TO GET INTO THE JUNIORS!
WE NEED TO MAKE IT OBVIOUS THAT...
...SHE DOESN'T BELONG HERE.
HAYASHIDA.
LET'S GET THAT ACROSS TO SUMIYOSHI!

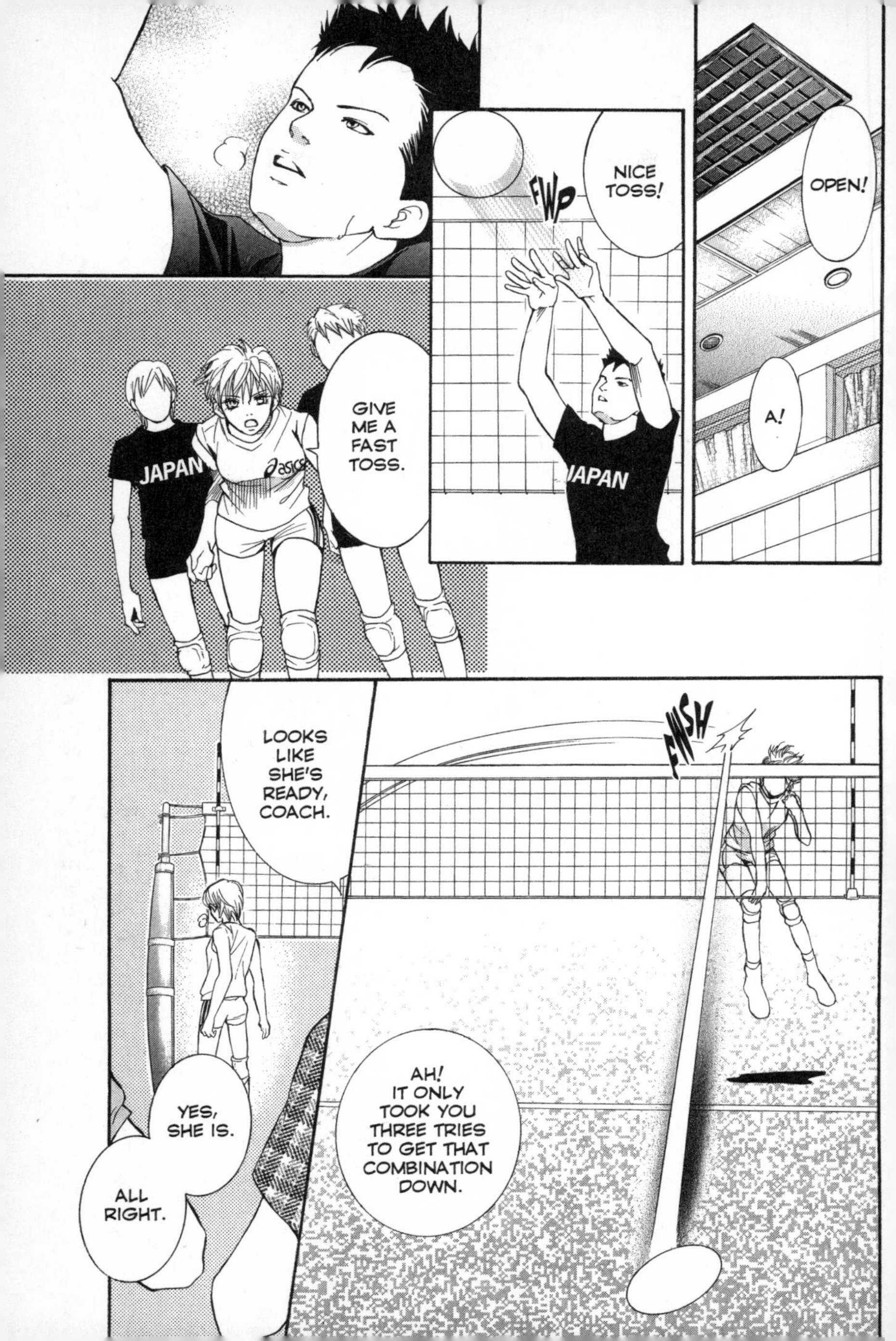
OPEN!
A!
FWP
NICE TOSS!
GIVE ME A FAST TOSS.
FWSH
AH! IT ONLY TOOK YOU THREE TRIES TO GET THAT COMBINATION DOWN.
LOOKS LIKE SHE'S READY, COACH.
YES, SHE IS.
ALL RIGHT.

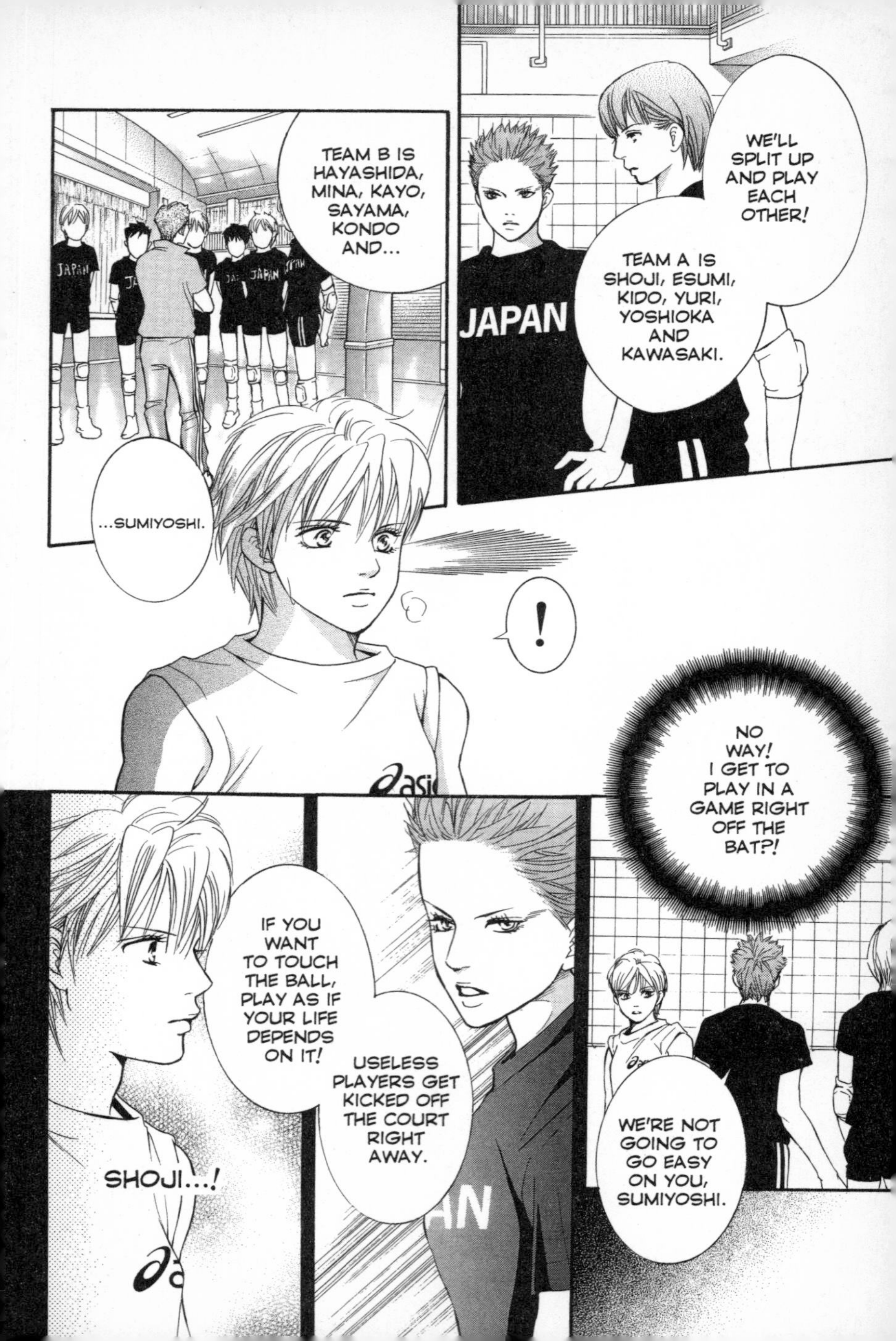
WE'LL SPLIT UP AND PLAY EACH OTHER!
TEAM A IS SHOJI, ESUMI, KIDO, YURI, YOSHIOKA AND KAWASAKI.
TEAM B IS HAYASHIDA, MINA, KAYO, SAYAMA, KONDO AND...
...SUMIYOSHI.
!
NO WAY! I GET TO PLAY IN A GAME RIGHT OFF THE BAT?!
WE'RE NOT GOING TO GO EASY ON YOU, SUMIYOSHI.
IF YOU WANT TO TOUCH THE BALL, PLAY AS IF YOUR LIFE DEPENDS ON IT!
USELESS PLAYERS GET KICKED OFF THE COURT RIGHT AWAY.
SHOJI...!

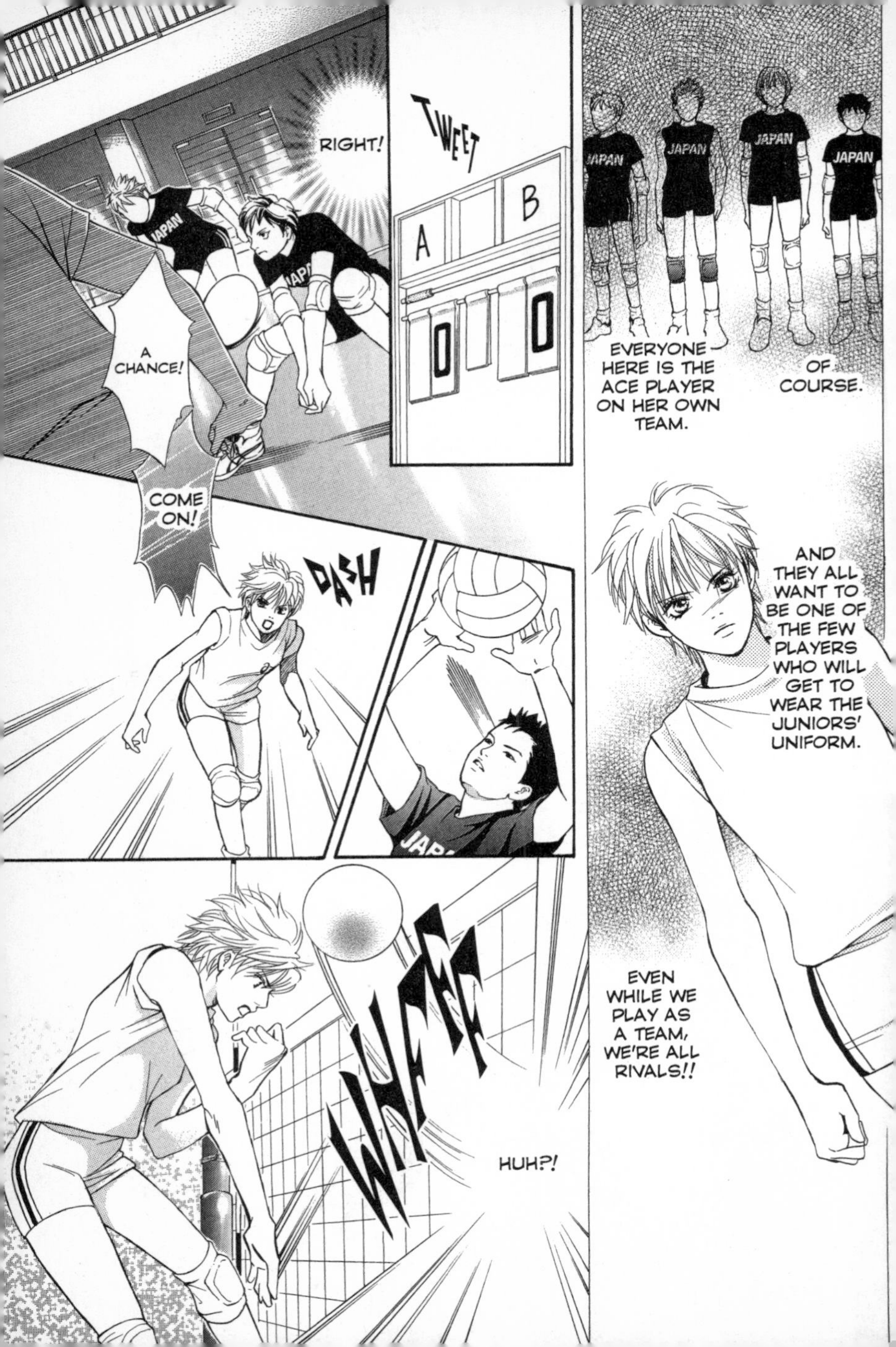
JAPAN
JAPAN
JAPAN
JAPAN
EVERYONE HERE IS THE ACE PLAYER ON HER OWN TEAM.
OF COURSE.
AND THEY ALL WANT TO BE ONE OF THE FEW PLAYERS WHO WILL GET TO WEAR THE JUNIORS' UNIFORM.
EVEN WHILE WE PLAY AS A TEAM, WE'RE ALL RIVALS!!
TWEET
A
B
0
0
RIGHT!
JAPAN
A CHANCE!
COME ON!
DASH
WHFFF
HUH?!

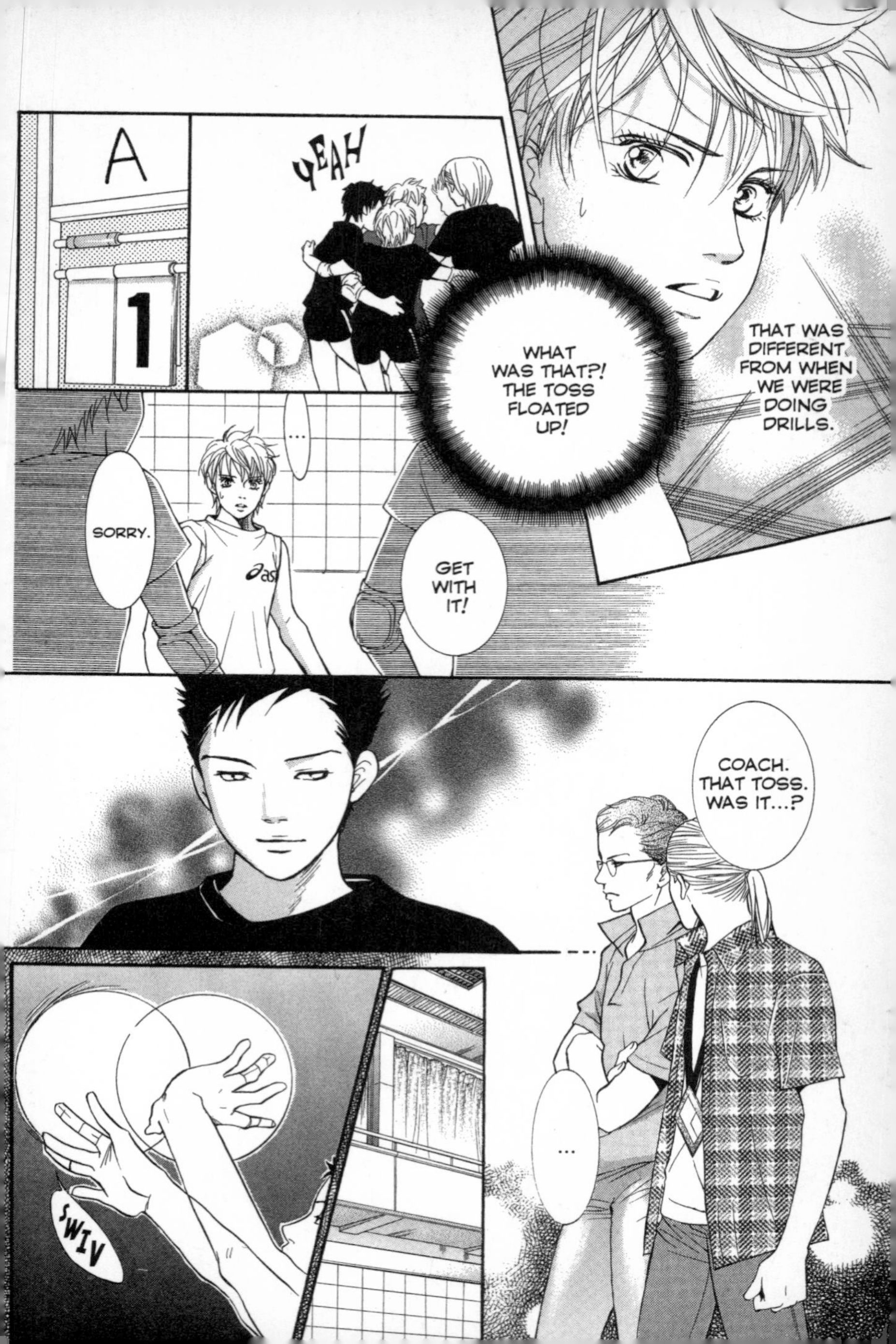
THAT WAS DIFFERENT FROM WHEN WE WERE DOING DRILLS.
YEAH
A
1
WHAT WAS THAT?! THE TOSS FLOATED UP!
...
GET WITH IT!
SORRY.
COACH. THAT TOSS. WAS IT...?
...
SWIV

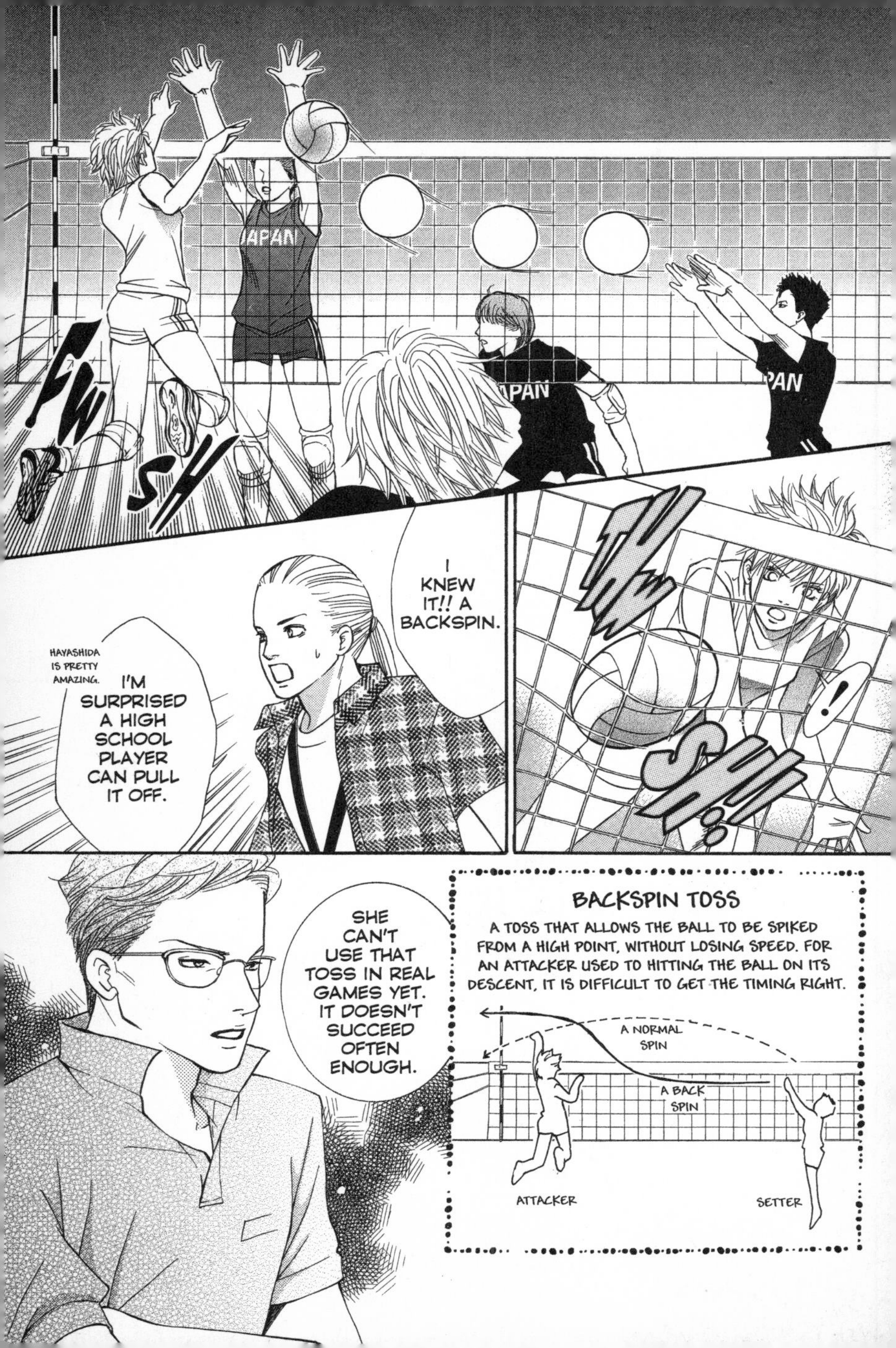

FWSH
!
I KNEW IT!! A BACKSPIN.
I'M SURPRISED A HIGH SCHOOL PLAYER CAN PULL IT OFF.
HAYASHIDA IS PRETTY AMAZING.
BACKSPIN TOSS
A TOSS THAT ALLOWS THE BALL TO BE SPIKED FROM A HIGH POINT, WITHOUT LOSING SPEED. FOR AN ATTACKER USED TO HITTING THE BALL ON ITS DESCENT, IT IS DIFFICULT TO GET THE TIMING RIGHT.
A NORMAL SPIN
A BACK SPIN
ATTACKER
SETTER
SHE CAN'T USE THAT TOSS IN REAL GAMES YET. IT DOESN'T SUCCEED OFTEN ENOUGH.

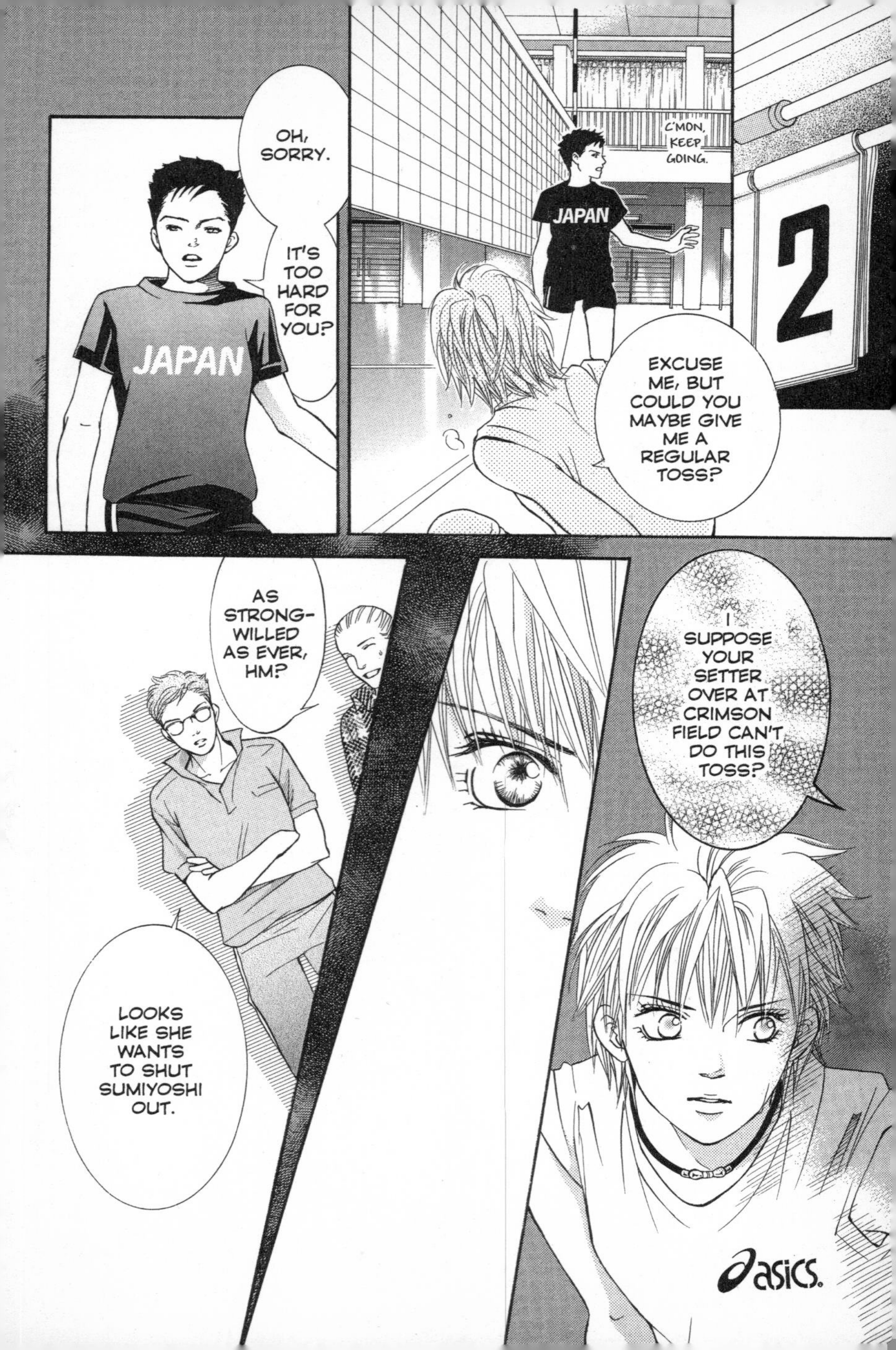
C'MON, KEEP GOING.
EXCUSE ME, BUT COULD YOU MAYBE GIVE ME A REGULAR TOSS?
OH, SORRY.
IT'S TOO HARD FOR YOU?
I SUPPOSE YOUR SETTER OVER AT CRIMSON FIELD CAN'T DO THIS TOSS?
AS STRONG-WILLED AS EVER, HM?
LOOKS LIKE SHE WANTS TO SHUT SUMIYOSHI OUT.

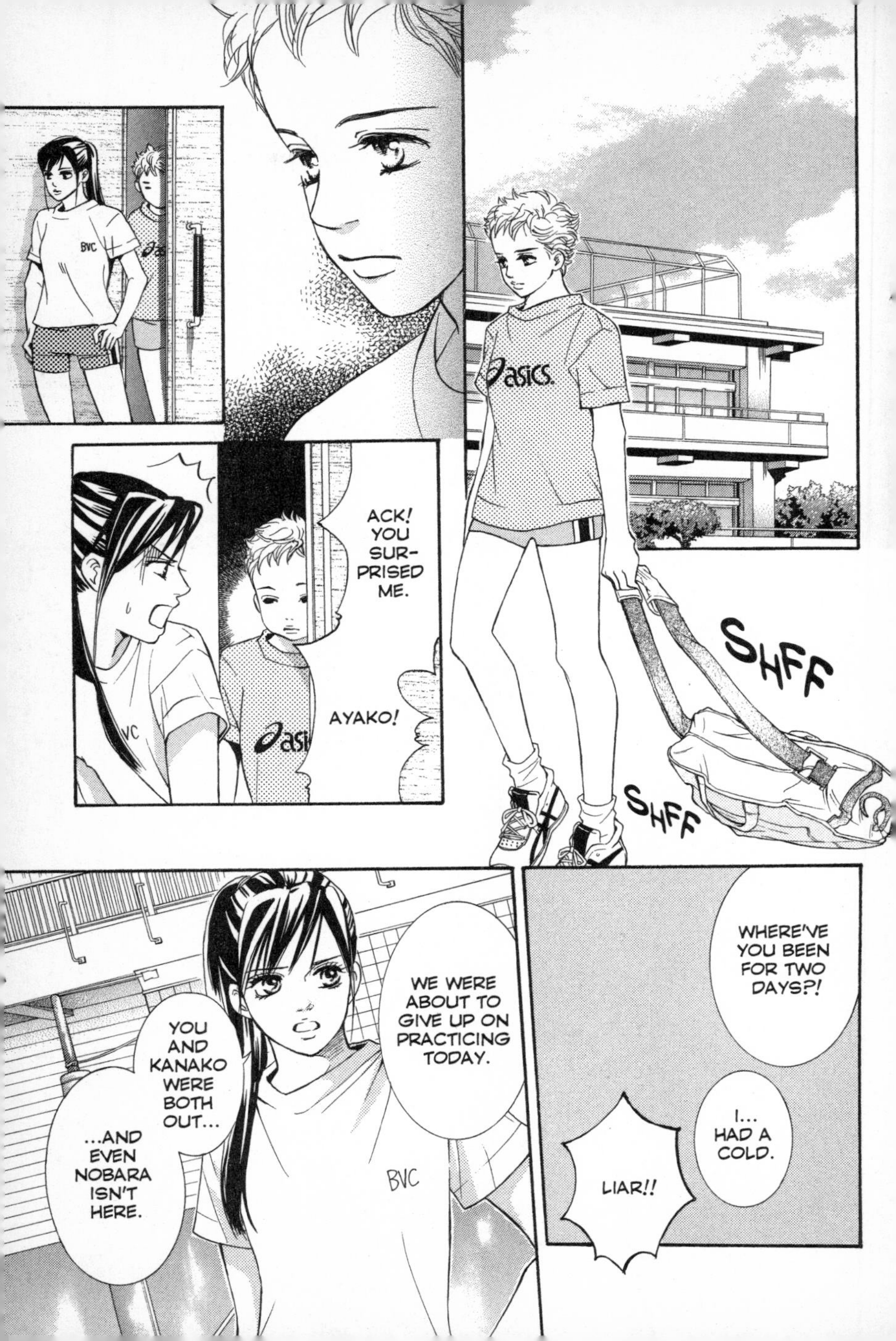

SHFF
SHFF
ACK! YOU SUR-PRISED ME.
AYAKO!
WHERE'VE YOU BEEN FOR TWO DAYS?!
I... HAD A COLD.
LIAR!!
WE WERE ABOUT TO GIVE UP ON PRACTICING TODAY.
YOU AND KANAKO WERE BOTH OUT...
...AND EVEN NOBARA ISN'T HERE.

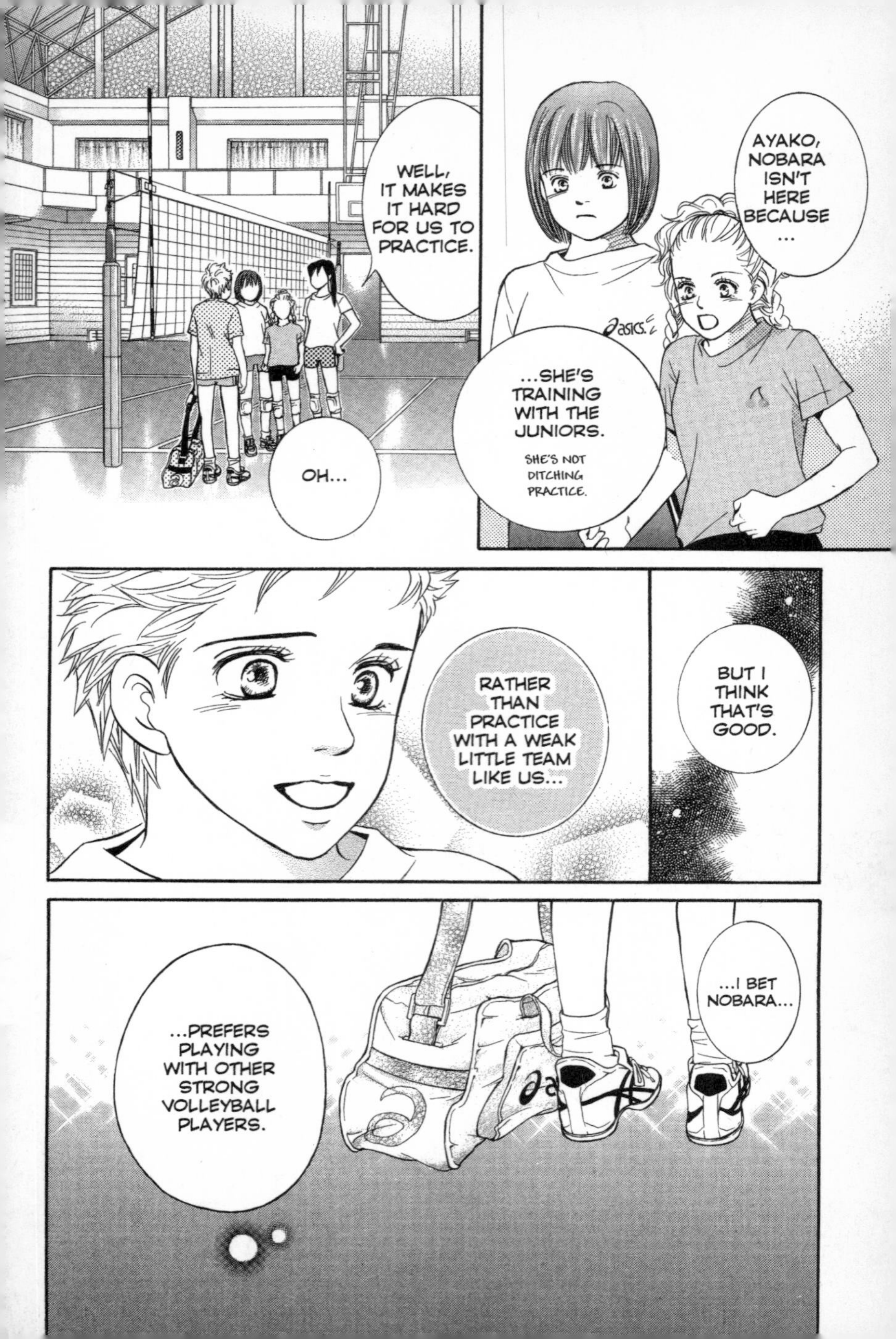
AYAKO, NOBARA ISN'T HERE BECAUSE ...
...SHE'S TRAINING WITH THE JUNIORS.
SHE'S NOT DITCHING PRACTICE.
WELL, IT MAKES IT HARD FOR US TO PRACTICE.
OH...
BUT I THINK THAT'S GOOD.
RATHER THAN PRACTICE WITH A WEAK LITTLE TEAM LIKE US...
...I BET NOBARA...
...PREFERS PLAYING WITH OTHER STRONG VOLLEYBALL PLAYERS.

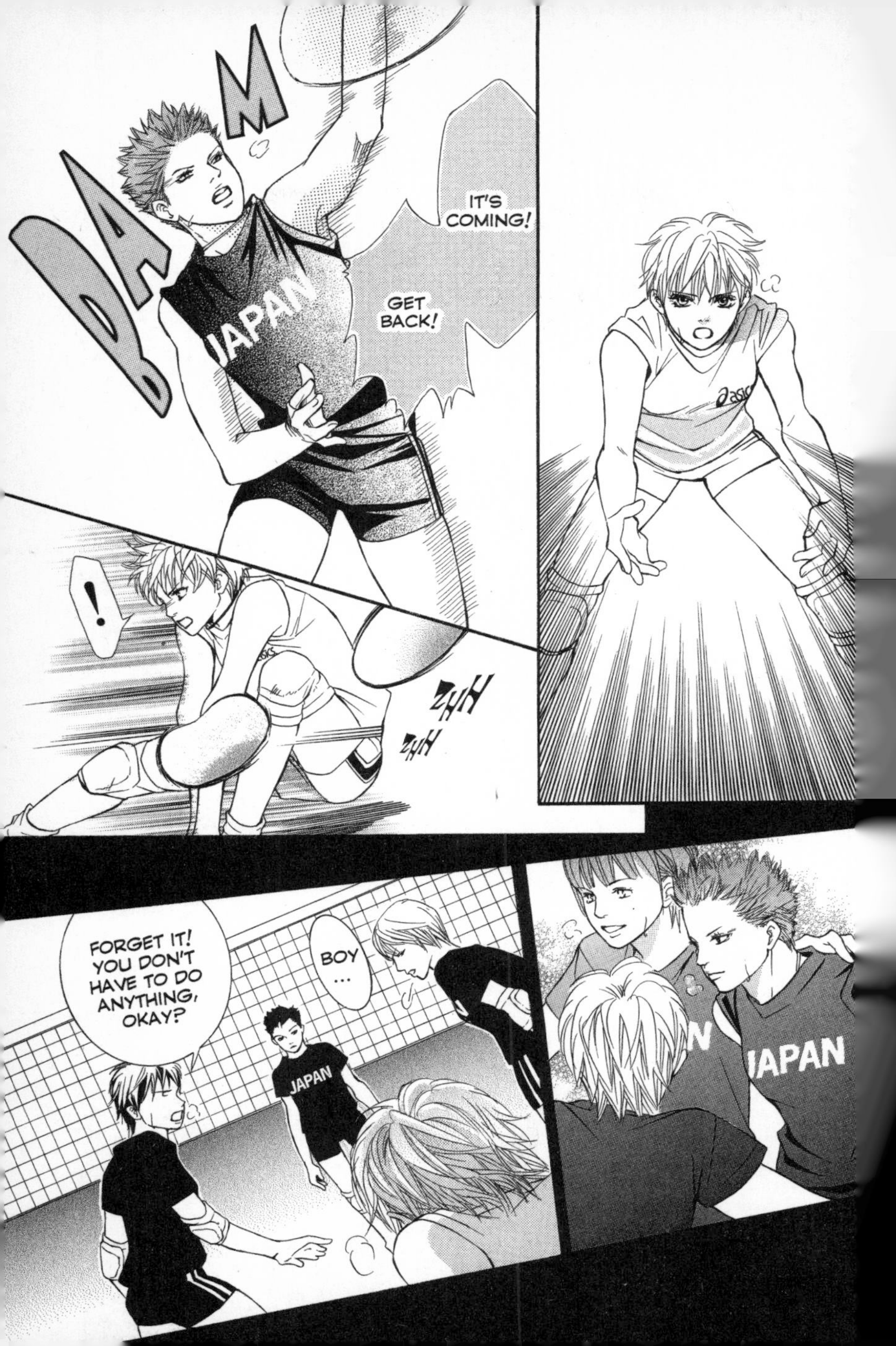
BAAM
IT'S COMING!
GET BACK!
!
ZHH
ZHH
BOY ...
FORGET IT! YOU DON'T HAVE TO DO ANYTHING, OKAY?

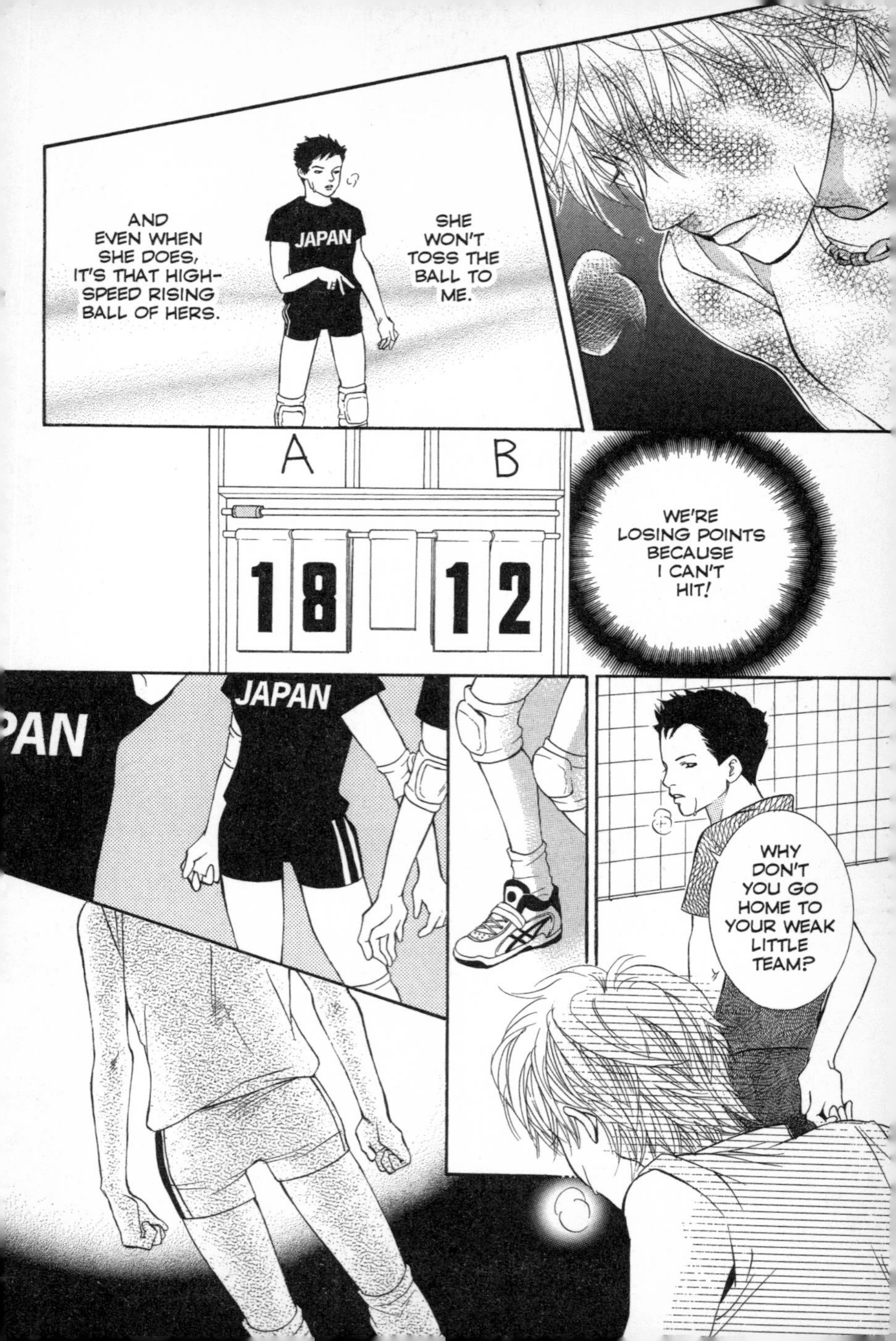
SHE WON'T TOSS THE BALL TO ME.
JAPAN
AND EVEN WHEN SHE DOES, IT'S THAT HIGH-SPEED RISING BALL OF HERS.
WE'RE LOSING POINTS BECAUSE I CAN'T HIT!
A
B
18
12
WHY DON'T YOU GO HOME TO YOUR WEAK LITTLE TEAM?
JAPAN
PAN

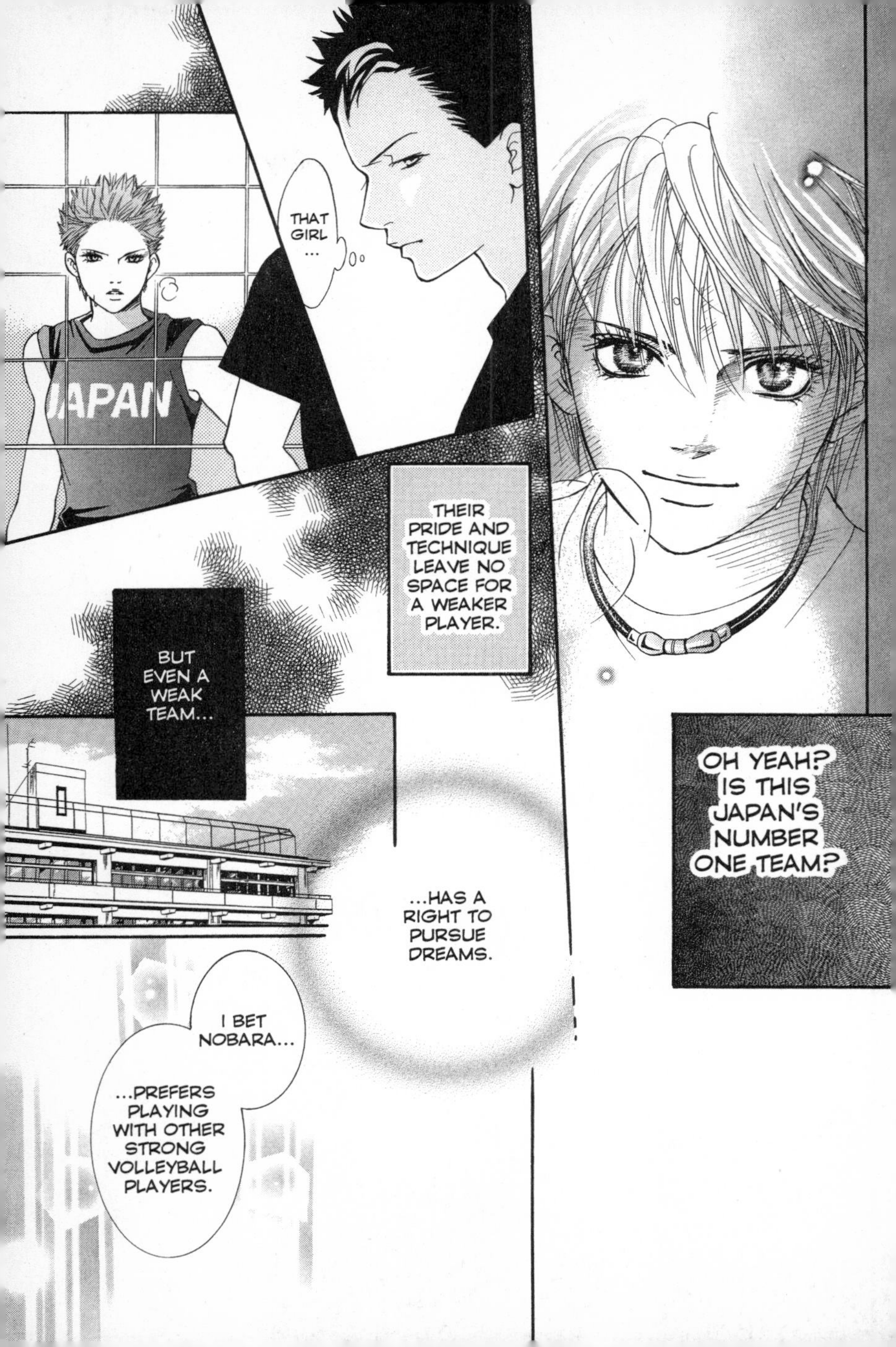
OH YEAH? IS THIS JAPAN'S NUMBER ONE TEAM?
THAT GIRL ...
JAPAN
THEIR PRIDE AND TECHNIQUE LEAVE NO SPACE FOR A WEAKER PLAYER.
BUT EVEN A WEAK TEAM...
...HAS A RIGHT TO PURSUE DREAMS.
I BET NOBARA...
...PREFERS PLAYING WITH OTHER STRONG VOLLEYBALL PLAYERS.

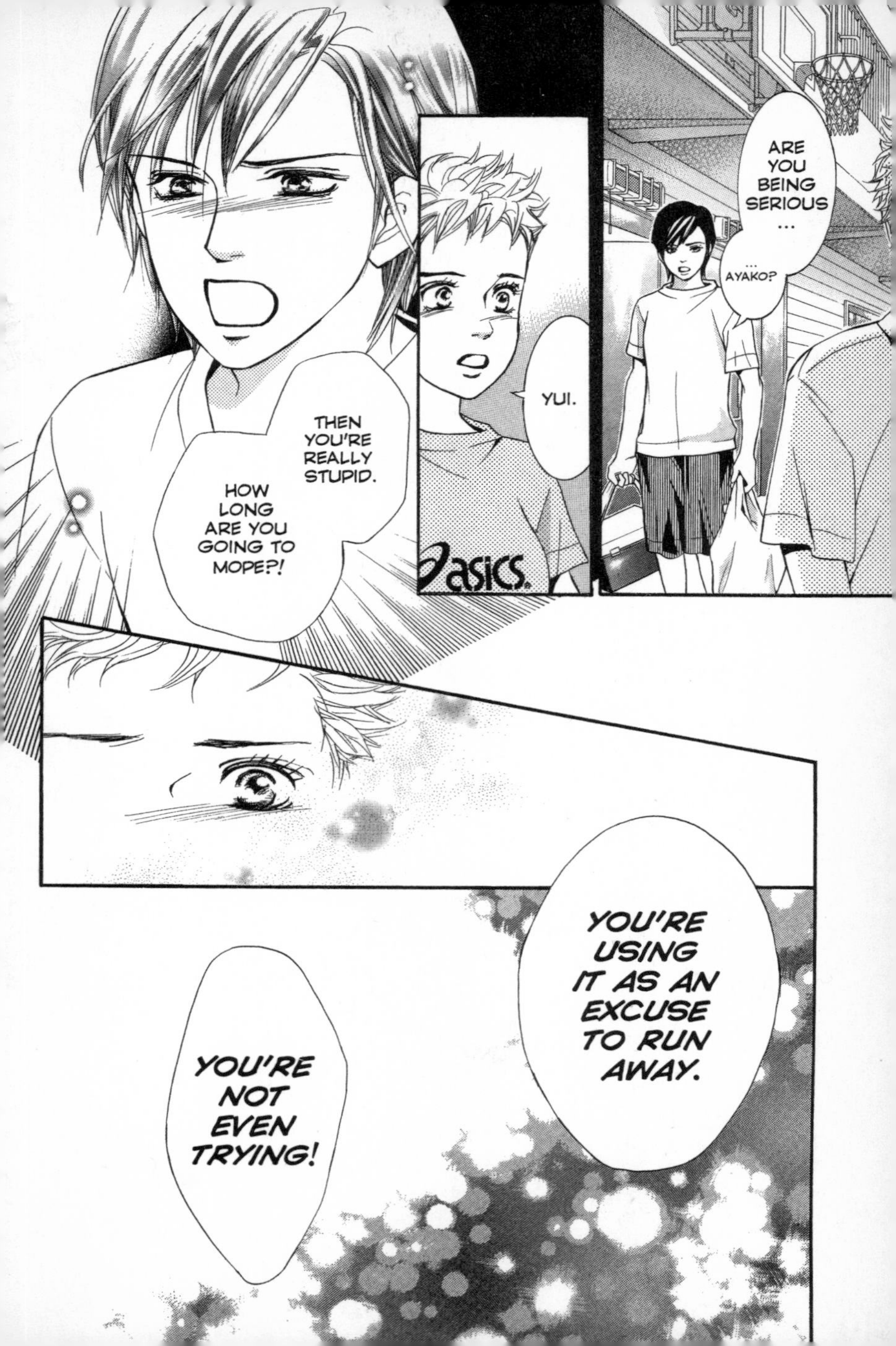
ARE YOU BEING SERIOUS ...
... AYAKO?
YUI.
asics
THEN YOU'RE REALLY STUPID.
HOW LONG ARE YOU GOING TO MOPE?!
YOU'RE USING IT AS AN EXCUSE TO RUN AWAY.
YOU'RE NOT EVEN TRYING!

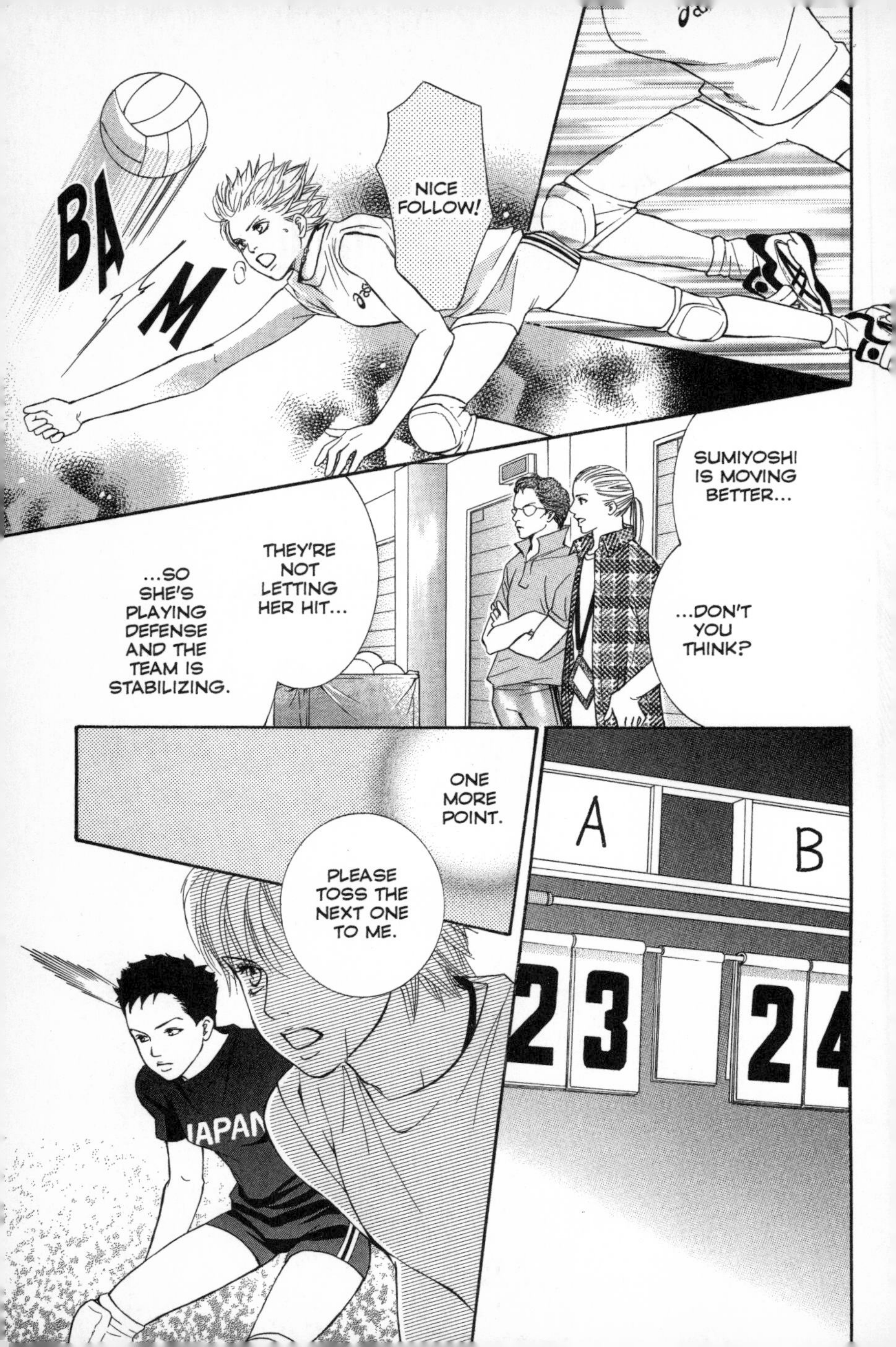
NICE FOLLOW!
BAM
SUMIYOSHI IS MOVING BETTER...
...DON'T YOU THINK?
THEY'RE NOT LETTING HER HIT...
...SO SHE'S PLAYING DEFENSE AND THE TEAM IS STABILIZING.
A
B
23
24
ONE MORE POINT.
PLEASE TOSS THE NEXT ONE TO ME.
JAPAN

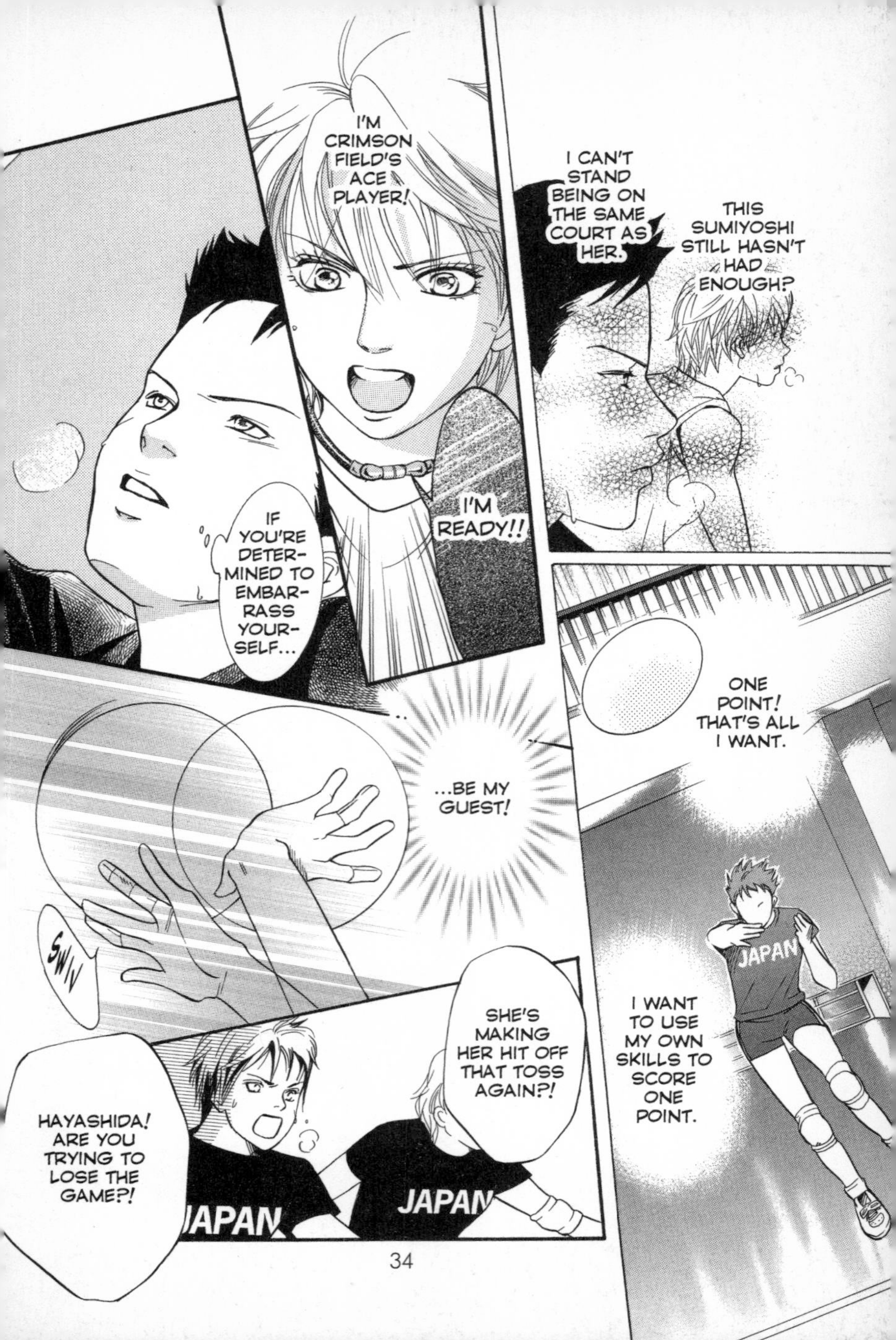
THIS SUMIYOSHI STILL HASN'T HAD ENOUGH?
I CAN'T STAND BEING ON THE SAME COURT AS HER.
I'M CRIMSON FIELD'S ACE PLAYER!
I'M READY!!
IF YOU'RE DETER-MINED TO EMBAR-RASS YOUR-SELF...
ONE POINT! THAT'S ALL I WANT.
I WANT TO USE MY OWN SKILLS TO SCORE ONE POINT.
...BE MY GUEST!
SWN
SHE'S MAKING HER HIT OFF THAT TOSS AGAIN?!
HAYASHIDA! ARE YOU TRYING TO LOSE THE GAME?!
JAPAN
JAPAN
JAPAN

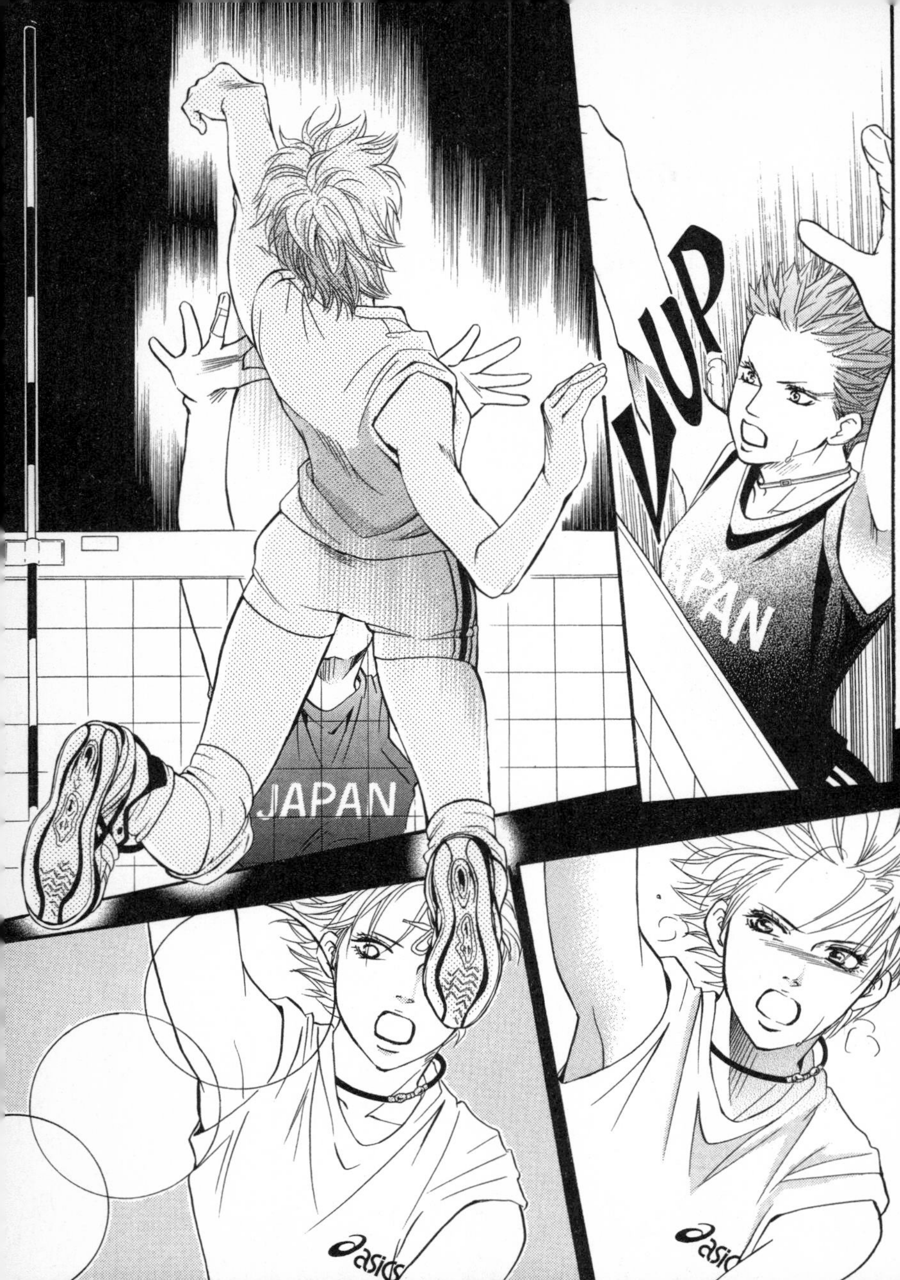
VUP
JAPAN

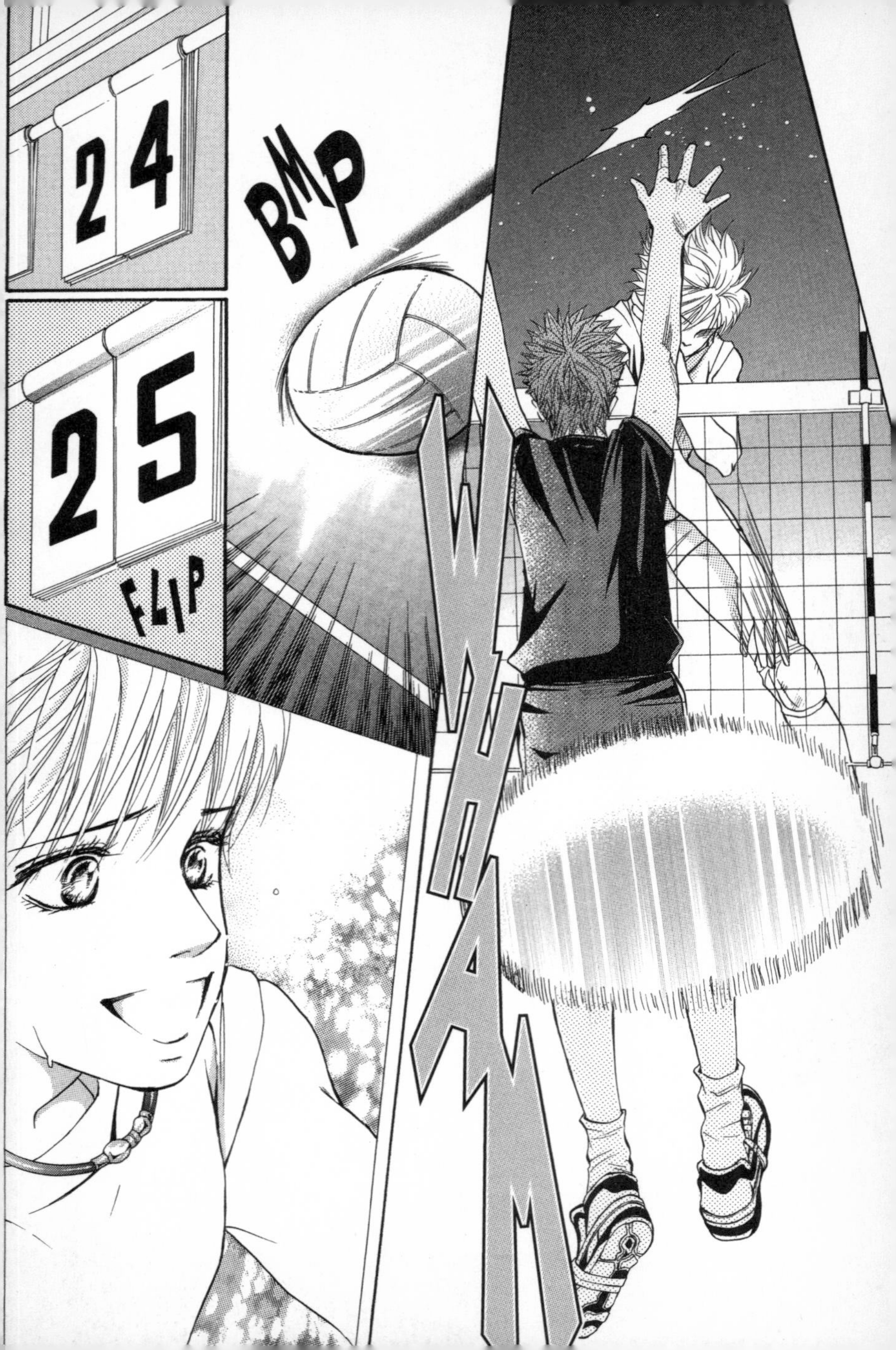
BMP
WHAM
24
25
FLIP

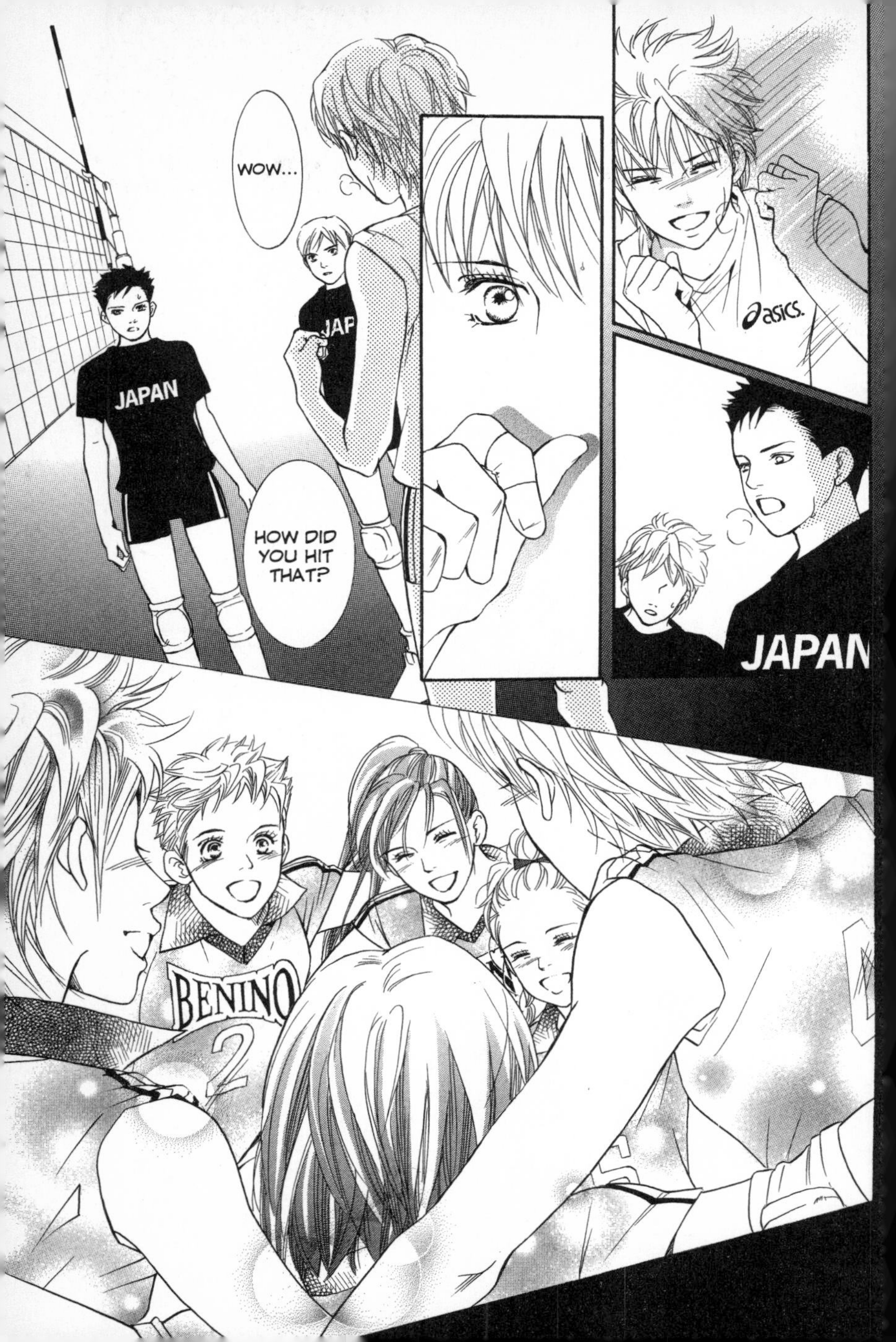
WOW...
HOW DID YOU HIT THAT?

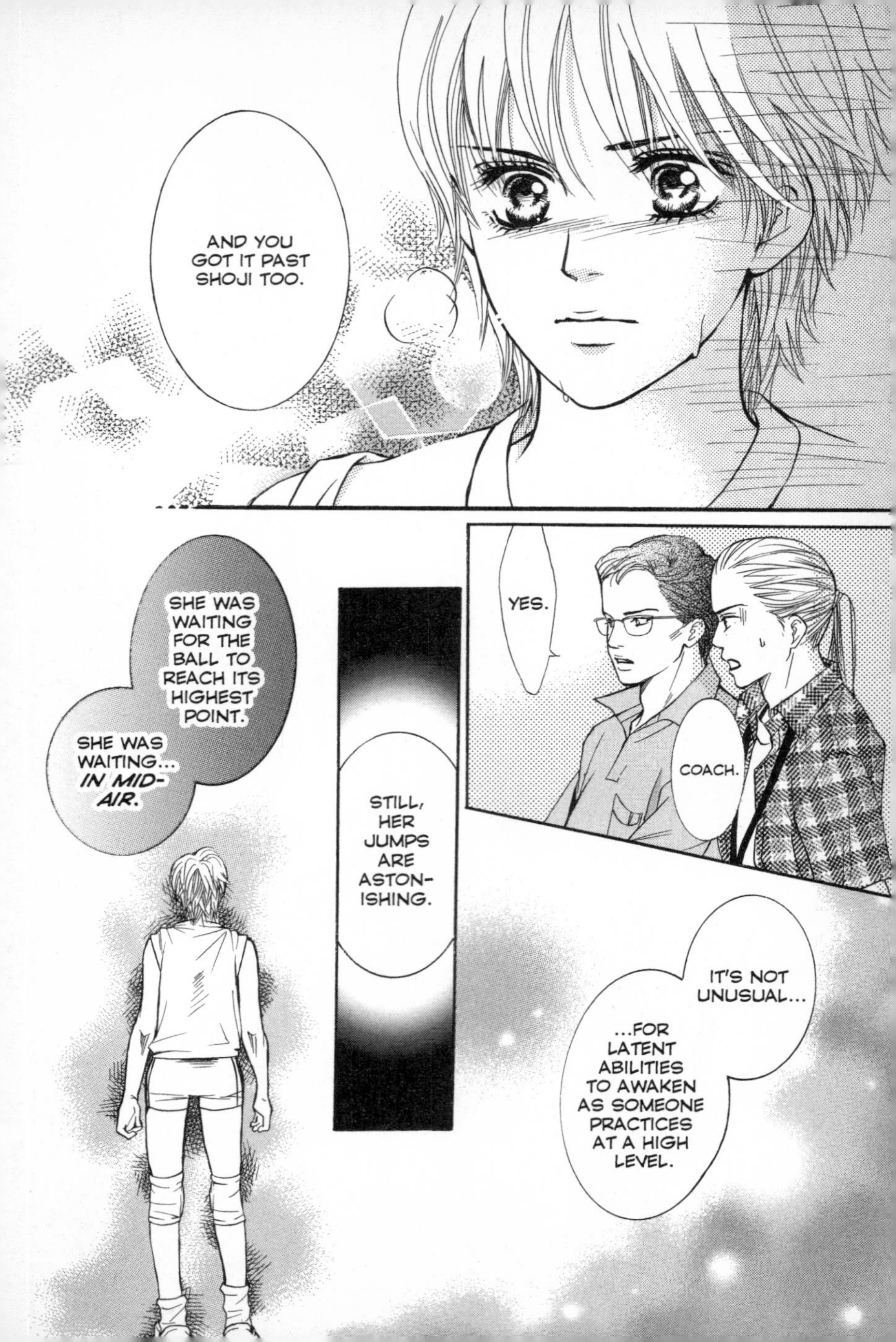
AND YOU GOT IT PAST SHOJI TOO.
YES.
COACH.
STILL, HER JUMPS ARE ASTON-ISHING.
SHE WAS WAITING FOR THE BALL TO REACH ITS HIGHEST POINT.
SHE WAS WAITING... *IN MID-AIR*.
IT'S NOT UNUSUAL...
...FOR LATENT ABILITIES TO AWAKEN AS SOMEONE PRACTICES AT A HIGH LEVEL.

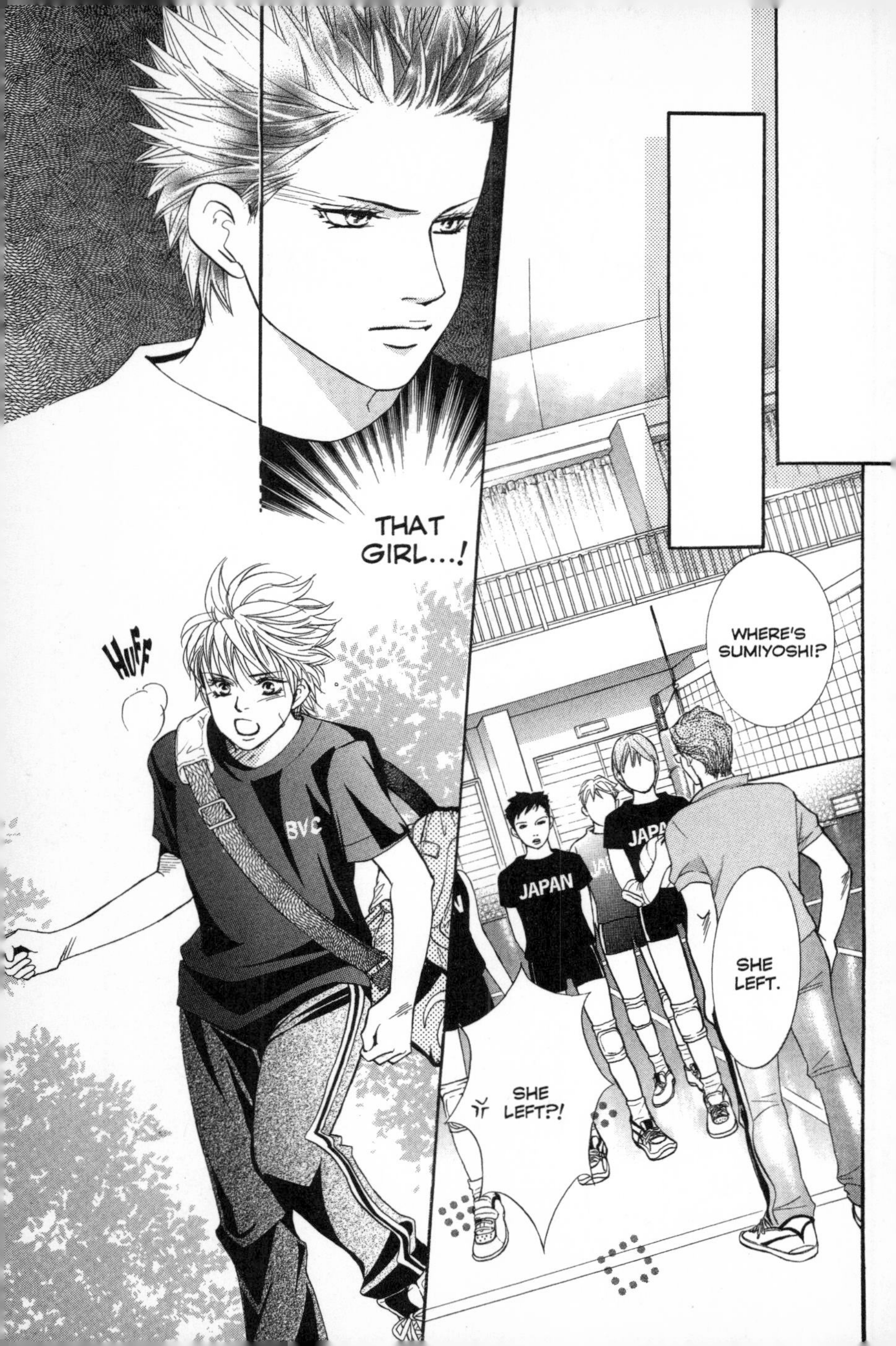
WHERE'S SUMIYOSHI?
SHE LEFT.
SHE LEFT?!
THAT GIRL...!
HUFF
BVC
JAPAN
JAPA

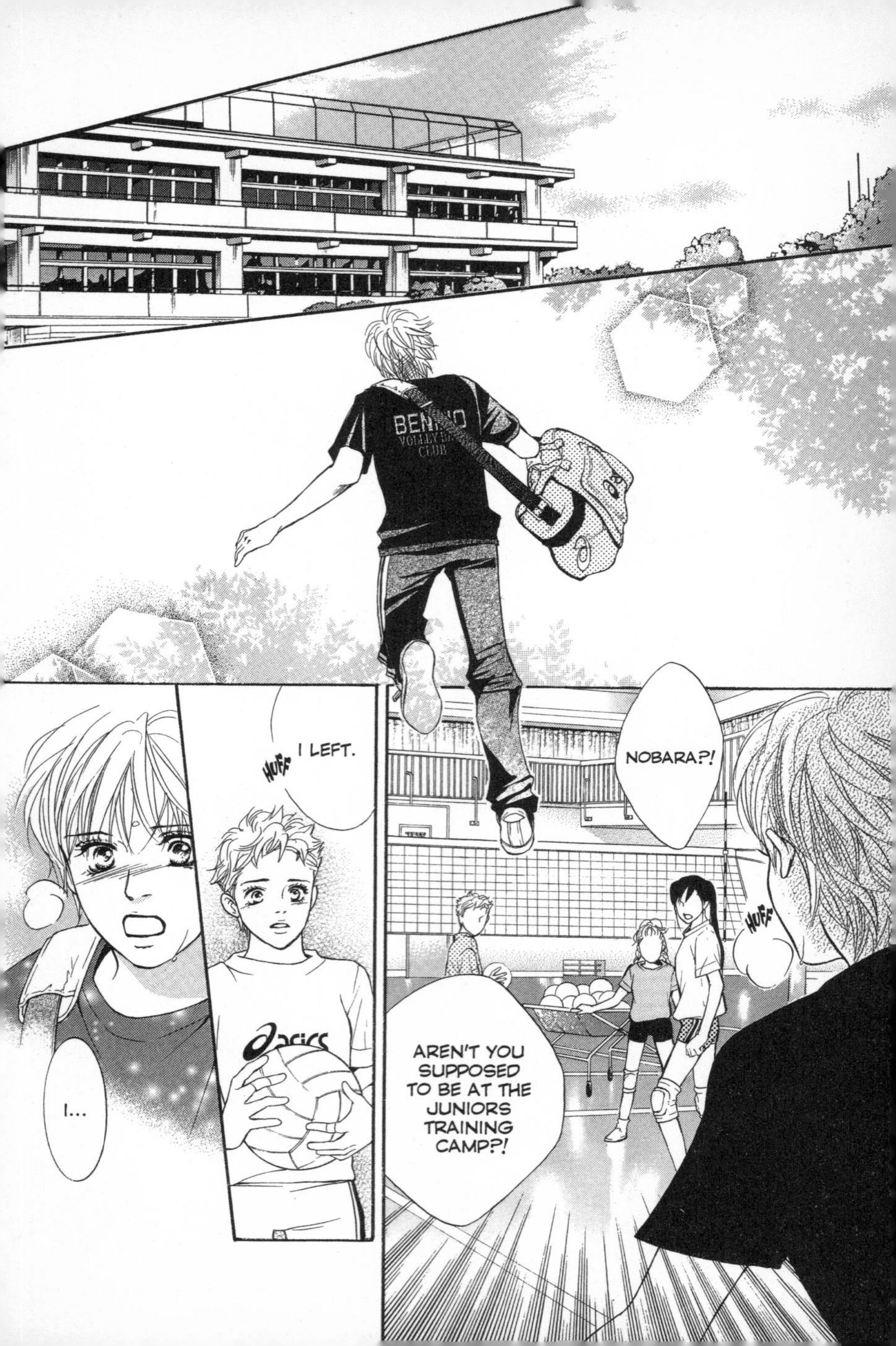
NOBARA?!
HUFF
AREN'T YOU SUPPOSED TO BE AT THE JUNIORS TRAINING CAMP?!
HUFF
I LEFT.
I...

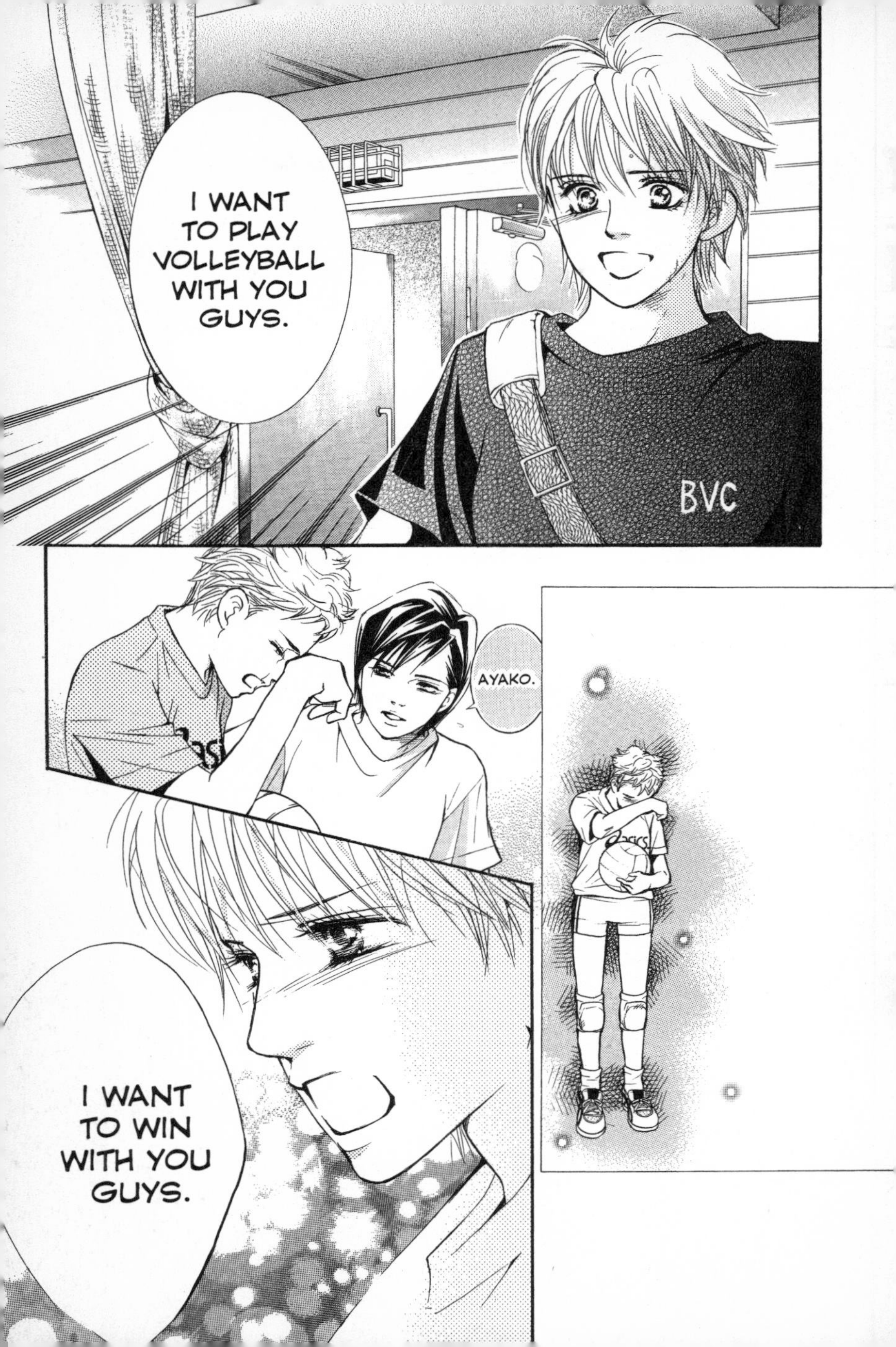
I WANT TO PLAY VOLLEYBALL WITH YOU GUYS.
AYAKO.
I WANT TO WIN WITH YOU GUYS.

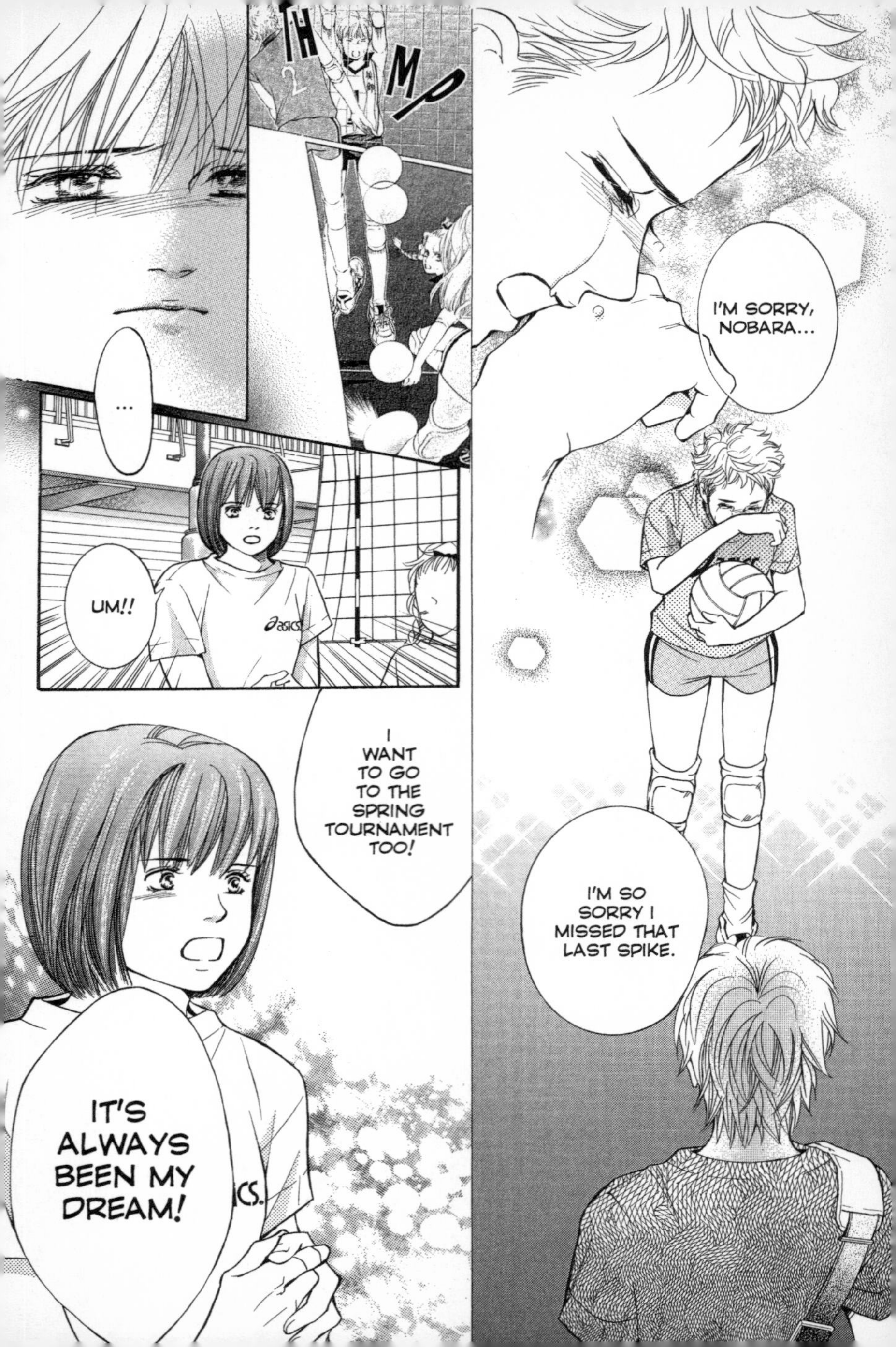
I'M SORRY, NOBARA...
I'M SO SORRY I MISSED THAT LAST SPIKE.
THMP
...
UM!!
I WANT TO GO TO THE SPRING TOURNAMENT TOO!
IT'S ALWAYS BEEN MY DREAM!

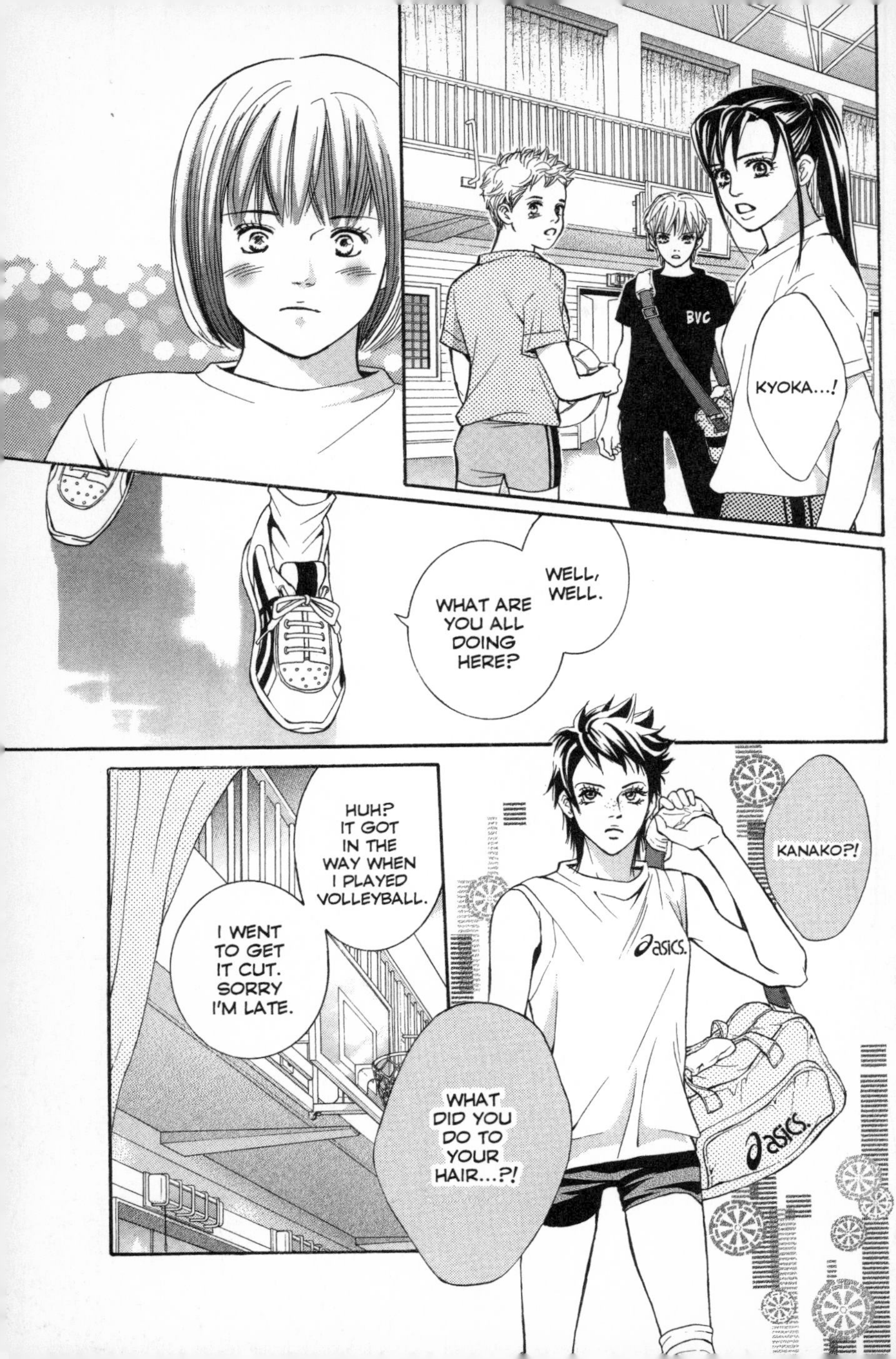
KYOKA...!
WELL, WELL. WHAT ARE YOU ALL DOING HERE?
KANAKO?!
WHAT DID YOU DO TO YOUR HAIR...?!
HUH? IT GOT IN THE WAY WHEN I PLAYED VOLLEYBALL.
I WENT TO GET IT CUT. SORRY I'M LATE.

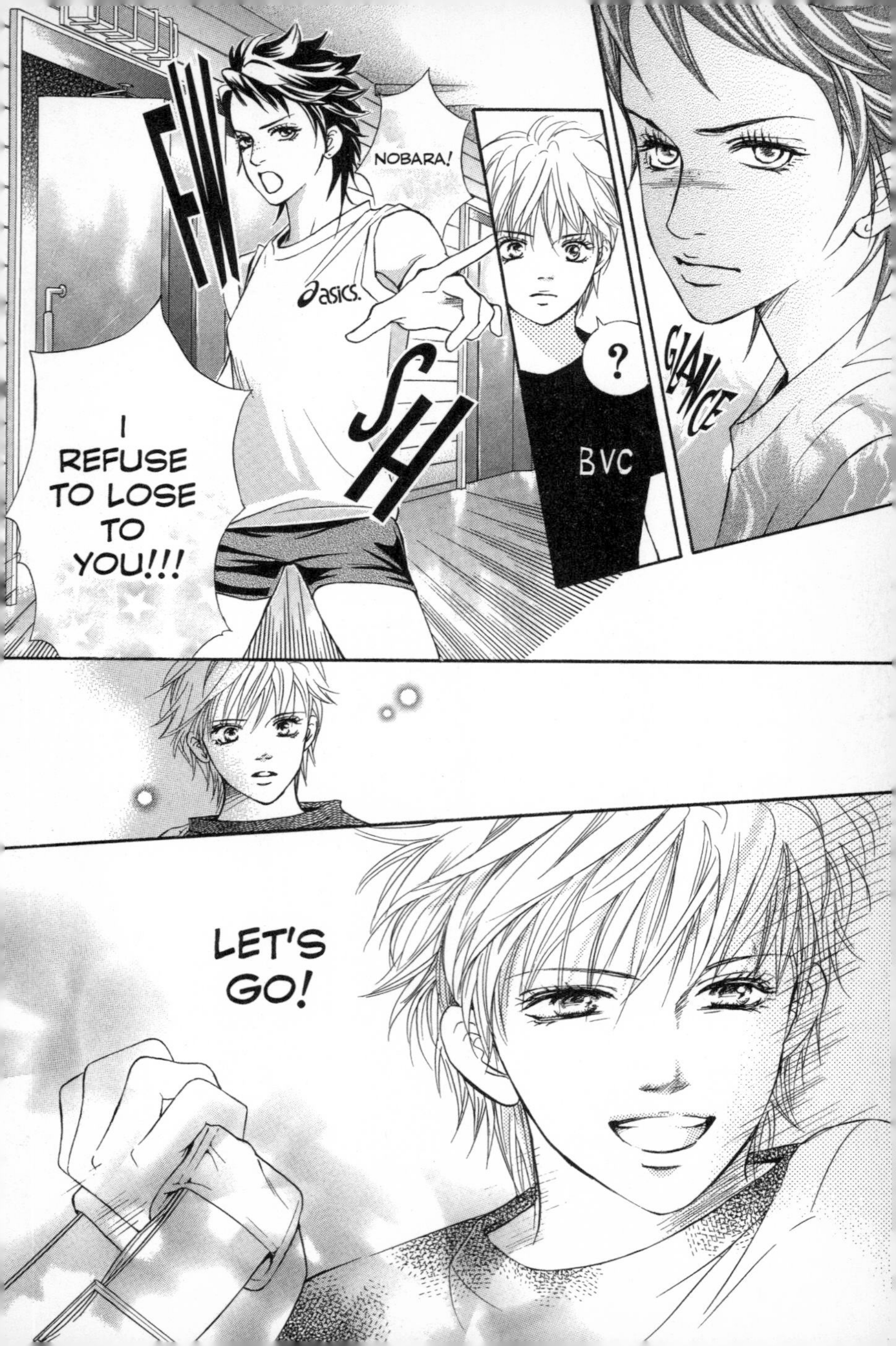
GLANCE
?
BVC
NOBARA!
FW
asics.
SH
I REFUSE TO LOSE TO YOU!!!
LET'S GO!

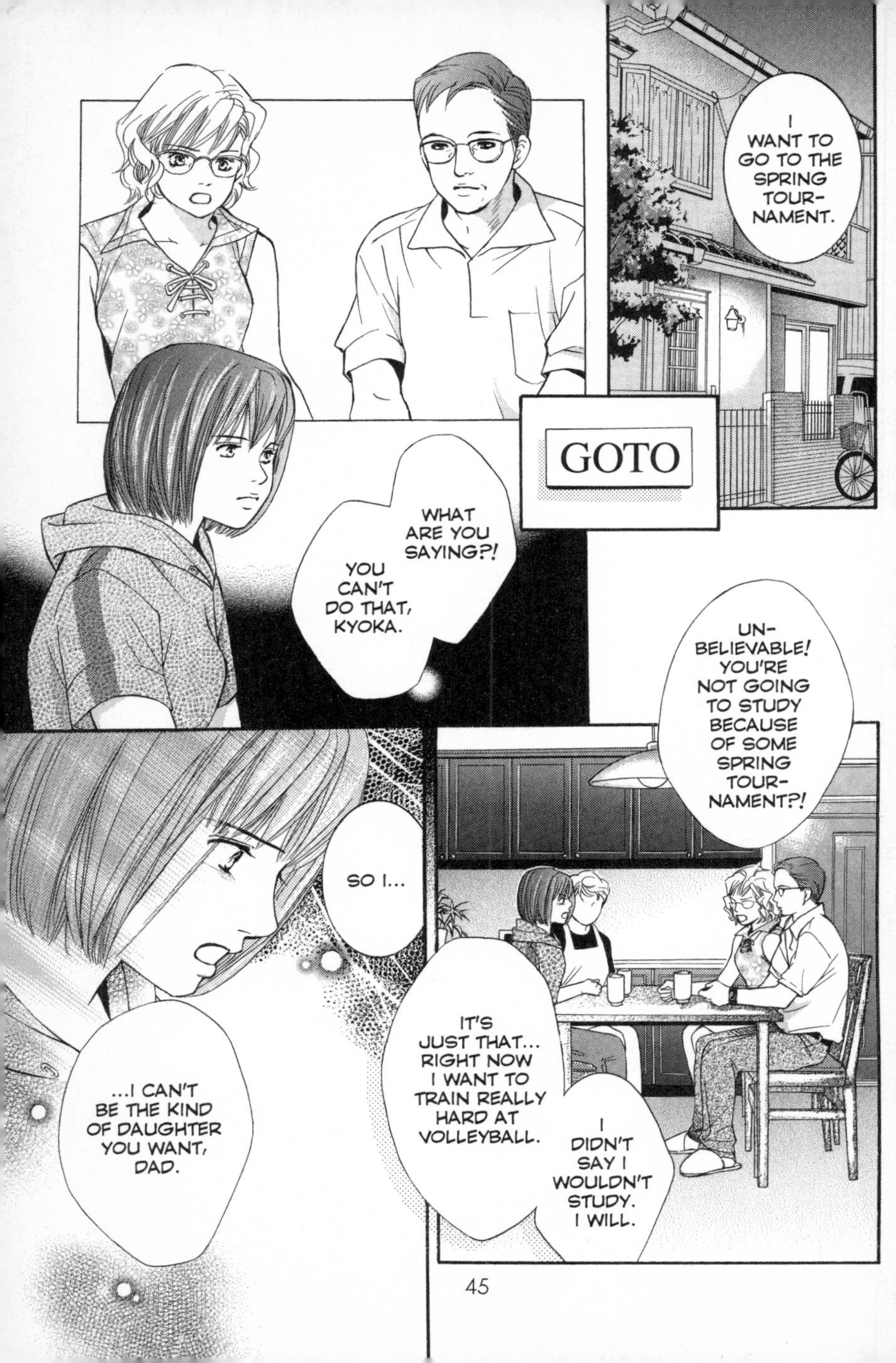
I WANT TO GO TO THE SPRING TOUR-NAMENT.
GOTO
WHAT ARE YOU SAYING?!
YOU CAN'T DO THAT, KYOKA.
UN-BELIEVABLE! YOU'RE NOT GOING TO STUDY BECAUSE OF SOME SPRING TOUR-NAMENT?!
I DIDN'T SAY I WOULDN'T STUDY. I WILL.
IT'S JUST THAT... RIGHT NOW I WANT TO TRAIN REALLY HARD AT VOLLEYBALL.
SO I...
...I CAN'T BE THE KIND OF DAUGHTER YOU WANT, DAD.

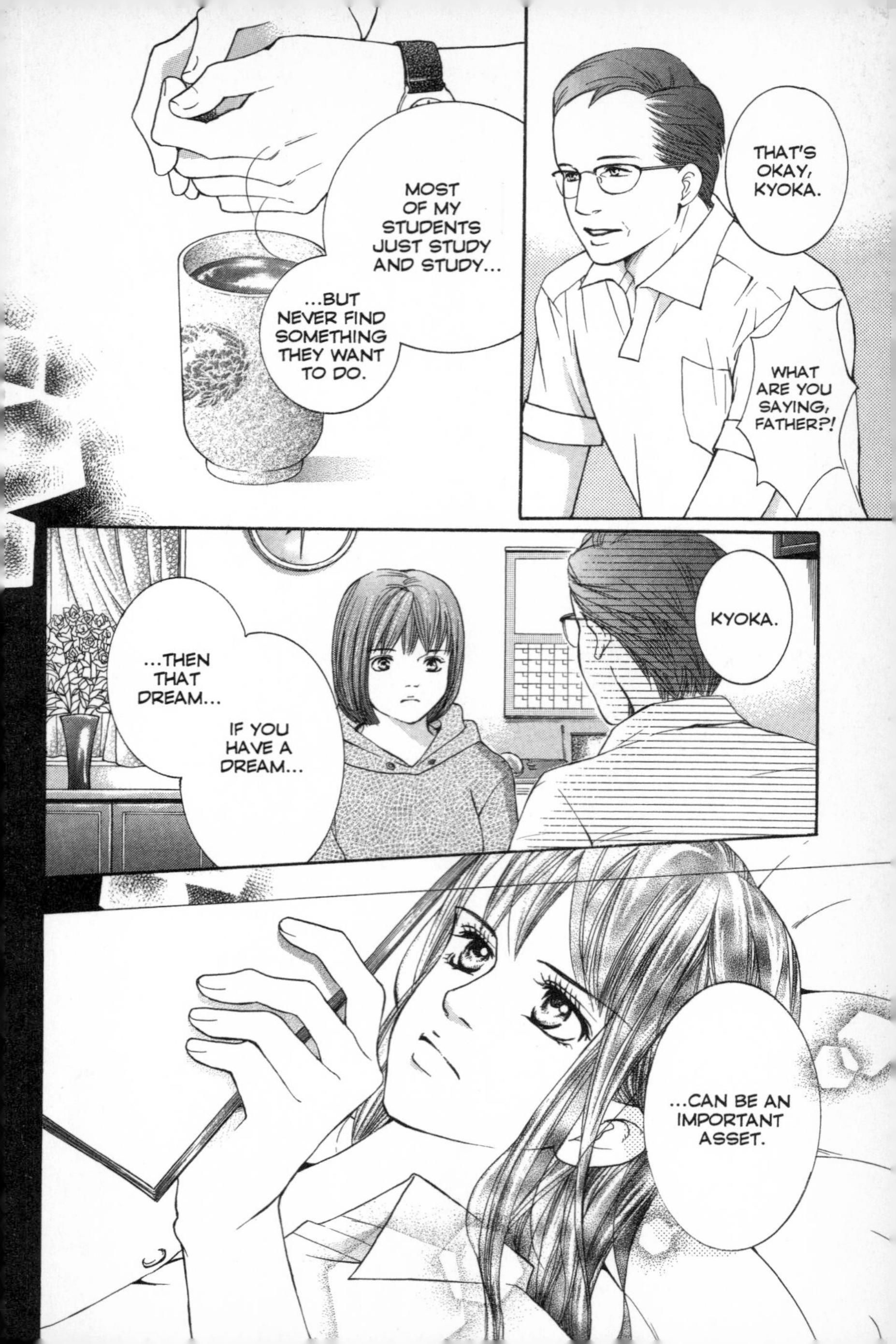
THAT'S OKAY, KYOKA.
WHAT ARE YOU SAYING, FATHER?!
MOST OF MY STUDENTS JUST STUDY AND STUDY...
...BUT NEVER FIND SOMETHING THEY WANT TO DO.
KYOKA.
IF YOU HAVE A DREAM...
...THEN THAT DREAM...
...CAN BE AN IMPORTANT ASSET.

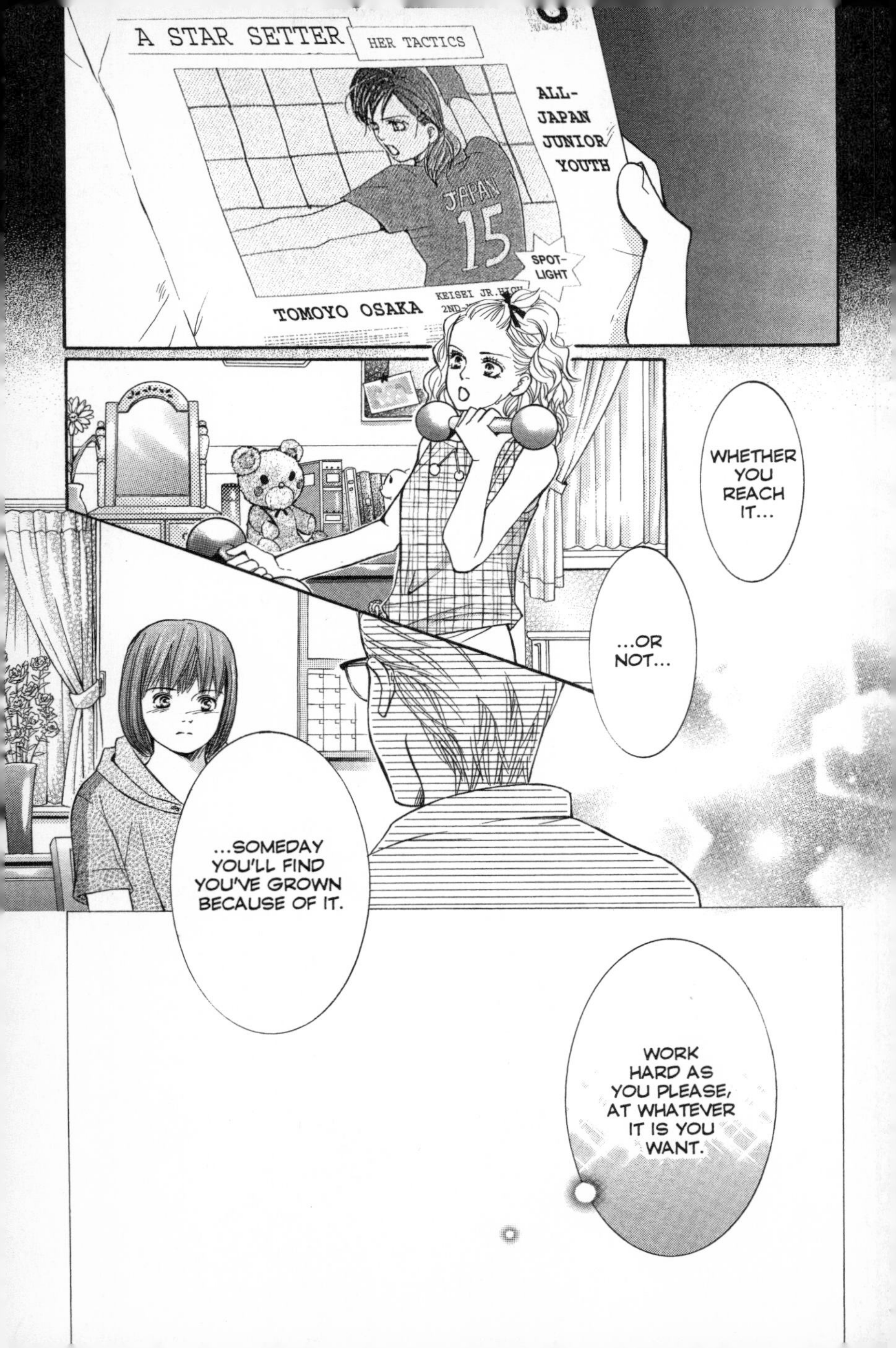
A STAR SETTER
HER TACTICS
ALL-JAPAN JUNIOR YOUTH
JAPAN 15
SPOT-LIGHT
TOMOYO OSAKA
WHETHER YOU REACH IT...
...OR NOT...
...SOMEDAY YOU'LL FIND YOU'VE GROWN BECAUSE OF IT.
WORK HARD AS YOU PLEASE, AT WHATEVER IT IS YOU WANT.

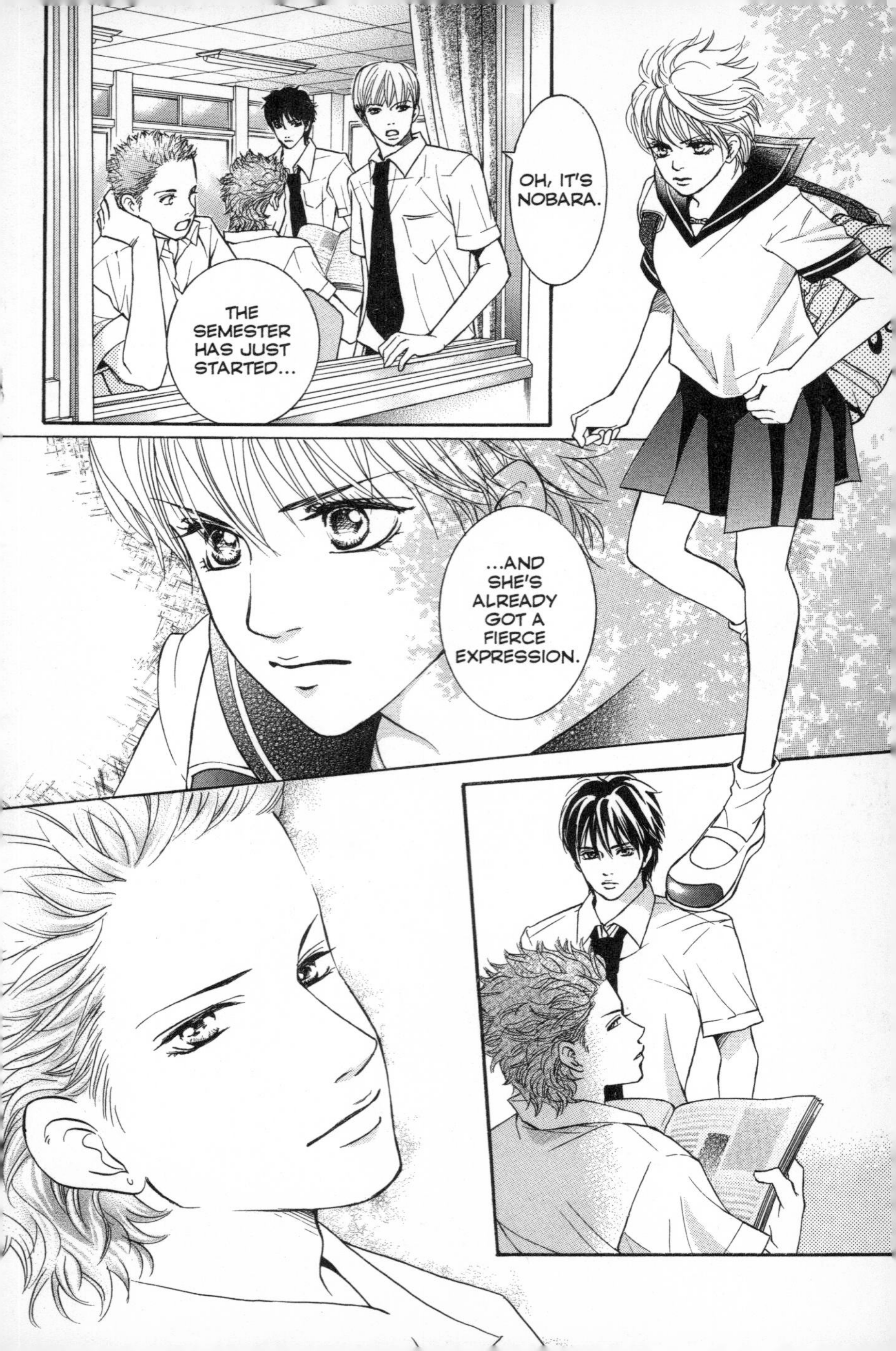
OH, IT'S NOBARA.
THE SEMESTER HAS JUST STARTED...
...AND SHE'S ALREADY GOT A FIERCE EXPRESSION.

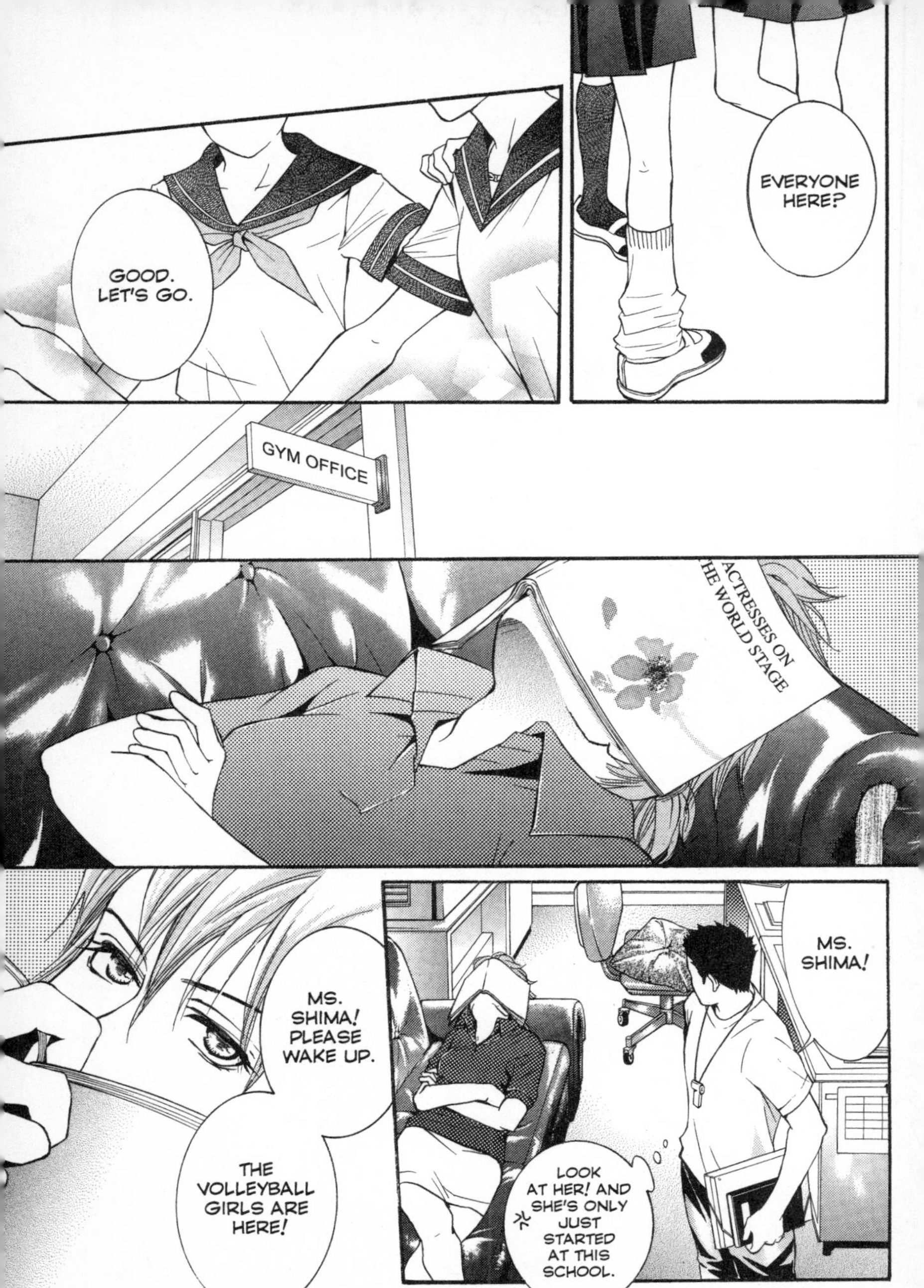
EVERYONE HERE?
GOOD. LET'S GO.
GYM OFFICE
ACTRESSES ON HE WORLD STAGE
MS. SHIMA!
LOOK AT HER! AND SHE'S ONLY JUST STARTED AT THIS SCHOOL.
MS. SHIMA! PLEASE WAKE UP.
THE VOLLEYBALL GIRLS ARE HERE!

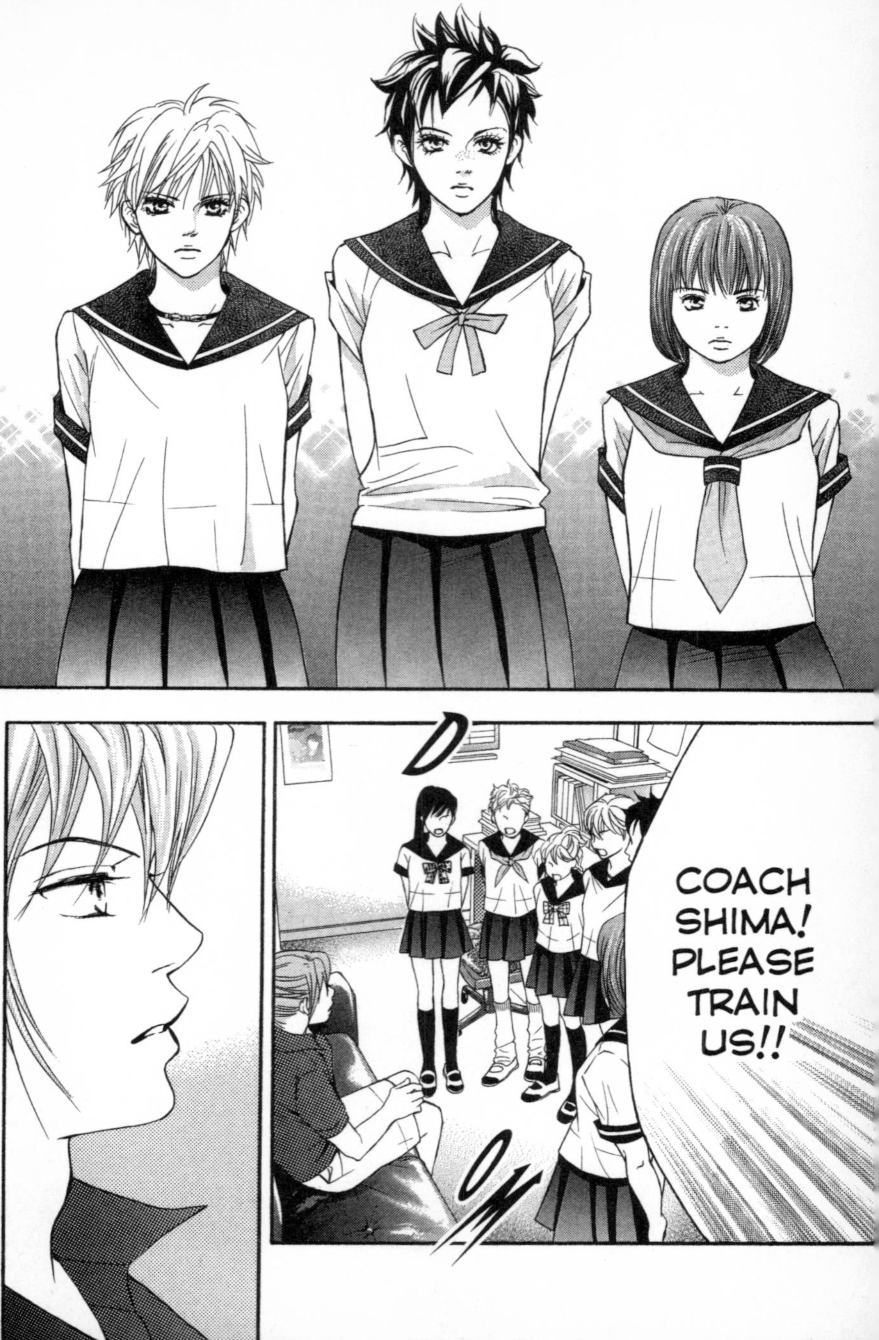
COACH SHIMA! PLEASE TRAIN US!!

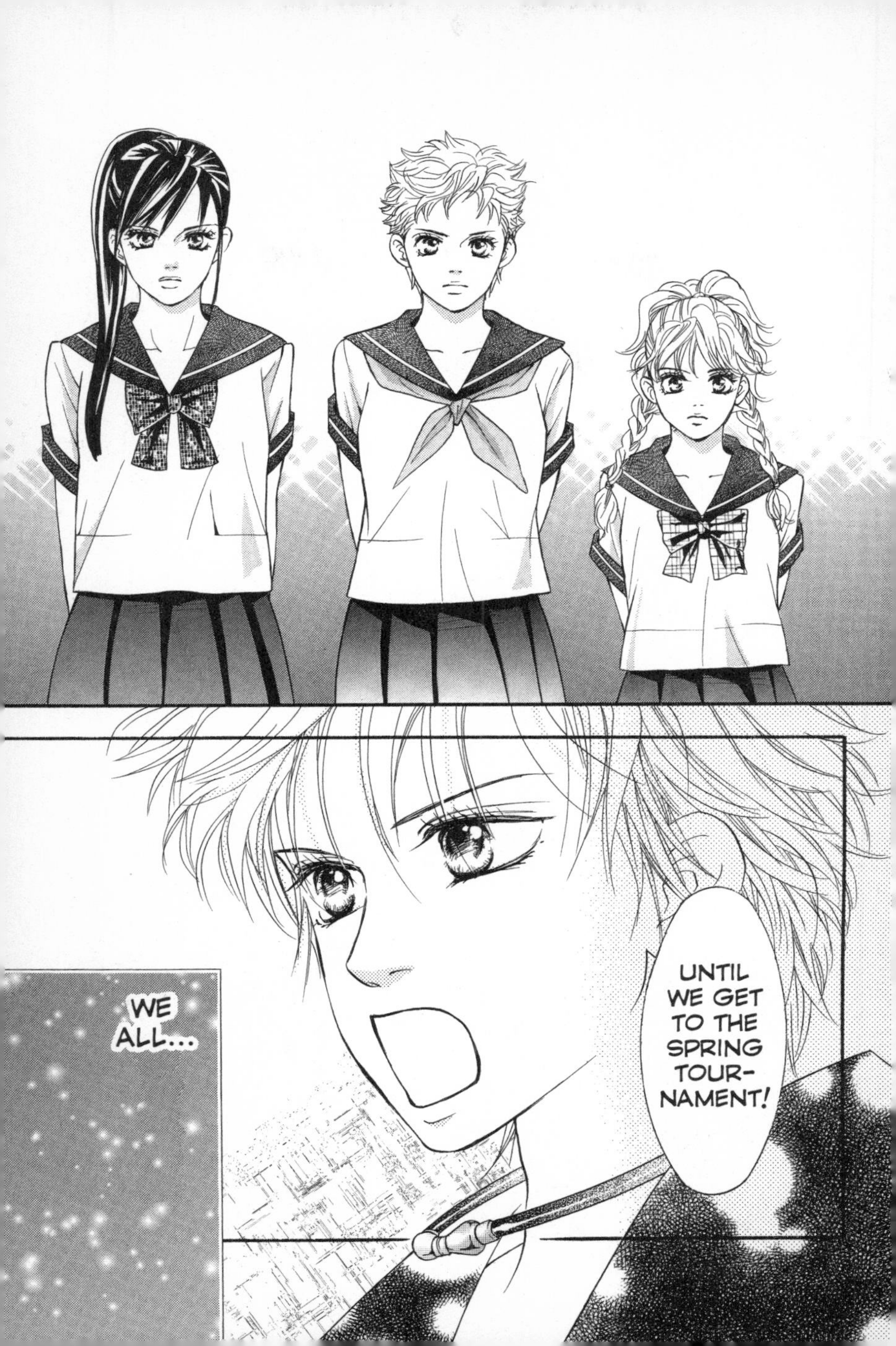
UNTIL WE GET TO THE SPRING TOUR-NAMENT!
WE ALL...

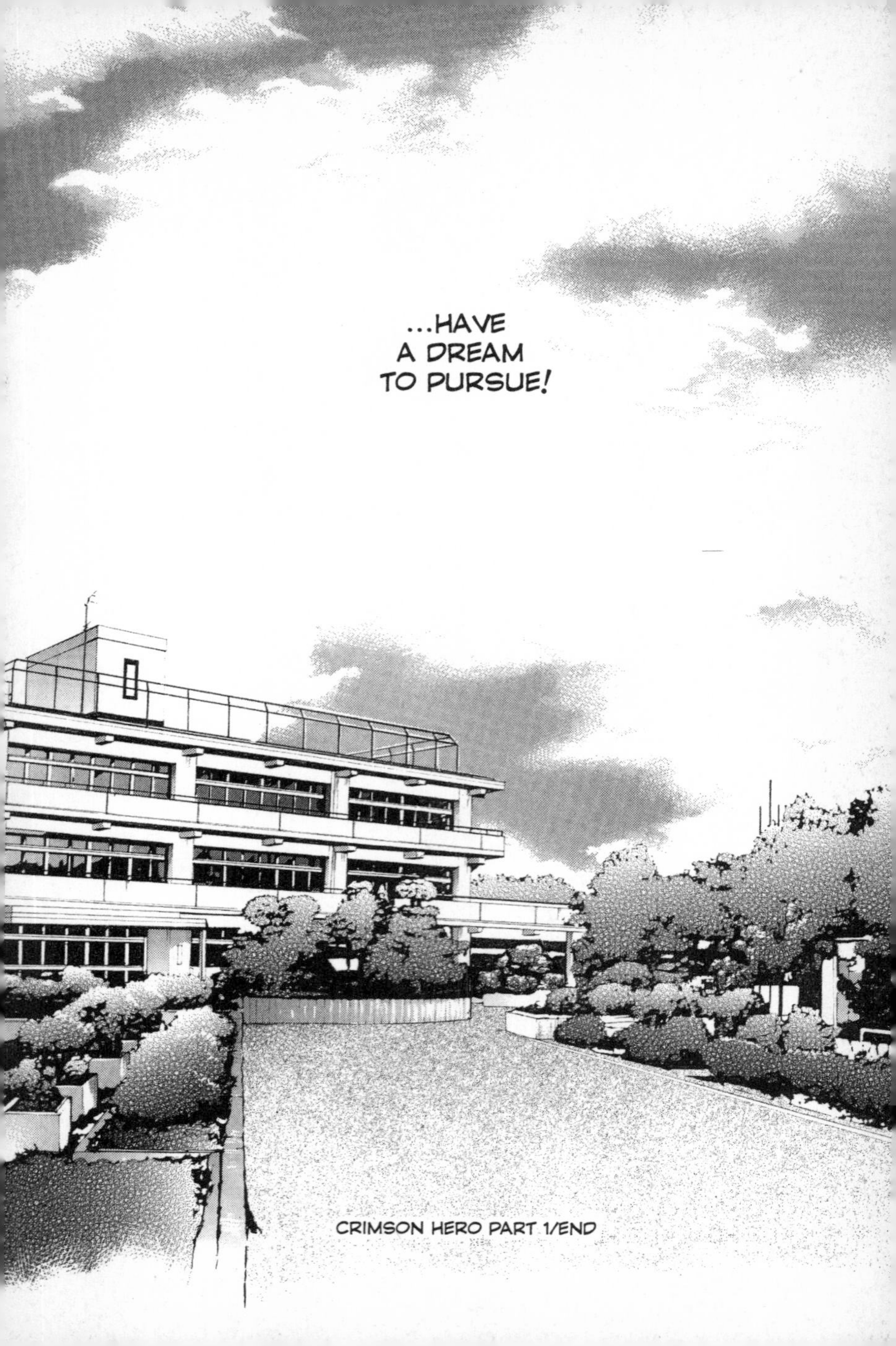
...HAVE A DREAM TO PURSUE!
CRIMSON HERO PART 1/END

CRIMSON HERO PART 2

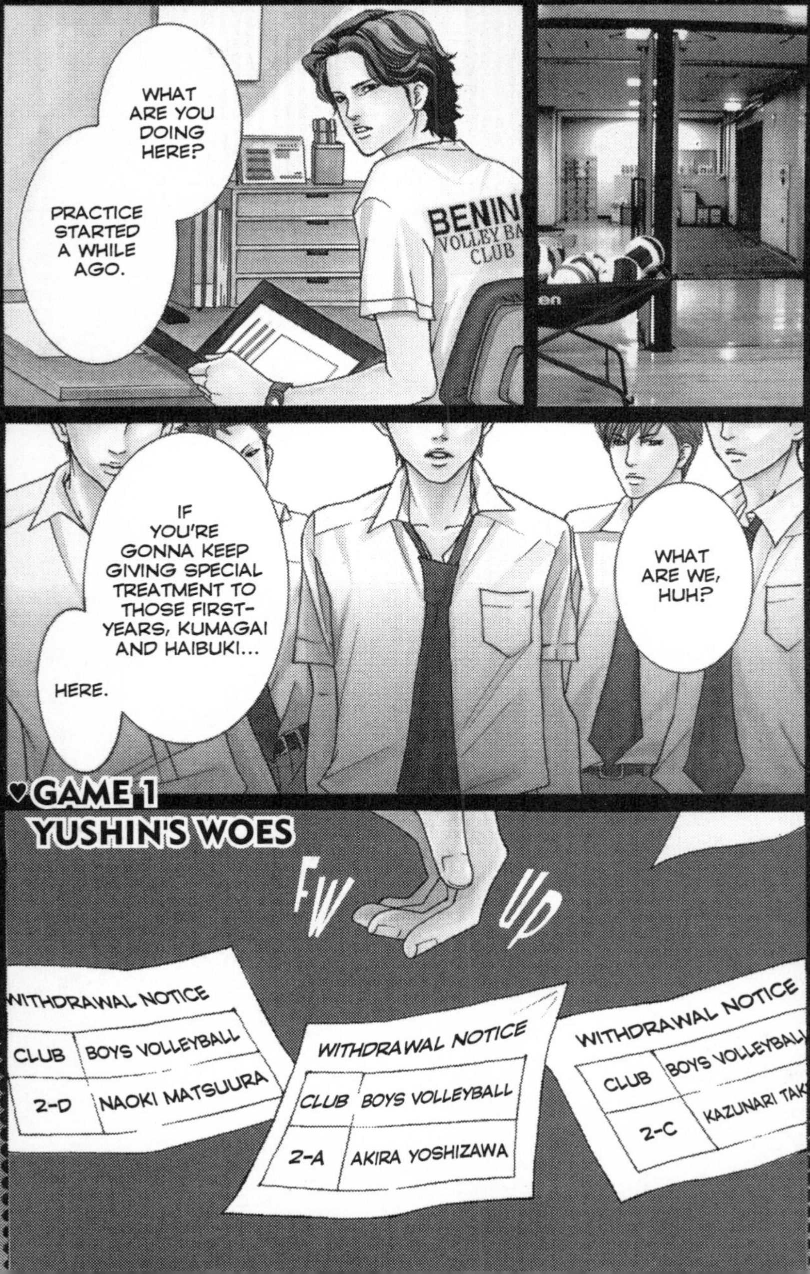
WHAT ARE YOU DOING HERE?
PRACTICE STARTED A WHILE AGO.
WHAT ARE WE, HUH?
IF YOU'RE GONNA KEEP GIVING SPECIAL TREATMENT TO THOSE FIRST-YEARS, KUMAGAI AND HAIBUKI...
HERE.
♥GAME 1
YUSHIN'S WOES
FWUP
WITHDRAWAL NOTICE
CLUB BOYS VOLLEYBALL
2-C KAZUNARI TAK
WITHDRAWAL NOTICE
CLUB BOYS VOLLEYBALL
2-A AKIRA YOSHIZAWA
WITHDRAWAL NOTICE
CLUB BOYS VOLLEYBALL
2-D NAOKI MATSUURA

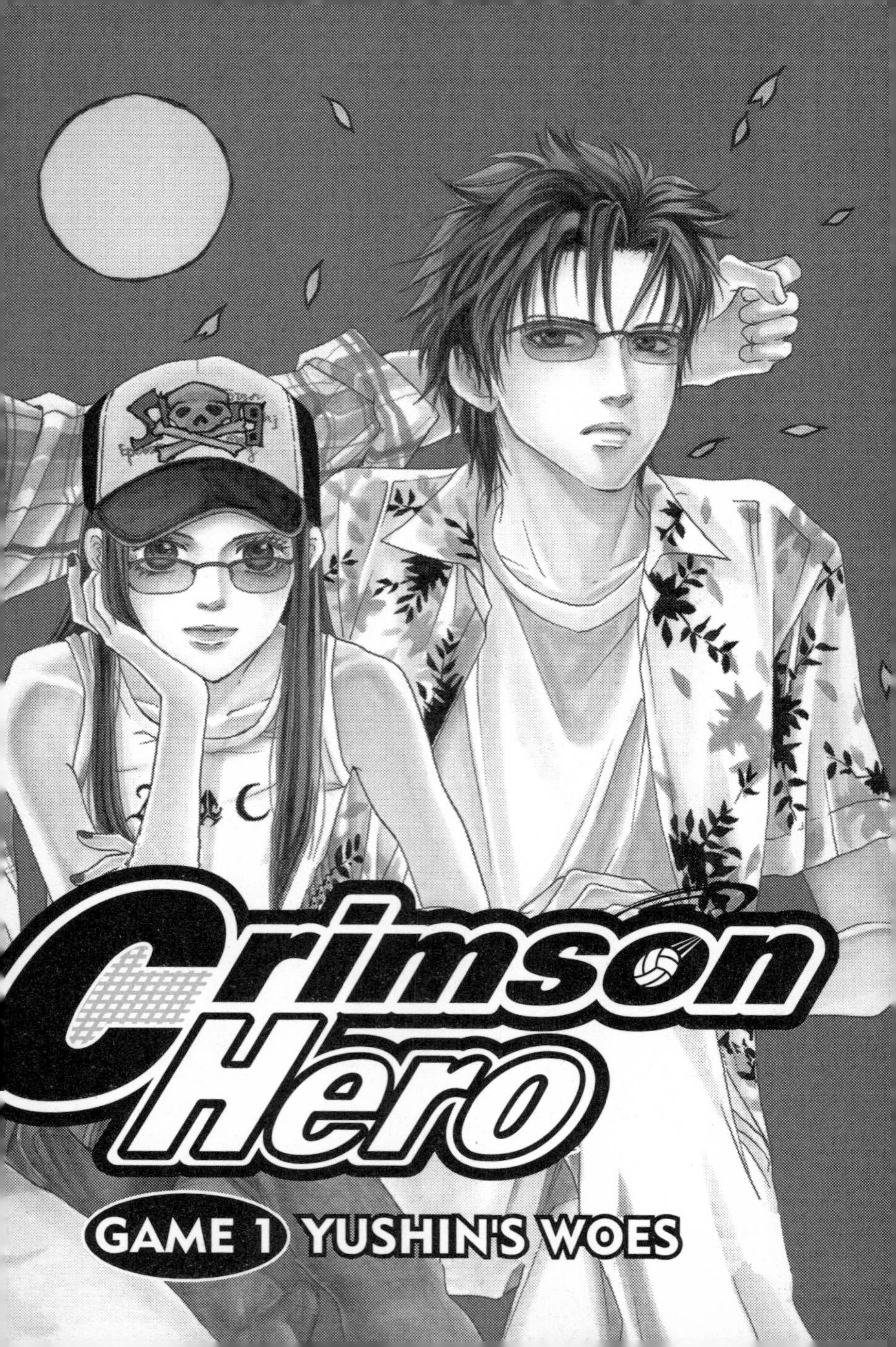
Crimson Hero
GAME 1 YUSHIN'S WOES

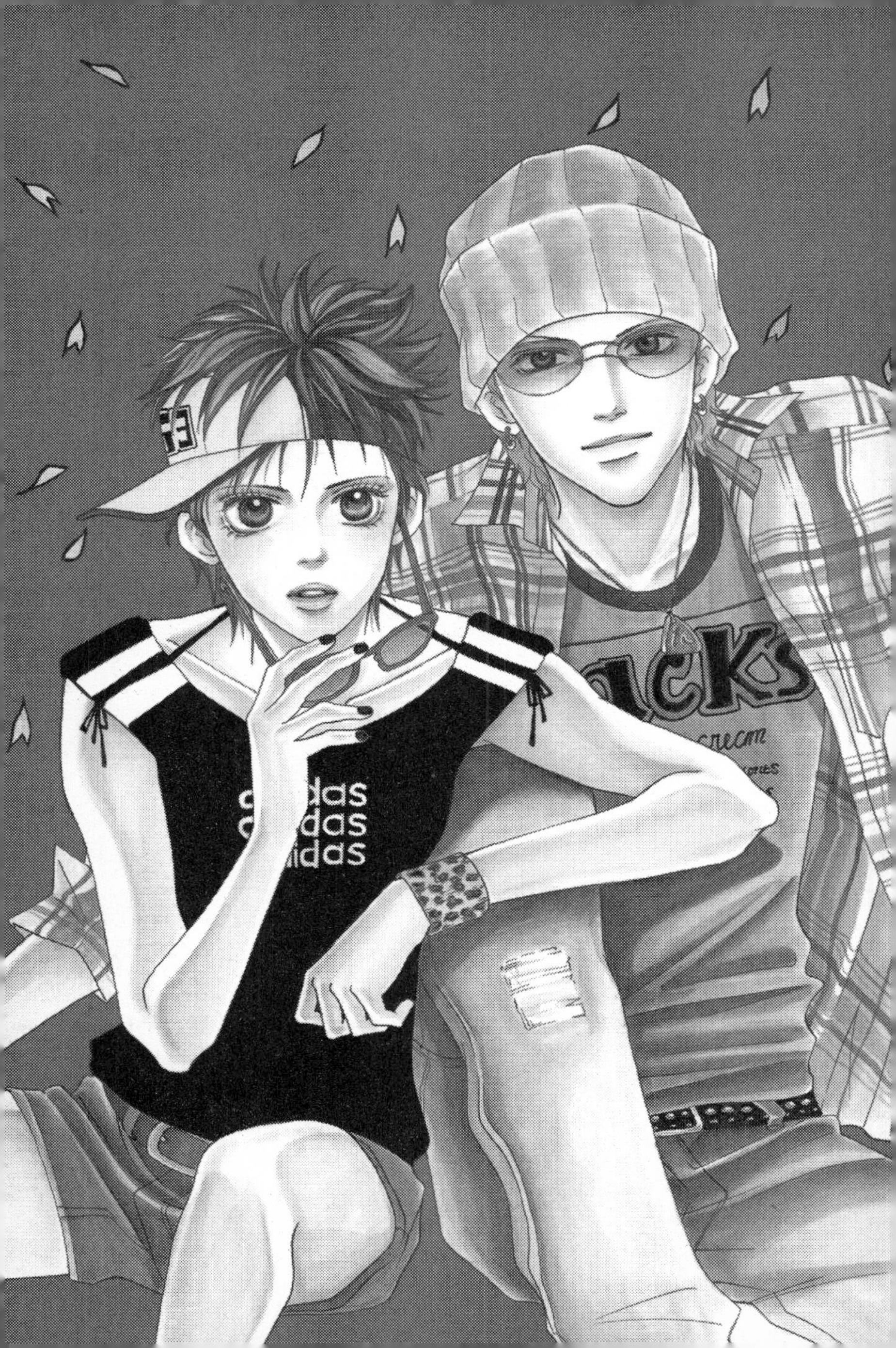

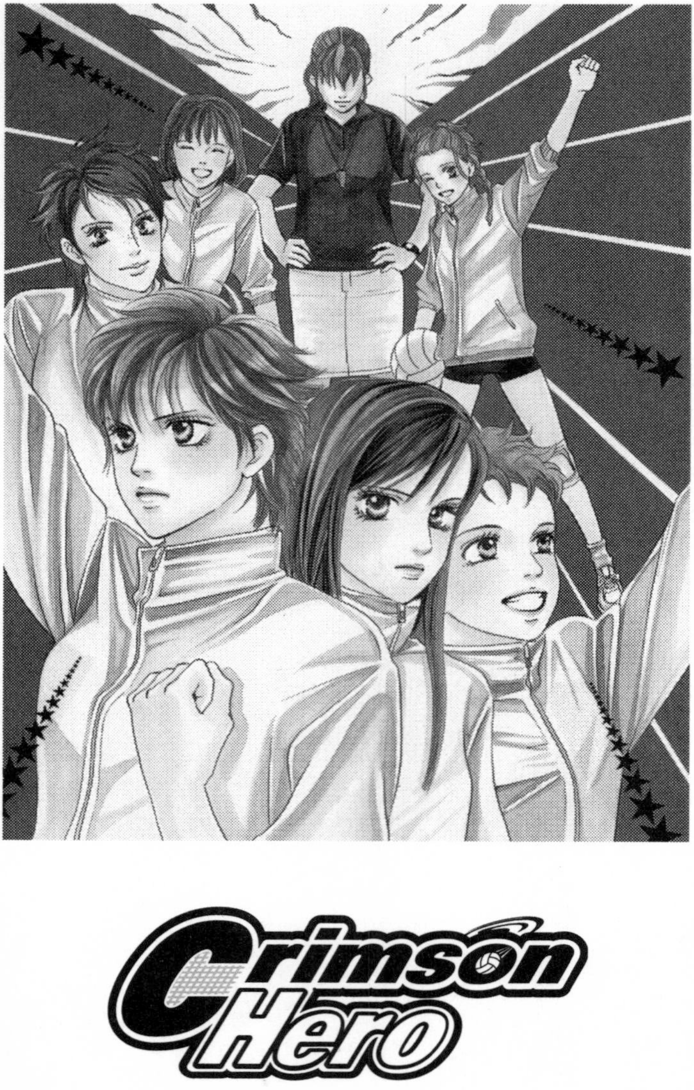

Crimson Hero

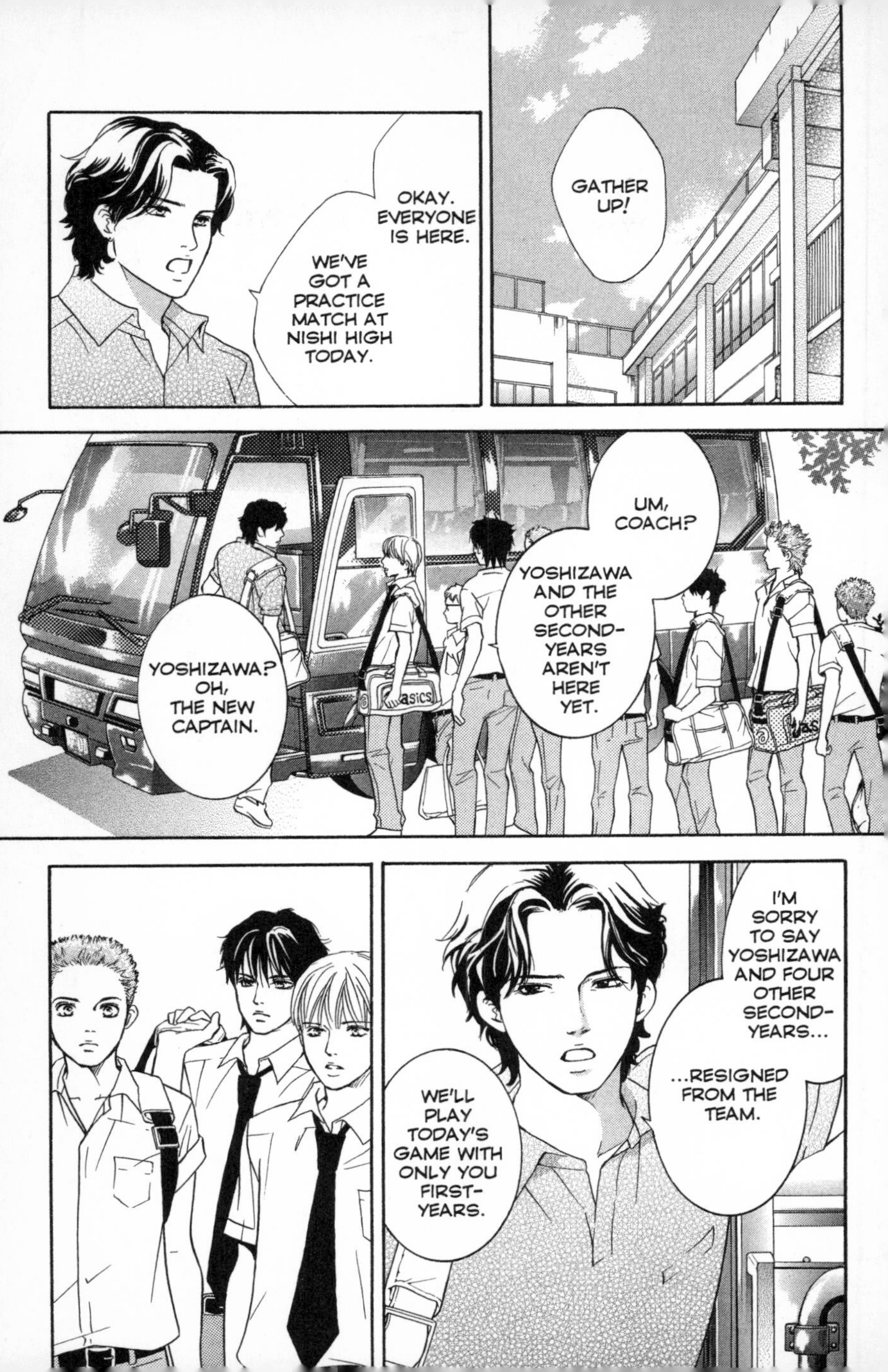
GATHER UP!
OKAY. EVERYONE IS HERE.
WE'VE GOT A PRACTICE MATCH AT NISHI HIGH TODAY.
UM, COACH?
YOSHIZAWA AND THE OTHER SECOND-YEARS AREN'T HERE YET.
YOSHIZAWA? OH, THE NEW CAPTAIN.
I'M SORRY TO SAY YOSHIZAWA AND FOUR OTHER SECOND-YEARS...
...RESIGNED FROM THE TEAM.
WE'LL PLAY TODAY'S GAME WITH ONLY YOU FIRST-YEARS.

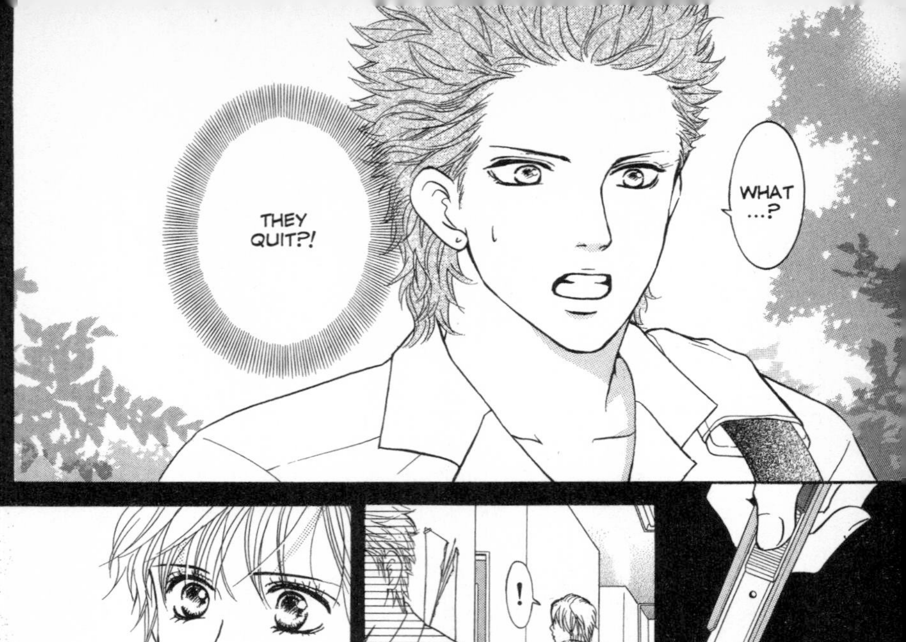
WHAT ...?
THEY QUIT?!
CH'K
!

THE MAKING OF *CRIMSON HERO*

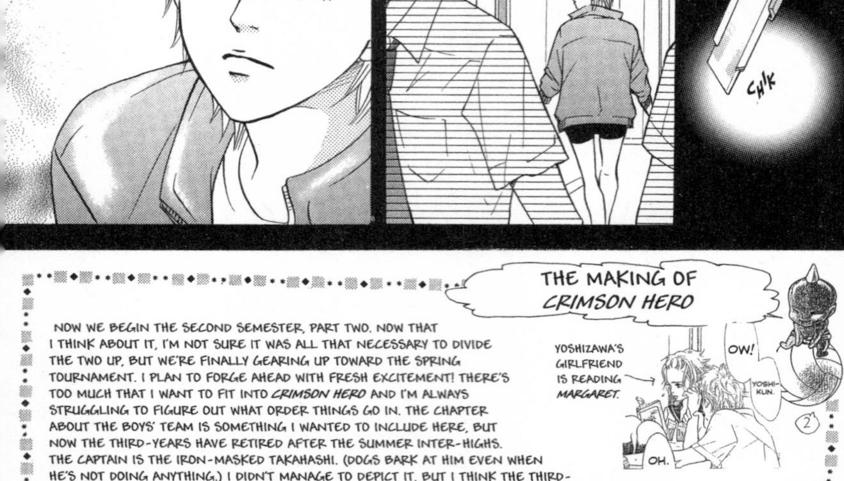
YOSHIZAWA'S GIRLFRIEND IS READING *MARGARET*.
OW!
YOSHI-KUN.
OH.
2

NOW WE BEGIN THE SECOND SEMESTER, PART TWO. NOW THAT I THINK ABOUT IT, I'M NOT SURE IT WAS ALL THAT NECESSARY TO DIVIDE THE TWO UP, BUT WE'RE FINALLY GEARING UP TOWARD THE SPRING TOURNAMENT. I PLAN TO FORGE AHEAD WITH FRESH EXCITEMENT! THERE'S TOO MUCH THAT I WANT TO FIT INTO *CRIMSON HERO* AND I'M ALWAYS STRUGGLING TO FIGURE OUT WHAT ORDER THINGS GO IN. THE CHAPTER ABOUT THE BOYS' TEAM IS SOMETHING I WANTED TO INCLUDE HERE, BUT NOW THE THIRD-YEARS HAVE RETIRED AFTER THE SUMMER INTER-HIGHS. THE CAPTAIN IS THE IRON-MASKED TAKAHASHI. (DOGS BARK AT HIM EVEN WHEN HE'S NOT DOING ANYTHING.) I DIDN'T MANAGE TO DEPICT IT, BUT I THINK THE THIRD-YEARS MUST HAVE BEEN AN AMAZINGLY STRONG TEAM. AND THEY WERE JOINED BY A FRESH FORCE OF VOLLEYBALL RECRUITS WHO QUICKLY BECAME THE TOP PLAYERS ON THE TEAM. SO THE SECOND-YEARS WERE SANDWICHED IN BETWEEN THOSE POWERFUL PLAYERS.

AND THEY DIDN'T NECESSARILY GET TO PLAY IN GAMES DESPITE PRACTICING REALLY HARD. I WANTED TO TRY DEPICTING PEOPLE IN THAT SITUATION. YOSHIZAWA'S ACTIONS ARE UNFORGIVABLE. I DON'T KNOW HOW HE APPEARS TO YOU READERS, BUT I IMAGINE IT MUST'VE BEEN HARD TO KNOW THE LIMITS OF YOUR ABILITIES WHILE ALSO HAVING SENIORITY. IT'D BE WRONG TO ASSUME EVERY MEMBER IS STRONG AND FULL OF ENERGY AND CONFIDENCE.

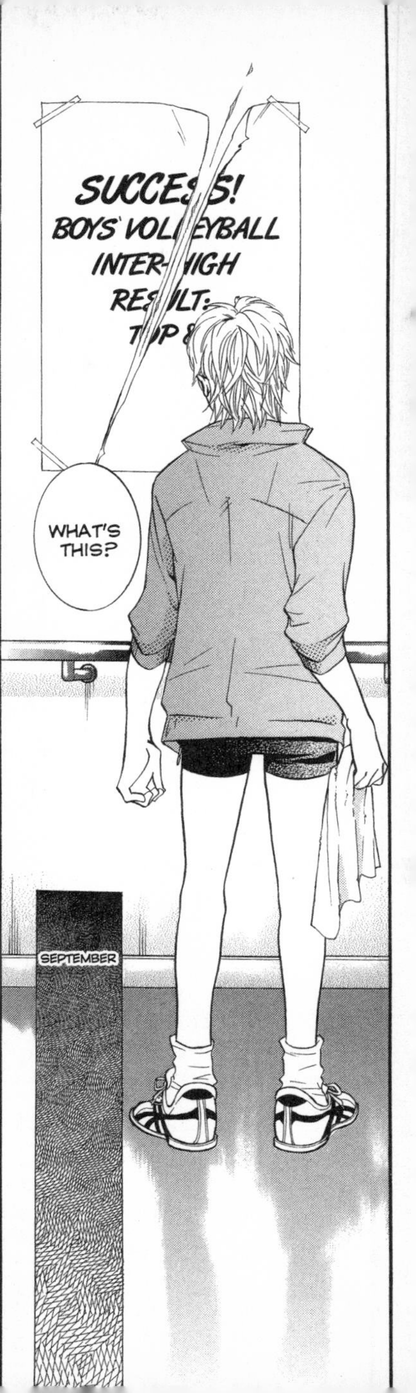
SUCCES S!
BOYS' VOLL EYBALL
INTER-HIGH
RESULT:
WHAT'S THIS?
SEPTEMBER

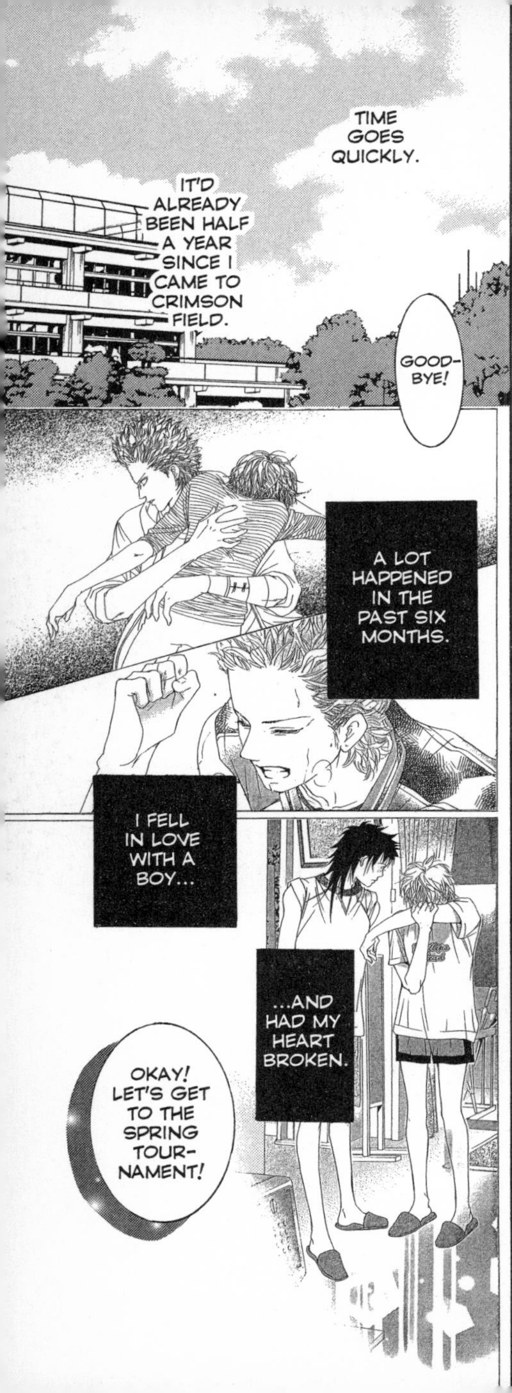
TIME GOES QUICKLY.
IT'D ALREADY BEEN HALF A YEAR SINCE I CAME TO CRIMSON FIELD.
GOOD-BYE!
A LOT HAPPENED IN THE PAST SIX MONTHS.
I FELL IN LOVE WITH A BOY...
...AND HAD MY HEART BROKEN.
OKAY! LET'S GET TO THE SPRING TOURNAMENT!

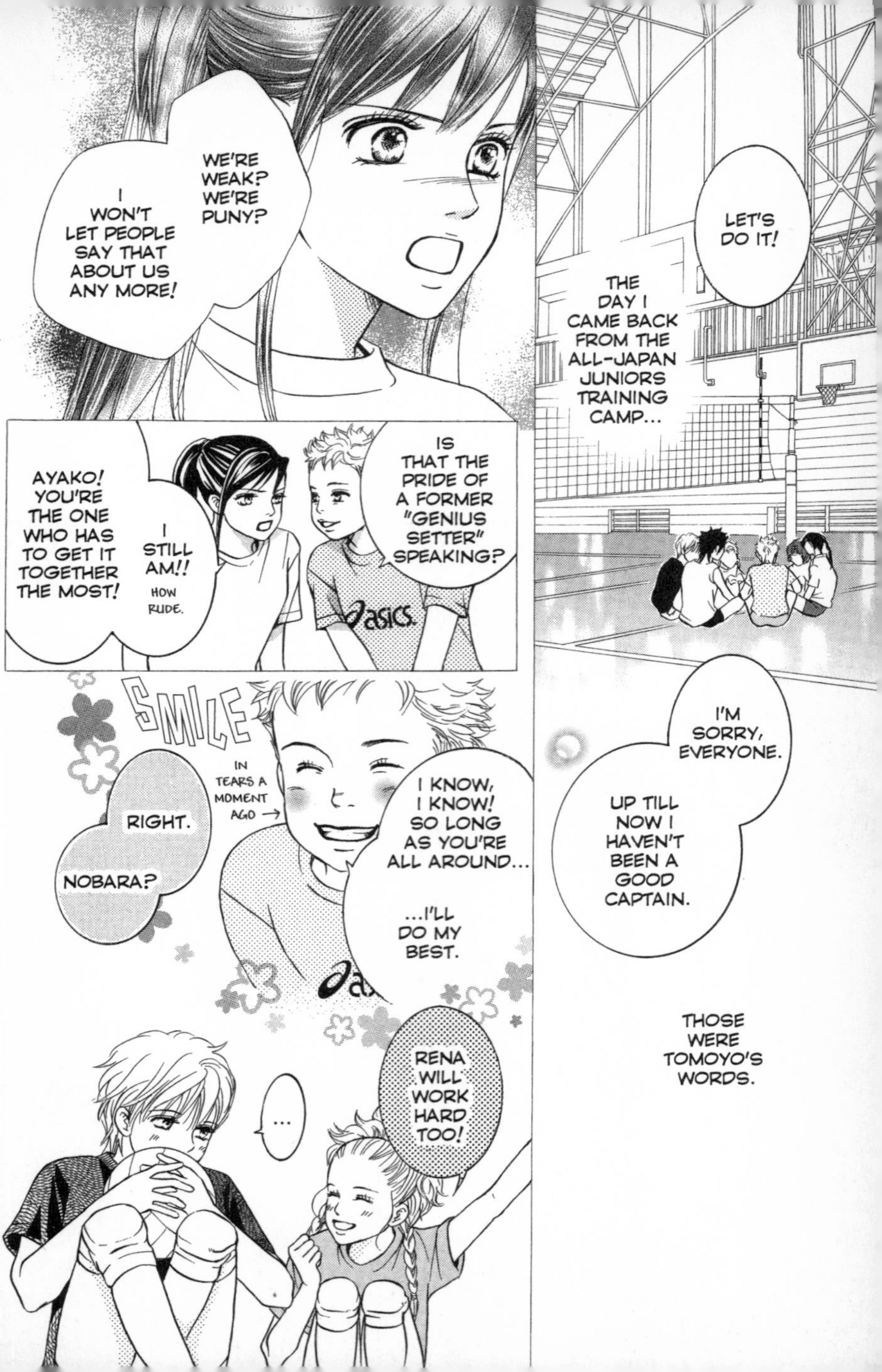
LET'S DO IT!
THE DAY I CAME BACK FROM THE ALL-JAPAN JUNIORS TRAINING CAMP...
I'M SORRY, EVERYONE.
UP TILL NOW I HAVEN'T BEEN A GOOD CAPTAIN.
THOSE WERE TOMOYO'S WORDS.
WE'RE WEAK? WE'RE PUNY?
I WON'T LET PEOPLE SAY THAT ABOUT US ANY MORE!
IS THAT THE PRIDE OF A FORMER "GENIUS SETTER" SPEAKING?
I STILL AM!!
HOW RUDE.
AYAKO! YOU'RE THE ONE WHO HAS TO GET IT TOGETHER THE MOST!
SMILE
I KNOW, I KNOW! SO LONG AS YOU'RE ALL AROUND...
...I'LL DO MY BEST.
IN TEARS A MOMENT AGO →
RIGHT.
NOBARA?
RENA WILL WORK HARD TOO!
...

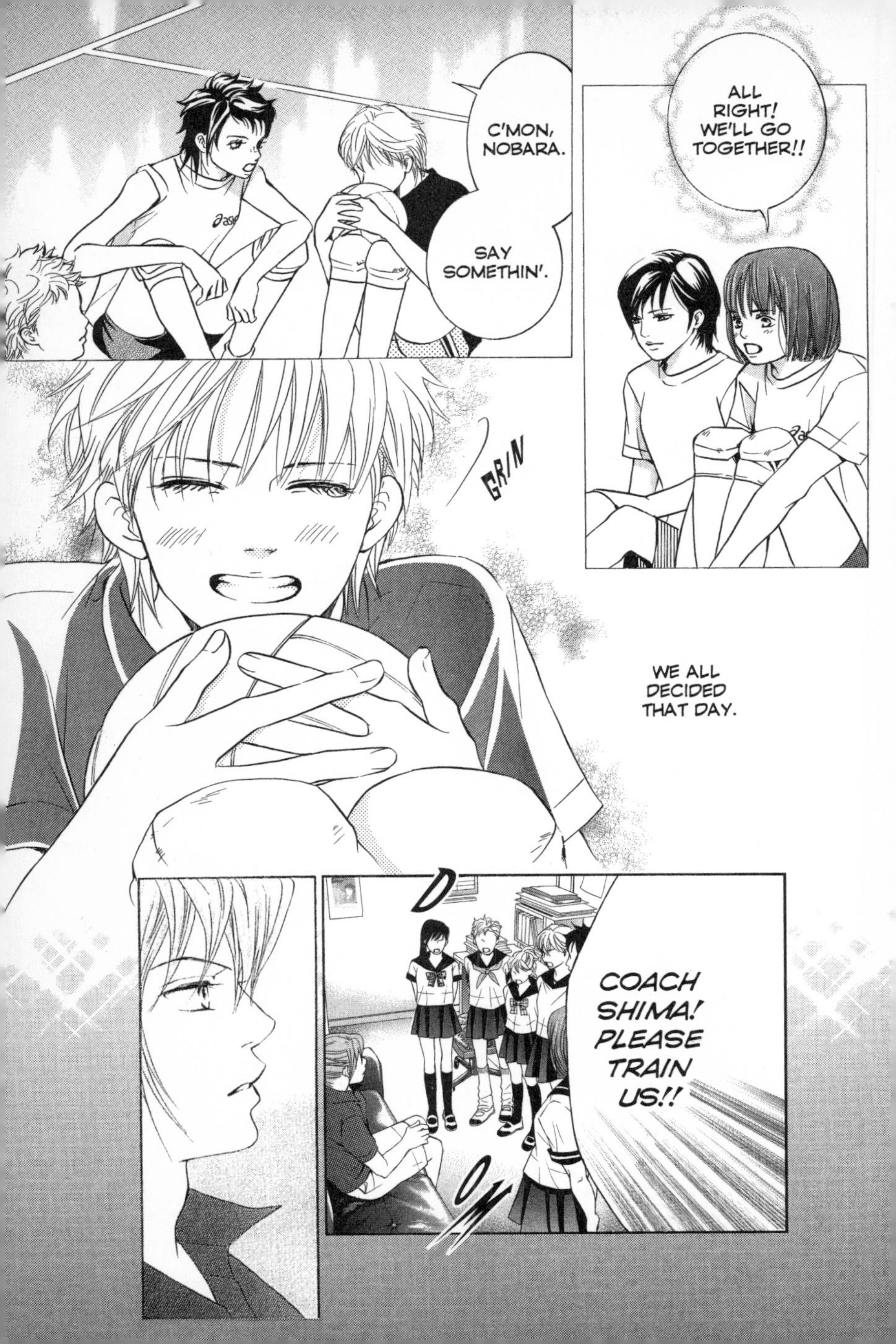
ALL RIGHT! WE'LL GO TOGETHER!!
C'MON, NOBARA.
SAY SOMETHIN'.
GRIN
WE ALL DECIDED THAT DAY.
D
COACH SHIMA! PLEASE TRAIN US!!
OM

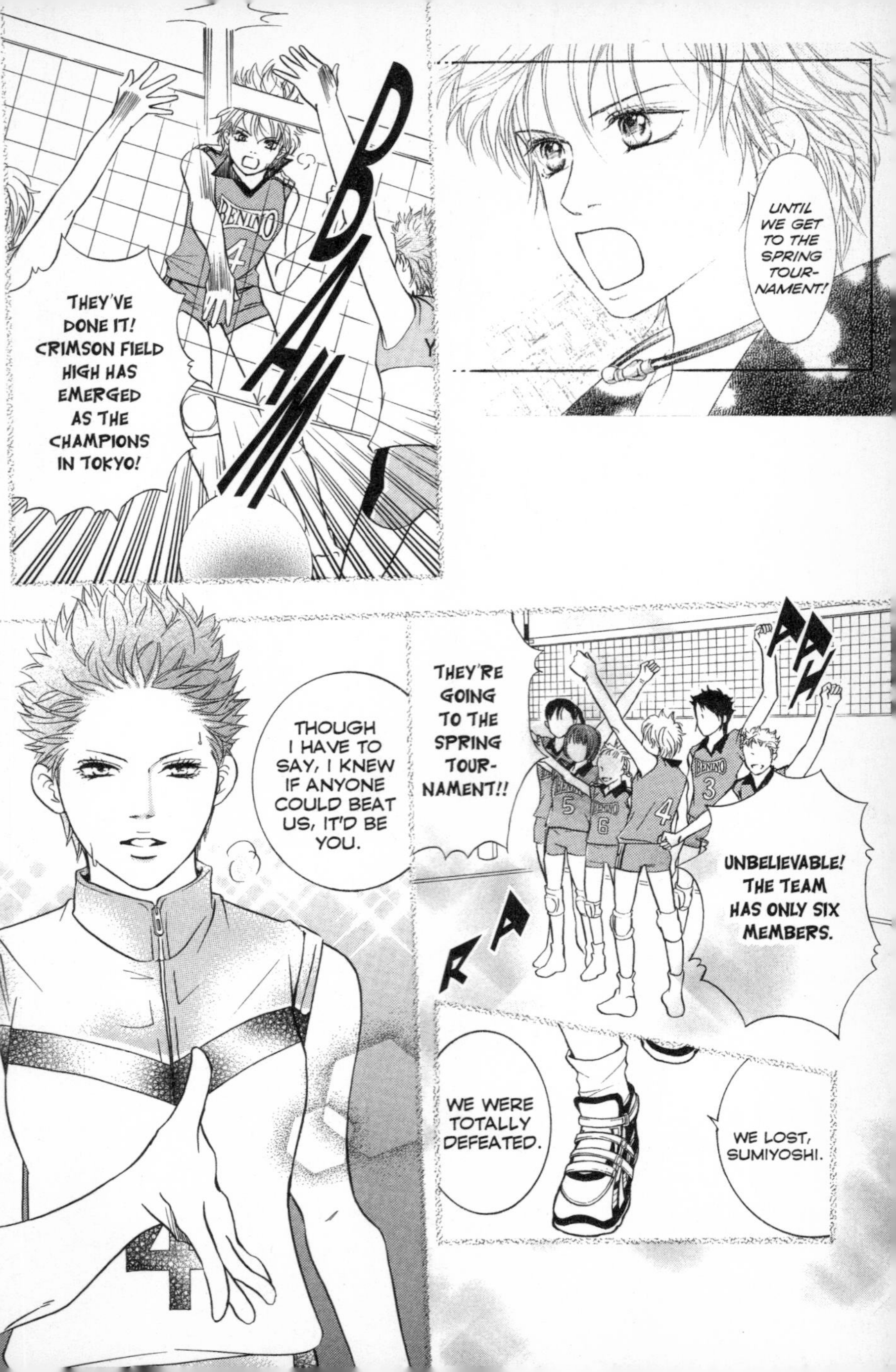
UNTIL WE GET TO THE SPRING TOUR-NAMENT!
BDAHM
THEY'VE DONE IT! CRIMSON FIELD HIGH HAS EMERGED AS THE CHAMPIONS IN TOKYO!
THEY'RE GOING TO THE SPRING TOUR-NAMENT!!
UNBELIEVABLE! THE TEAM HAS ONLY SIX MEMBERS.
WE LOST, SUMIYOSHI.
WE WERE TOTALLY DEFEATED.
THOUGH I HAVE TO SAY, I KNEW IF ANYONE COULD BEAT US, IT'D BE YOU.

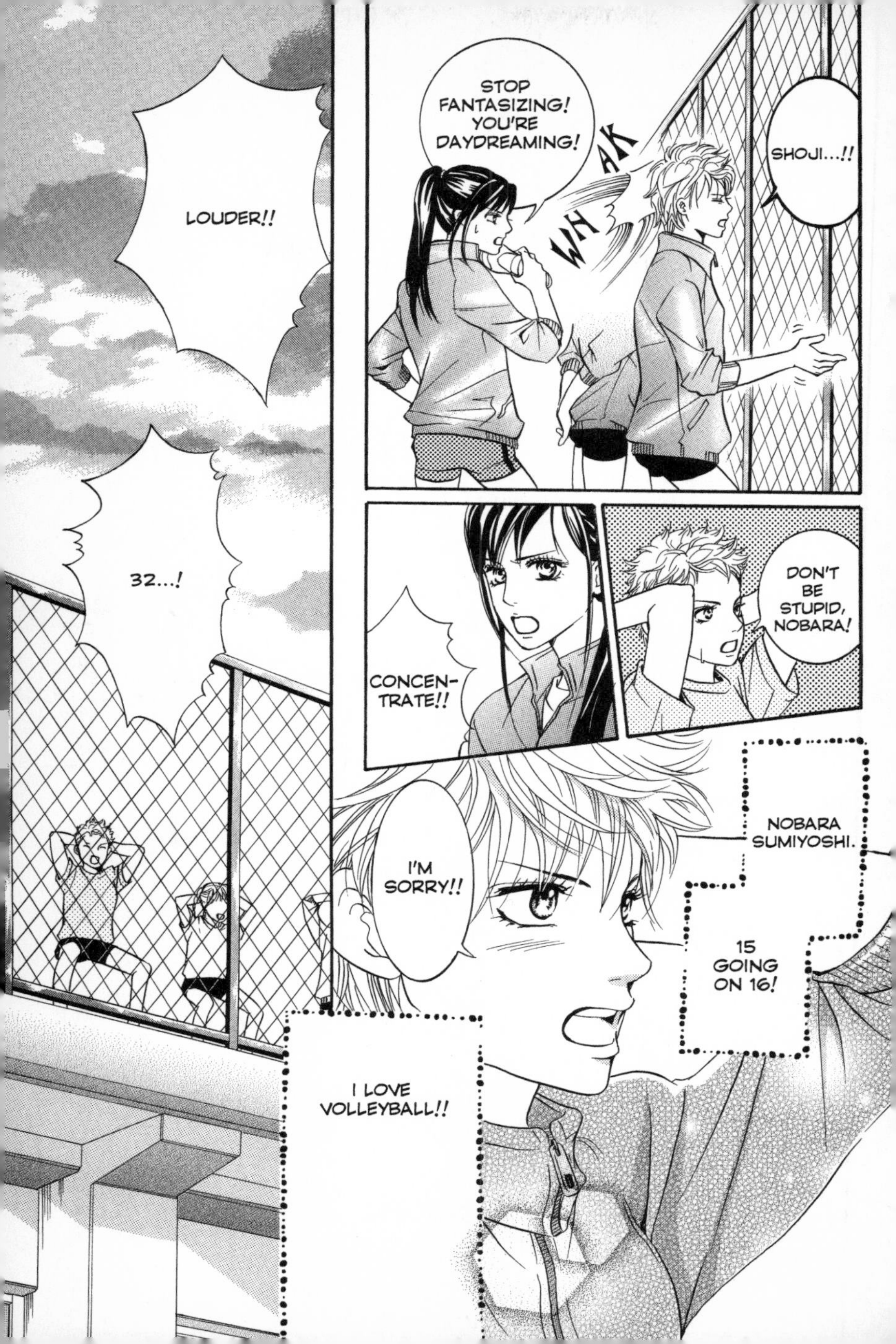
SHOJI...!!
STOP FANTASIZING! YOU'RE DAYDREAMING!
WHAK
DON'T BE STUPID, NOBARA!
CONCENTRATE!!
NOBARA SUMIYOSHI.
I'M SORRY!!
15 GOING ON 16!
I LOVE VOLLEYBALL!!
LOUDER!!
32...!

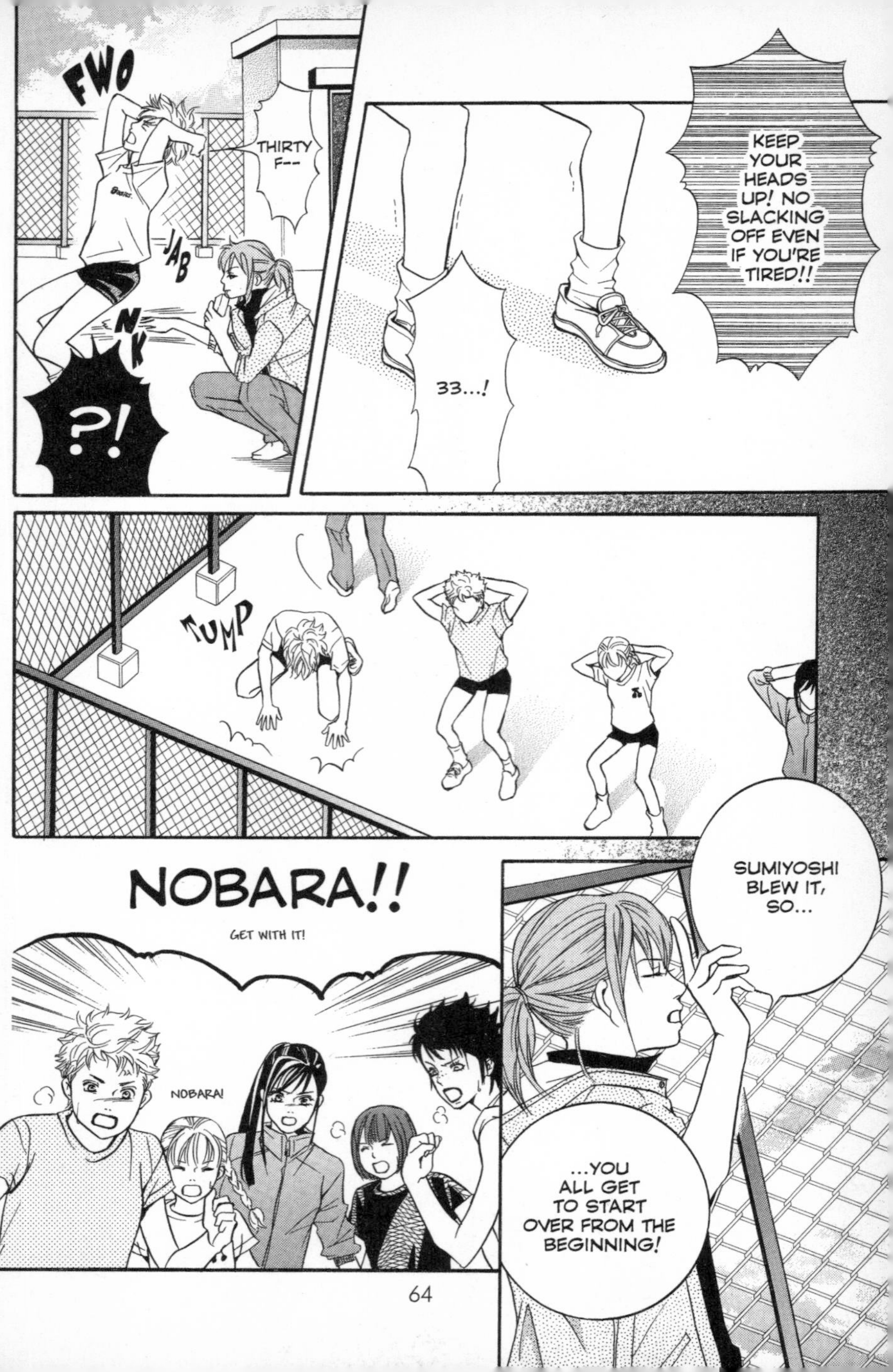
KEEP YOUR HEADS UP! NO SLACKING OFF EVEN IF YOU'RE TIRED!!
33...!
FWO
THIRTY F--
JAB
NK
?!
TUMP
SUMIYOSHI BLEW IT, SO...
...YOU ALL GET TO START OVER FROM THE BEGINNING!
NOBARA!!
GET WITH IT!
NOBARA!

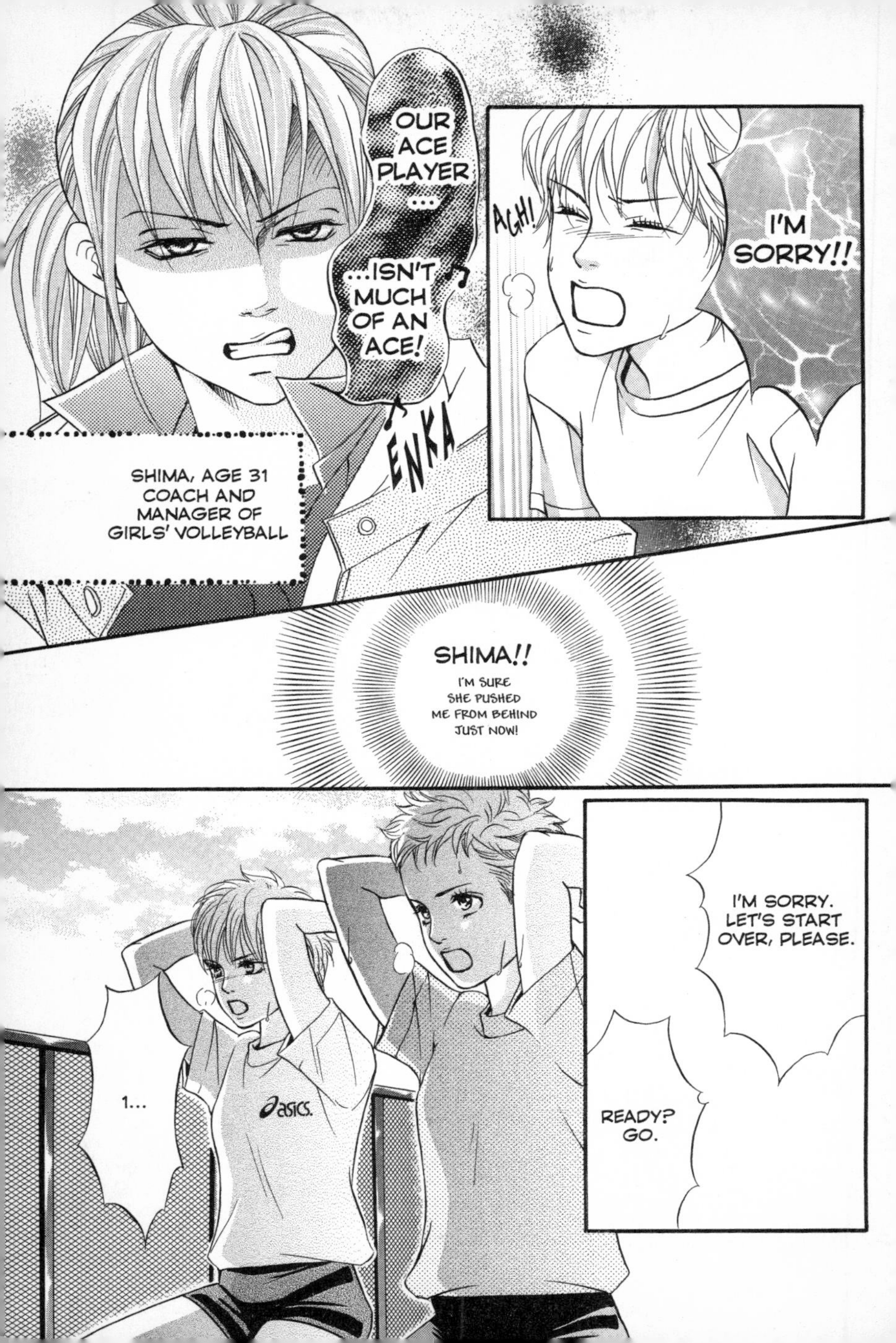
I'M SORRY!!
AGH!
OUR ACE PLAYER ...
...ISN'T MUCH OF AN ACE!
ENKA
SHIMA, AGE 31
COACH AND MANAGER OF GIRLS' VOLLEYBALL
SHIMA!!
I'M SURE SHE PUSHED ME FROM BEHIND JUST NOW!
I'M SORRY. LET'S START OVER, PLEASE.
READY? GO.
asics.
1...

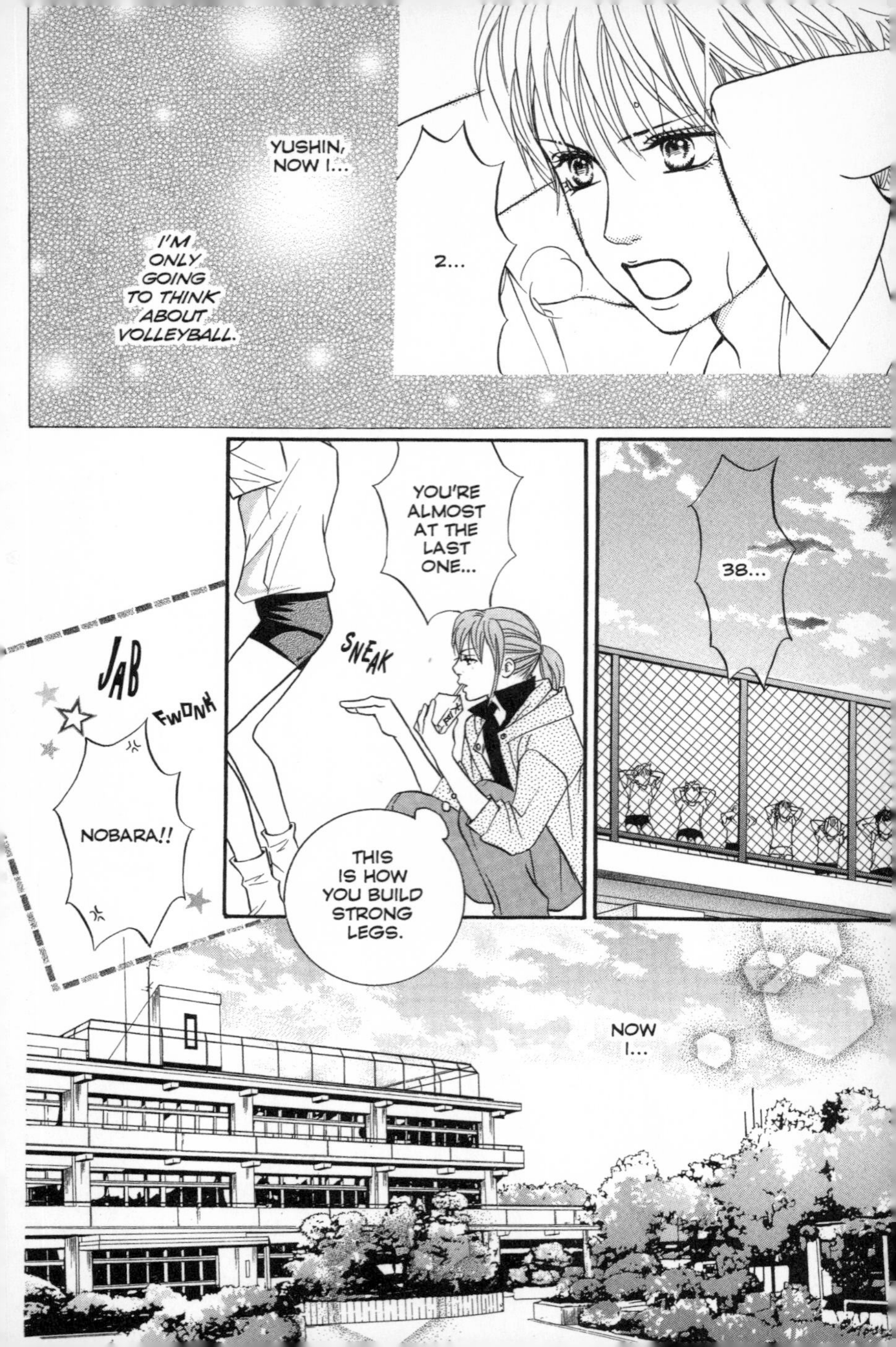
2...
YUSHIN, NOW I...
I'M ONLY GOING TO THINK ABOUT VOLLEYBALL.
38...
YOU'RE ALMOST AT THE LAST ONE...
SNEAK
THIS IS HOW YOU BUILD STRONG LEGS.
JAB
FWONK
NOBARA!!
NOW I...

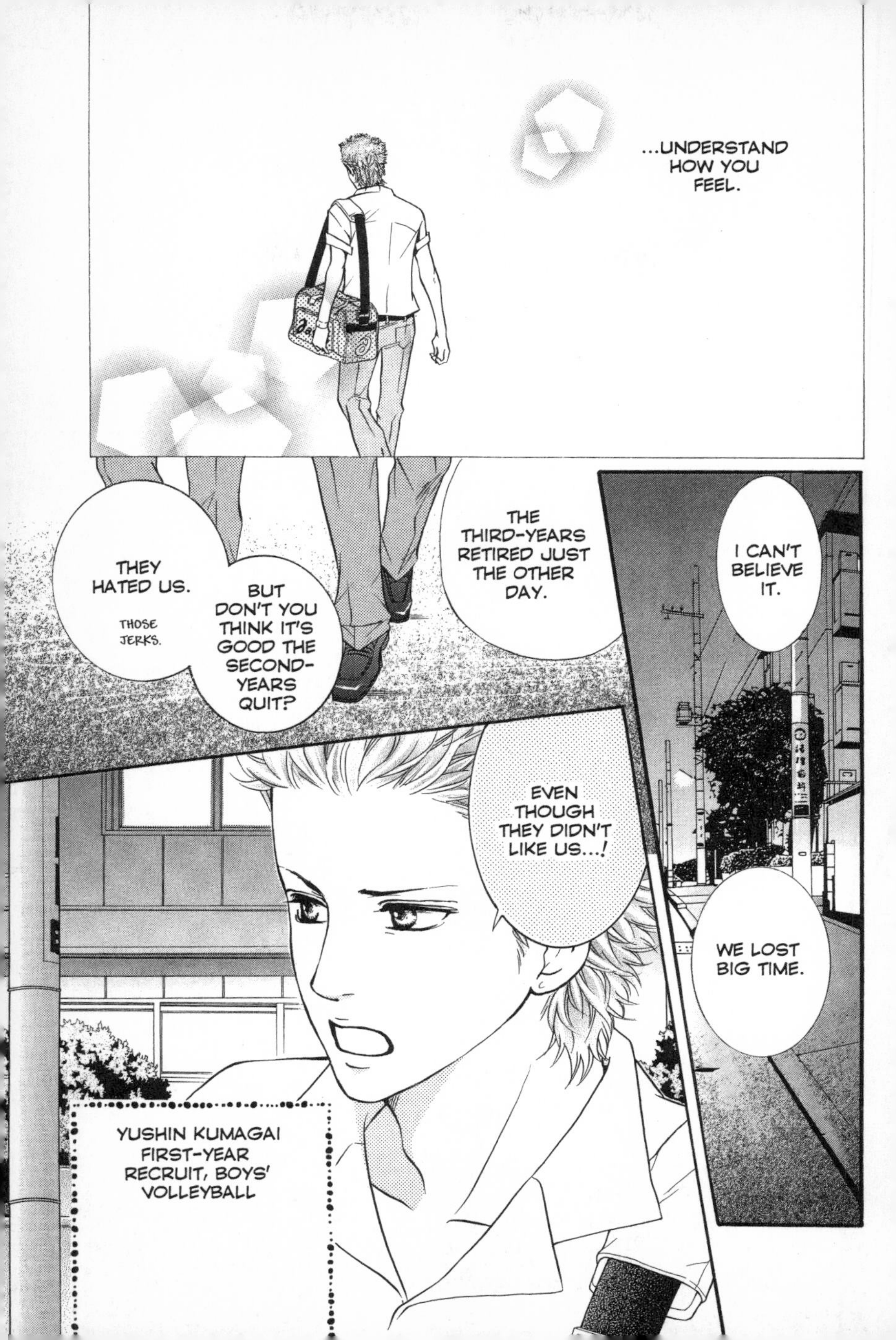
...UNDERSTAND HOW YOU FEEL.
I CAN'T BELIEVE IT.
WE LOST BIG TIME.
THE THIRD-YEARS RETIRED JUST THE OTHER DAY.
BUT DON'T YOU THINK IT'S GOOD THE SECOND-YEARS QUIT?
THEY HATED US.
THOSE JERKS.
EVEN THOUGH THEY DIDN'T LIKE US...!
YUSHIN KUMAGAI FIRST-YEAR RECRUIT, BOYS' VOLLEYBALL

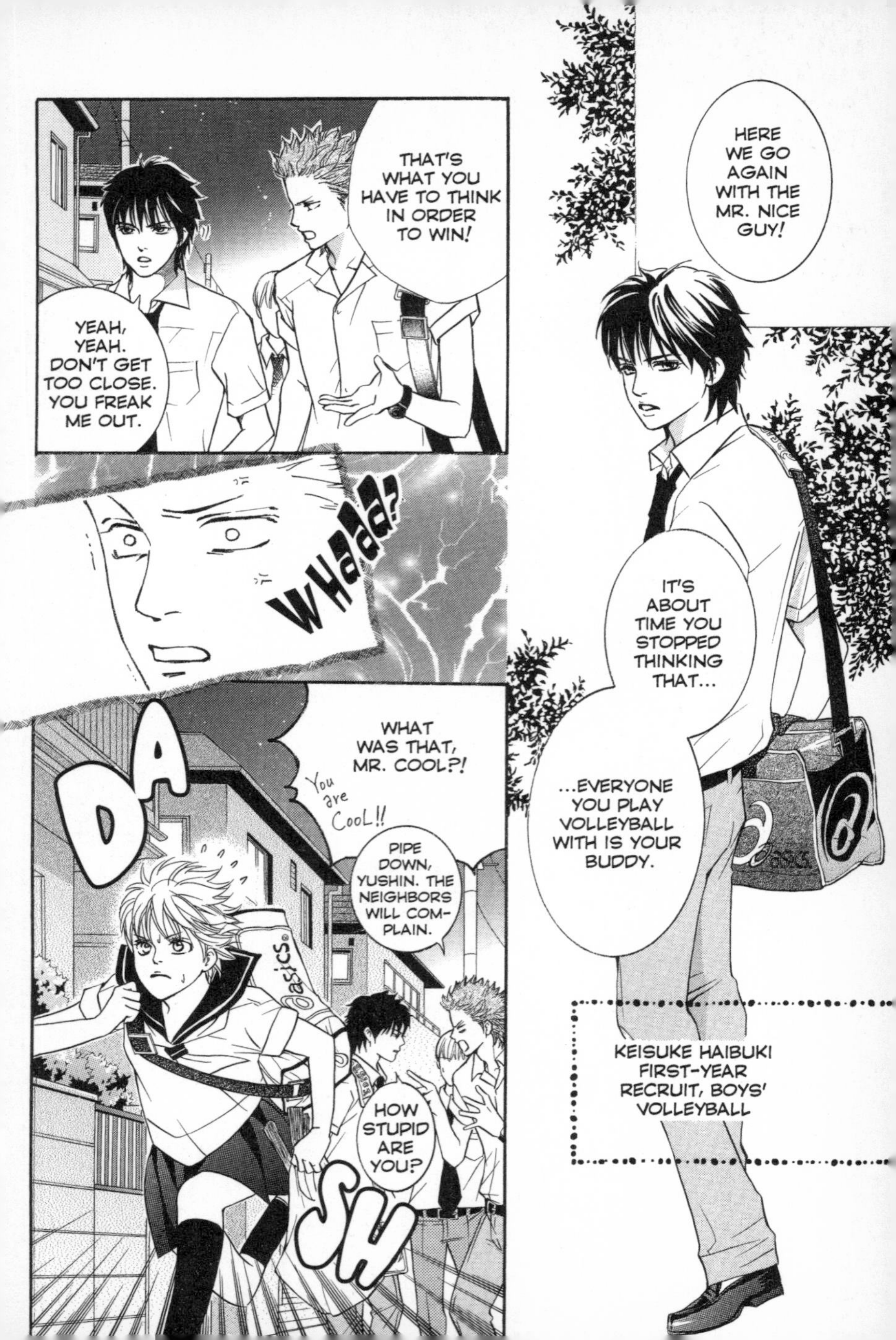
HERE WE GO AGAIN WITH THE MR. NICE GUY!
IT'S ABOUT TIME YOU STOPPED THINKING THAT...
...EVERYONE YOU PLAY VOLLEYBALL WITH IS YOUR BUDDY.
KEISUKE HAIBUKI FIRST-YEAR RECRUIT, BOYS' VOLLEYBALL
THAT'S WHAT YOU HAVE TO THINK IN ORDER TO WIN!
YEAH, YEAH. DON'T GET TOO CLOSE. YOU FREAK ME OUT.
WHAAAA?
WHAT WAS THAT, MR. COOL?!
You are CooL!!
DA
PIPE DOWN, YUSHIN. THE NEIGHBORS WILL COMPLAIN.
HOW STUPID ARE YOU?
SH

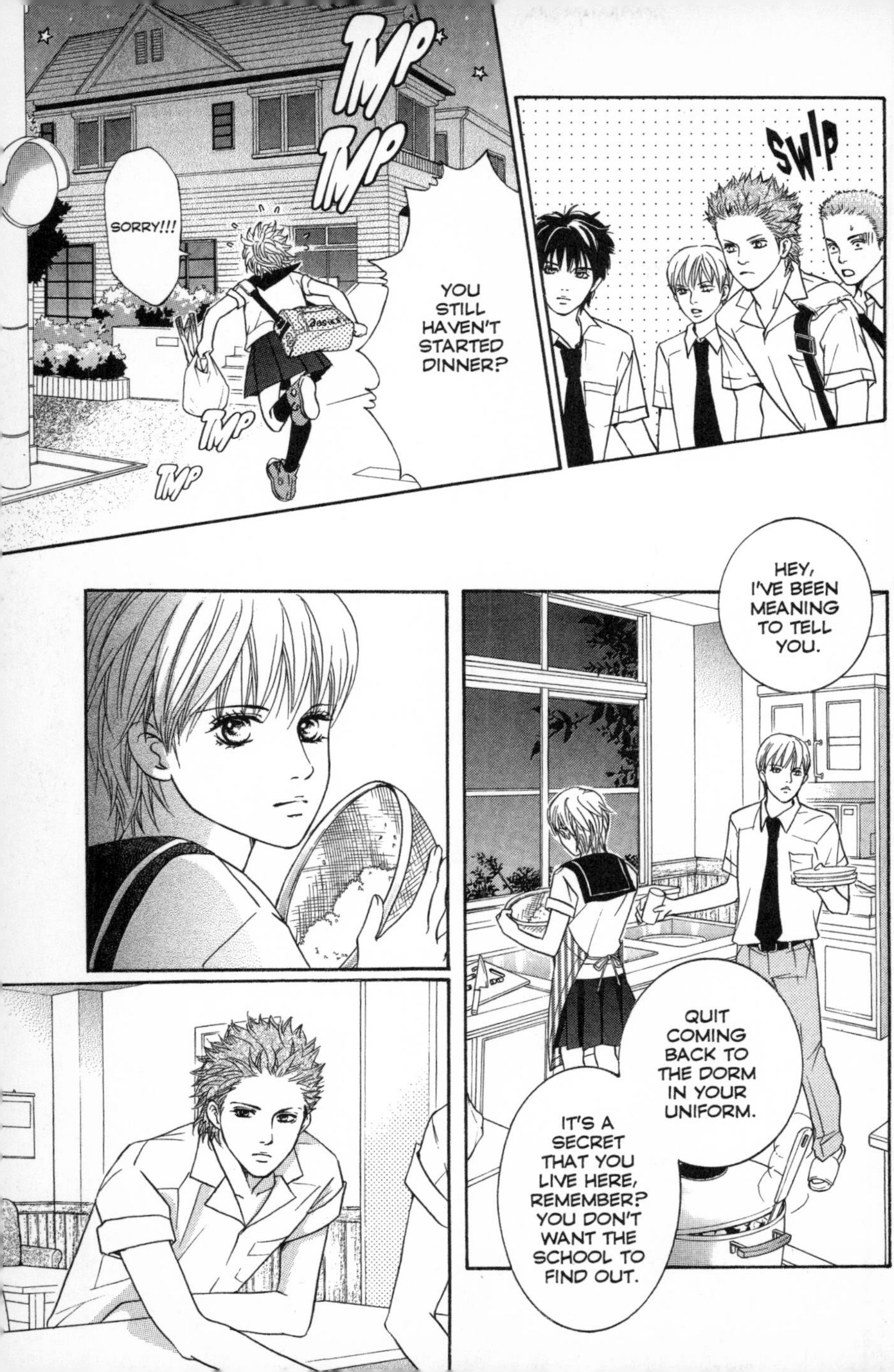
SWIP
TMP TMP
YOU STILL HAVEN'T STARTED DINNER?
SORRY!!!
TMP
TMP
HEY, I'VE BEEN MEANING TO TELL YOU.
QUIT COMING BACK TO THE DORM IN YOUR UNIFORM.
IT'S A SECRET THAT YOU LIVE HERE, REMEMBER? YOU DON'T WANT THE SCHOOL TO FIND OUT.

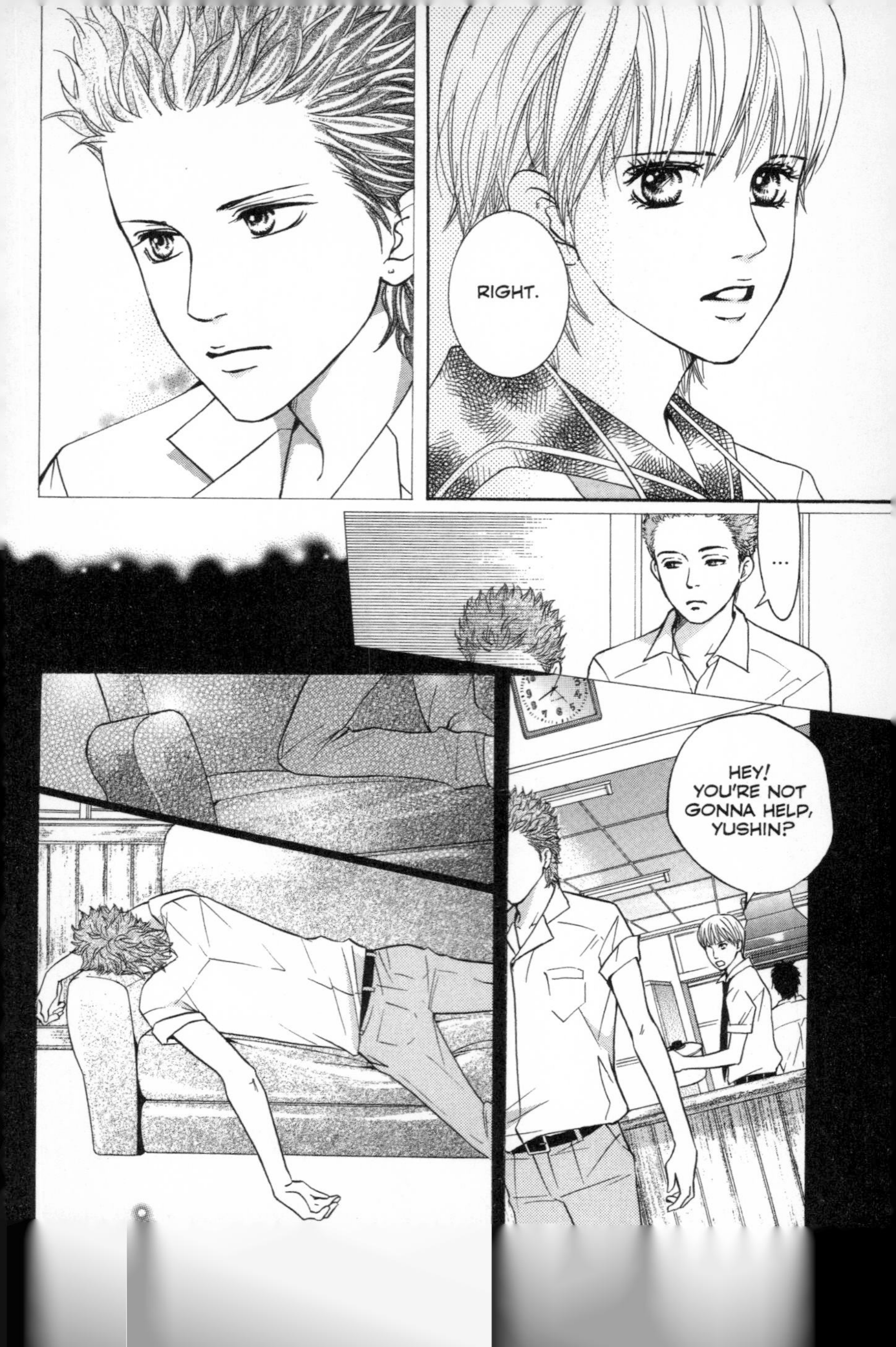
RIGHT.
...
HEY! YOU'RE NOT GONNA HELP, YUSHIN?

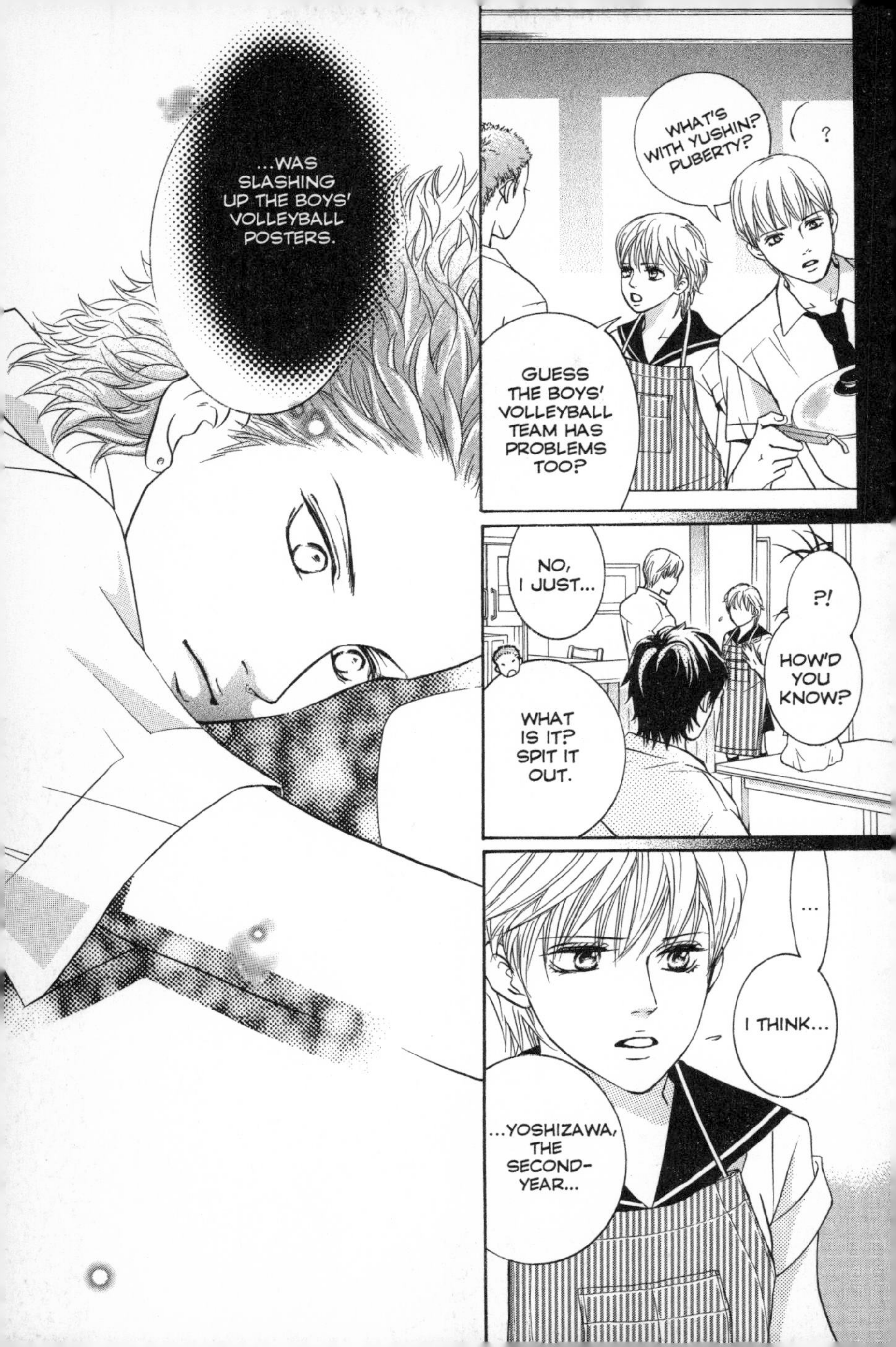
?
WHAT'S WITH YUSHIN? PUBERTY?
GUESS THE BOYS' VOLLEYBALL TEAM HAS PROBLEMS TOO?
?!
HOW'D YOU KNOW?
NO, I JUST...
WHAT IS IT? SPIT IT OUT.
...
I THINK...
...YOSHIZAWA, THE SECOND-YEAR...
...WAS SLASHING UP THE BOYS' VOLLEYBALL POSTERS.

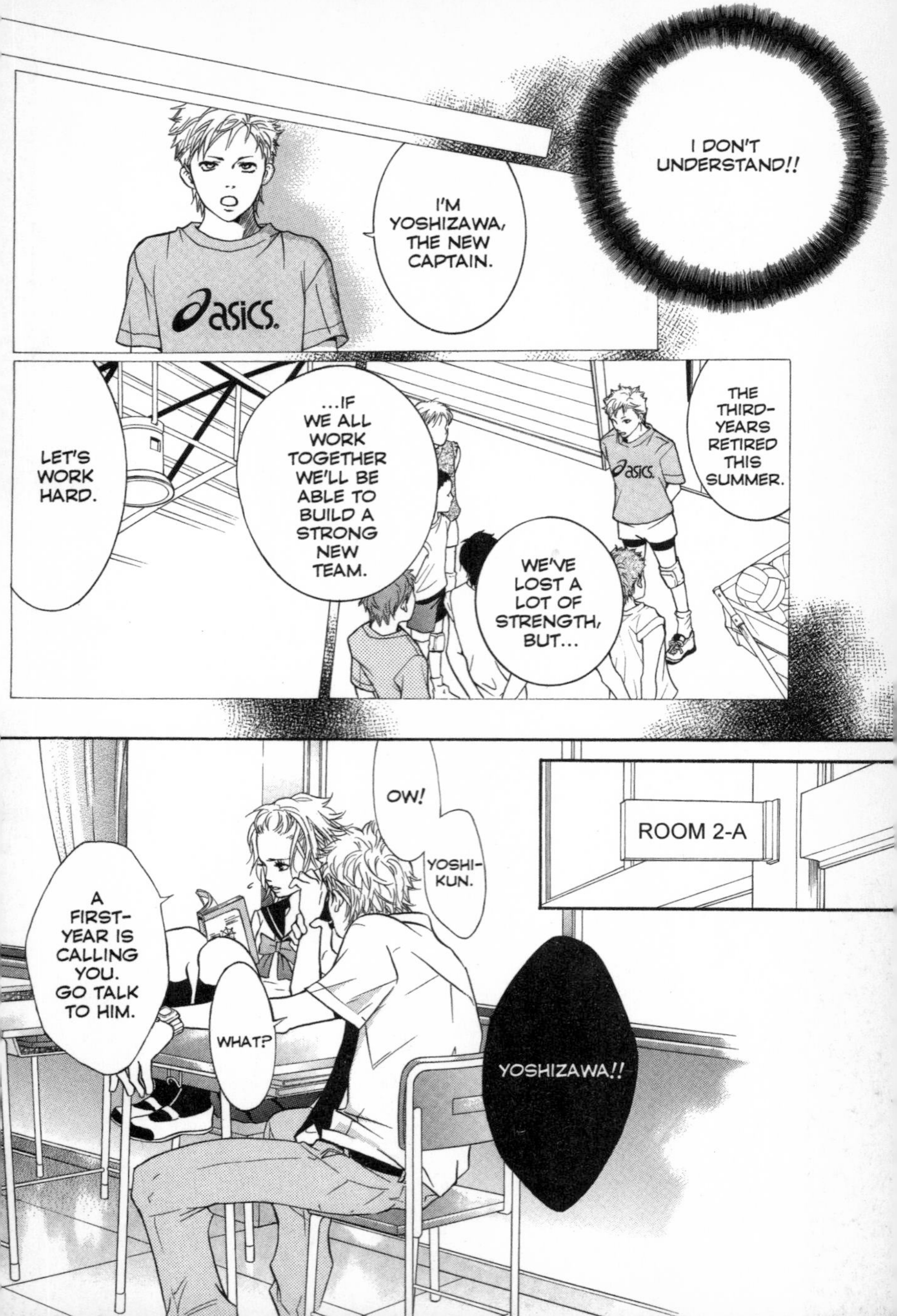
I DON'T UNDERSTAND!!
I'M YOSHIZAWA, THE NEW CAPTAIN.
THE THIRD-YEARS RETIRED THIS SUMMER.
WE'VE LOST A LOT OF STRENGTH, BUT...
...IF WE ALL WORK TOGETHER WE'LL BE ABLE TO BUILD A STRONG NEW TEAM.
LET'S WORK HARD.
ROOM 2-A
YOSHIZAWA!!
OW!
YOSHI-KUN.
A FIRST-YEAR IS CALLING YOU. GO TALK TO HIM.
WHAT?

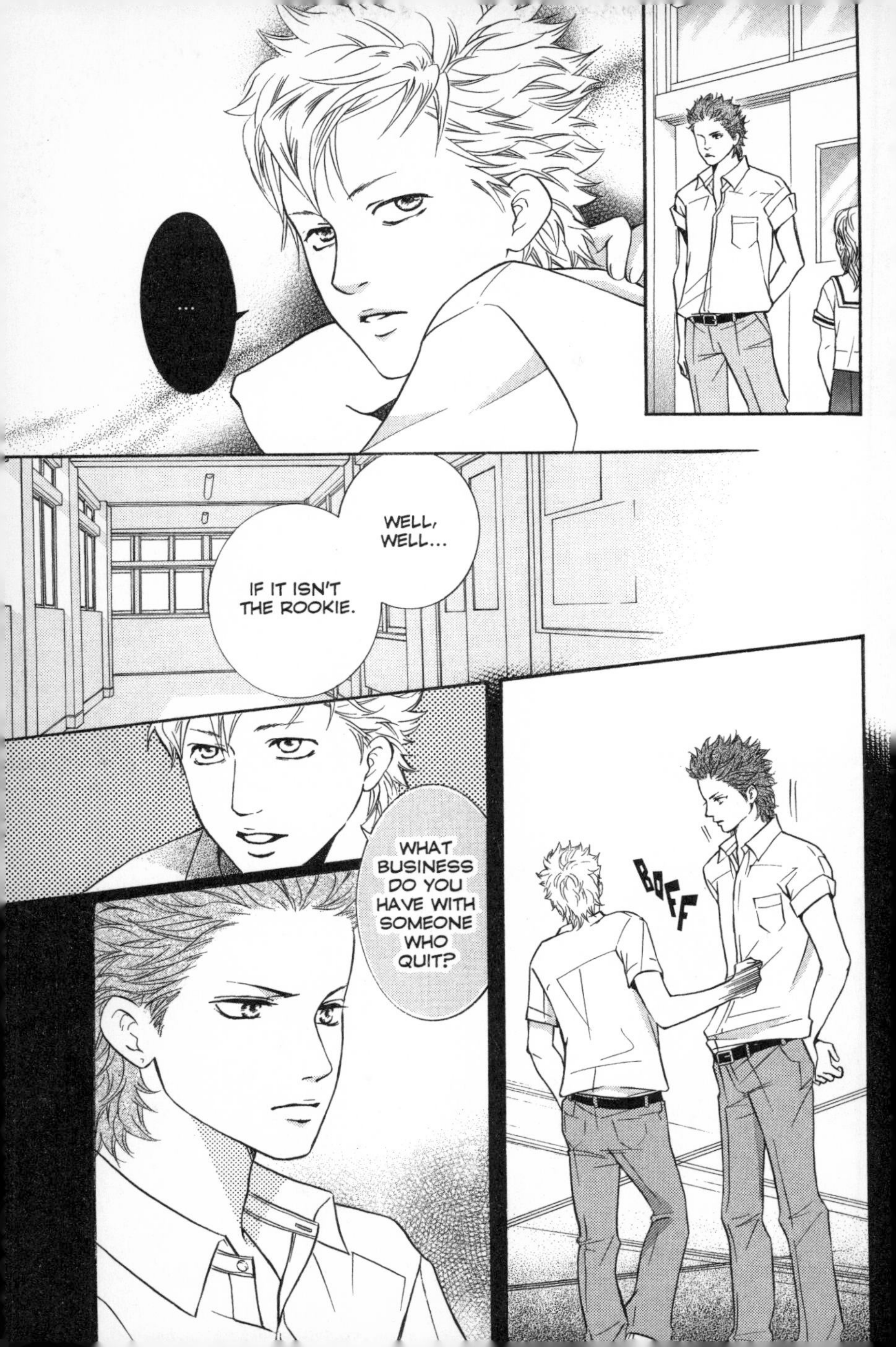
...
WELL, WELL...
IF IT ISN'T THE ROOKIE.
BOFF
WHAT BUSINESS DO YOU HAVE WITH SOMEONE WHO QUIT?

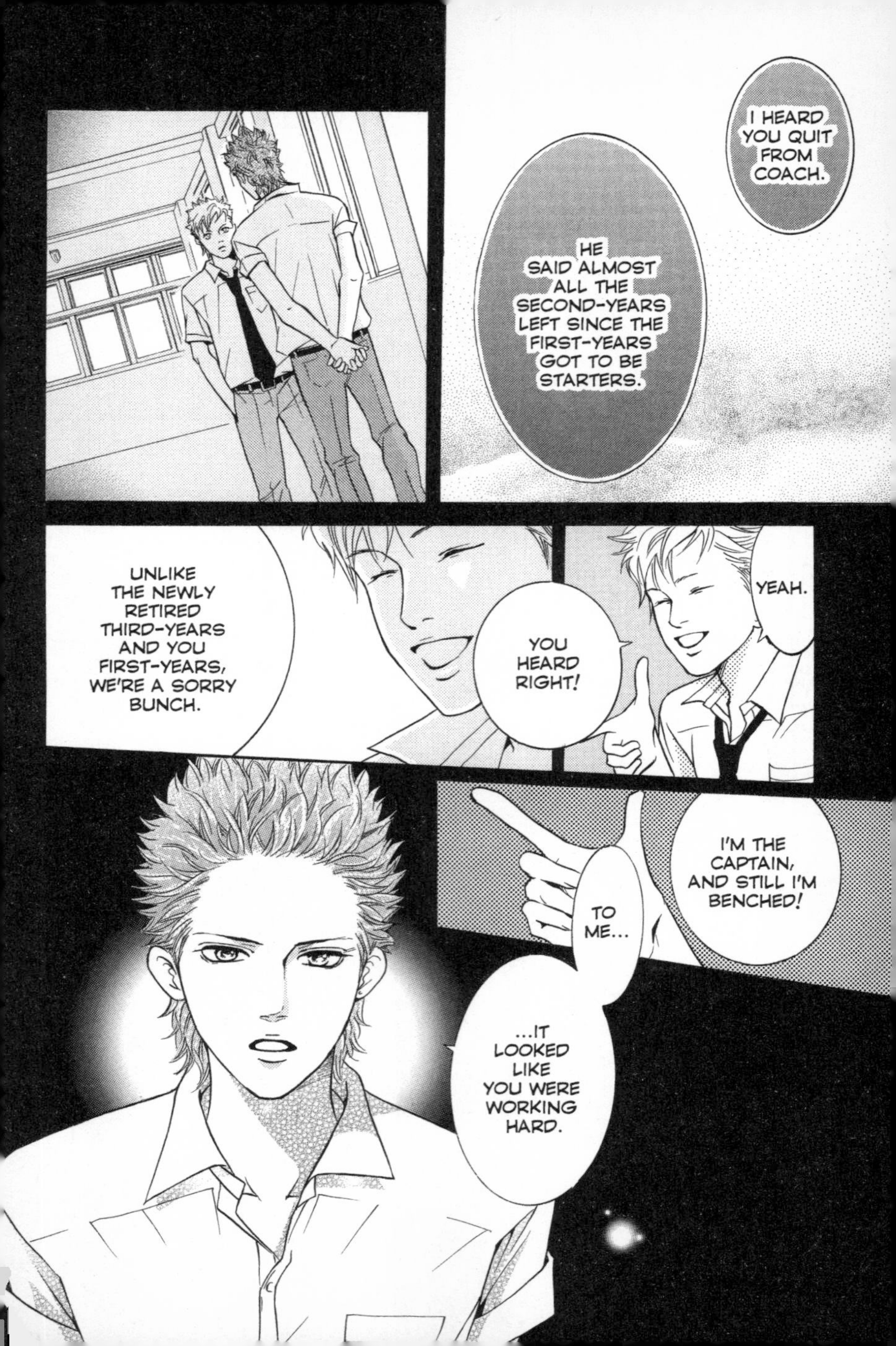
I HEARD YOU QUIT FROM COACH.
HE SAID ALMOST ALL THE SECOND-YEARS LEFT SINCE THE FIRST-YEARS GOT TO BE STARTERS.
YEAH.
YOU HEARD RIGHT!
UNLIKE THE NEWLY RETIRED THIRD-YEARS AND YOU FIRST-YEARS, WE'RE A SORRY BUNCH.
I'M THE CAPTAIN, AND STILL I'M BENCHED!
TO ME...
...IT LOOKED LIKE YOU WERE WORKING HARD.

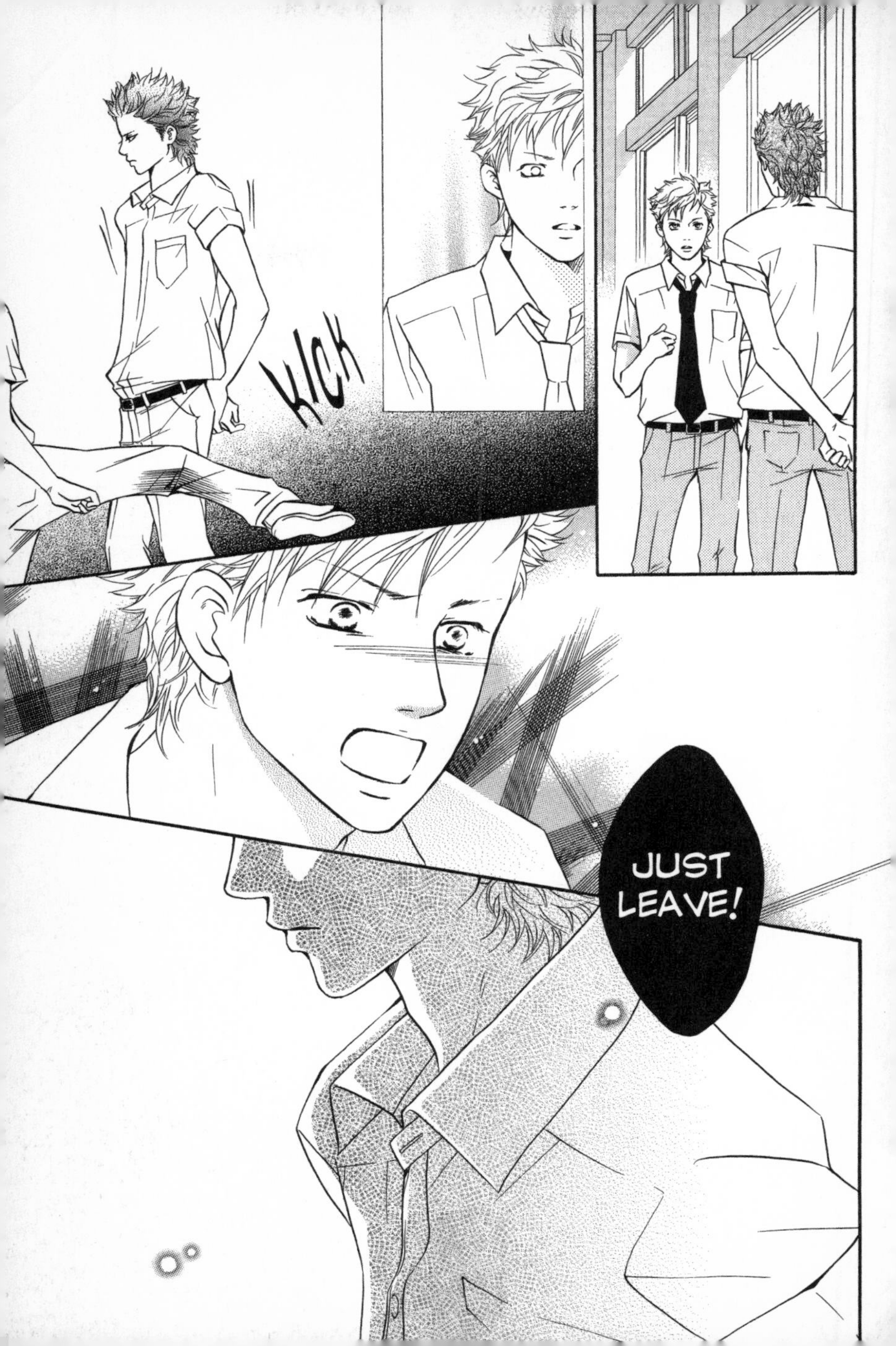
KICK
JUST LEAVE!

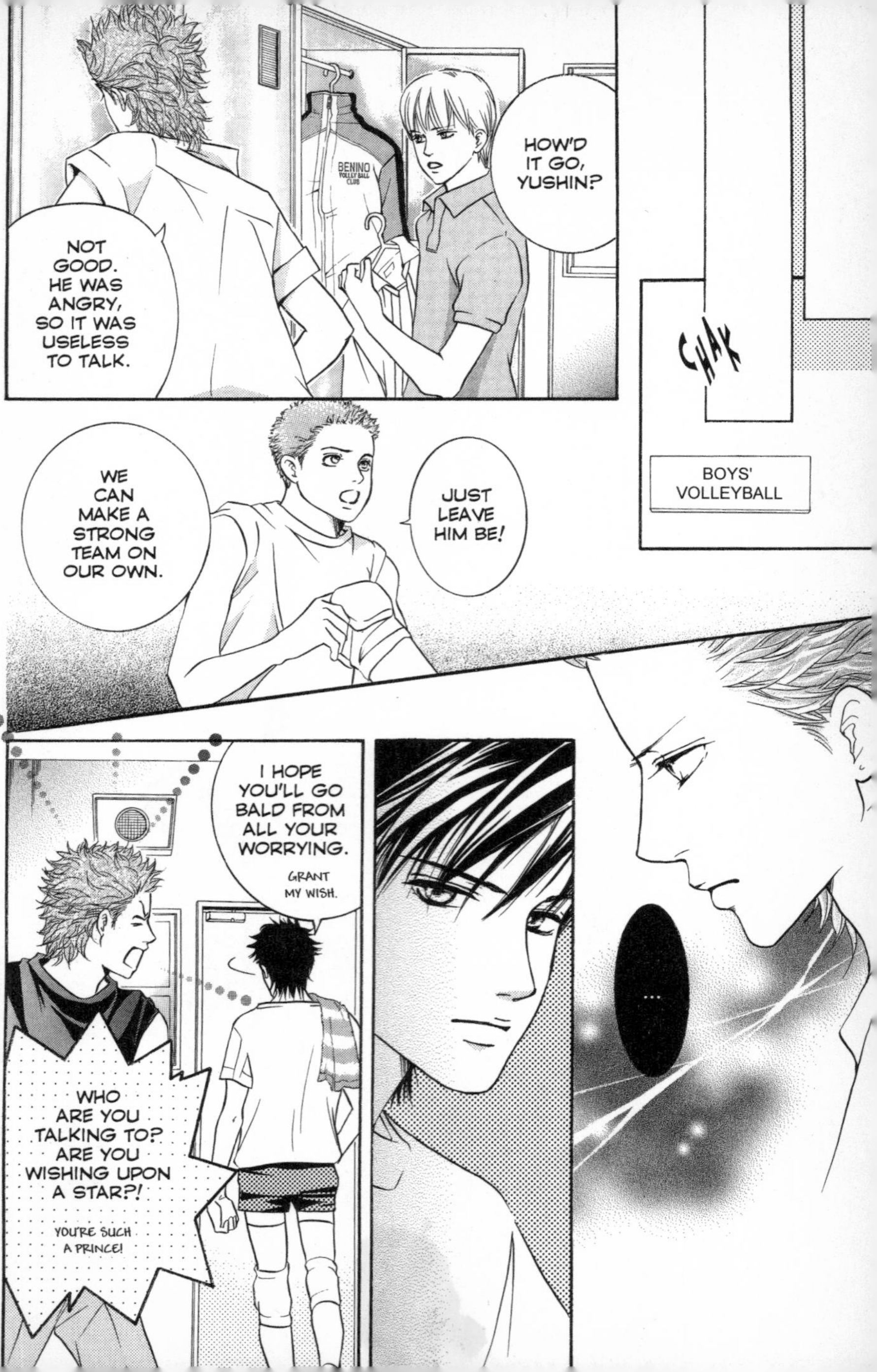
CHAK
BOYS' VOLLEYBALL
HOW'D IT GO, YUSHIN?
BENINO VOLLEY BALL CLUB
NOT GOOD. HE WAS ANGRY, SO IT WAS USELESS TO TALK.
JUST LEAVE HIM BE!
WE CAN MAKE A STRONG TEAM ON OUR OWN.
...
I HOPE YOU'LL GO BALD FROM ALL YOUR WORRYING.
GRANT MY WISH.
WHO ARE YOU TALKING TO? ARE YOU WISHING UPON A STAR?!
YOU'RE SUCH A PRINCE!

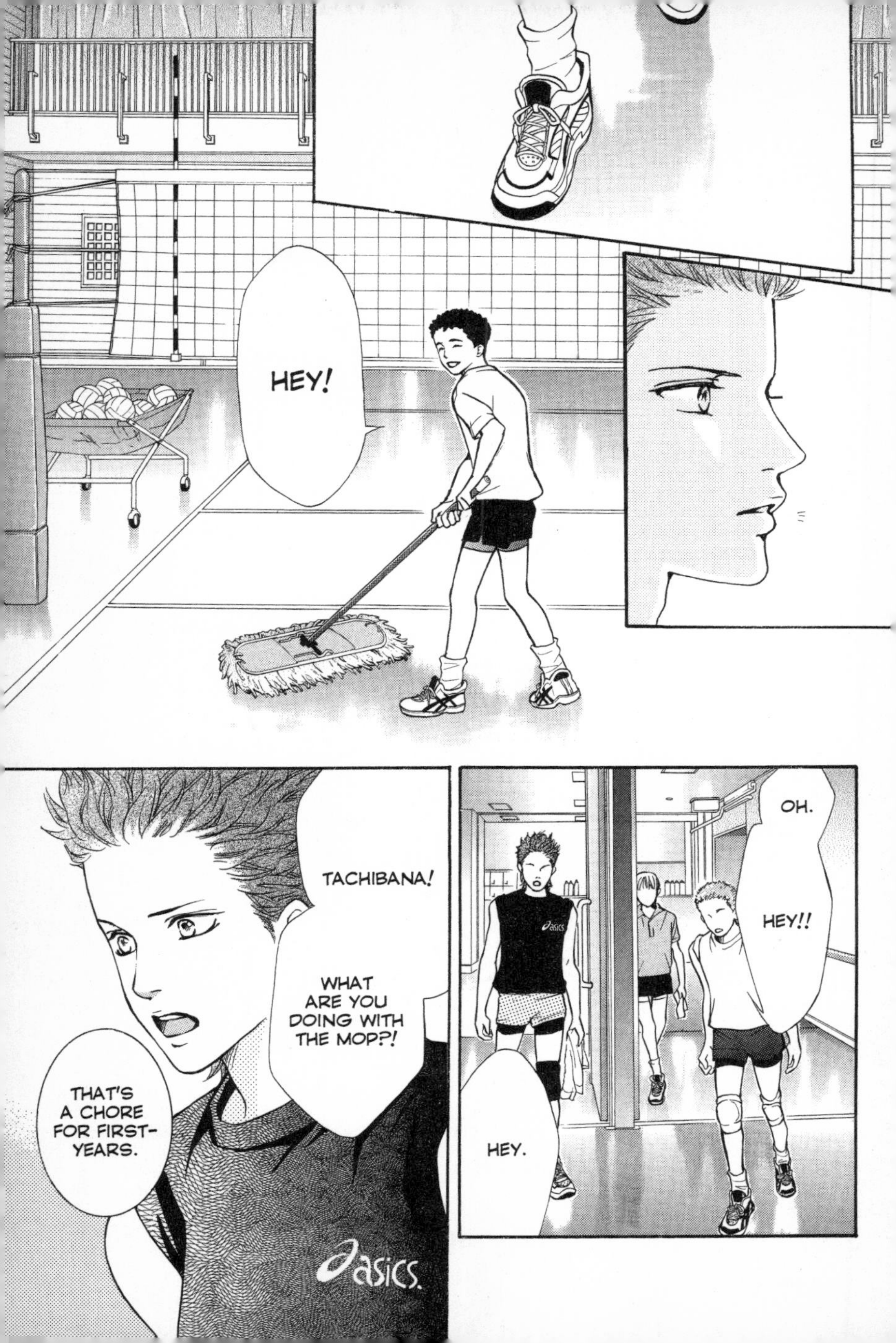
HEY!
OH.
HEY!!
HEY.
TACHIBANA!
WHAT ARE YOU DOING WITH THE MOP?!
THAT'S A CHORE FOR FIRST-YEARS.
asics.

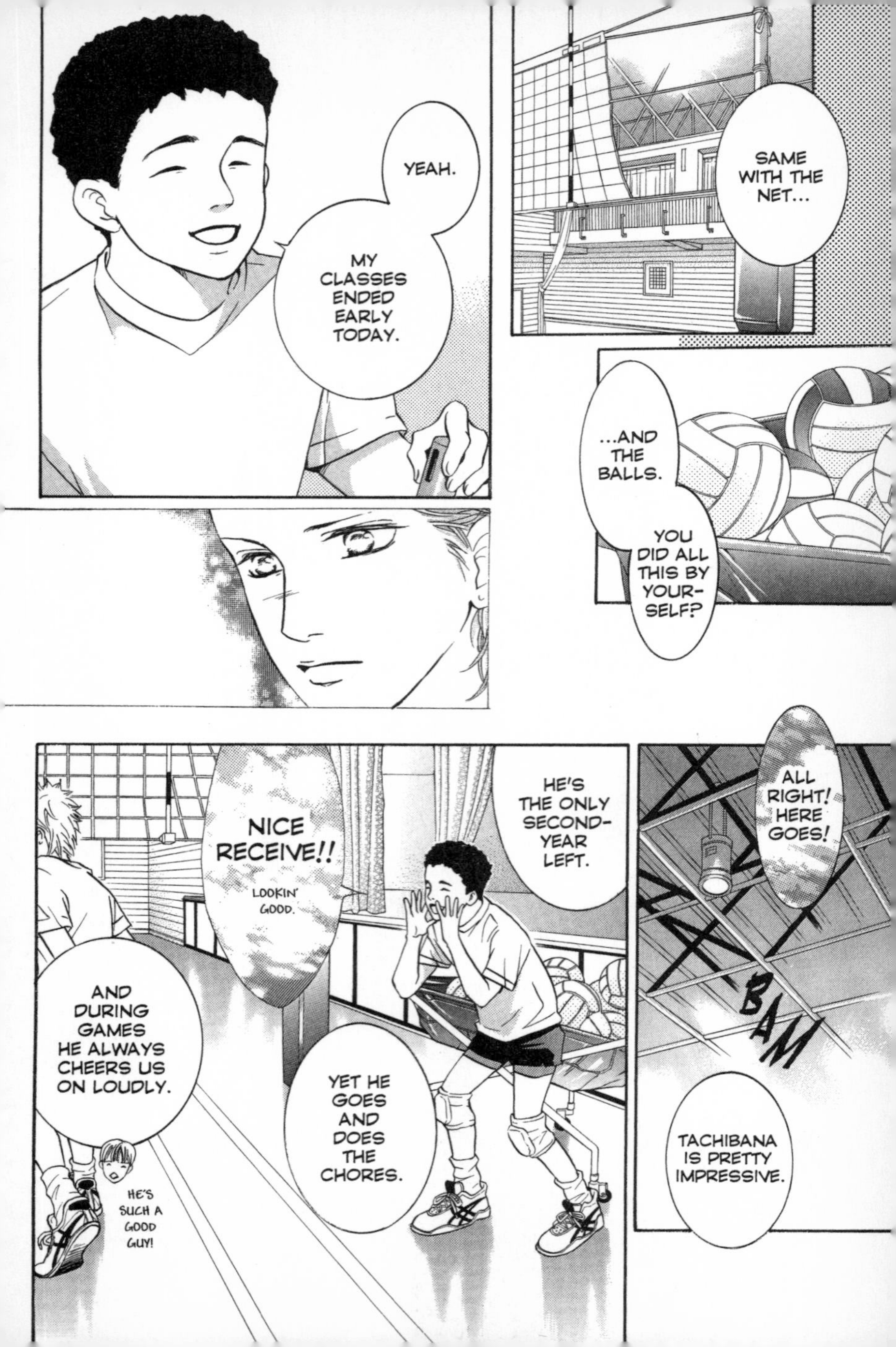
SAME WITH THE NET...
...AND THE BALLS.
YOU DID ALL THIS BY YOUR-SELF?
YEAH.
MY CLASSES ENDED EARLY TODAY.
ALL RIGHT! HERE GOES!
BAM
TACHIBANA IS PRETTY IMPRESSIVE.
HE'S THE ONLY SECOND-YEAR LEFT.
NICE RECEIVE!!
LOOKIN' GOOD.
AND DURING GAMES HE ALWAYS CHEERS US ON LOUDLY.
YET HE GOES AND DOES THE CHORES.
HE'S SUCH A GOOD GUY!

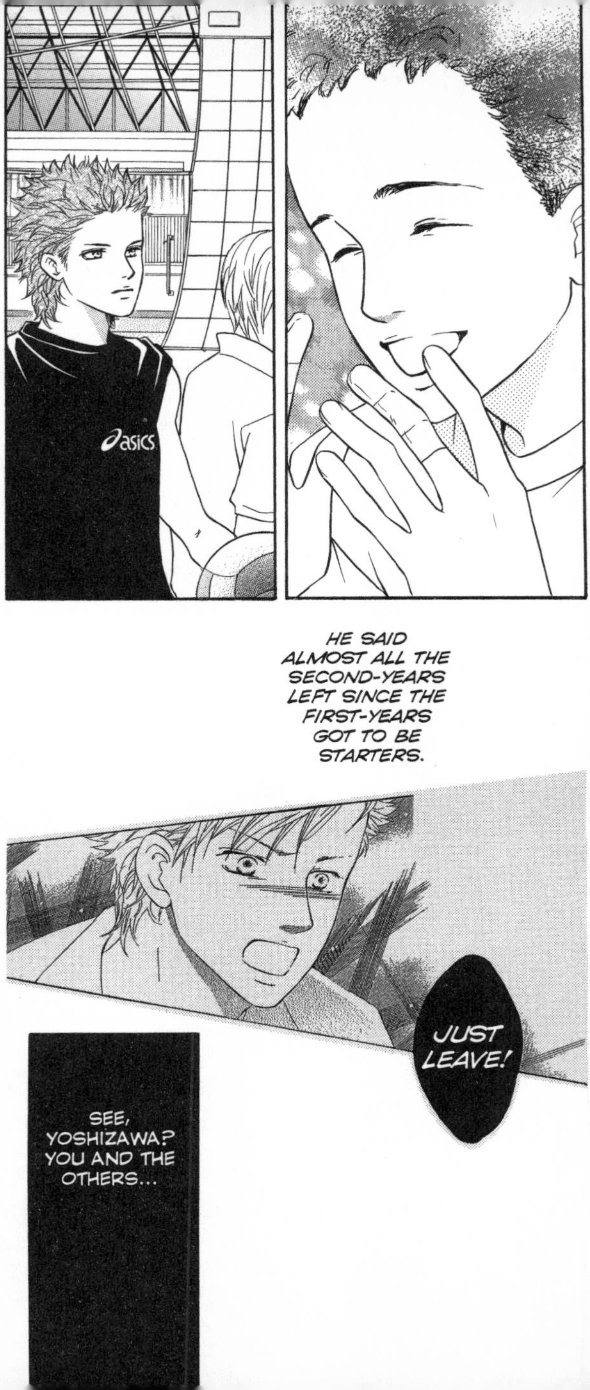
HE SAID ALMOST ALL THE SECOND-YEARS LEFT SINCE THE FIRST-YEARS GOT TO BE STARTERS.
JUST LEAVE!
SEE, YOSHIZAWA? YOU AND THE OTHERS...

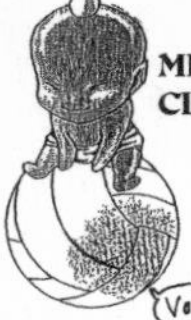

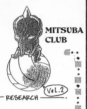

MITSUBA CLUB

— RESEARCH — Vol. 2

BACK IN THE SUMMER I GOT TO VISIT TOKAI UNIVERSITY'S MEN'S VOLLEYBALL TEAM. AT FIRST I WAS SURPRISED BY HOW SPACIOUS THE CAMPUS WAS. EVERYONE WAS SO KIND!!! ESPECIALLY THE MANAGER, WHO ANSWERED ALL MY QUESTIONS AND EXPLAINED THINGS IN A WAY THAT WAS EASY TO UNDERSTAND. I WAS VERY IMPRESSED. AND ONCE AGAIN EVERYONE WAS SO HANDSOME!! WHAT AM I TO DO? AT COLLEGE-LEVEL VOLLEYBALL CLUBS, THE STUDENTS TAKE CARE OF MANAGEMENT, TRAINING, AND ALL THE TASKS OF RUNNING THE TEAM.

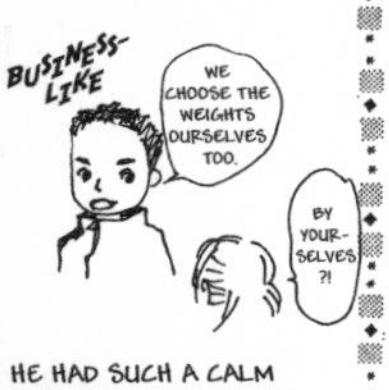
BUSINESS-LIKE
WE CHOOSE THE WEIGHTS OURSELVES TOO.
BY YOURSELVES ?!

HE HAD SUCH A CALM MANNER THAT I DIDN'T REALIZE HE WAS A STUDENT.

EVERYONE BUT THE COACH WAS A STUDENT. IT'S THEIR TEAM, AND THEY KEEP EVERYTHING UP THEMSELVES. I WAIT WITH EAGER ANTICIPATION FOR THE NEAR FUTURE WHEN I WILL SEE PLAYERS FROM TOKAI UNIVERSITY PLAYING AT V-LEAGUE OR ALL JAPAN.

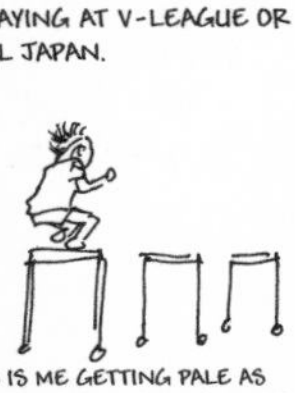

THIS IS ME GETTING PALE AS WE MADE THEM JUMP HURDLES OVER AND OVER AGAIN WHEN THE PHOTOGRAPHER HAD CAMERA PROBLEMS. I'M SO SORRY!

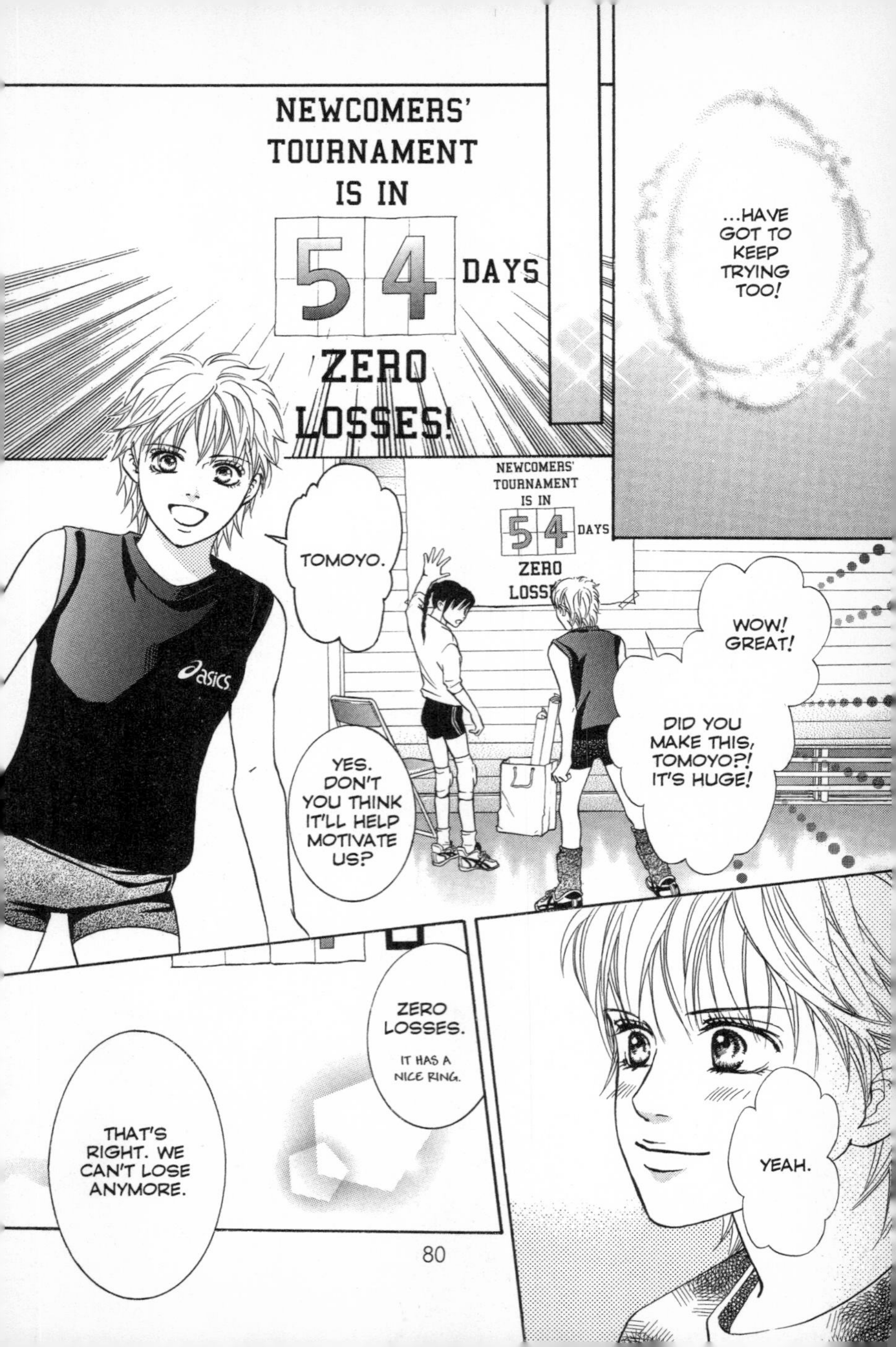
...HAVE GOT TO KEEP TRYING TOO!
NEWCOMERS' TOURNAMENT IS IN 54 DAYS
ZERO LOSSES!
WOW! GREAT!
DID YOU MAKE THIS, TOMOYO?! IT'S HUGE!
NEWCOMERS' TOURNAMENT IS IN 54 DAYS
ZERO LOSSES
YES. DON'T YOU THINK IT'LL HELP MOTIVATE US?
TOMOYO.
YEAH.
ZERO LOSSES.
IT HAS A NICE RING.
THAT'S RIGHT. WE CAN'T LOSE ANYMORE.

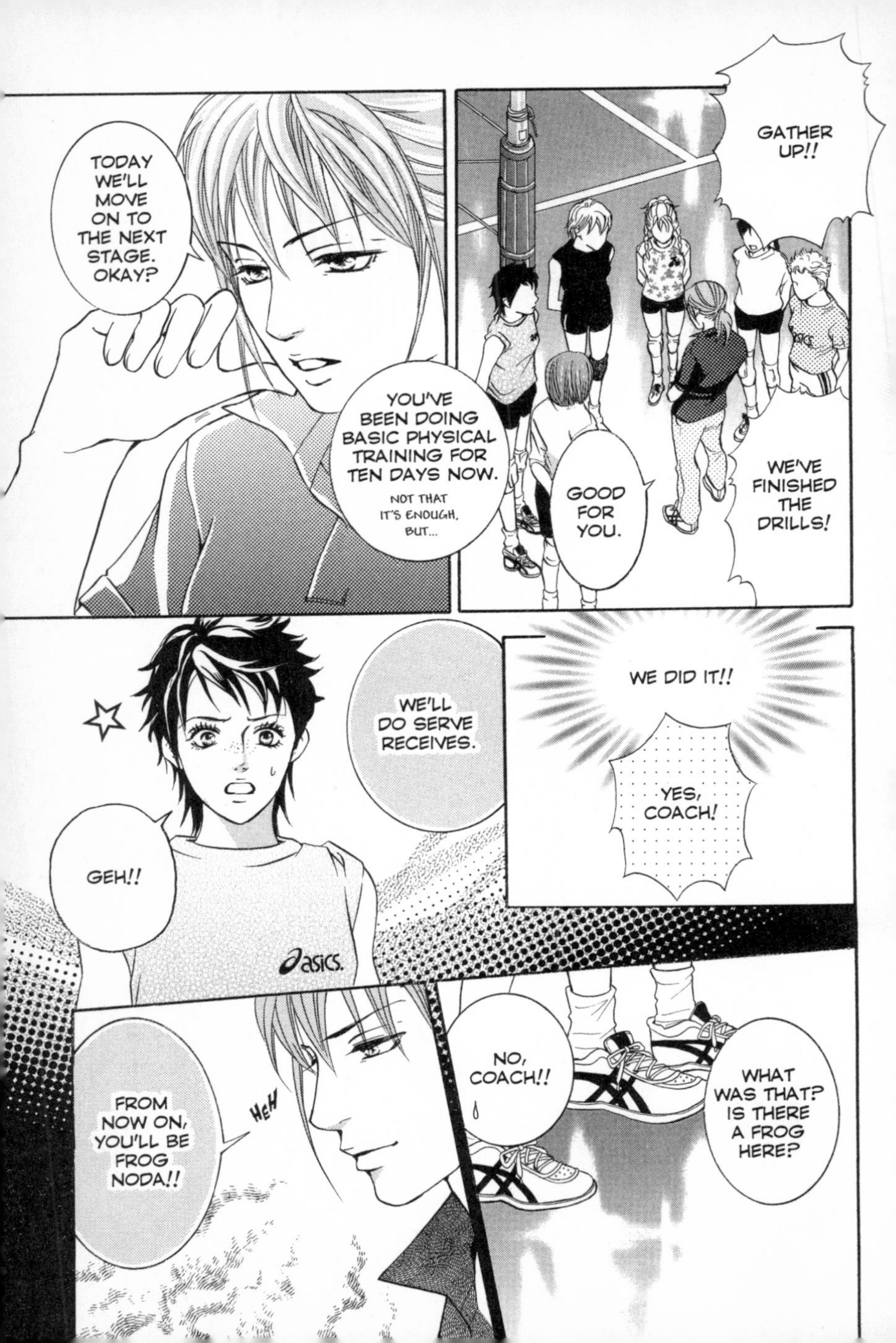
GATHER UP!!
WE'VE FINISHED THE DRILLS!
GOOD FOR YOU.
YOU'VE BEEN DOING BASIC PHYSICAL TRAINING FOR TEN DAYS NOW.
NOT THAT IT'S ENOUGH, BUT...
TODAY WE'LL MOVE ON TO THE NEXT STAGE. OKAY?
WE DID IT!!
YES, COACH!
WE'LL DO SERVE RECEIVES.
GEH!!
WHAT WAS THAT? IS THERE A FROG HERE?
NO, COACH!!
HEH
FROM NOW ON, YOU'LL BE FROG NODA!!

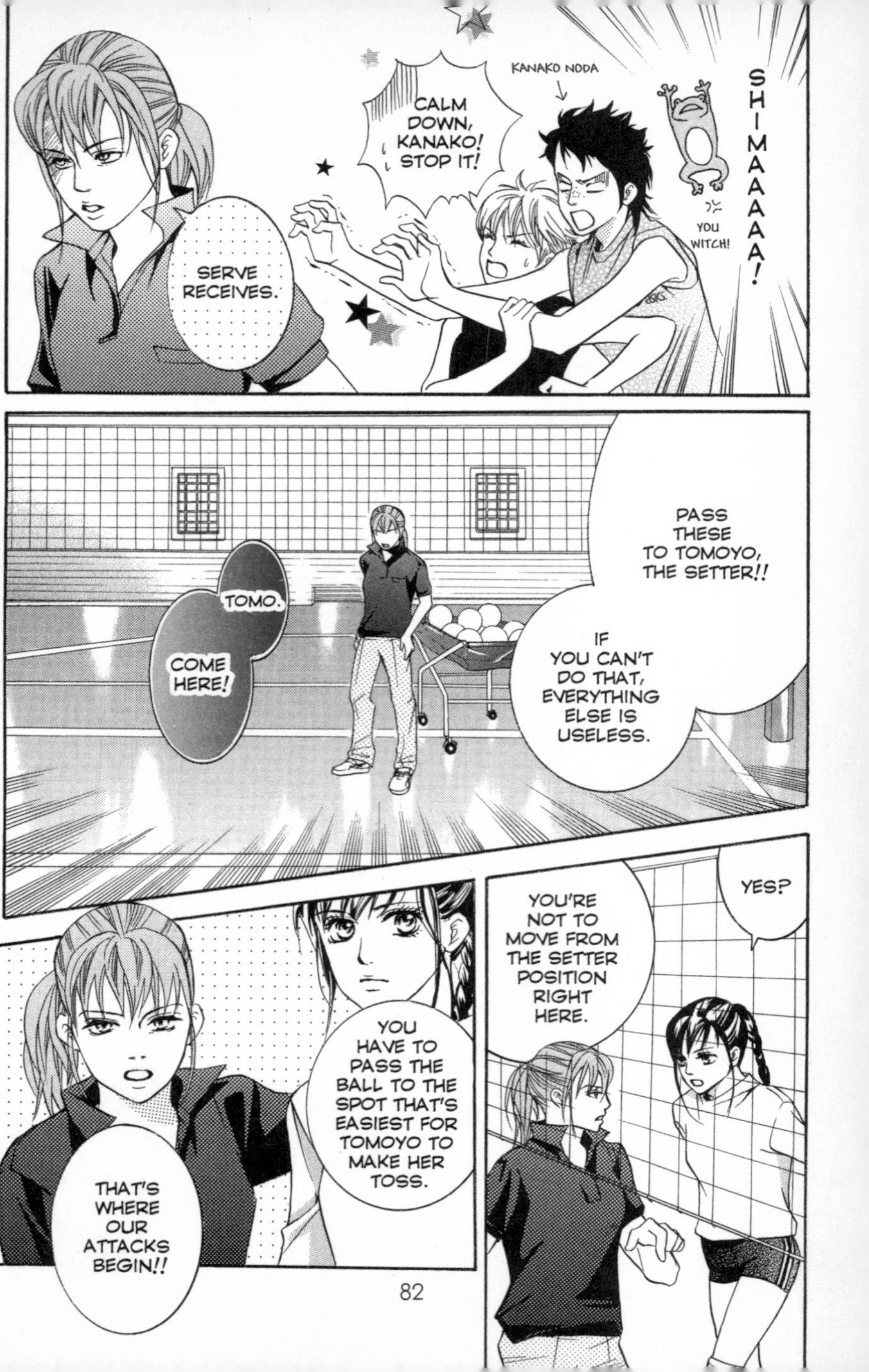
SHIMAAAAAA!
YOU WITCH!
KANAKO NODA
CALM DOWN, KANAKO! STOP IT!
SERVE RECEIVES.
PASS THESE TO TOMOYO, THE SETTER!!
IF YOU CAN'T DO THAT, EVERYTHING ELSE IS USELESS.
TOMO.
COME HERE!
YES?
YOU'RE NOT TO MOVE FROM THE SETTER POSITION RIGHT HERE.
YOU HAVE TO PASS THE BALL TO THE SPOT THAT'S EASIEST FOR TOMOYO TO MAKE HER TOSS.
THAT'S WHERE OUR ATTACKS BEGIN!!

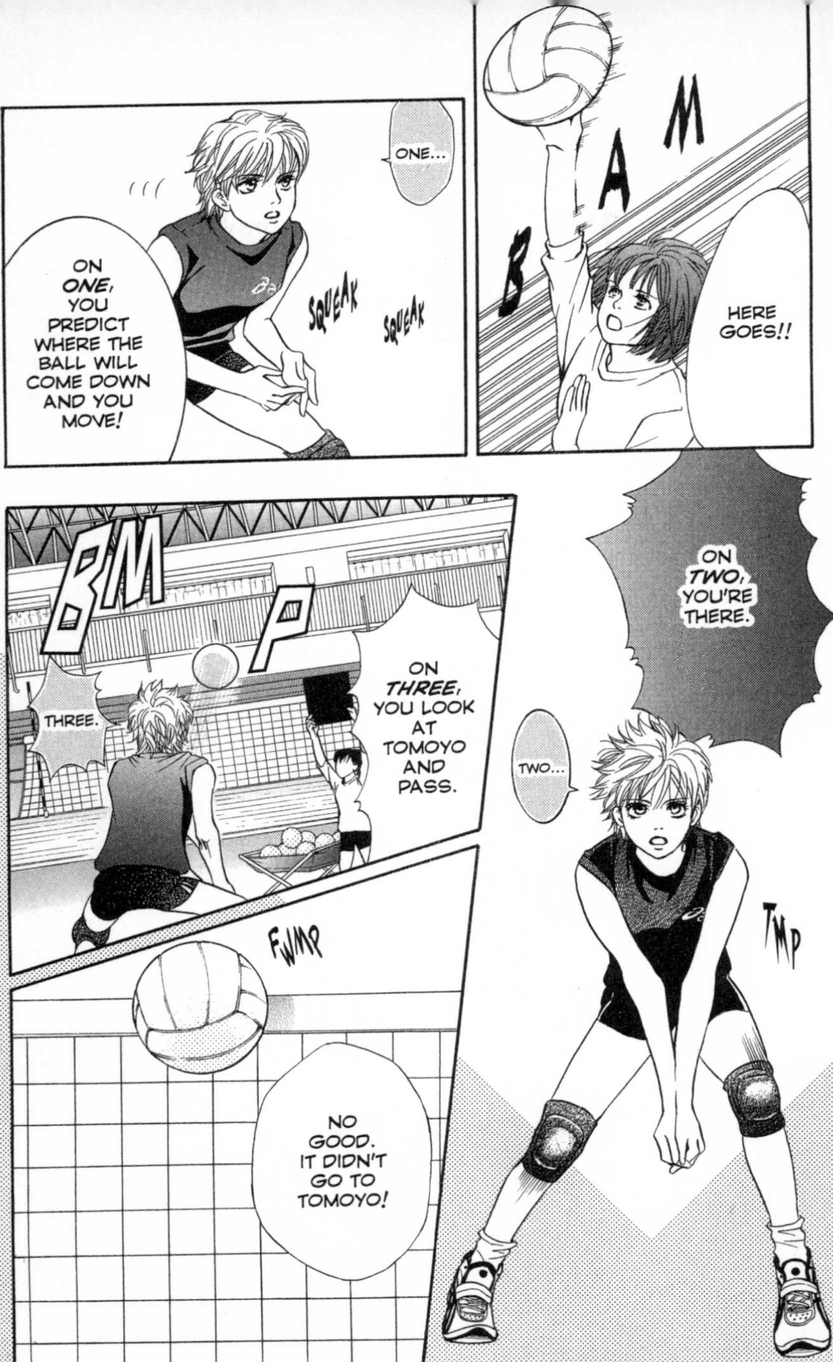
BAM
HERE GOES!!
ONE...
ON ONE, YOU PREDICT WHERE THE BALL WILL COME DOWN AND YOU MOVE!
SQUEAK
SQUEAK
ON TWO, YOU'RE THERE.
TWO...
TMP
BMP
ON THREE, YOU LOOK AT TOMOYO AND PASS.
THREE.
FWMP
NO GOOD. IT DIDN'T GO TO TOMOYO!

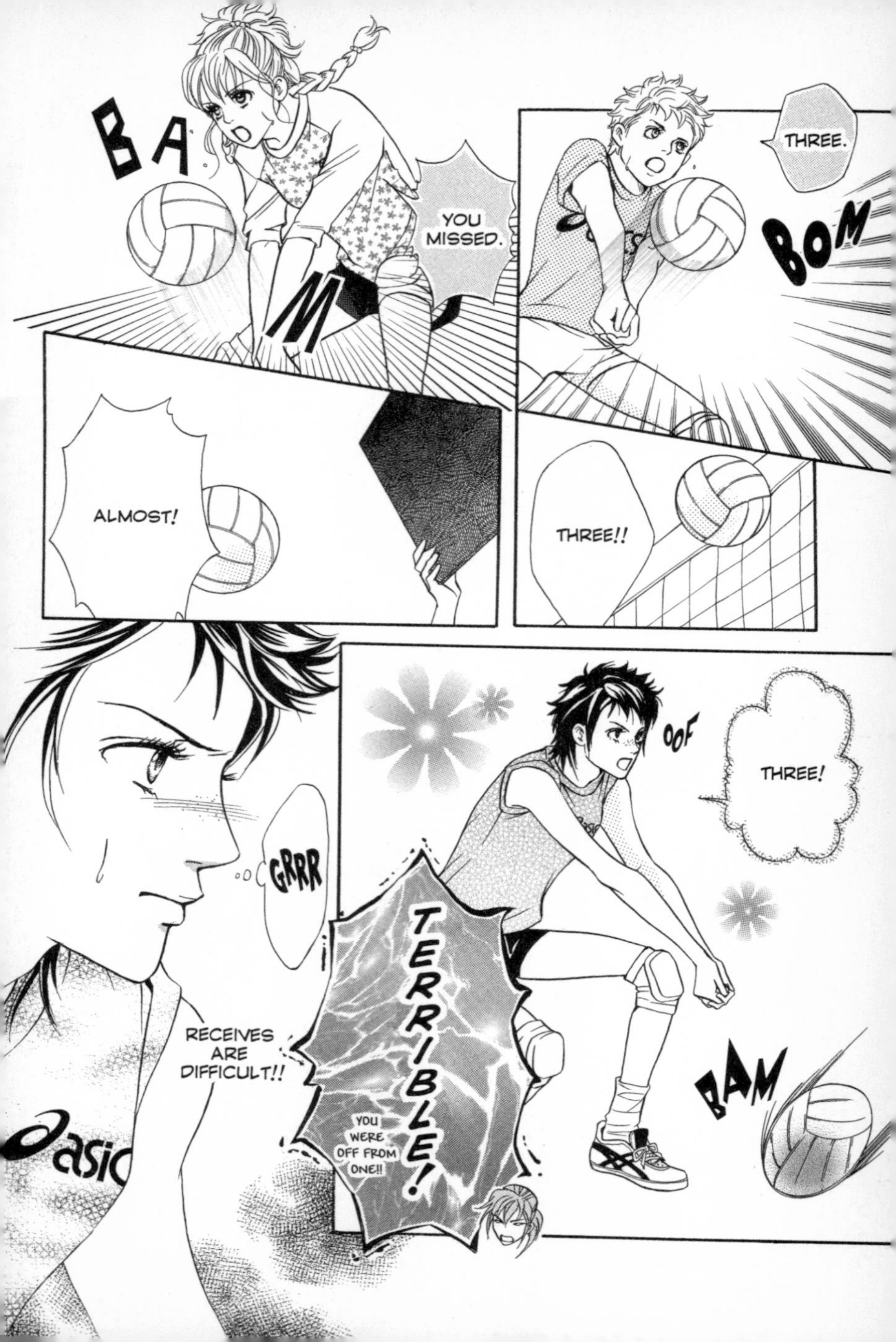
THREE.
BOM
YOU MISSED.
BAM
THREE!!
ALMOST!
THREE!
OOF
BAM
TERRIBLE!
YOU WERE OFF FROM ONE!!
GRRR
RECEIVES ARE DIFFICULT!!

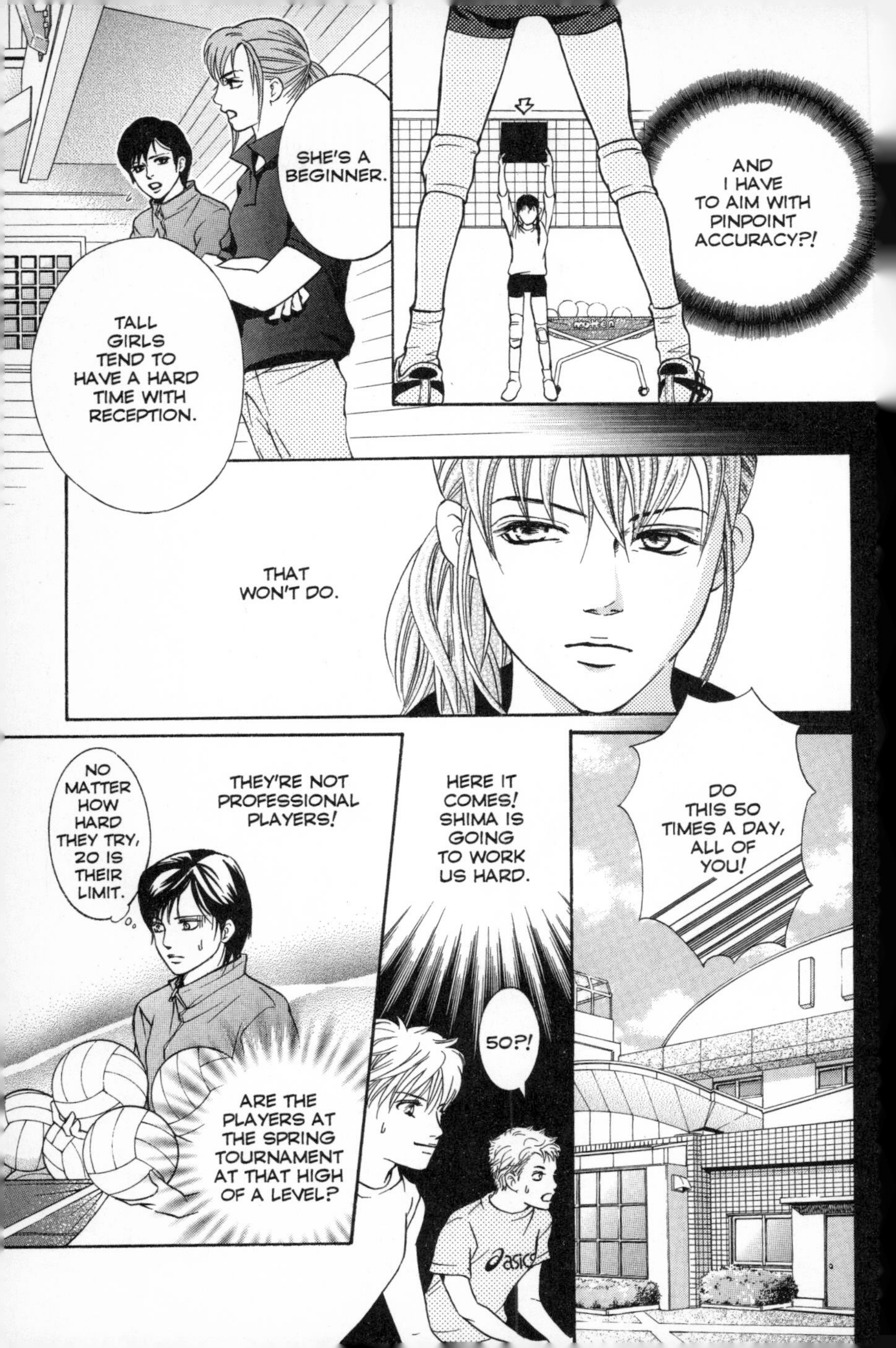
AND I HAVE TO AIM WITH PINPOINT ACCURACY?!
SHE'S A BEGINNER.
TALL GIRLS TEND TO HAVE A HARD TIME WITH RECEPTION.
THAT WON'T DO.
DO THIS 50 TIMES A DAY, ALL OF YOU!
50?!
HERE IT COMES! SHIMA IS GOING TO WORK US HARD.
THEY'RE NOT PROFESSIONAL PLAYERS!
NO MATTER HOW HARD THEY TRY, 20 IS THEIR LIMIT.
ARE THE PLAYERS AT THE SPRING TOURNAMENT AT THAT HIGH OF A LEVEL?

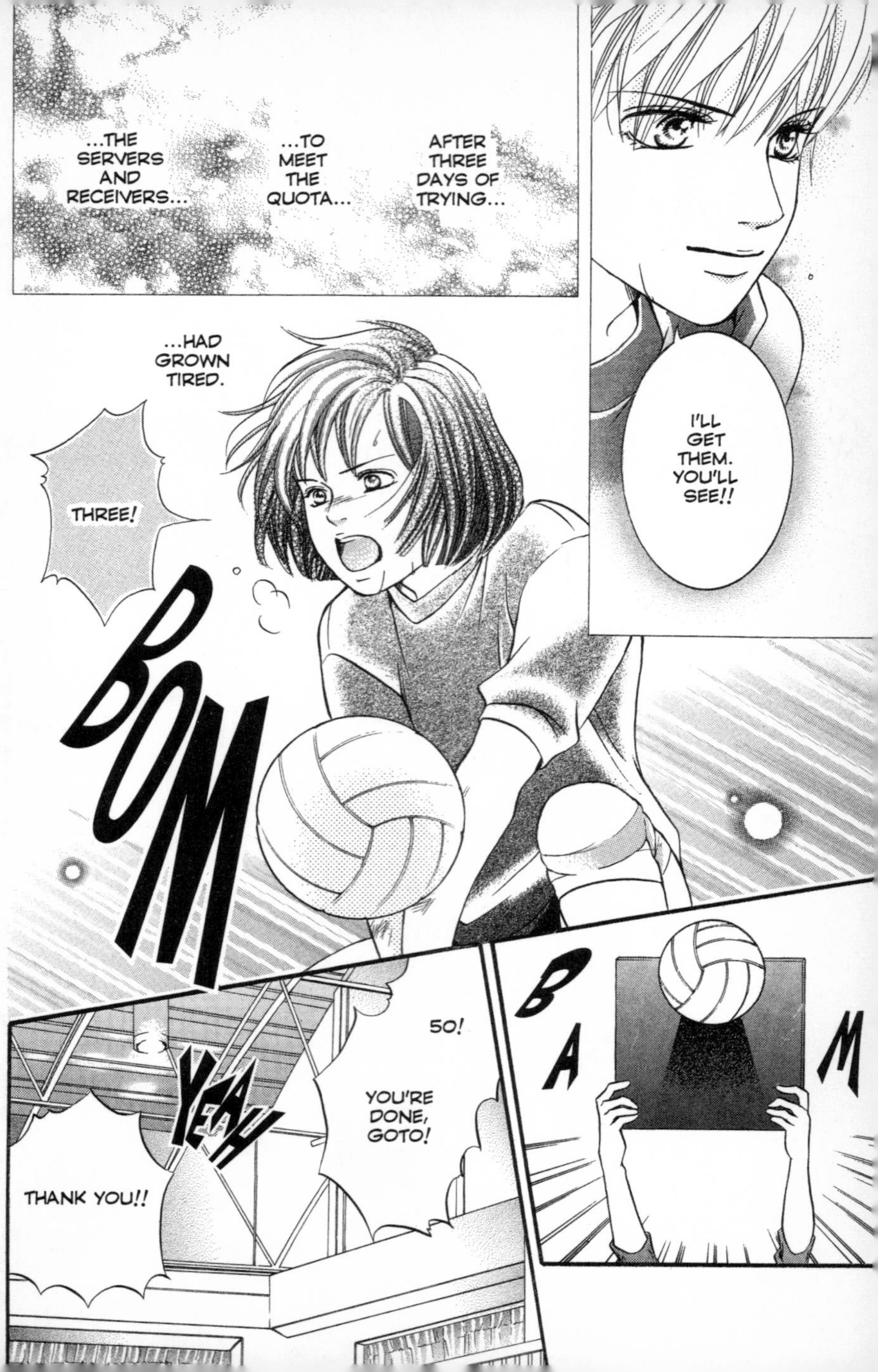
I'LL GET THEM. YOU'LL SEE!!
AFTER THREE DAYS OF TRYING...
...TO MEET THE QUOTA...
...THE SERVERS AND RECEIVERS...
...HAD GROWN TIRED.
THREE!
BOM
BAM
50!
YOU'RE DONE, GOTO!
YEAH
THANK YOU!!

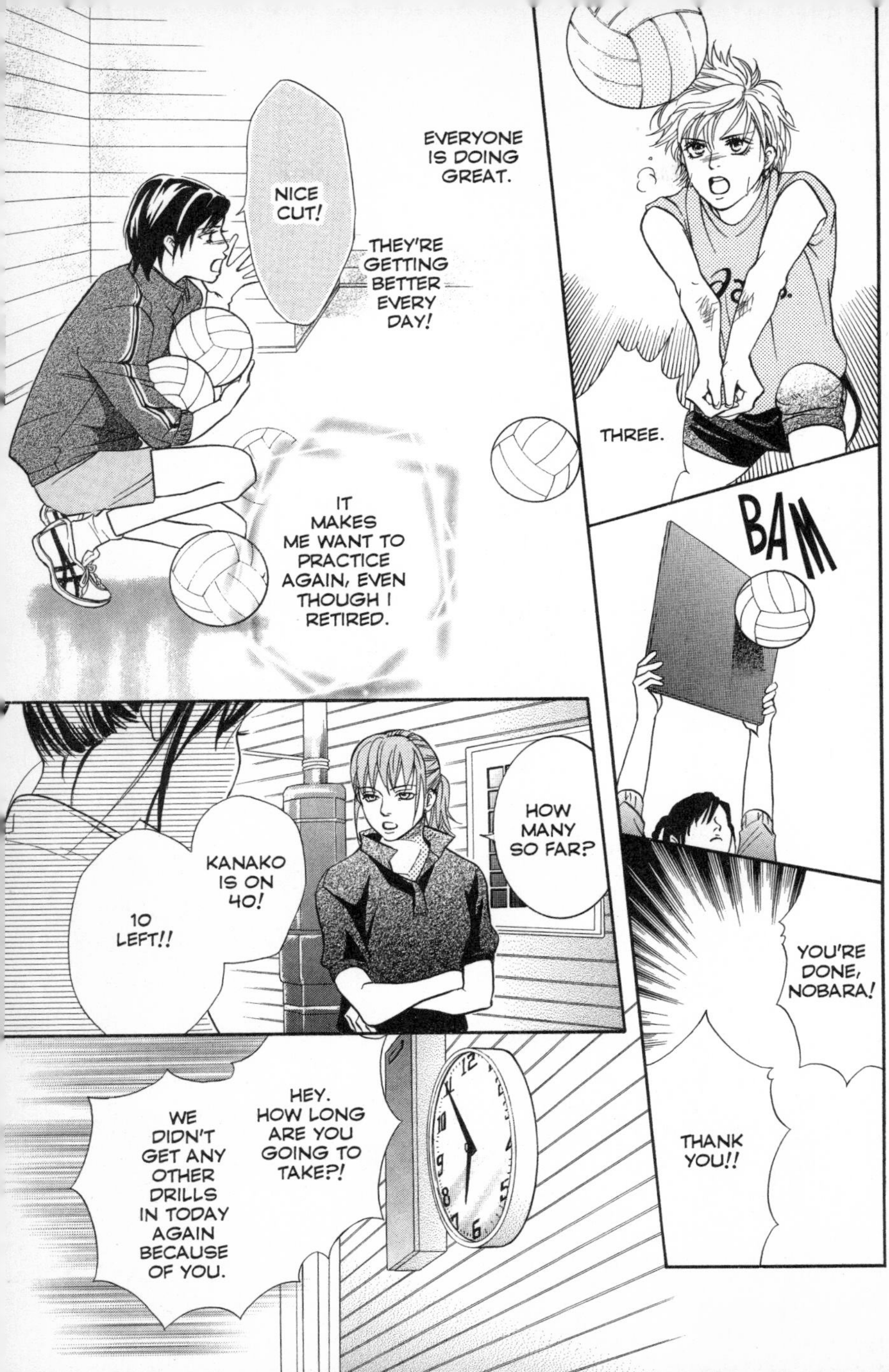
THREE.
EVERYONE IS DOING GREAT.
NICE CUT!
THEY'RE GETTING BETTER EVERY DAY!
IT MAKES ME WANT TO PRACTICE AGAIN, EVEN THOUGH I RETIRED.
BAM
HOW MANY SO FAR?
KANAKO IS ON 40!
10 LEFT!!
YOU'RE DONE, NOBARA!
THANK YOU!!
HEY. HOW LONG ARE YOU GOING TO TAKE?!
WE DIDN'T GET ANY OTHER DRILLS IN TODAY AGAIN BECAUSE OF YOU.

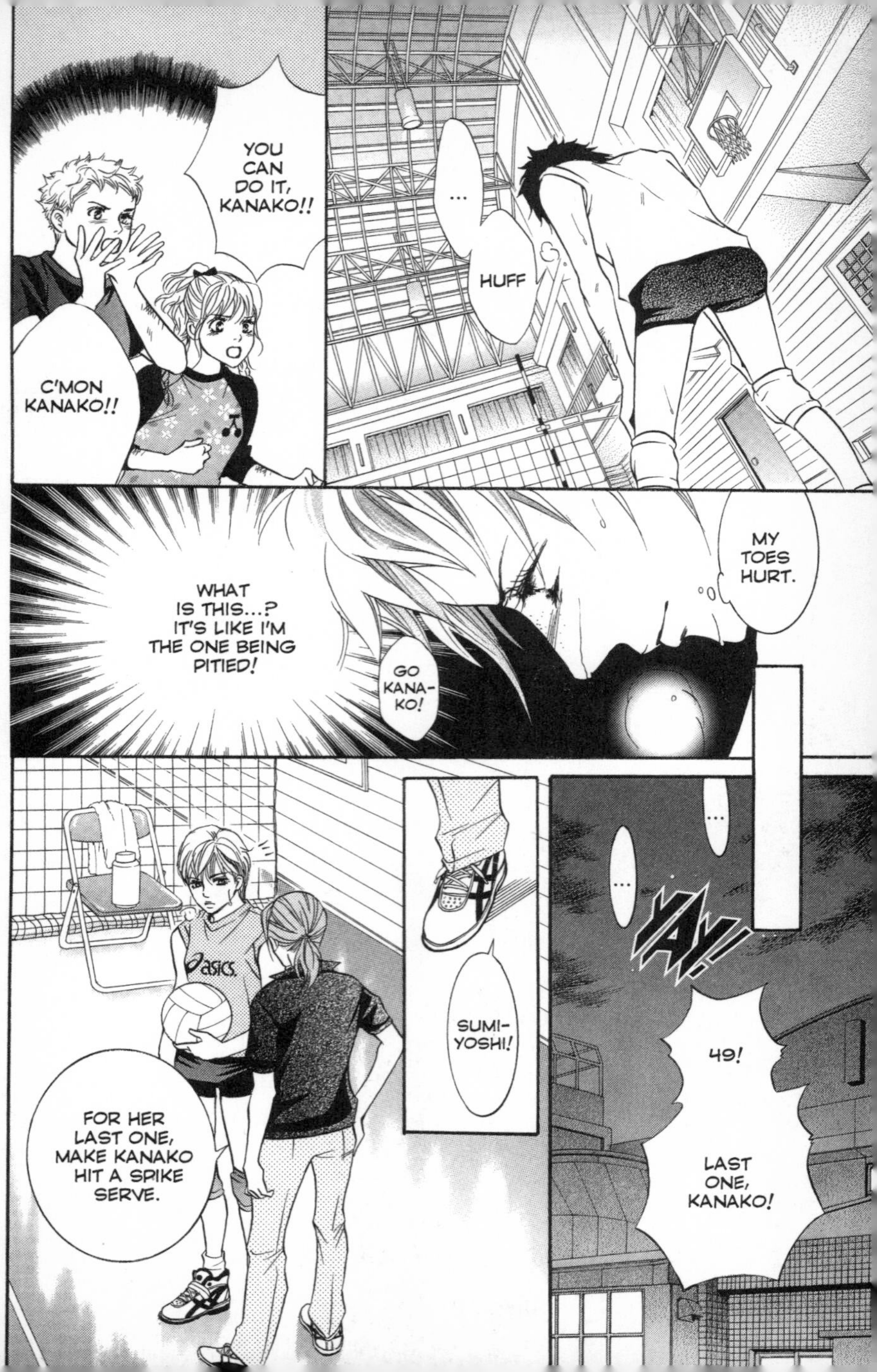
...
HUFF
YOU CAN DO IT, KANAKO!!
C'MON KANAKO!!
MY TOES HURT.
GO KANA-KO!
WHAT IS THIS...? IT'S LIKE I'M THE ONE BEING PITIED!
...
...
YAY!
49!
LAST ONE, KANAKO!
SUMI-YOSHI!
FOR HER LAST ONE, MAKE KANAKO HIT A SPIKE SERVE.

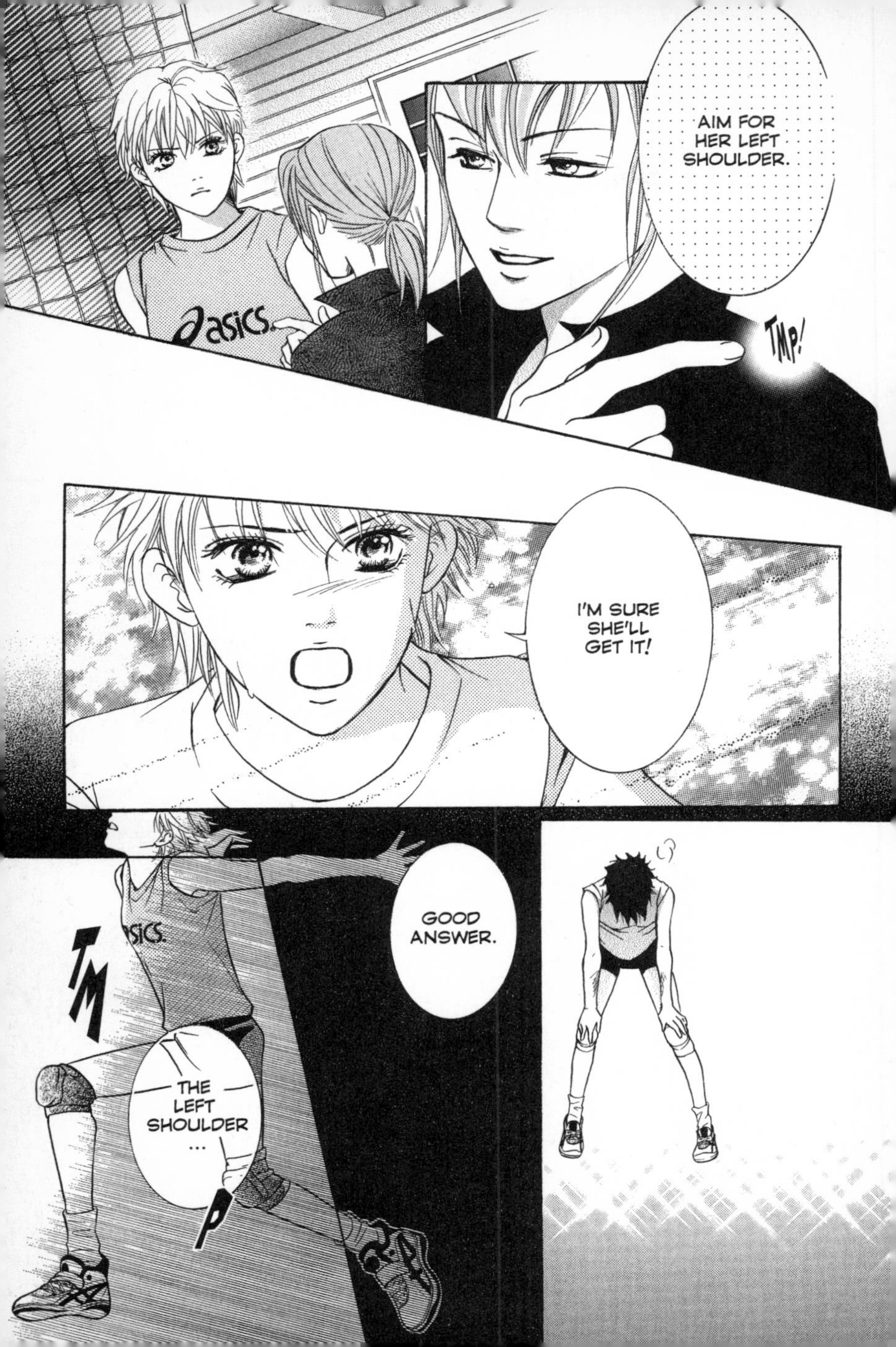
AIM FOR HER LEFT SHOULDER.
TMP!
I'M SURE SHE'LL GET IT!
GOOD ANSWER.
TM
P
THE LEFT SHOULDER ...

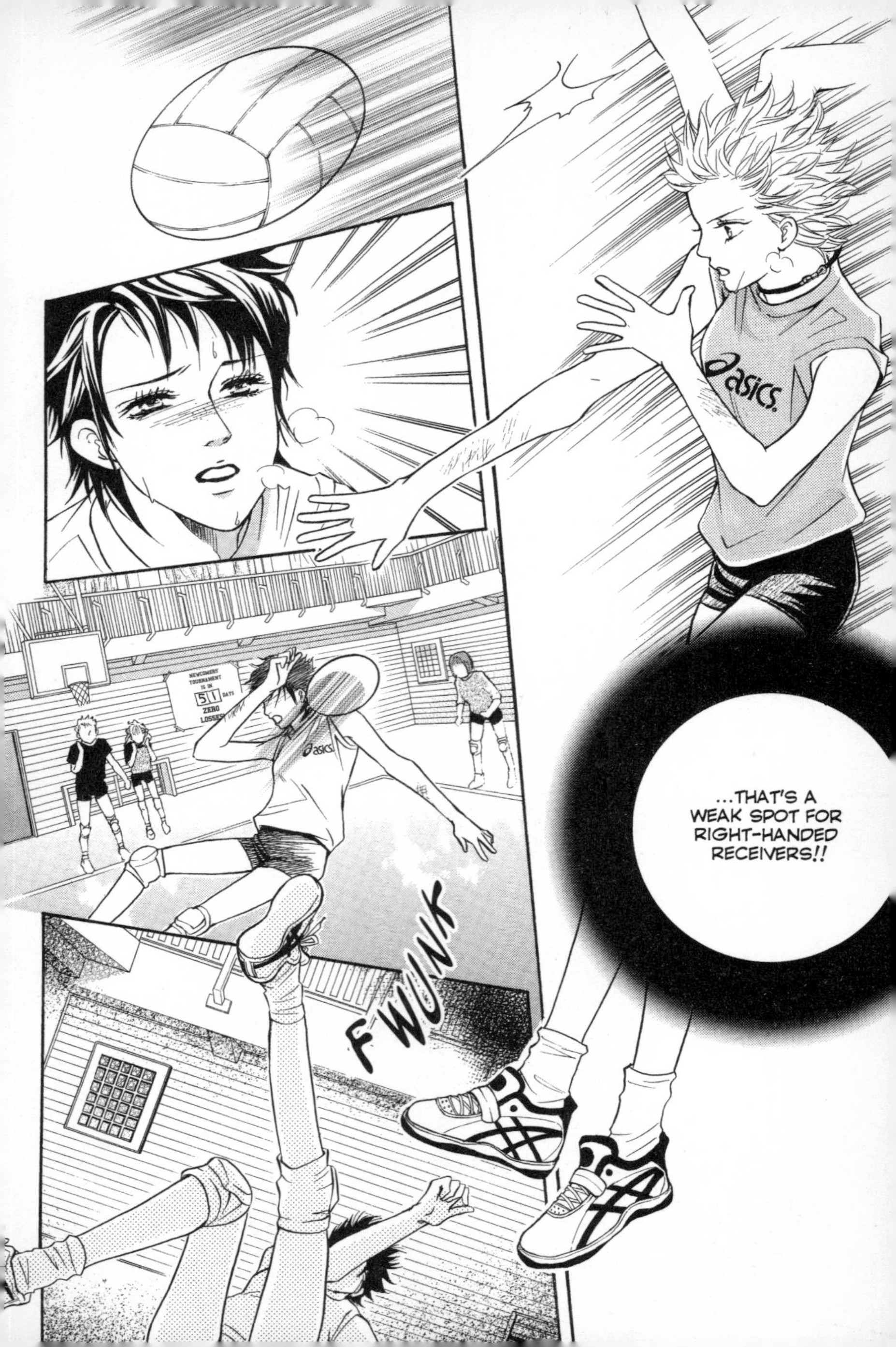
...THAT'S A WEAK SPOT FOR RIGHT-HANDED RECEIVERS!!
NEWCOMERS' TOURNAMENT IS IN 51 DAYS ZERO LOSSES
FWUNK

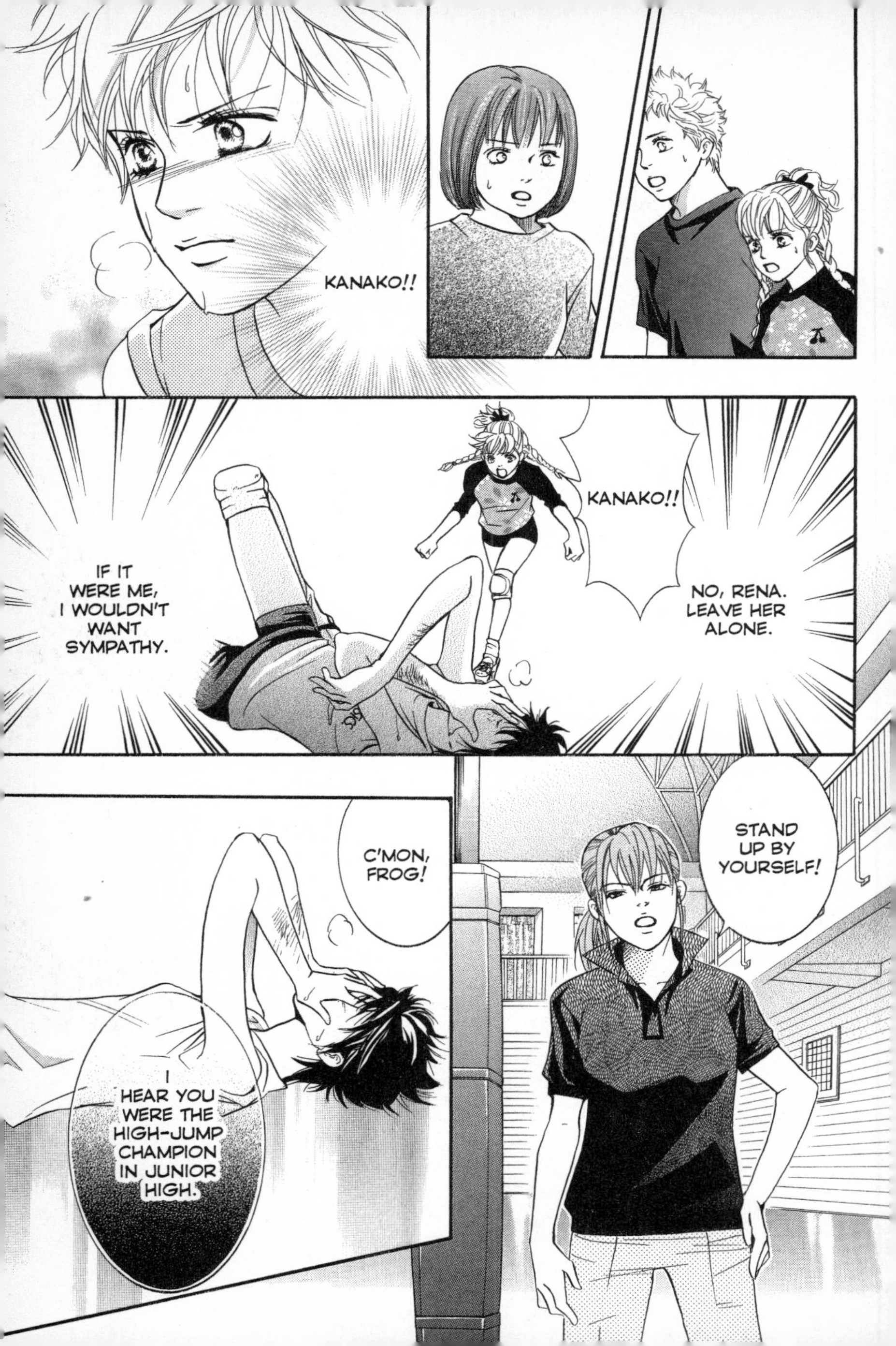
KANAKO!!
KANAKO!!
NO, RENA. LEAVE HER ALONE.
IF IT WERE ME, I WOULDN'T WANT SYMPATHY.
STAND UP BY YOURSELF!
C'MON, FROG!
I HEAR YOU WERE THE HIGH-JUMP CHAMPION IN JUNIOR HIGH.

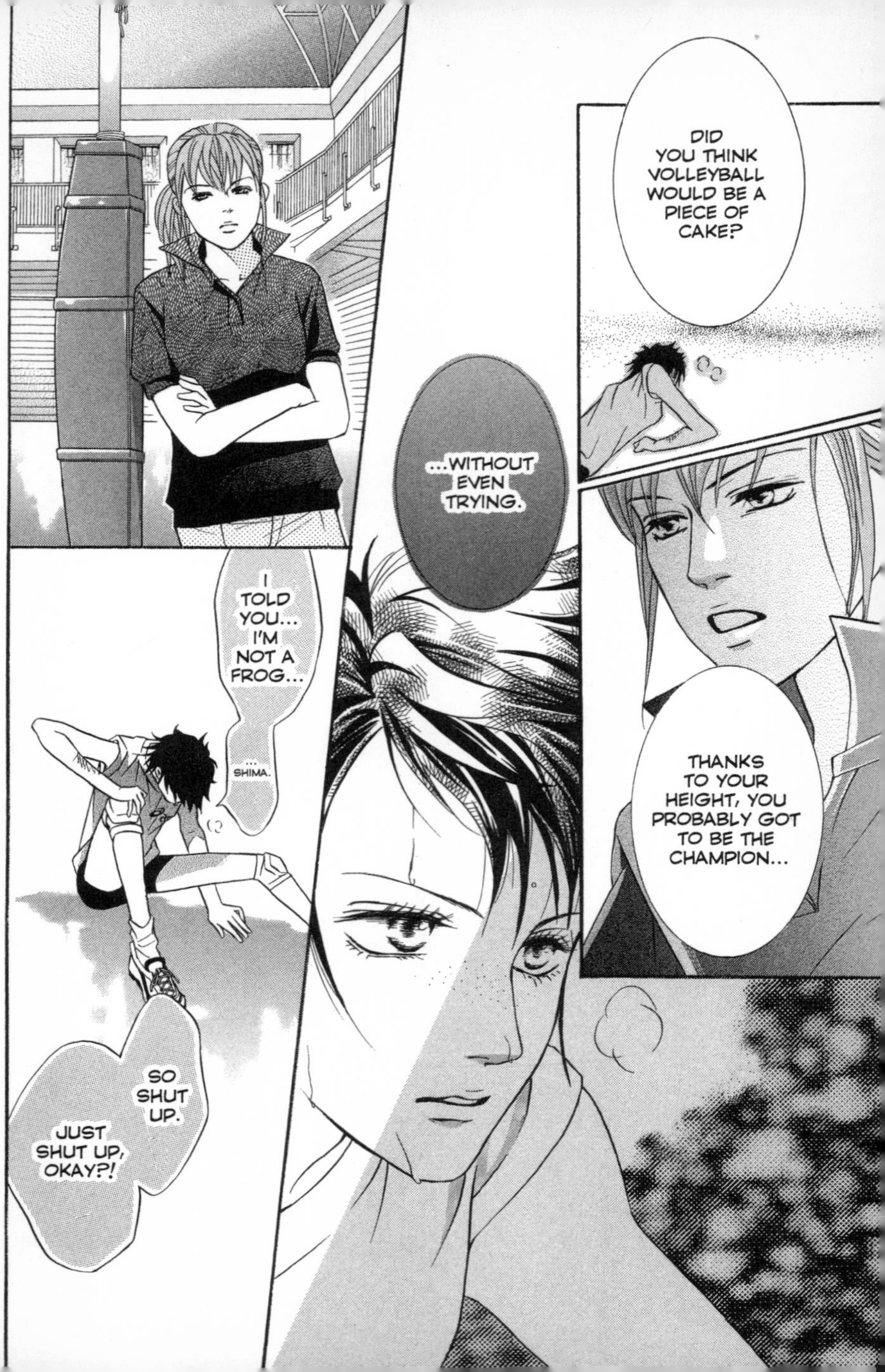
DID YOU THINK VOLLEYBALL WOULD BE A PIECE OF CAKE?
THANKS TO YOUR HEIGHT, YOU PROBABLY GOT TO BE THE CHAMPION...
...WITHOUT EVEN TRYING.
I TOLD YOU... I'M NOT A FROG...
...SHIMA.
SO SHUT UP.
JUST SHUT UP, OKAY?!

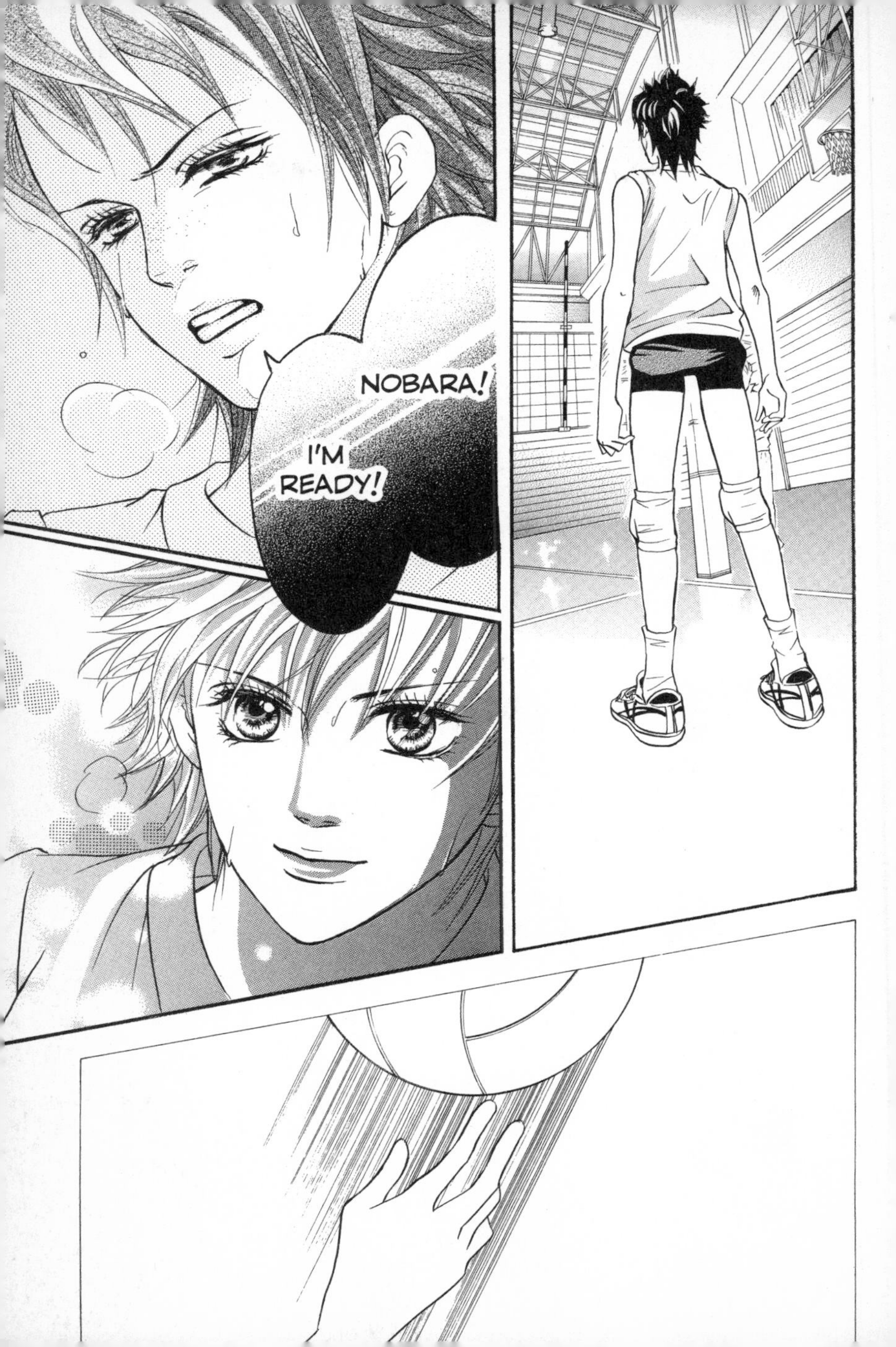
NOBARA!
I'M READY!

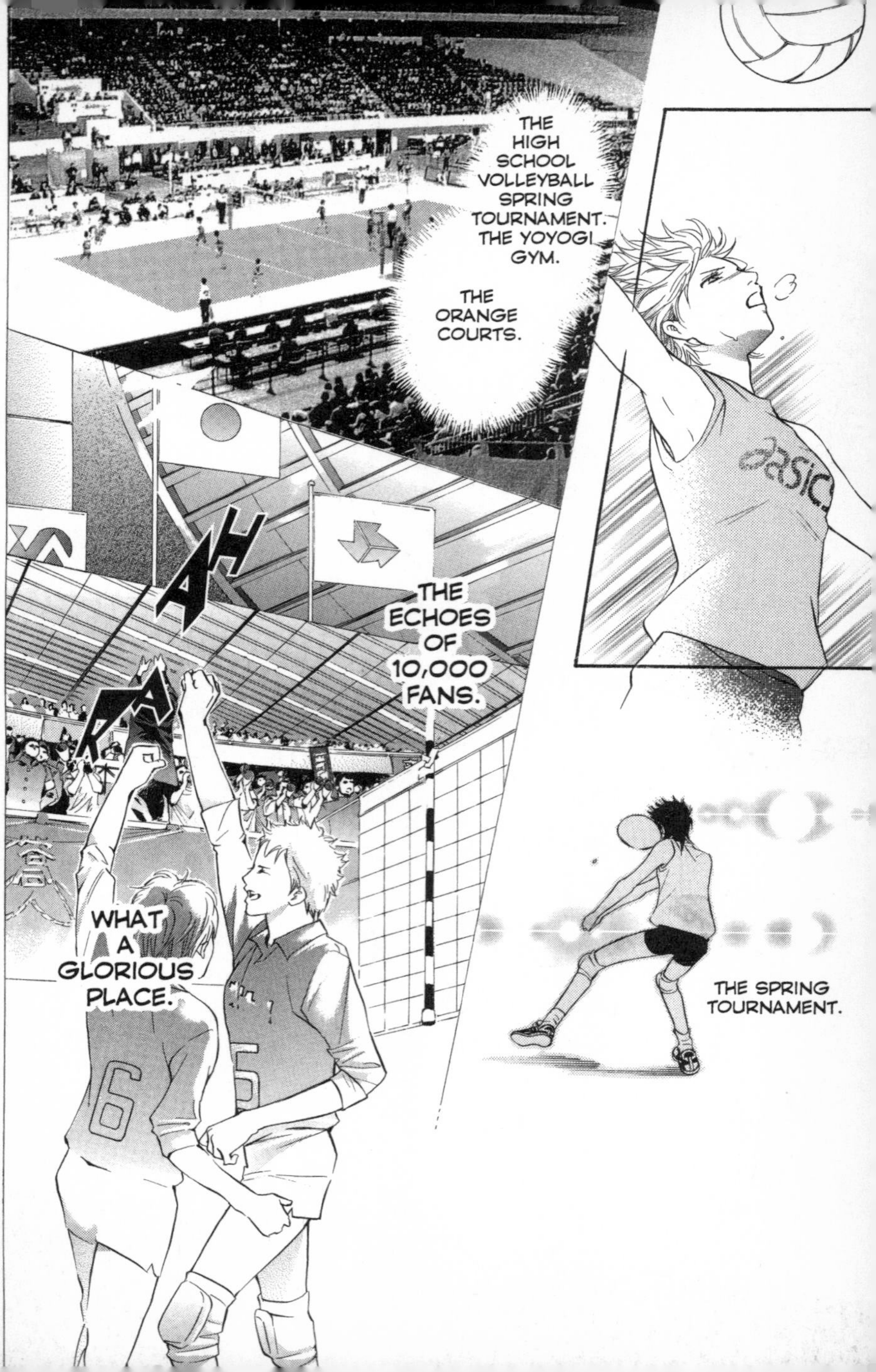
THE HIGH SCHOOL VOLLEYBALL SPRING TOURNAMENT. THE YOYOGI GYM.
THE ORANGE COURTS.
AH
THE SPRING TOURNAMENT.
RA
THE ECHOES OF 10,000 FANS.
WHAT A GLORIOUS PLACE.

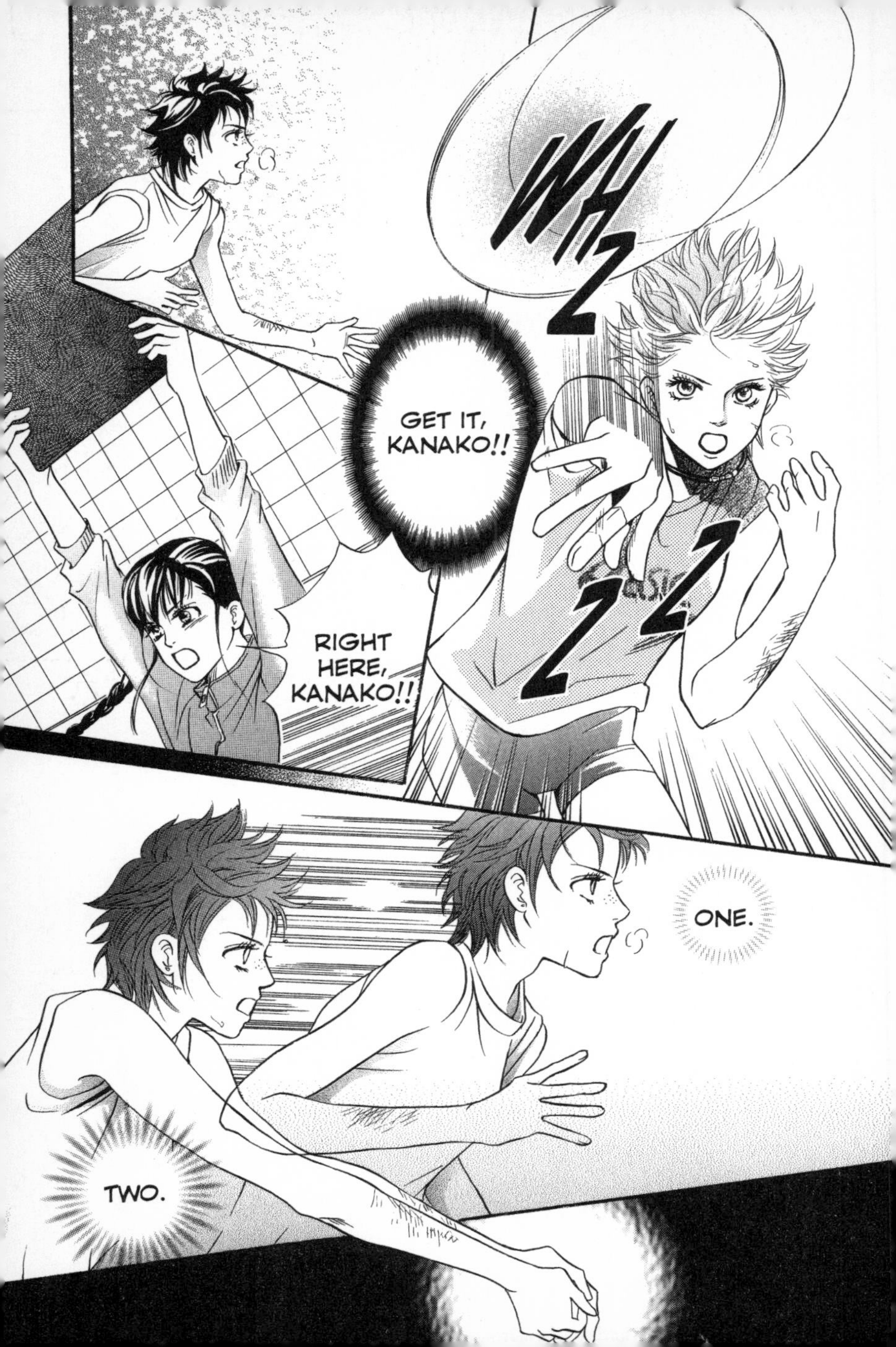
WHIZ
ZZ
GET IT, KANAKO!!
RIGHT HERE, KANAKO!!
ONE.
TWO.

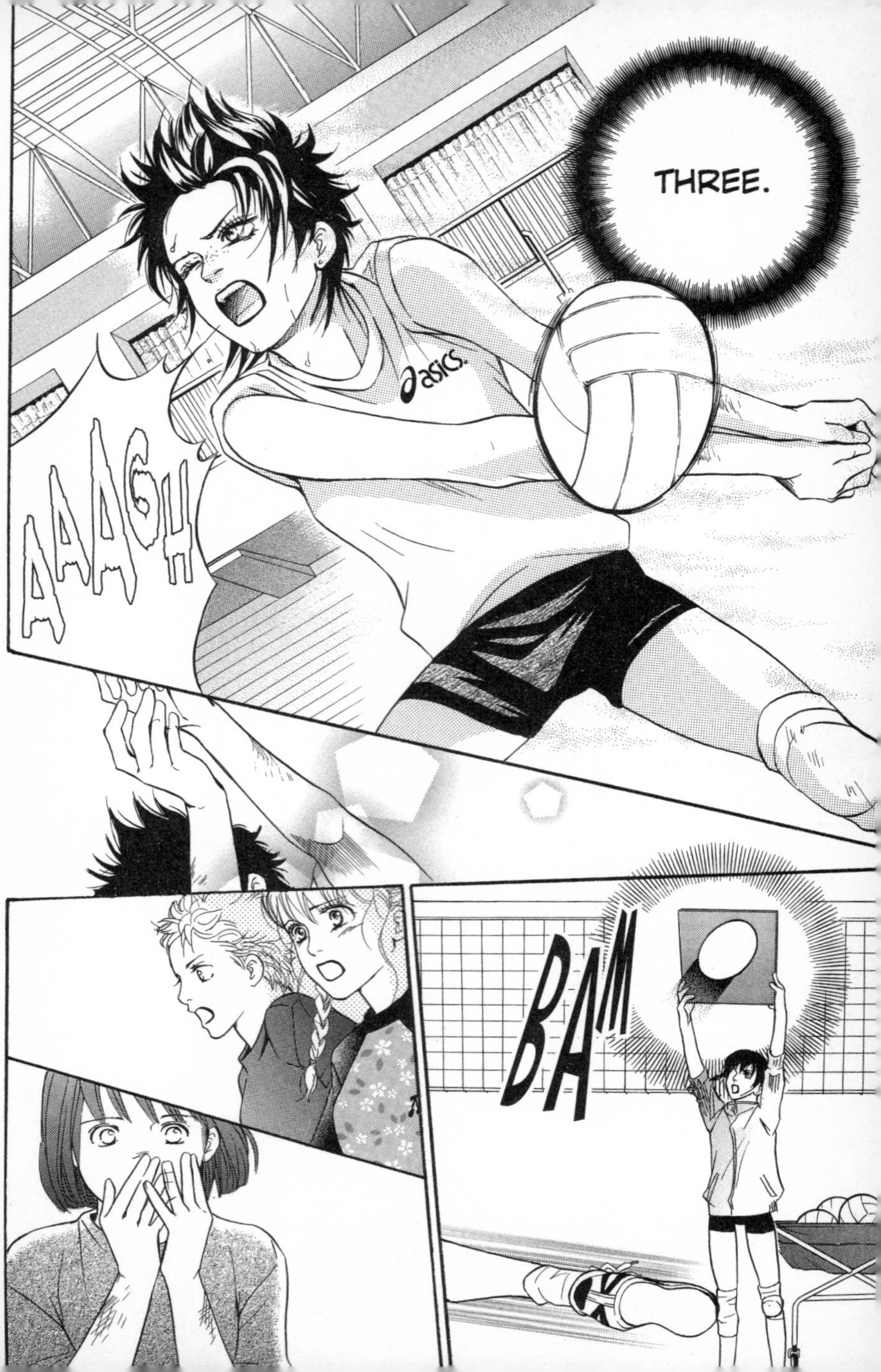
THREE.
AAAGH
asics
BAM

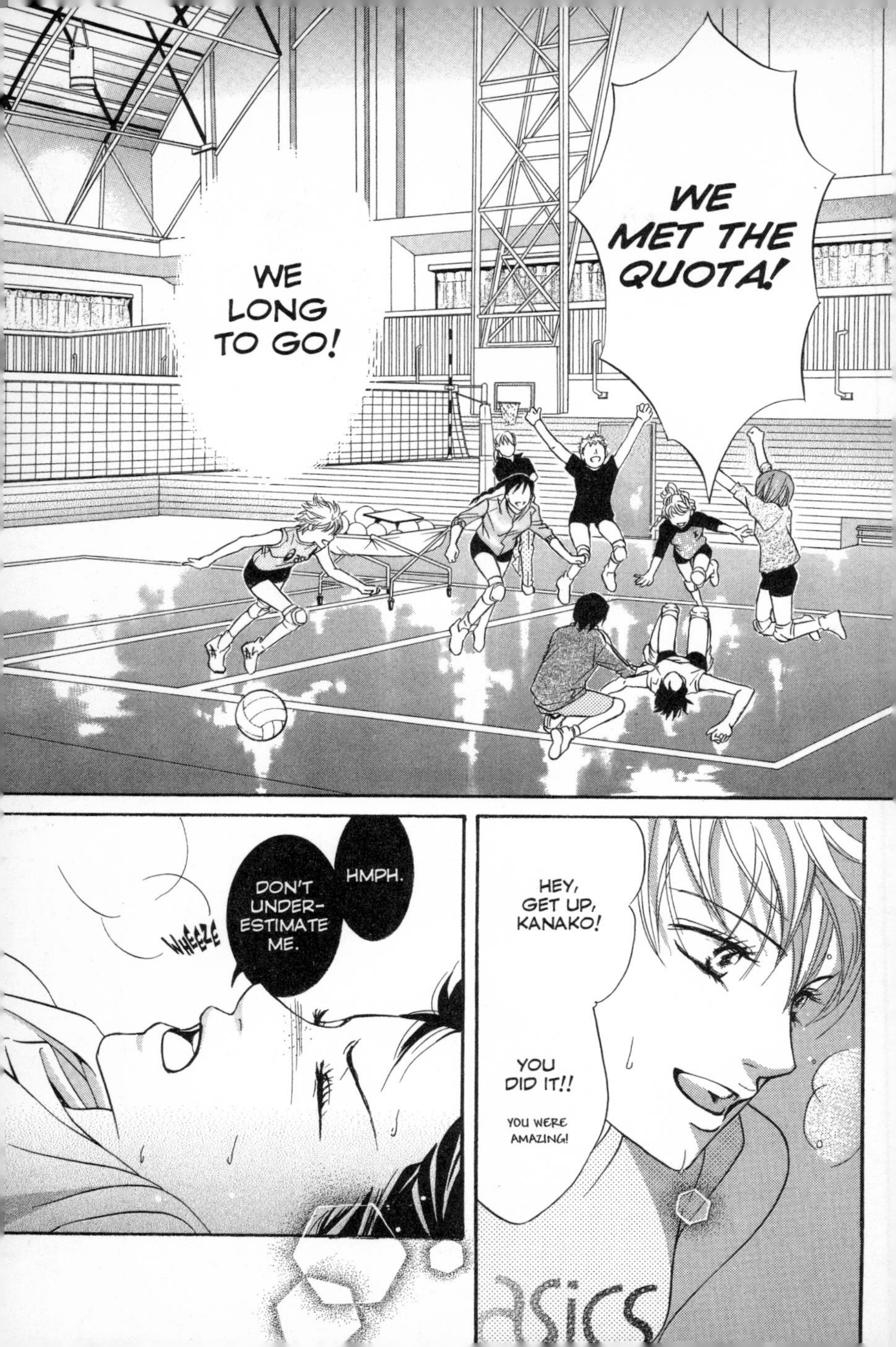
WE MET THE QUOTA!
WE LONG TO GO!
HEY, GET UP, KANAKO!
YOU DID IT!!
YOU WERE AMAZING!
HMPH.
DON'T UNDER-ESTIMATE ME.
WHEEZE

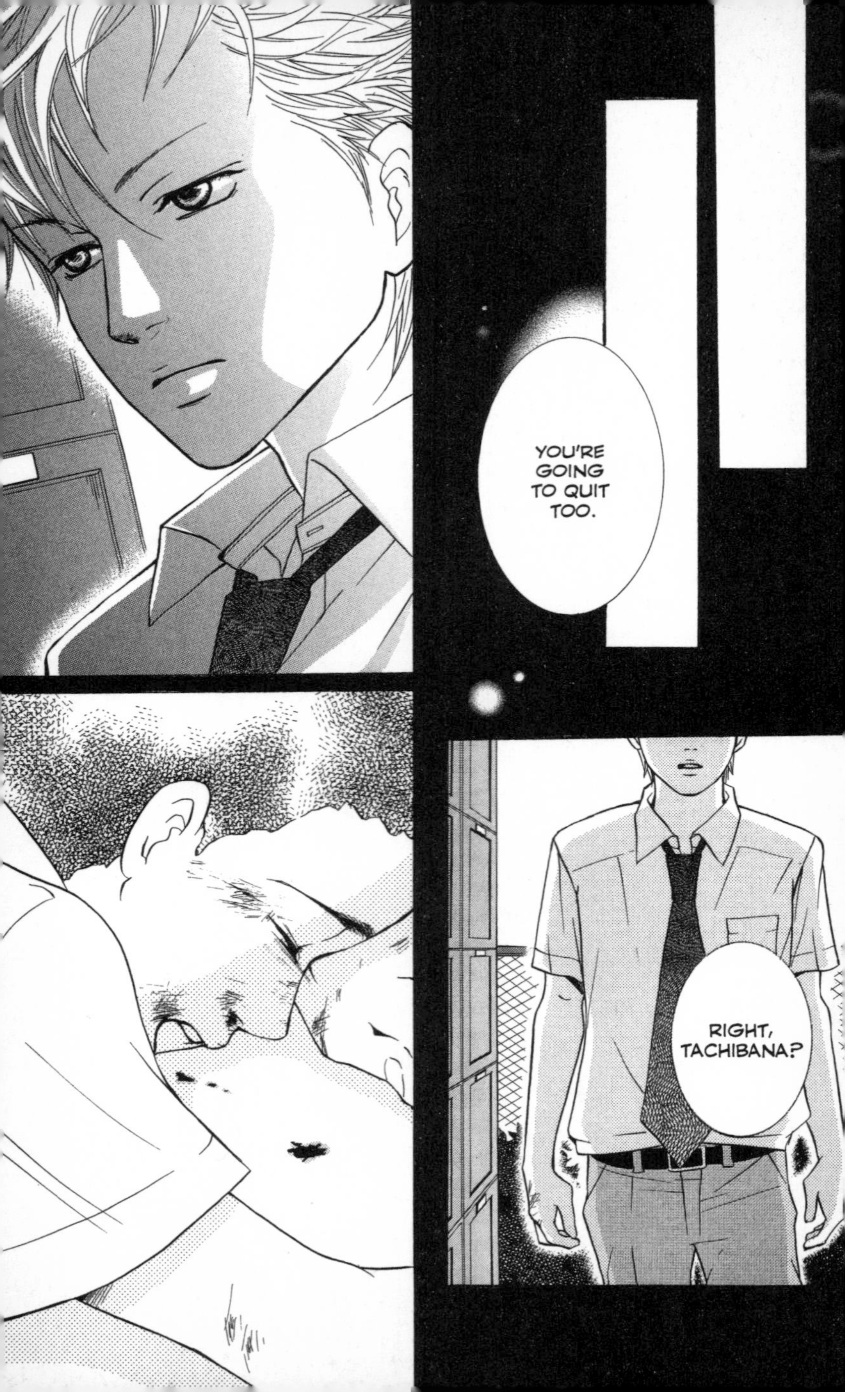
YOU'RE GOING TO QUIT TOO.
RIGHT, TACHIBANA?

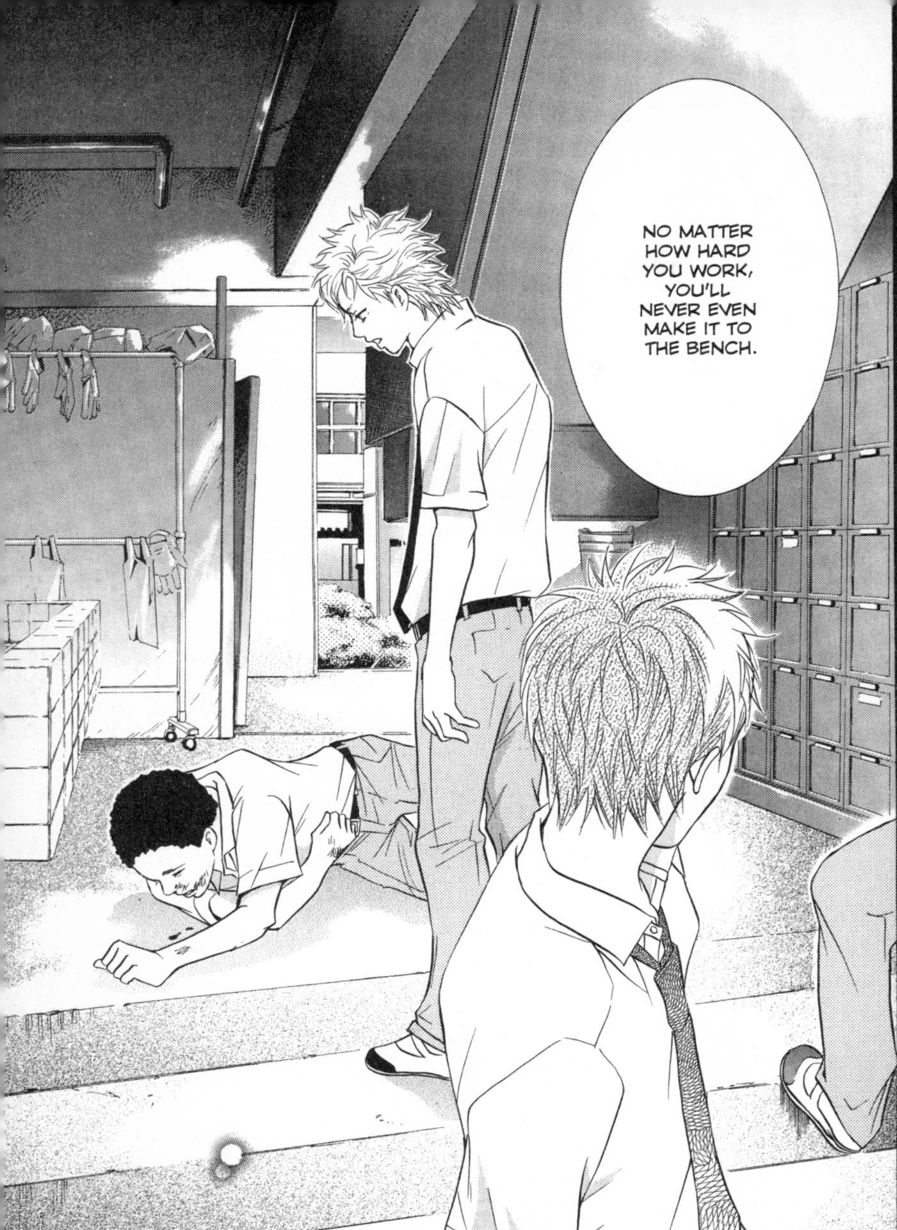
NO MATTER HOW HARD YOU WORK, YOU'LL NEVER EVEN MAKE IT TO THE BENCH.

eral recommending reduced
intake of dietary fats, especially saturated fats.
stant film and cameras — and
Kodak out of the in-
ohy business.
00 million of
ated $200
seless
nt.
ar-
titled
unitive
total to

the Mala
Growers C
an informa
has underv
dies to sup

In a pre
ruled in
Kodak ha
Polaroid's
of fats and
ucts in the
only 550 n
million kg
tropical oi

U.S. con-
by a
months
n February
981, right be
the 1981-82

Michael
economist
constructic
that histor;
about 650
million kg)
the record
(720 millio
1970s.

The thre
push
li

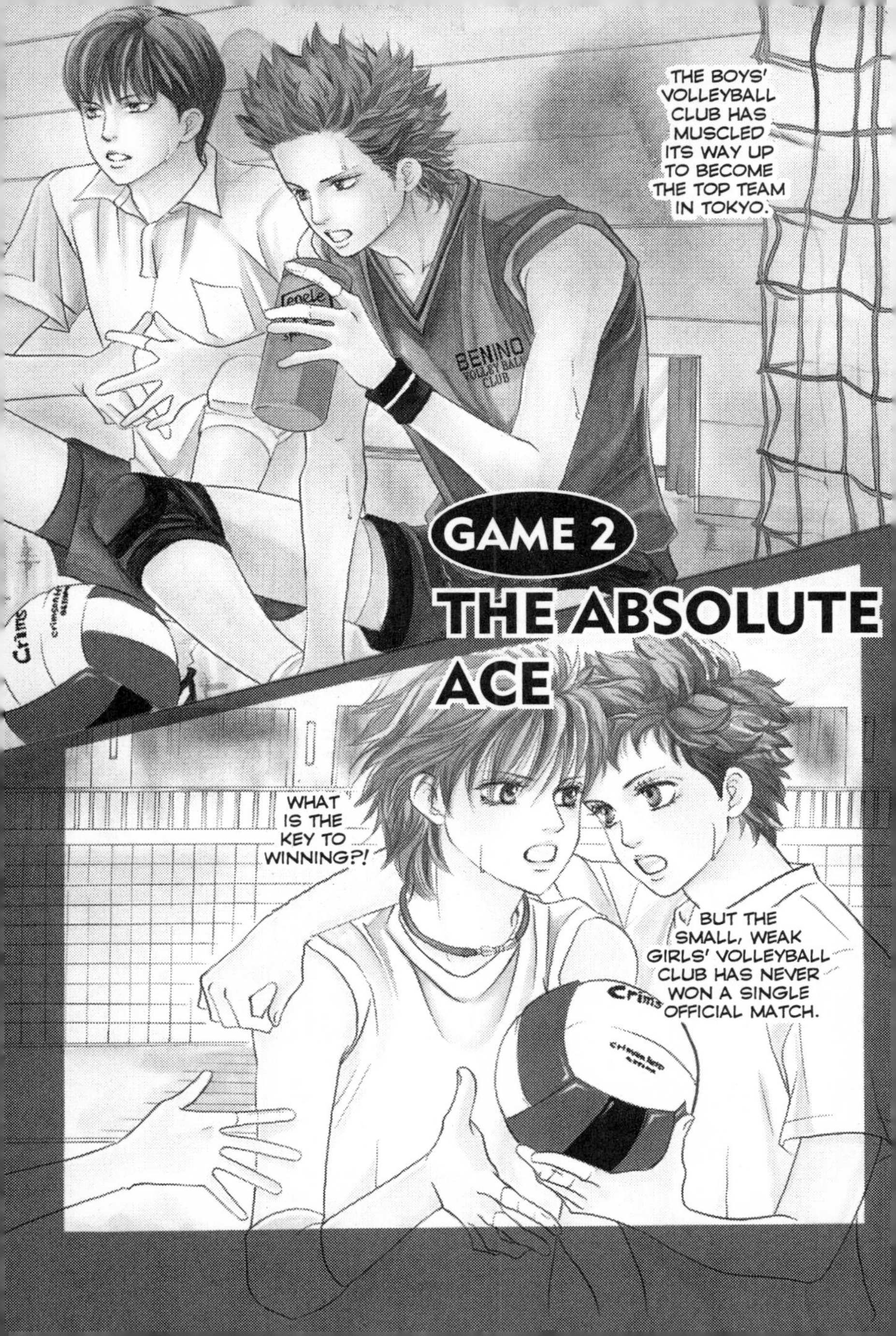
THE BOYS' VOLLEYBALL CLUB HAS MUSCLED ITS WAY UP TO BECOME THE TOP TEAM IN TOKYO.
BENINO VOLLEY BALL CLUB
GAME 2
THE ABSOLUTE ACE
BUT THE SMALL, WEAK GIRLS' VOLLEYBALL CLUB HAS NEVER WON A SINGLE OFFICIAL MATCH.
WHAT IS THE KEY TO WINNING?!

Crimson Hero

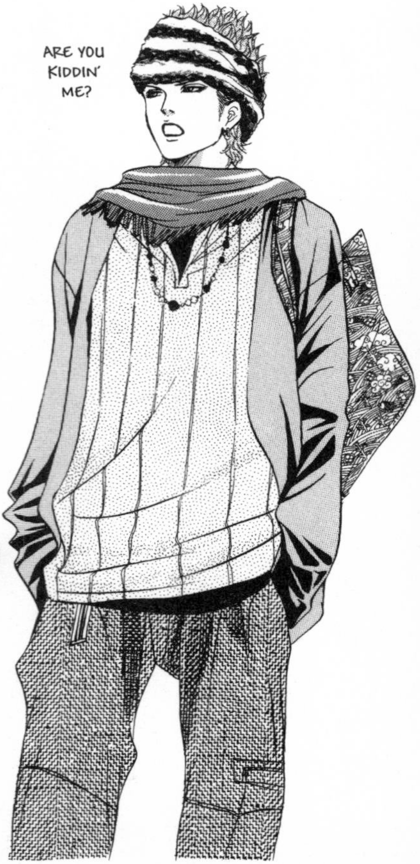
ARE YOU KIDDIN' ME?

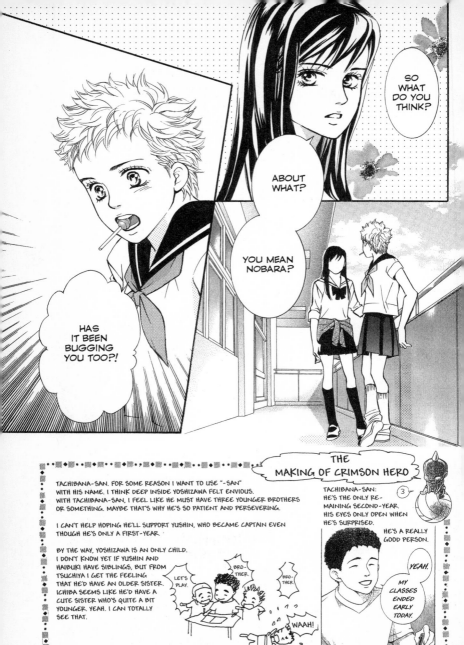

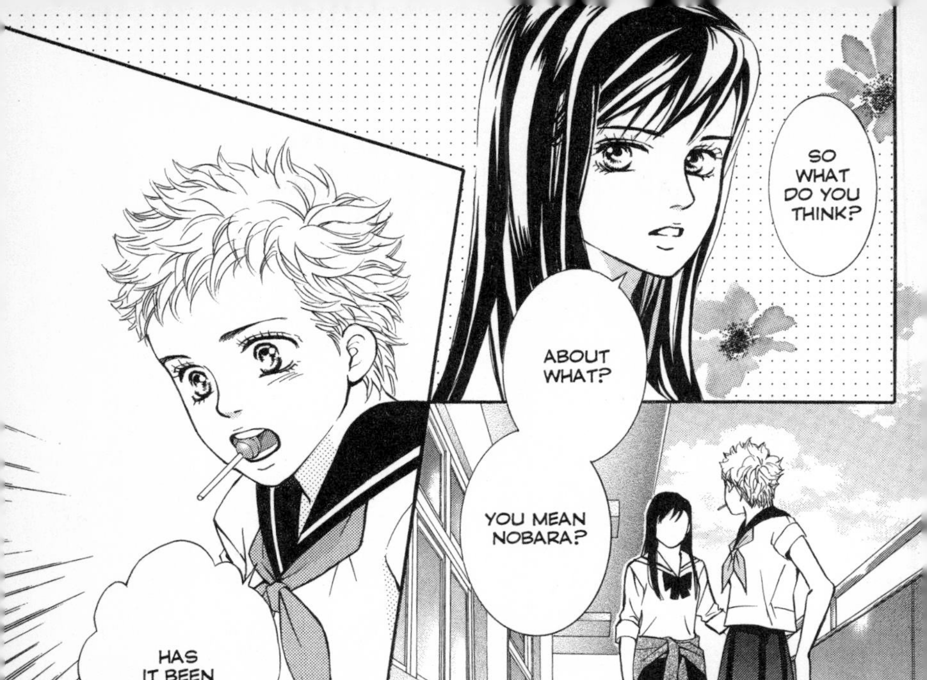
SO WHAT DO YOU THINK?
ABOUT WHAT?
YOU MEAN NOBARA?
HAS IT BEEN BUGGING YOU TOO?!

THE MAKING OF CRIMSON HERO

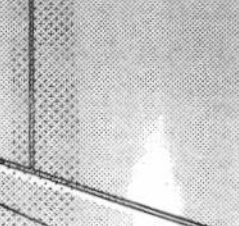
3

TACHIBANA-SAN. FOR SOME REASON I WANT TO USE "-SAN" WITH HIS NAME. I THINK DEEP INSIDE YOSHIZAWA FELT ENVIOUS. WITH TACHIBANA-SAN, I FEEL LIKE HE MUST HAVE THREE YOUNGER BROTHERS OR SOMETHING. MAYBE THAT'S WHY HE'S SO PATIENT AND PERSEVERING.

I CAN'T HELP HOPING HE'LL SUPPORT YUSHIN, WHO BECAME CAPTAIN EVEN THOUGH HE'S ONLY A FIRST-YEAR.

BY THE WAY, YOSHIZAWA IS AN ONLY CHILD. I DON'T KNOW YET IF YUSHIN AND HAIBUKI HAVE SIBLINGS, BUT FROM TSUCHIYA I GET THE FEELING THAT HE'D HAVE AN OLDER SISTER. ICHIBA SEEMS LIKE HE'D HAVE A CUTE SISTER WHO'S QUITE A BIT YOUNGER. YEAH. I CAN TOTALLY SEE THAT.

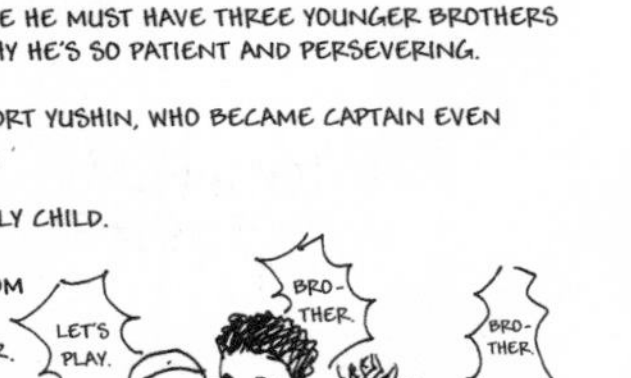
BROTHER.
BROTHER.
LET'S PLAY.
WAAH!

TACHIBANA-SAN: HE'S THE ONLY REMAINING SECOND-YEAR. HIS EYES ONLY OPEN WHEN HE'S SURPRISED.

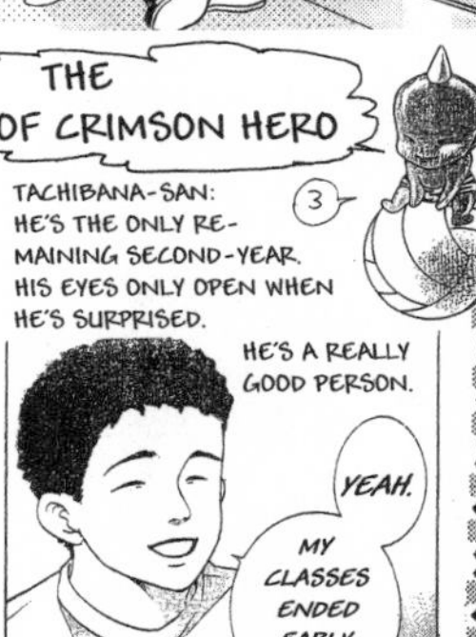
HE'S A REALLY GOOD PERSON.
YEAH.
MY CLASSES ENDED EARLY TODAY.

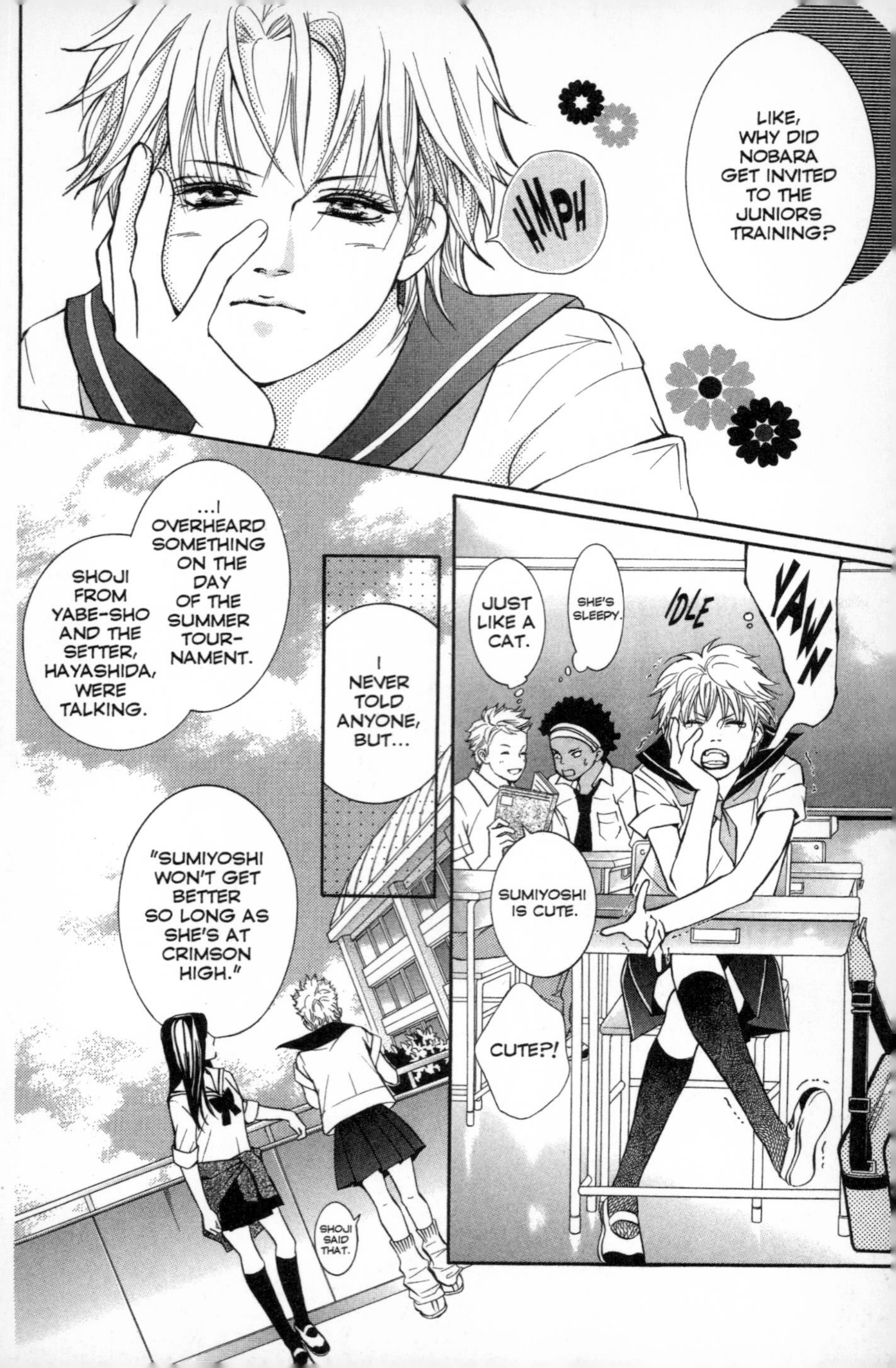
LIKE, WHY DID NOBARA GET INVITED TO THE JUNIORS TRAINING?
HMPH
YAWN
IDLE
SHE'S SLEEPY.
JUST LIKE A CAT.
SUMIYOSHI IS CUTE.
CUTE?!
I NEVER TOLD ANYONE, BUT...
...I OVERHEARD SOMETHING ON THE DAY OF THE SUMMER TOURNAMENT.
SHOJI FROM YABE-SHO AND THE SETTER, HAYASHIDA, WERE TALKING.
"SUMIYOSHI WON'T GET BETTER SO LONG AS SHE'S AT CRIMSON HIGH."
SHOJI SAID THAT.

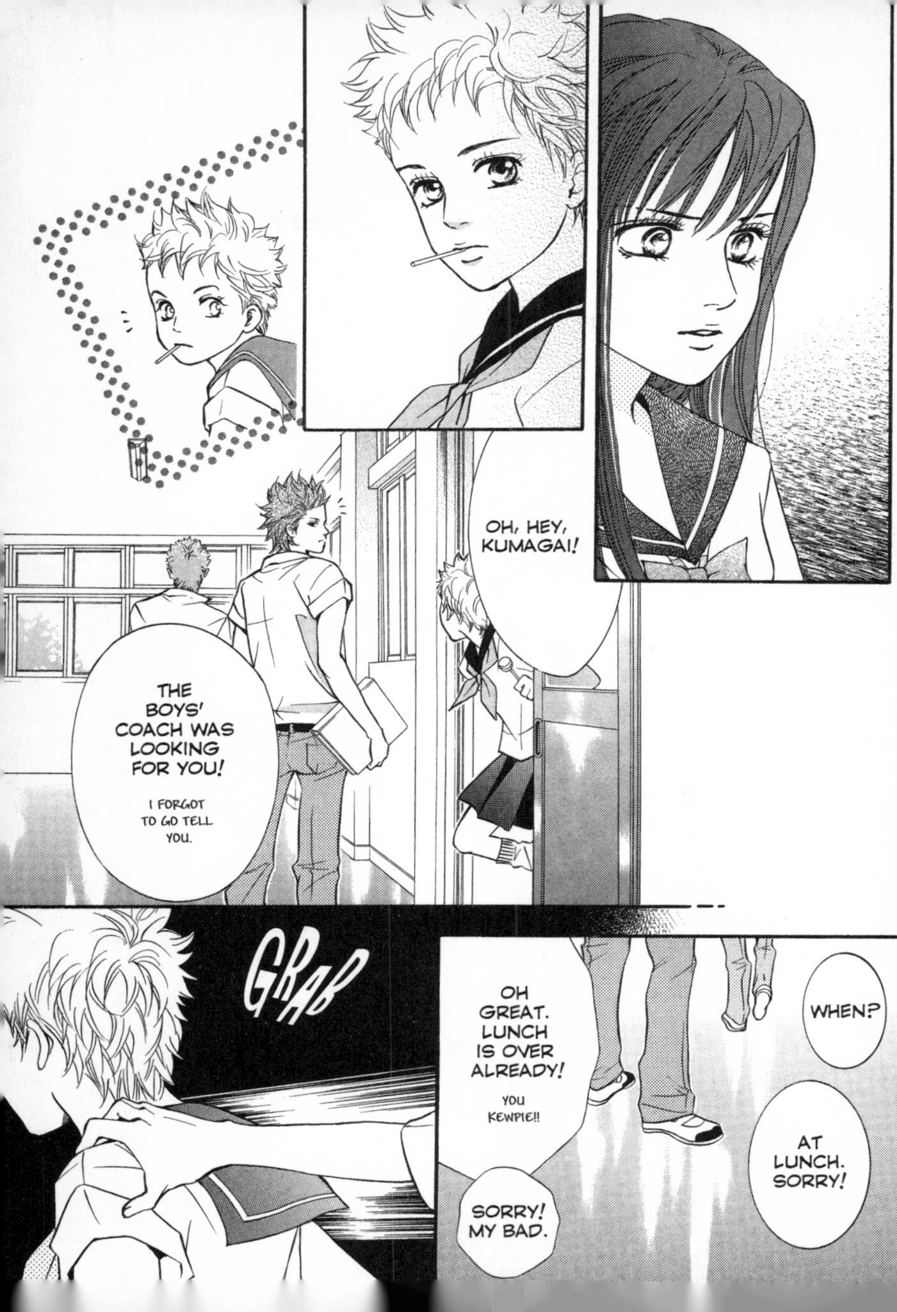
OH, HEY, KUMAGAI!
THE BOYS' COACH WAS LOOKING FOR YOU!
I FORGOT TO GO TELL YOU.
WHEN?
AT LUNCH. SORRY!
OH GREAT. LUNCH IS OVER ALREADY!
YOU KEWPIE!!
SORRY! MY BAD.
GRAB

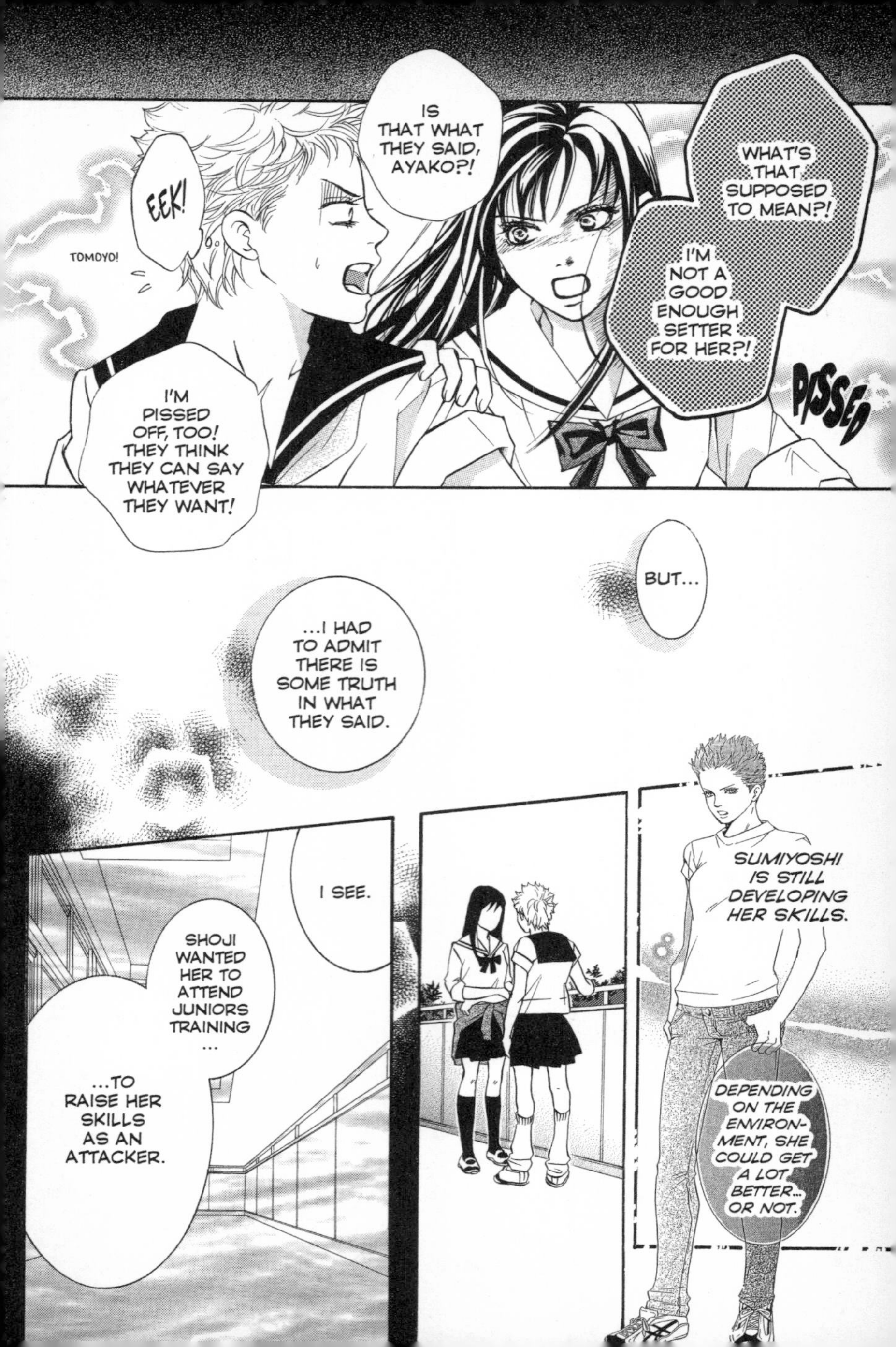
WHAT'S THAT SUPPOSED TO MEAN?!
I'M NOT A GOOD ENOUGH SETTER FOR HER?!
PISSED
IS THAT WHAT THEY SAID, AYAKO?!
EEK!
TOMOYO!
I'M PISSED OFF, TOO! THEY THINK THEY CAN SAY WHATEVER THEY WANT!
BUT...
...I HAD TO ADMIT THERE IS SOME TRUTH IN WHAT THEY SAID.
SUMIYOSHI IS STILL DEVELOPING HER SKILLS.
DEPENDING ON THE ENVIRON-MENT, SHE COULD GET A LOT BETTER... OR NOT.
I SEE.
SHOJI WANTED HER TO ATTEND JUNIORS TRAINING...
...TO RAISE HER SKILLS AS AN ATTACKER.

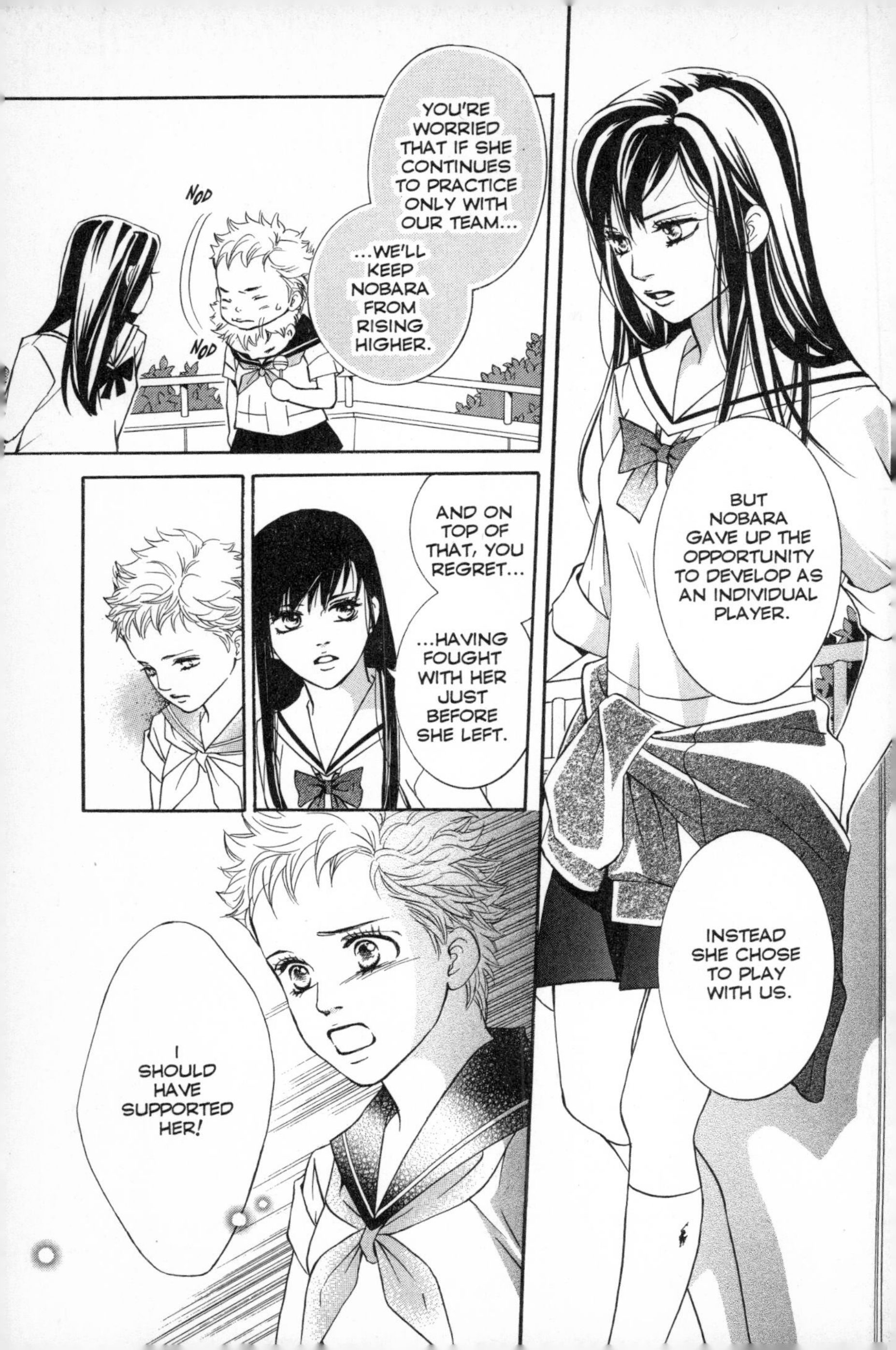

BUT NOBARA GAVE UP THE OPPORTUNITY TO DEVELOP AS AN INDIVIDUAL PLAYER.
INSTEAD SHE CHOSE TO PLAY WITH US.
YOU'RE WORRIED THAT IF SHE CONTINUES TO PRACTICE ONLY WITH OUR TEAM...
...WE'LL KEEP NOBARA FROM RISING HIGHER.
NOD
NOD
AND ON TOP OF THAT, YOU REGRET...
...HAVING FOUGHT WITH HER JUST BEFORE SHE LEFT.
I SHOULD HAVE SUPPORTED HER!

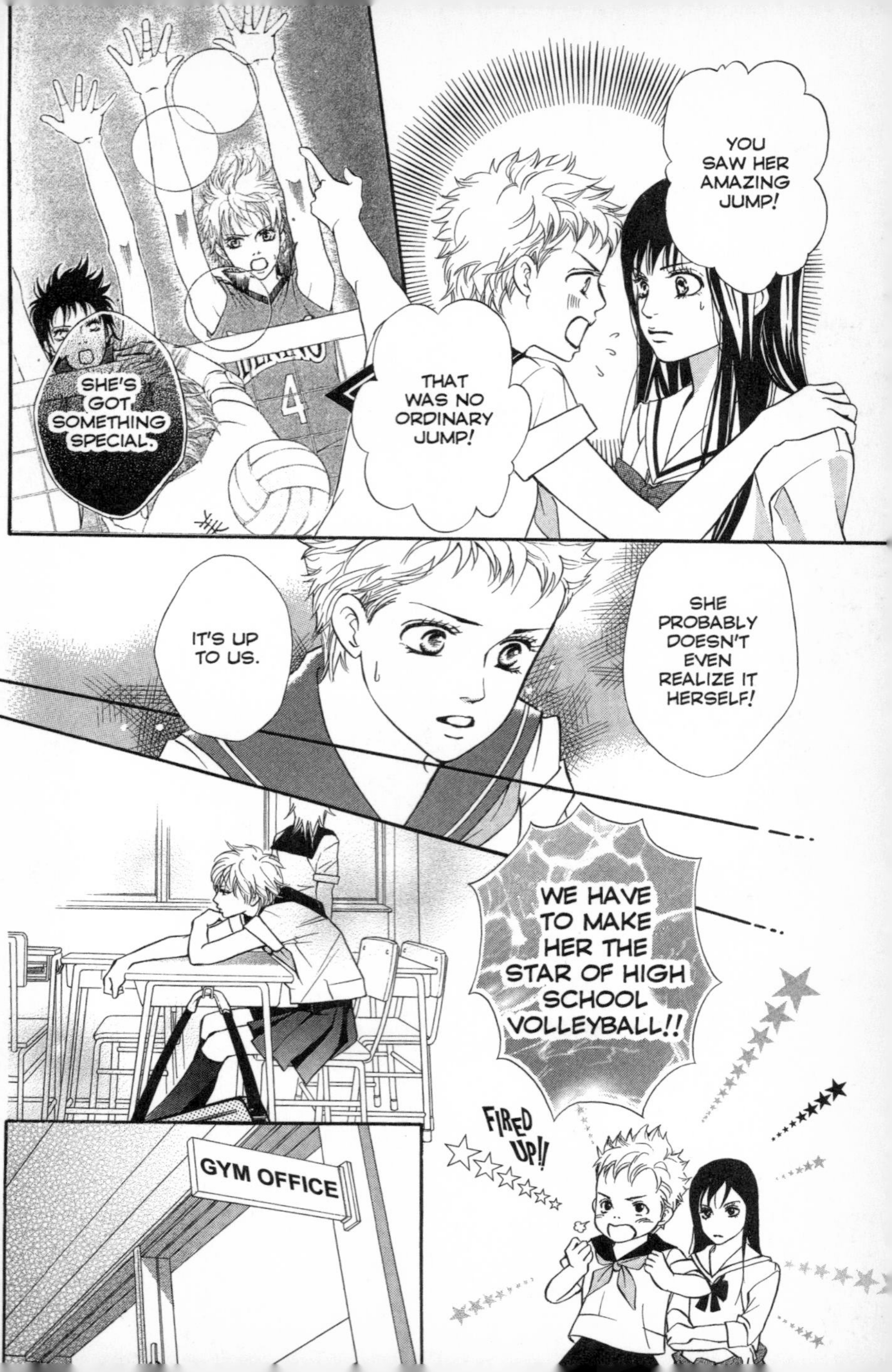

YOU SAW HER AMAZING JUMP!
THAT WAS NO ORDINARY JUMP!
SHE'S GOT SOMETHING SPECIAL.
SHE PROBABLY DOESN'T EVEN REALIZE IT HERSELF!
IT'S UP TO US.
WE HAVE TO MAKE HER THE STAR OF HIGH SCHOOL VOLLEYBALL!!
FIRED UP!!
GYM OFFICE

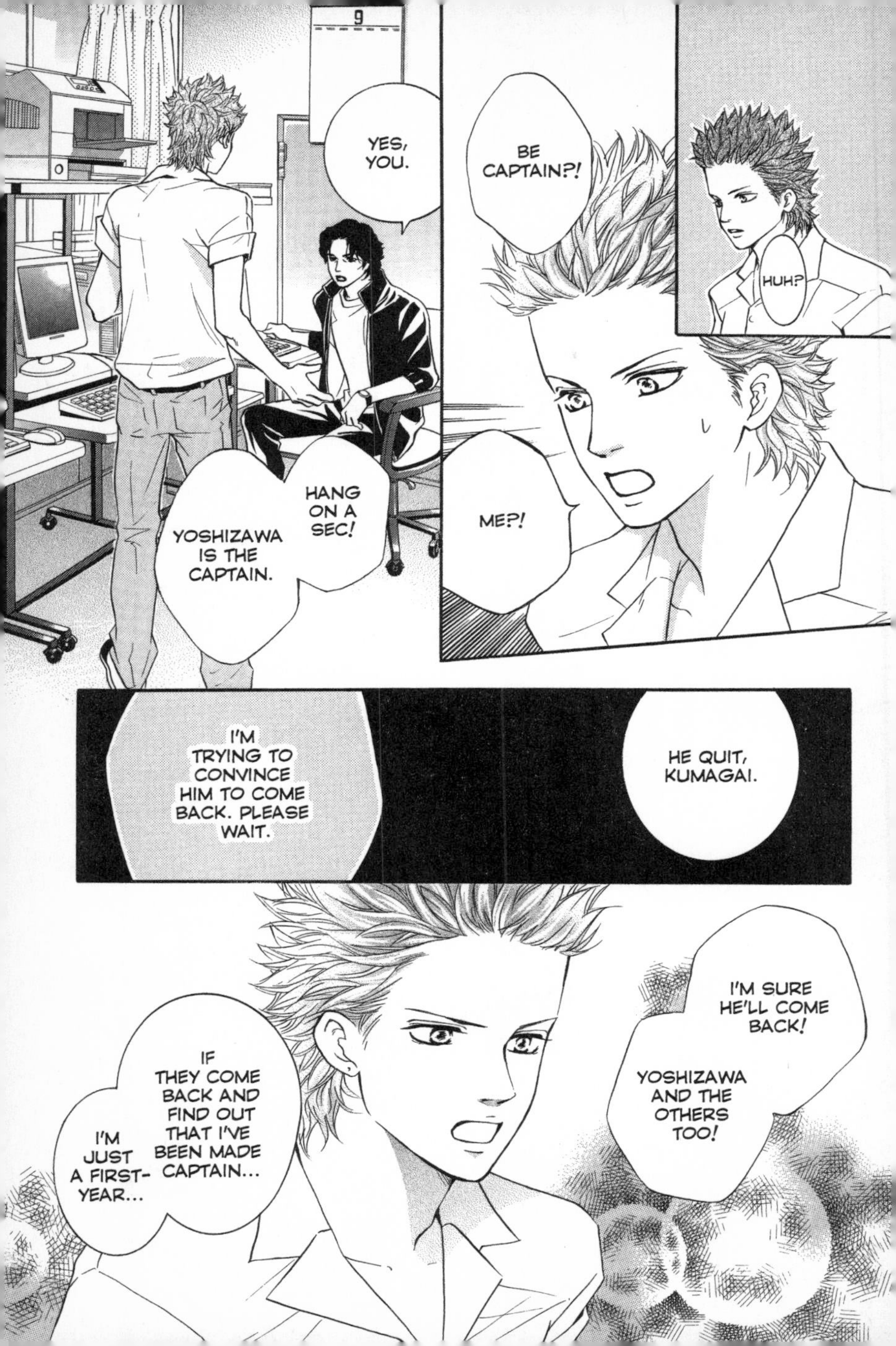
HUH?
BE CAPTAIN?!
ME?!
YES, YOU.
HANG ON A SEC!
YOSHIZAWA IS THE CAPTAIN.
HE QUIT, KUMAGAI.
I'M TRYING TO CONVINCE HIM TO COME BACK. PLEASE WAIT.
I'M SURE HE'LL COME BACK!
YOSHIZAWA AND THE OTHERS TOO!
IF THEY COME BACK AND FIND OUT THAT I'VE BEEN MADE CAPTAIN...
I'M JUST A FIRST-YEAR...

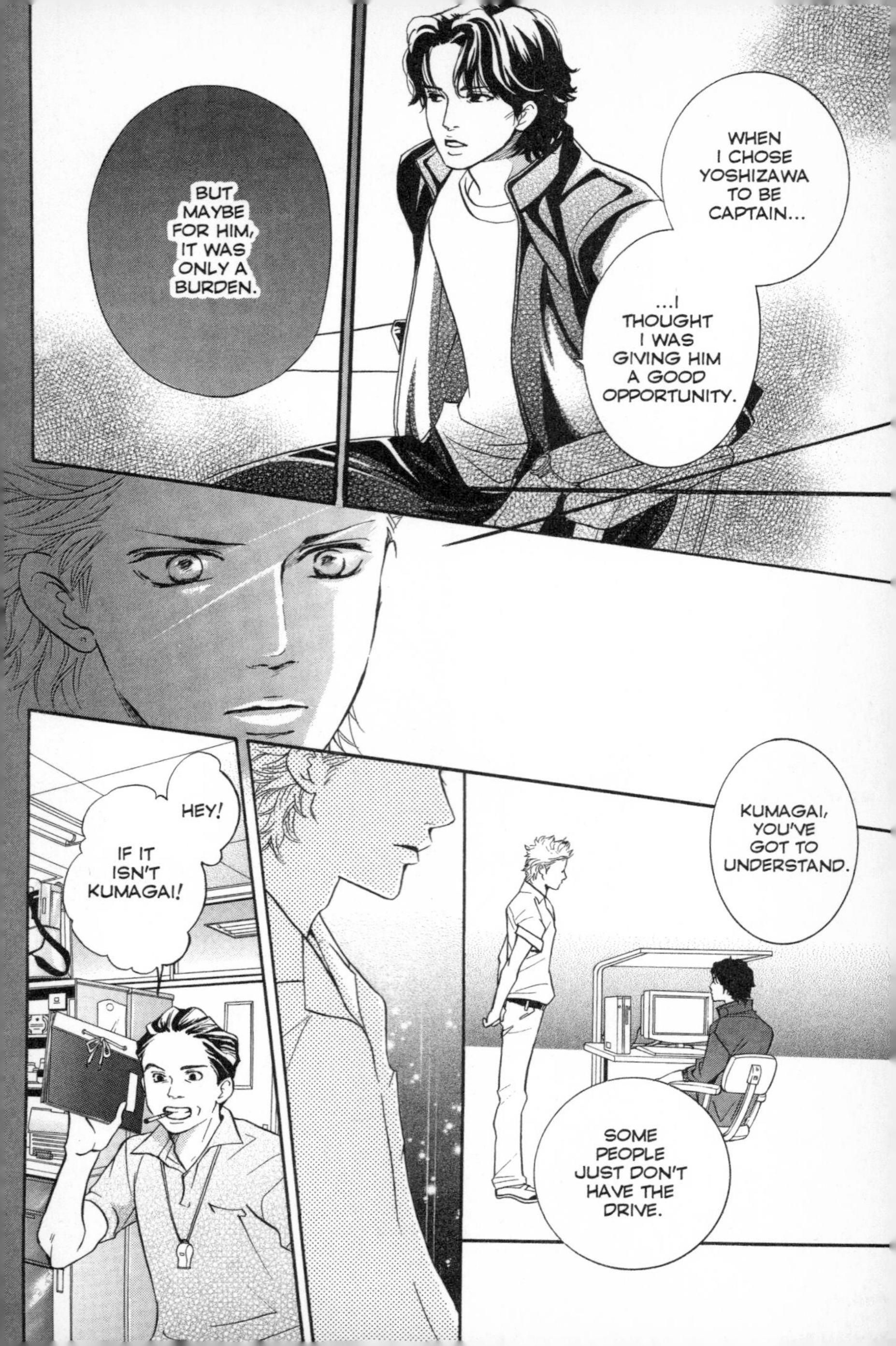
WHEN I CHOSE YOSHIZAWA TO BE CAPTAIN...
...I THOUGHT I WAS GIVING HIM A GOOD OPPORTUNITY.
BUT MAYBE FOR HIM, IT WAS ONLY A BURDEN.
KUMAGAI, YOU'VE GOT TO UNDERSTAND.
SOME PEOPLE JUST DON'T HAVE THE DRIVE.
HEY!
IF IT ISN'T KUMAGAI!

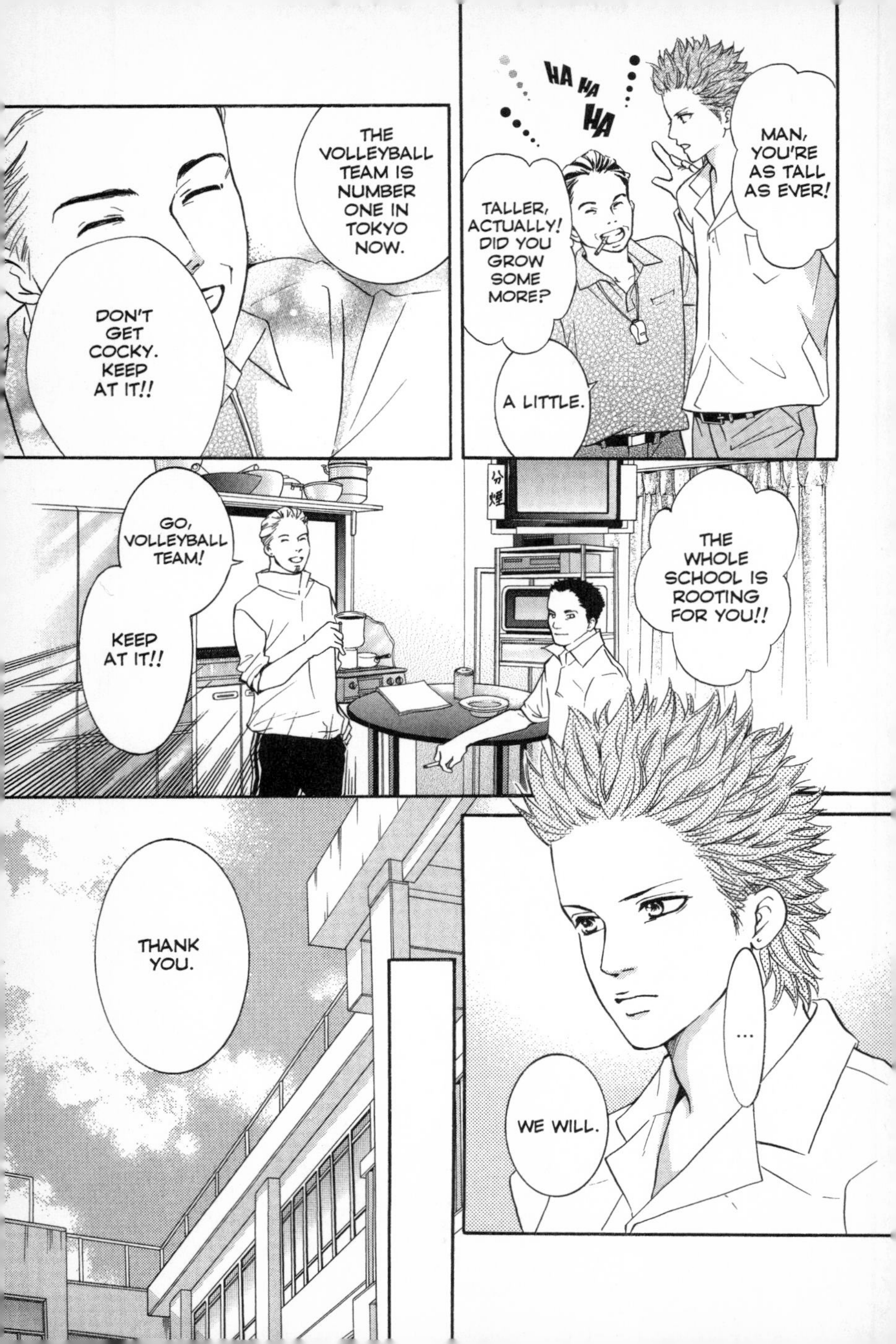
MAN, YOU'RE AS TALL AS EVER!
HA HA HA
TALLER, ACTUALLY! DID YOU GROW SOME MORE?
A LITTLE.
THE VOLLEYBALL TEAM IS NUMBER ONE IN TOKYO NOW.
DON'T GET COCKY. KEEP AT IT!!
分煙
THE WHOLE SCHOOL IS ROOTING FOR YOU!!
GO, VOLLEYBALL TEAM!
KEEP AT IT!!
...
WE WILL.
THANK YOU.

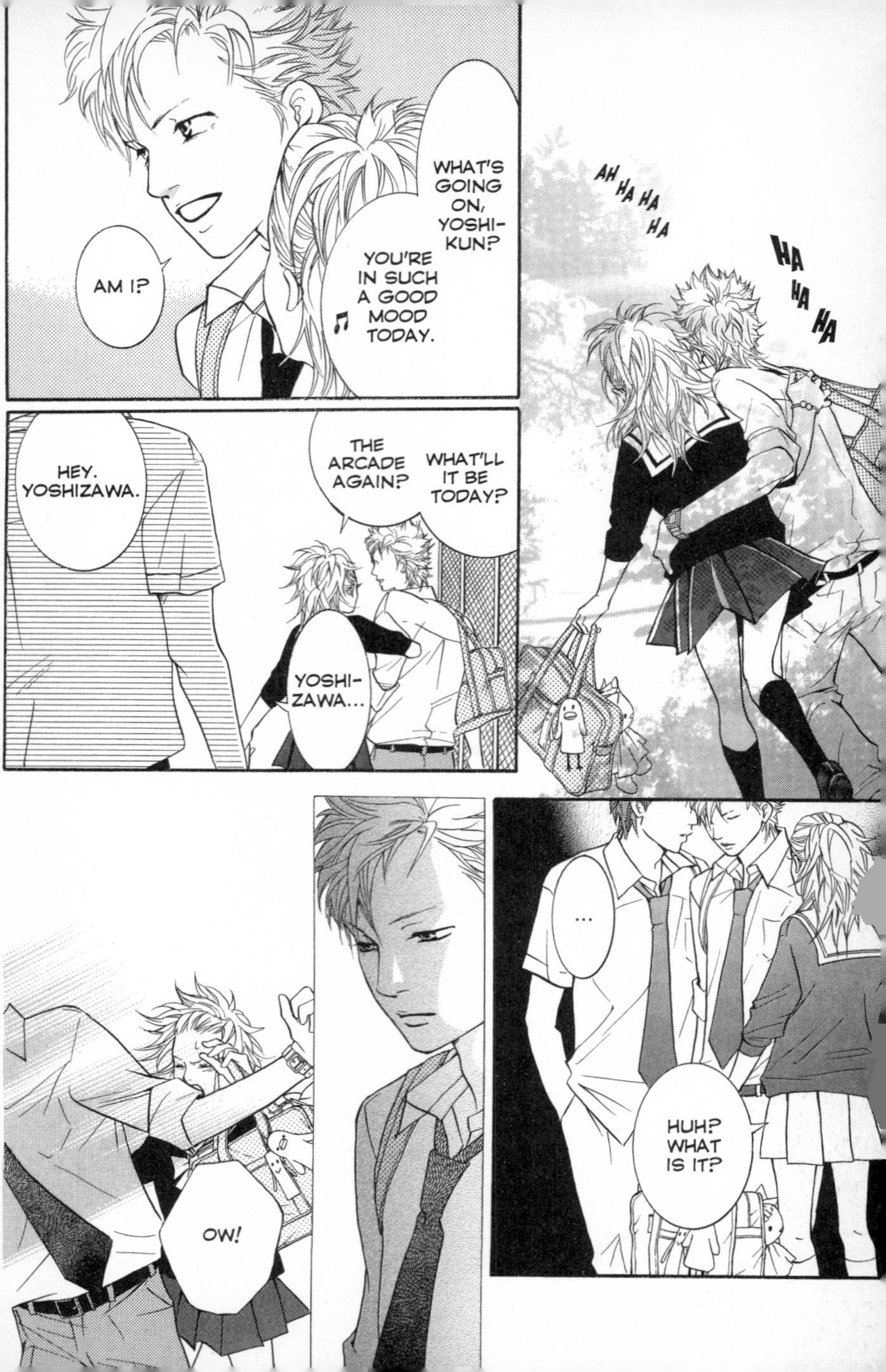
AH HA HA HA
HA HA HA
WHAT'S GOING ON, YOSHI-KUN?
YOU'RE IN SUCH A GOOD MOOD TODAY. ♪
AM I?
WHAT'LL IT BE TODAY?
THE ARCADE AGAIN?
HEY. YOSHIZAWA.
YOSHI-ZAWA...
...
HUH? WHAT IS IT?
OW!

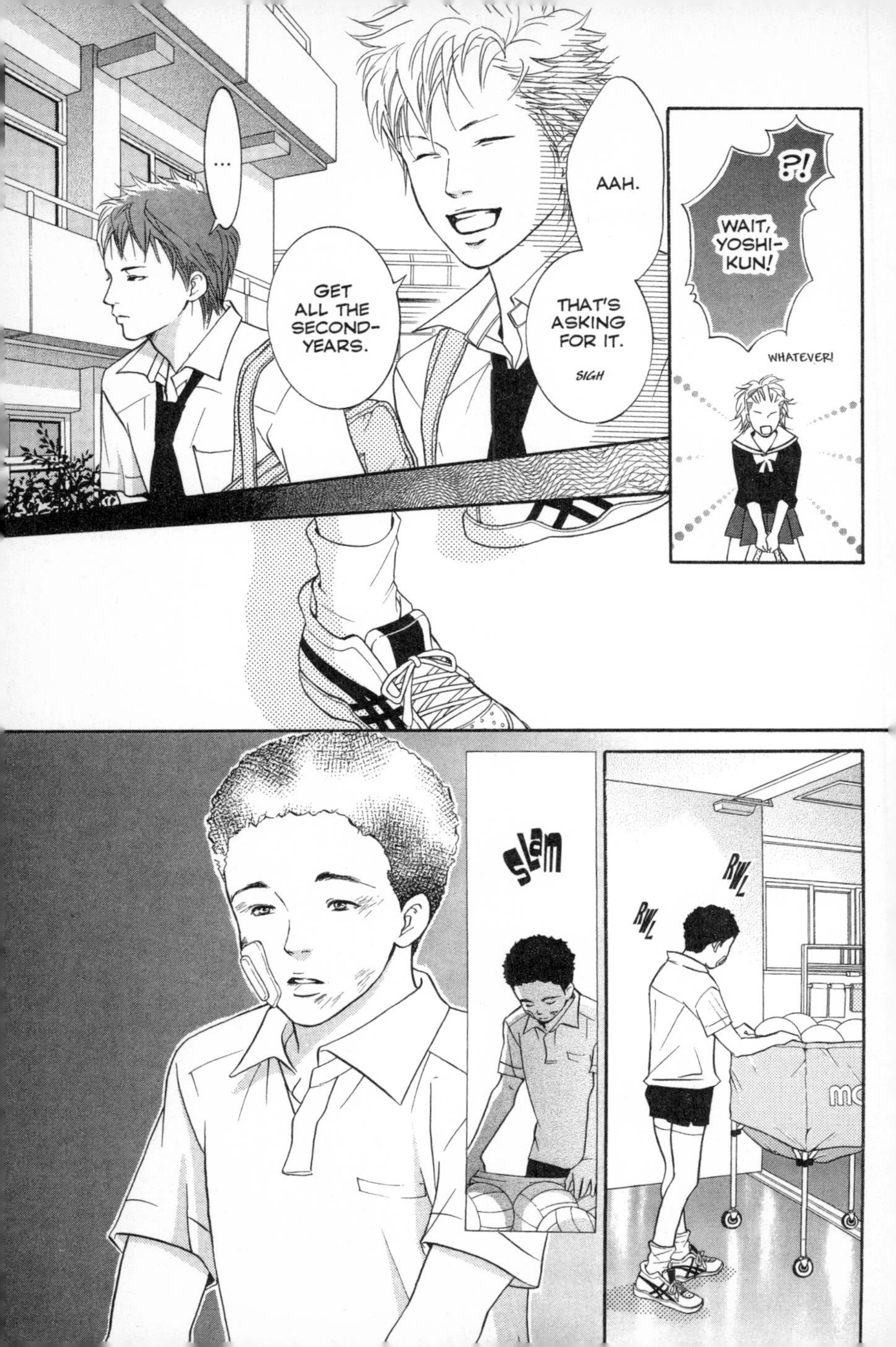
?!
WAIT, YOSHI-KUN!
WHATEVER!
AAH.
THAT'S ASKING FOR IT.
SIGH
GET ALL THE SECOND-YEARS.
...
RWL
RWL
SLAM

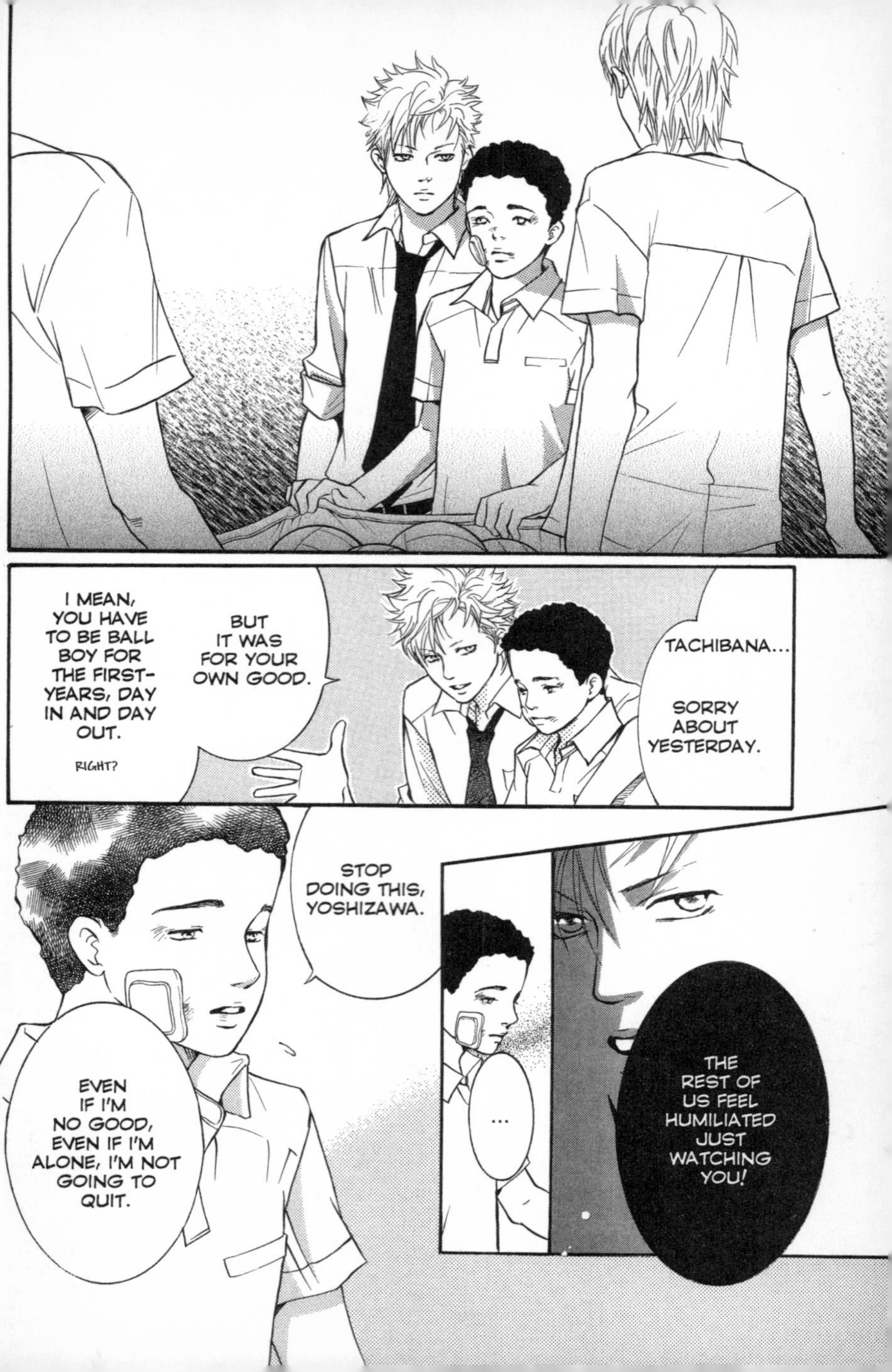
TACHIBANA...
SORRY ABOUT YESTERDAY.
BUT IT WAS FOR YOUR OWN GOOD.
I MEAN, YOU HAVE TO BE BALL BOY FOR THE FIRST-YEARS, DAY IN AND DAY OUT.
RIGHT?
THE REST OF US FEEL HUMILIATED JUST WATCHING YOU!
...
STOP DOING THIS, YOSHIZAWA.
EVEN IF I'M NO GOOD, EVEN IF I'M ALONE, I'M NOT GOING TO QUIT.

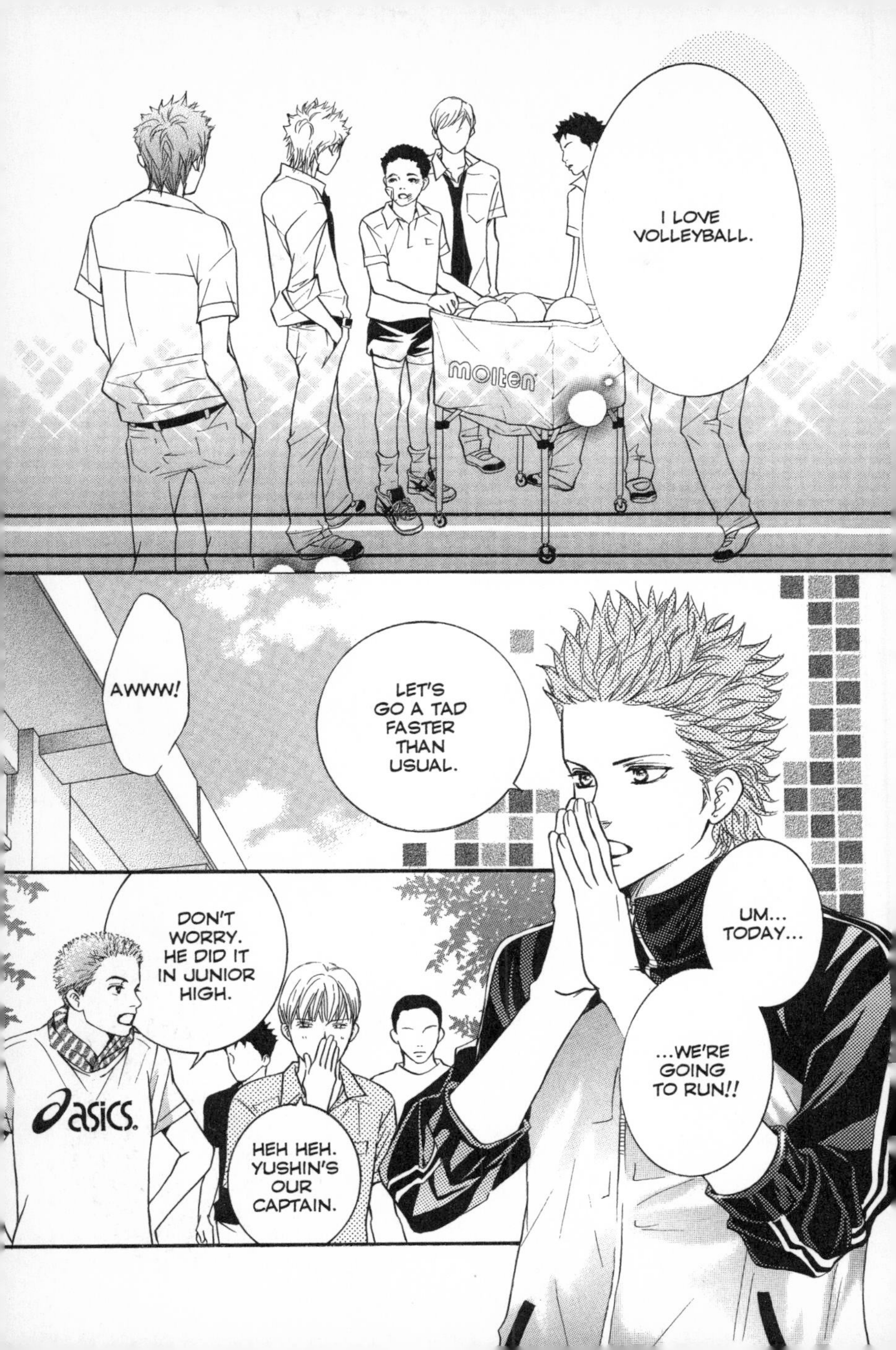
I LOVE VOLLEYBALL.
molten
UM... TODAY...
...WE'RE GOING TO RUN!!
LET'S GO A TAD FASTER THAN USUAL.
AWWW!
DON'T WORRY. HE DID IT IN JUNIOR HIGH.
HEH HEH. YUSHIN'S OUR CAPTAIN.
asics.

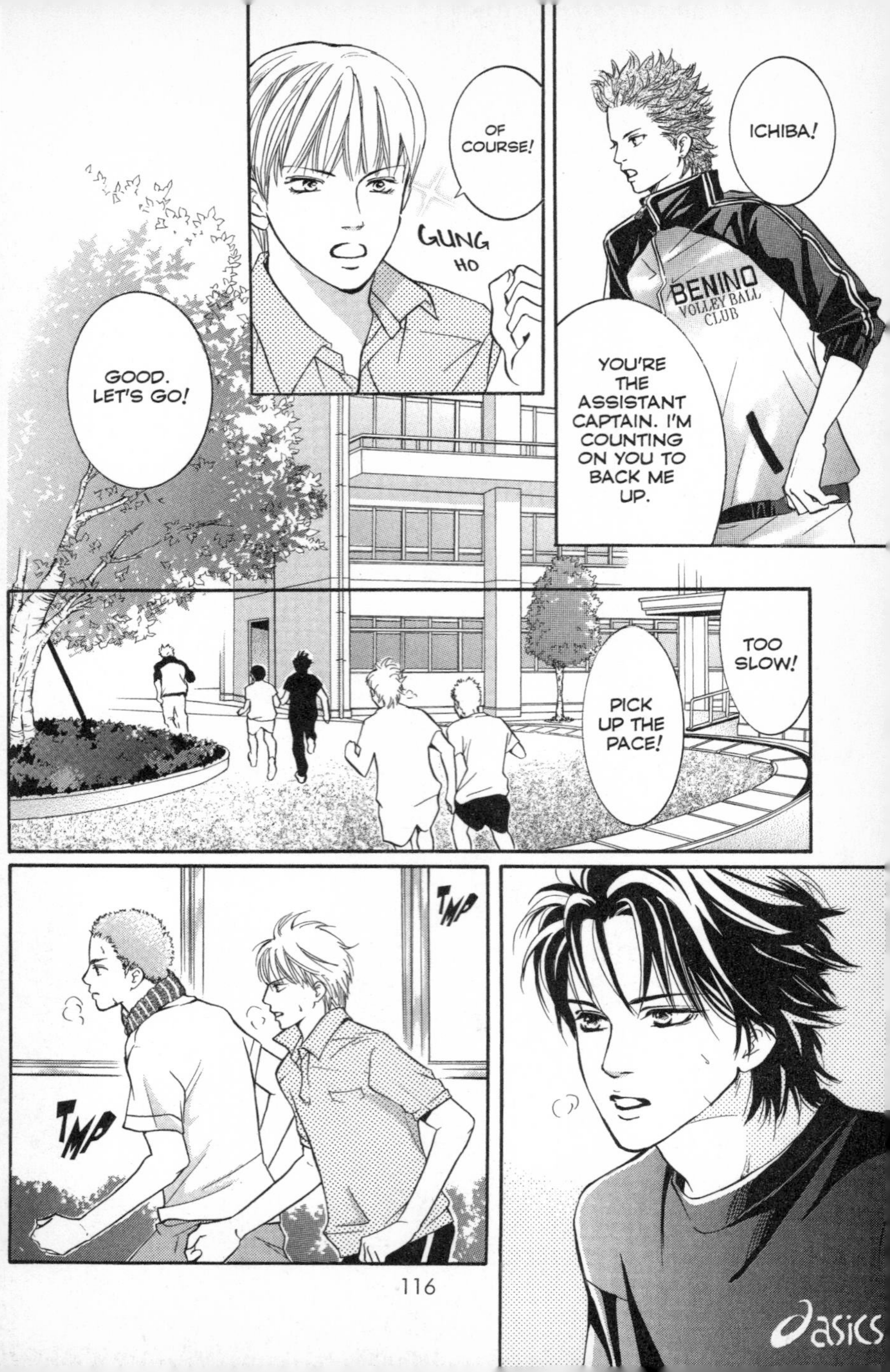
ICHIBA!
YOU'RE THE ASSISTANT CAPTAIN. I'M COUNTING ON YOU TO BACK ME UP.
BENINO VOLLEY BALL CLUB
OF COURSE!
GUNG HO
GOOD. LET'S GO!
TOO SLOW!
PICK UP THE PACE!
TMP
TMP

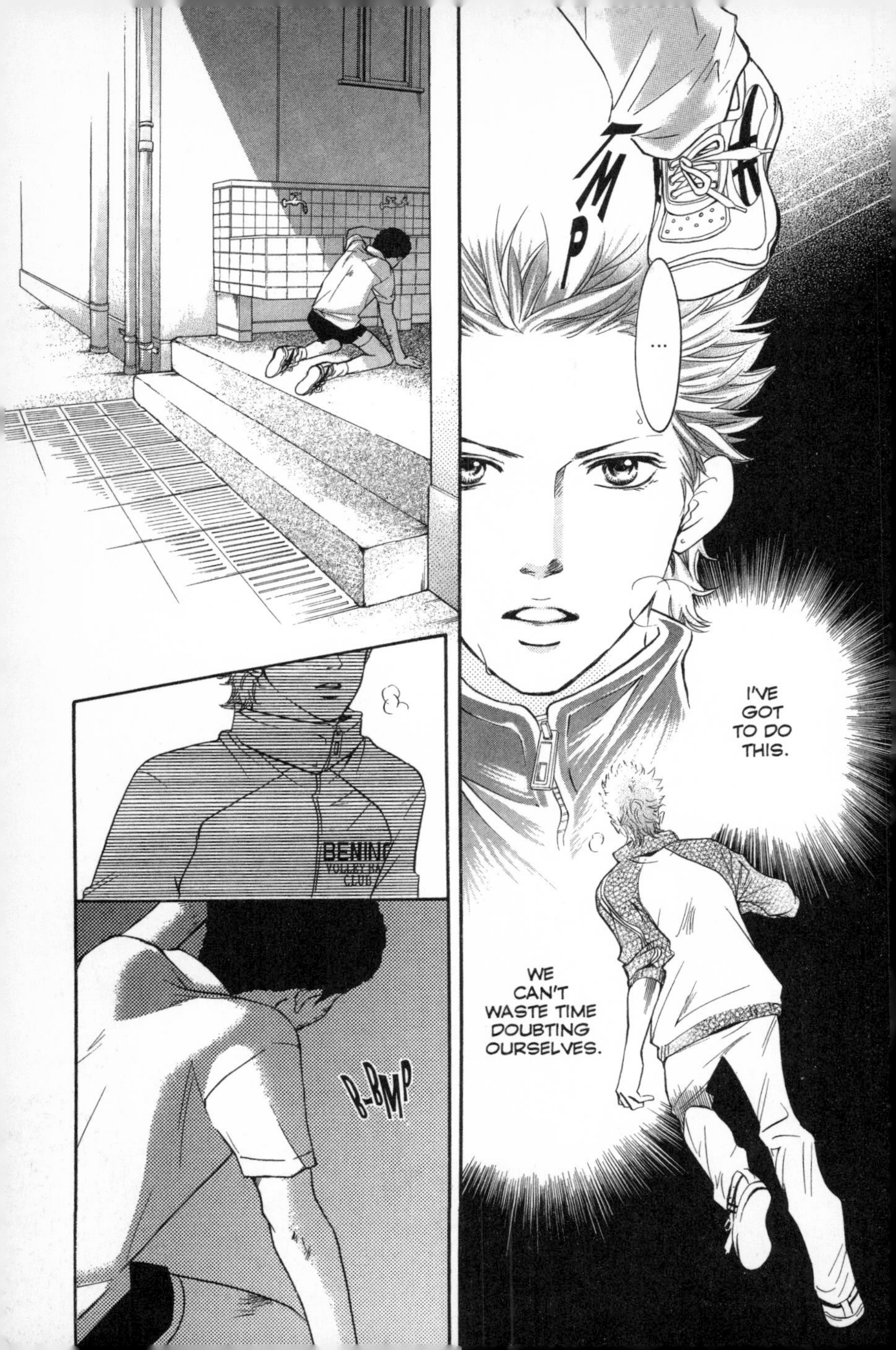
TMP
...
I'VE GOT TO DO THIS.
WE CAN'T WASTE TIME DOUBTING OURSELVES.
VOLLEY
CLUB
B-BMP

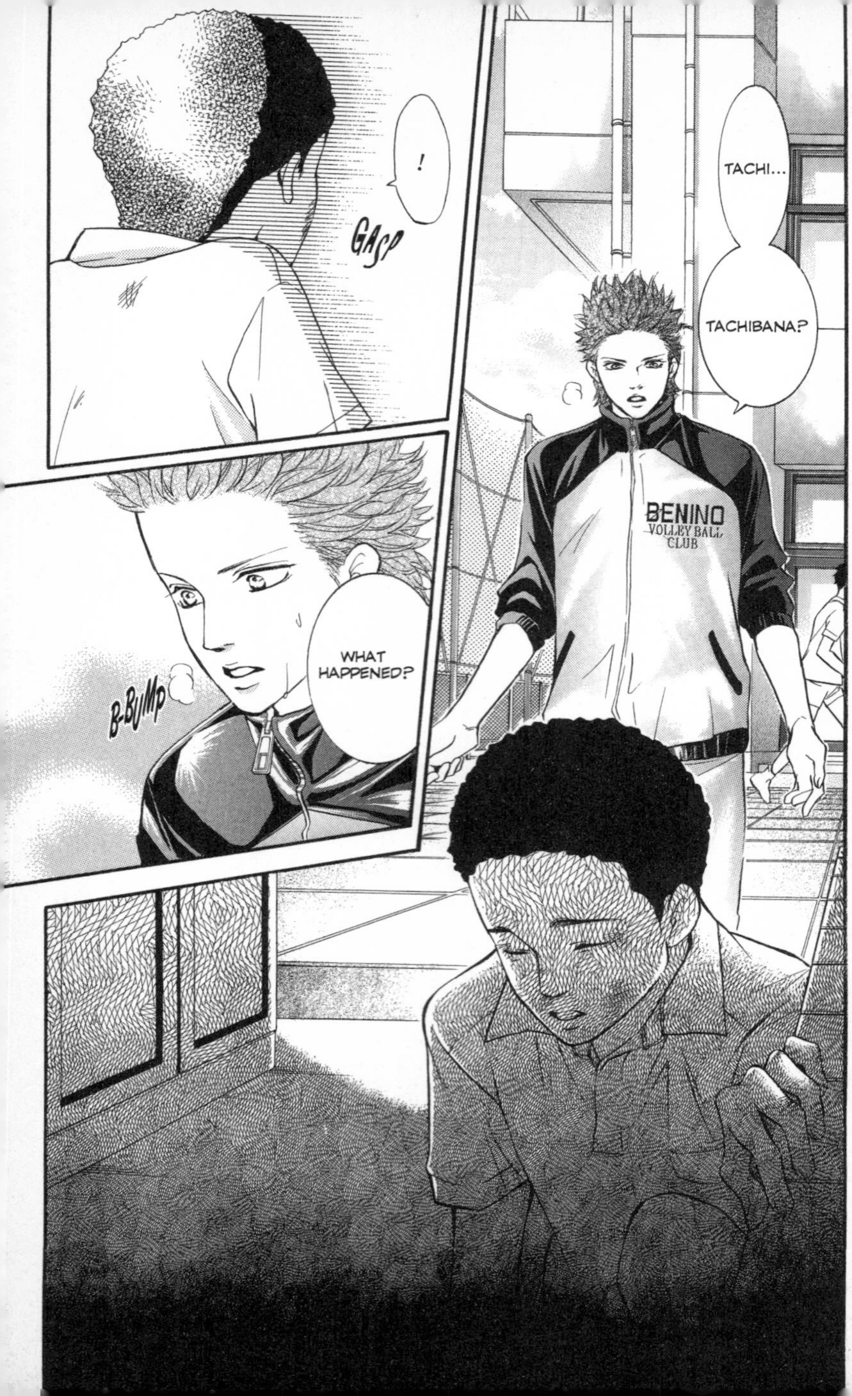

TACHI...
TACHIBANA?
BENINO
VOLLEY BALL
CLUB
!
GASP
WHAT HAPPENED?
B-BUMP

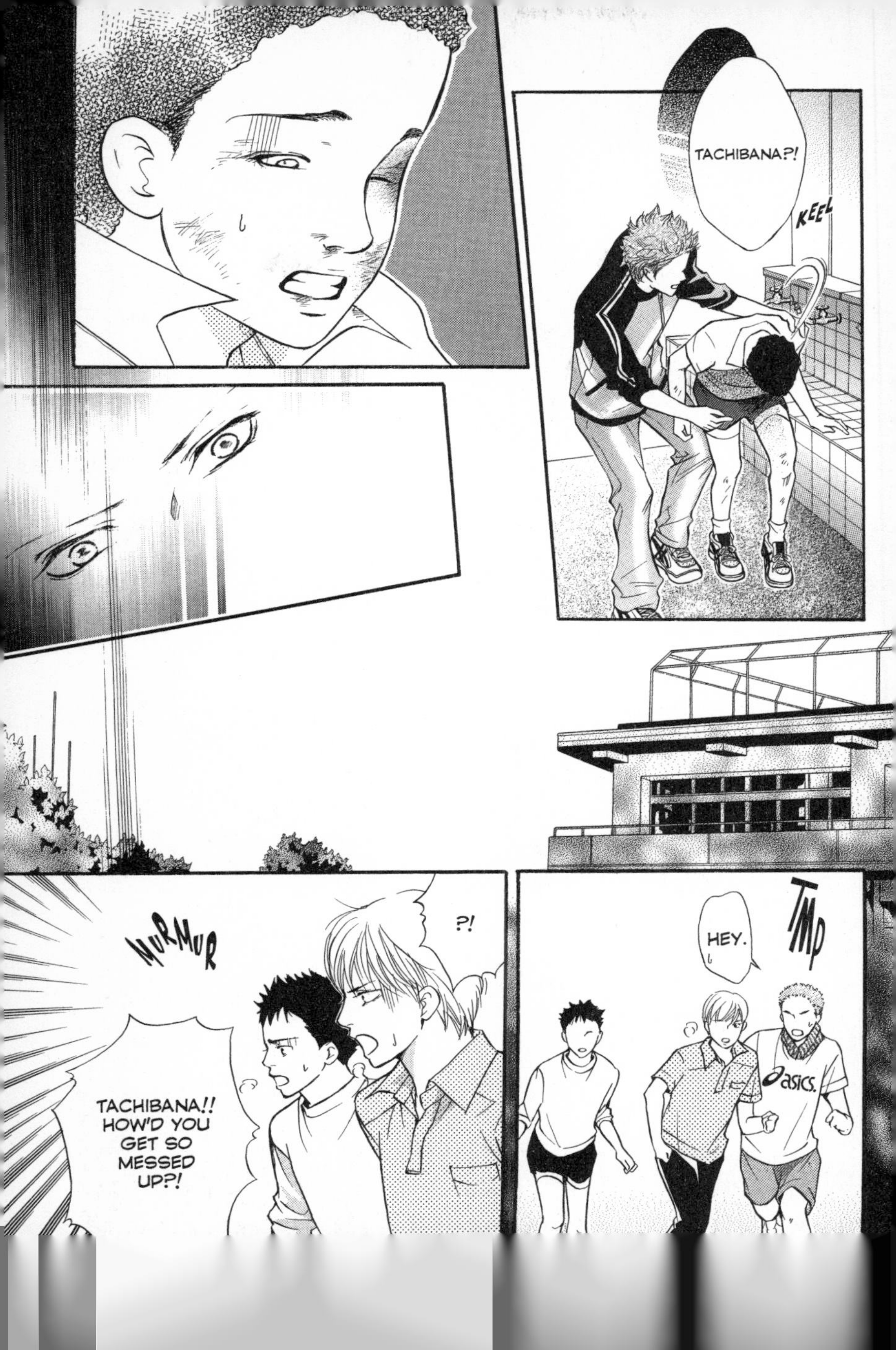
TACHIBANA?!
KEEL
TMP
HEY.
?!
MURMUR
TACHIBANA!! HOW'D YOU GET SO MESSED UP?!

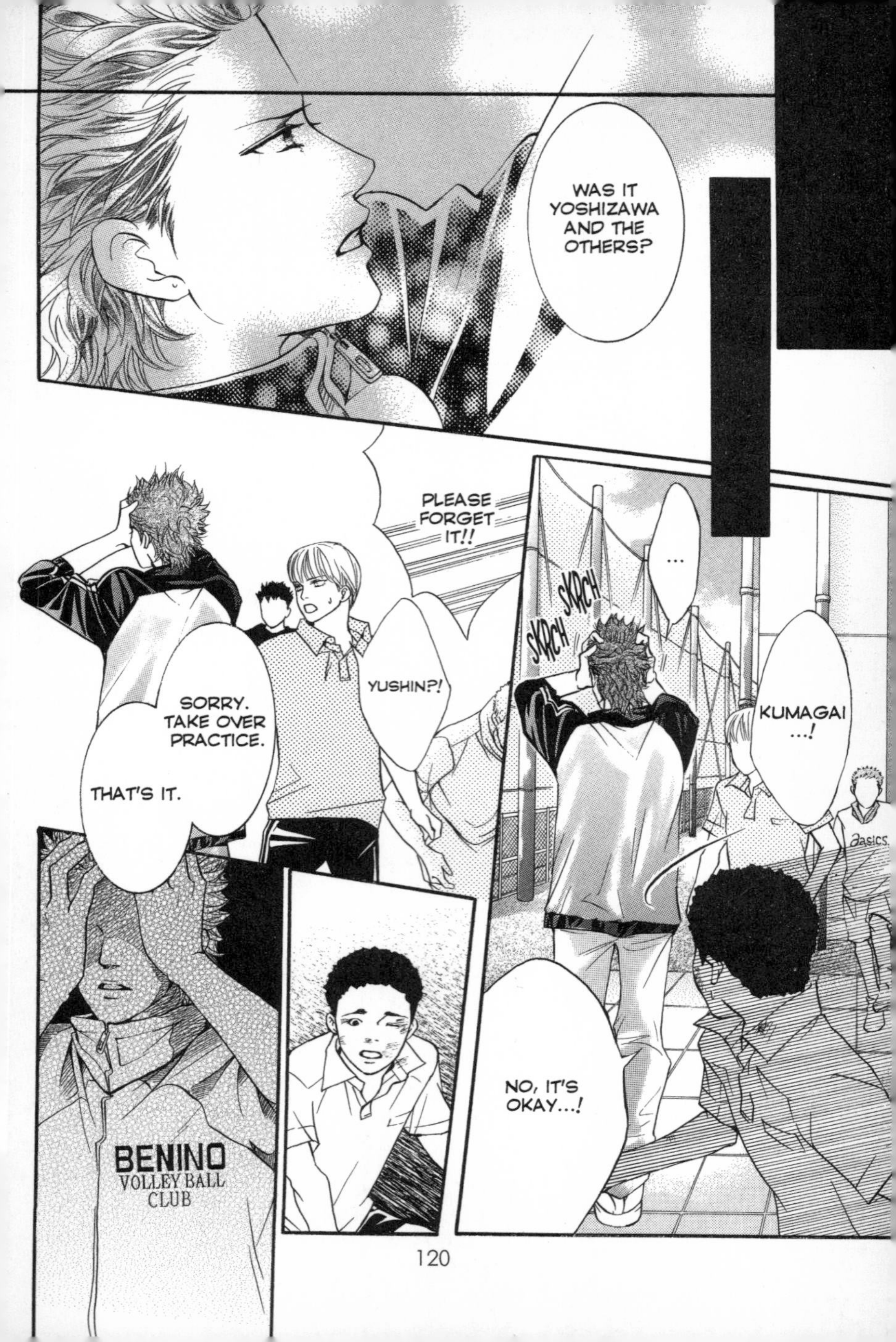
WAS IT YOSHIZAWA AND THE OTHERS?
SKRCH SKRCH
...
KUMAGAI ...!
asics.
PLEASE FORGET IT!!
YUSHIN?!
SORRY. TAKE OVER PRACTICE.
THAT'S IT.
NO, IT'S OKAY...!
BENINO VOLLEY BALL CLUB

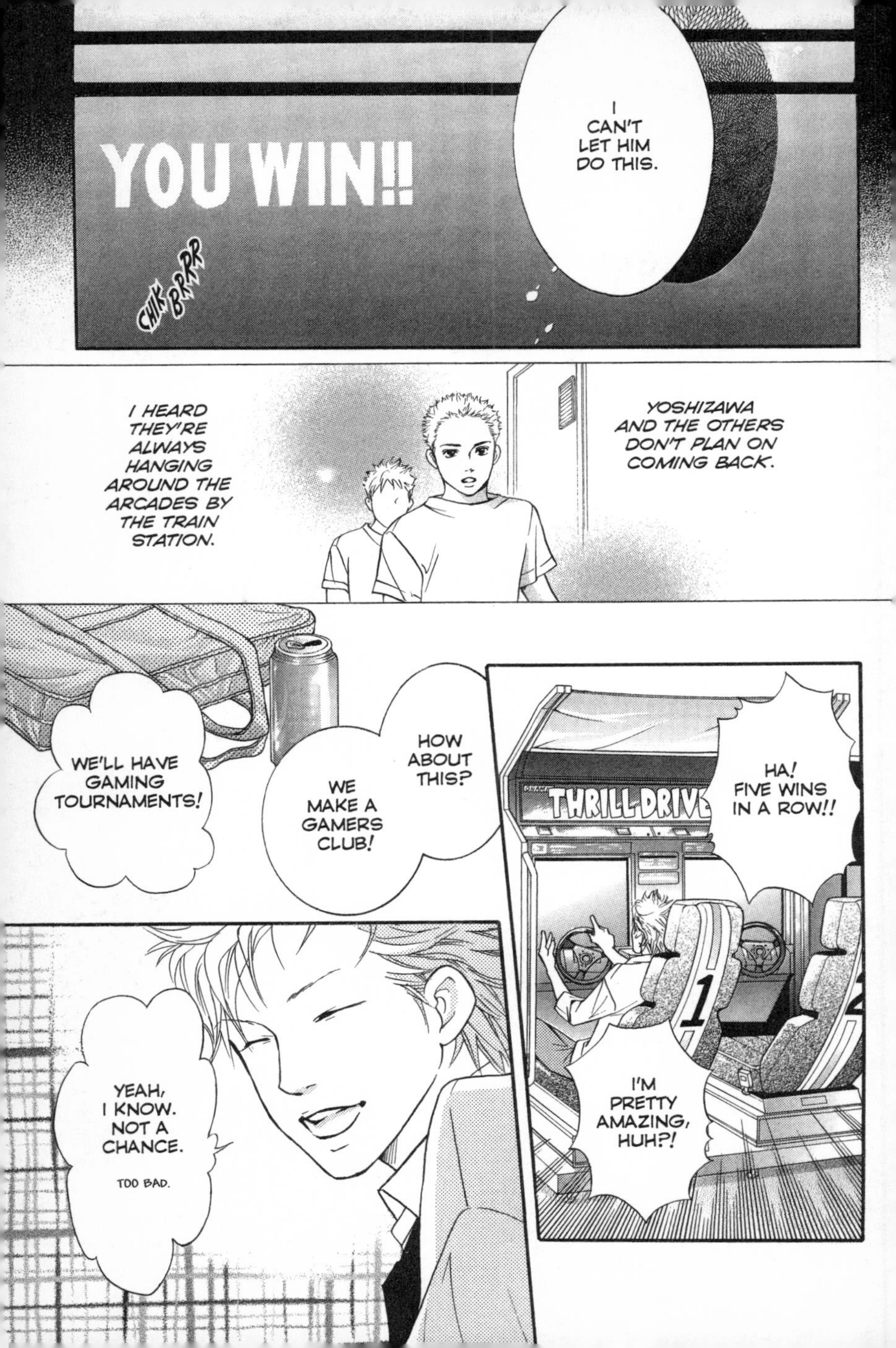
I CAN'T LET HIM DO THIS.
YOU WIN!!
CHIK BRRR
YOSHIZAWA AND THE OTHERS DON'T PLAN ON COMING BACK.
I HEARD THEY'RE ALWAYS HANGING AROUND THE ARCADES BY THE TRAIN STATION.
THRILL DRIVE
HA! FIVE WINS IN A ROW!!
I'M PRETTY AMAZING, HUH?!
HOW ABOUT THIS?
WE MAKE A GAMERS CLUB!
WE'LL HAVE GAMING TOURNAMENTS!
YEAH, I KNOW. NOT A CHANCE.
TOO BAD.

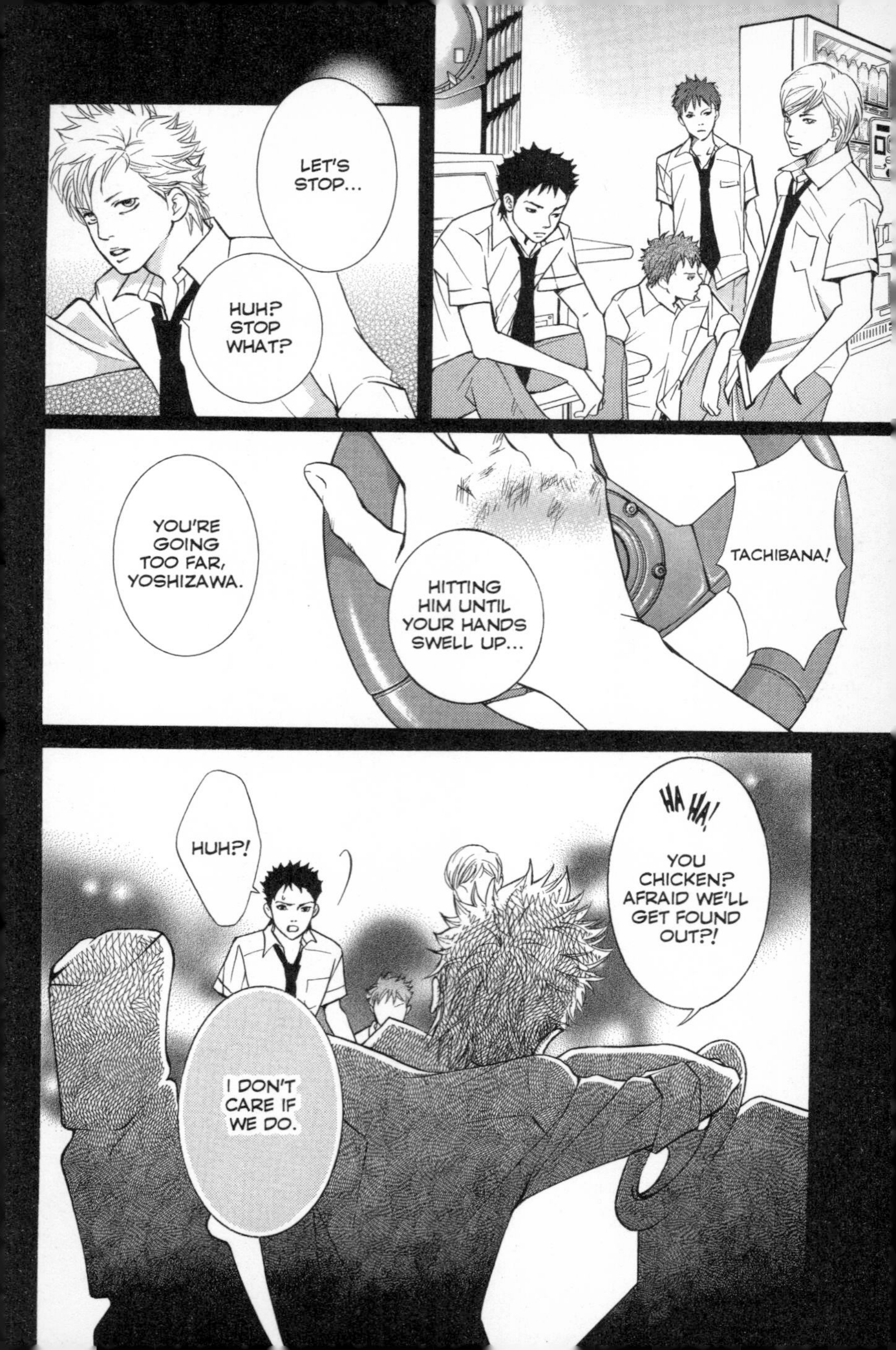
LET'S STOP...
HUH? STOP WHAT?
TACHIBANA!
YOU'RE GOING TOO FAR, YOSHIZAWA.
HITTING HIM UNTIL YOUR HANDS SWELL UP...
HA HA! YOU CHICKEN? AFRAID WE'LL GET FOUND OUT?!
HUH?!
I DON'T CARE IF WE DO.

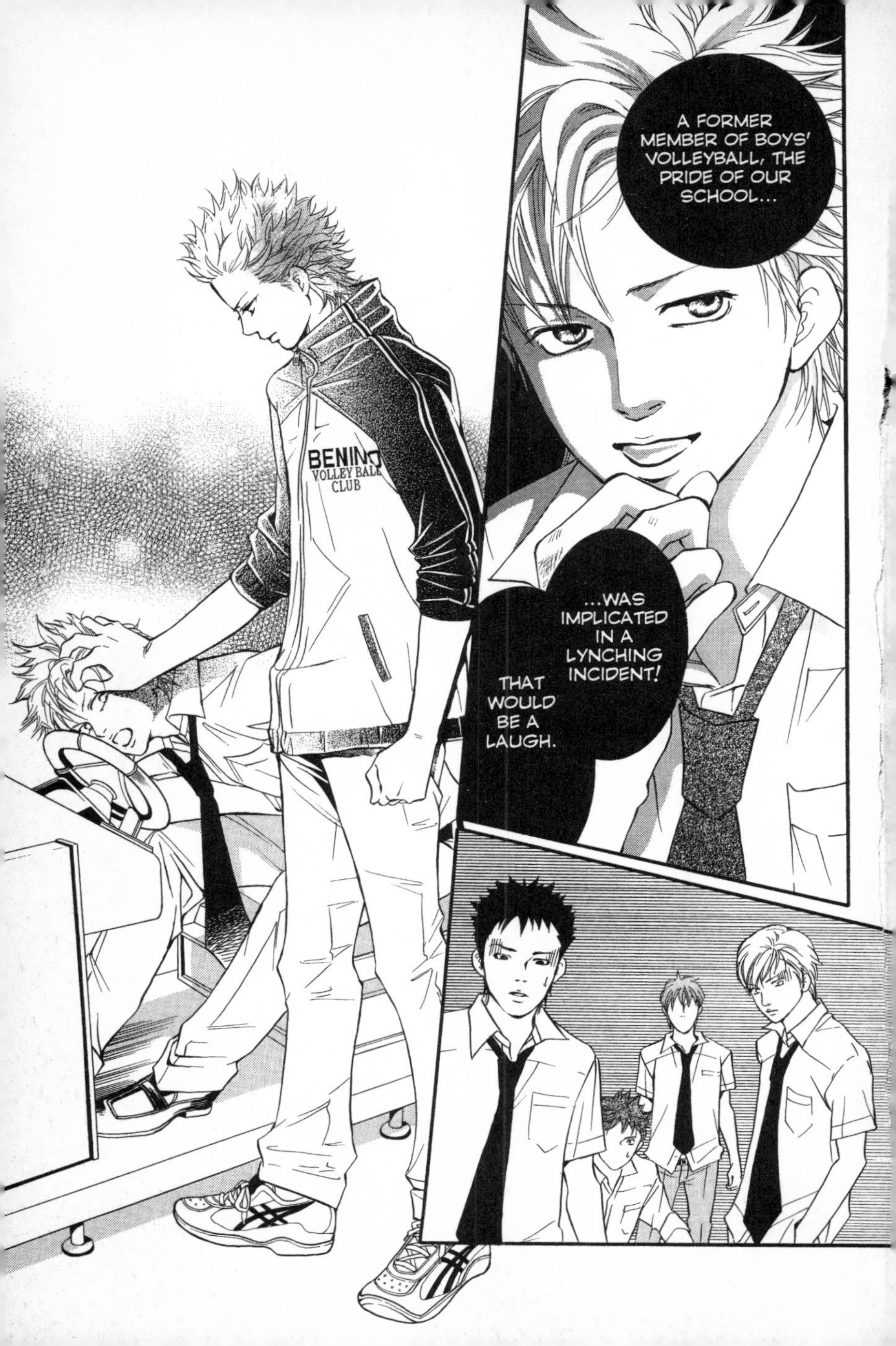
A FORMER MEMBER OF BOYS' VOLLEYBALL, THE PRIDE OF OUR SCHOOL...
...WAS IMPLICATED IN A LYNCHING INCIDENT!
THAT WOULD BE A LAUGH.
BENINO
VOLLEY BALL CLUB

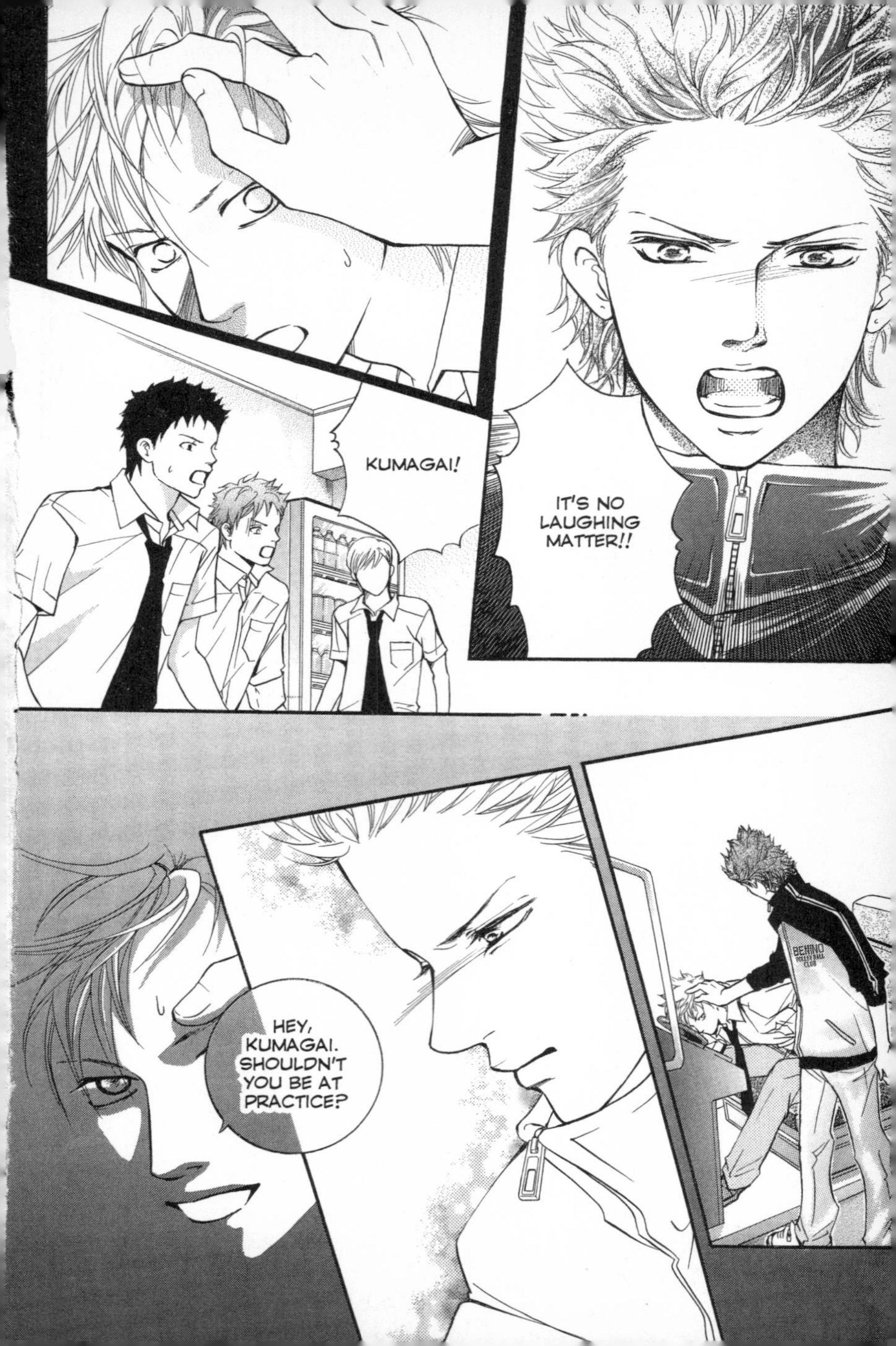
IT'S NO LAUGHING MATTER!!
KUMAGAI!
HEY, KUMAGAI. SHOULDN'T YOU BE AT PRACTICE?

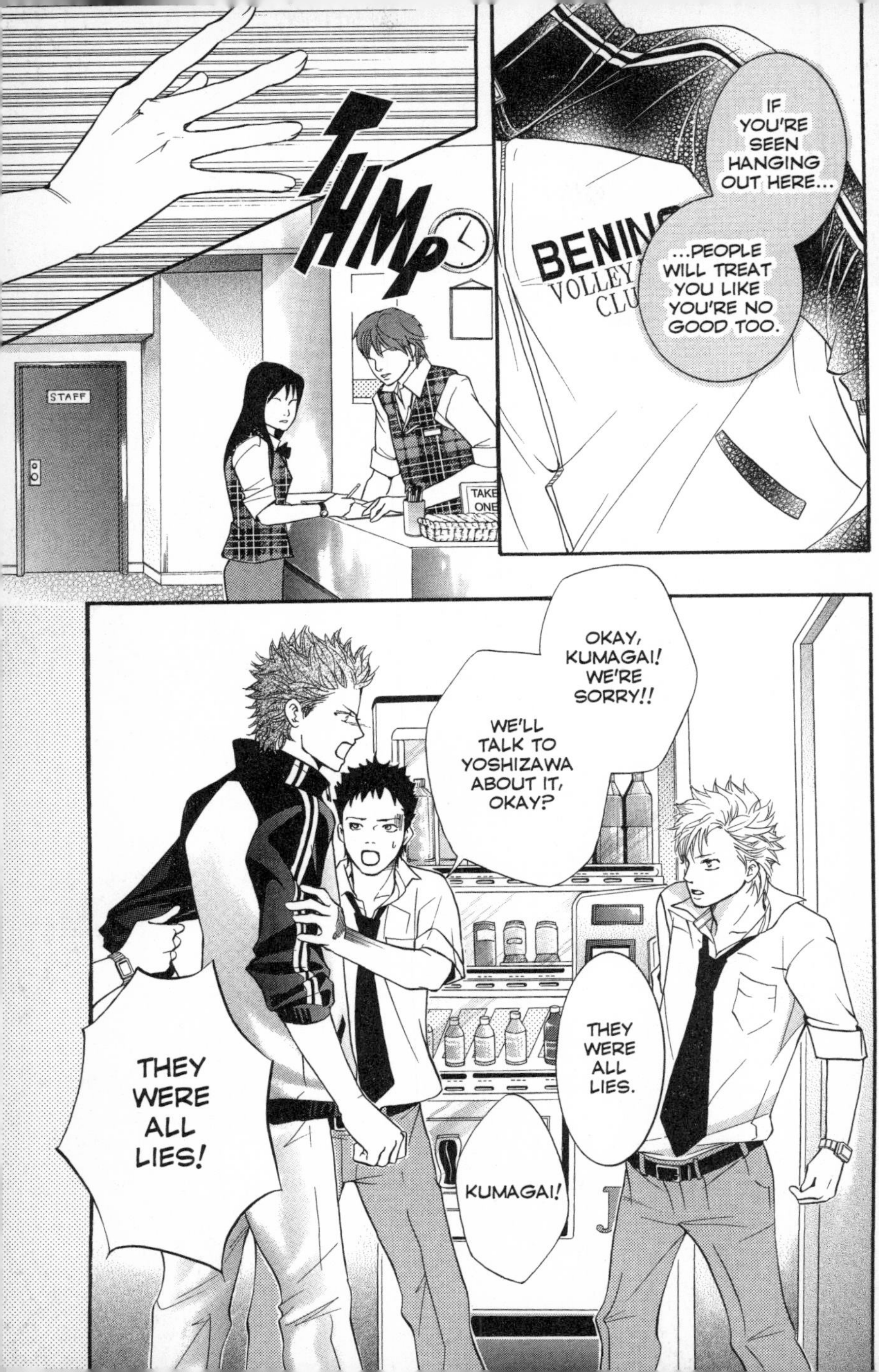
IF YOU'RE SEEN HANGING OUT HERE...
...PEOPLE WILL TREAT YOU LIKE YOU'RE NO GOOD TOO.
THMP
STAFF
TAKE ONE
OKAY, KUMAGAI! WE'RE SORRY!!
WE'LL TALK TO YOSHIZAWA ABOUT IT, OKAY?
THEY WERE ALL LIES.
KUMAGAI!
THEY WERE ALL LIES!

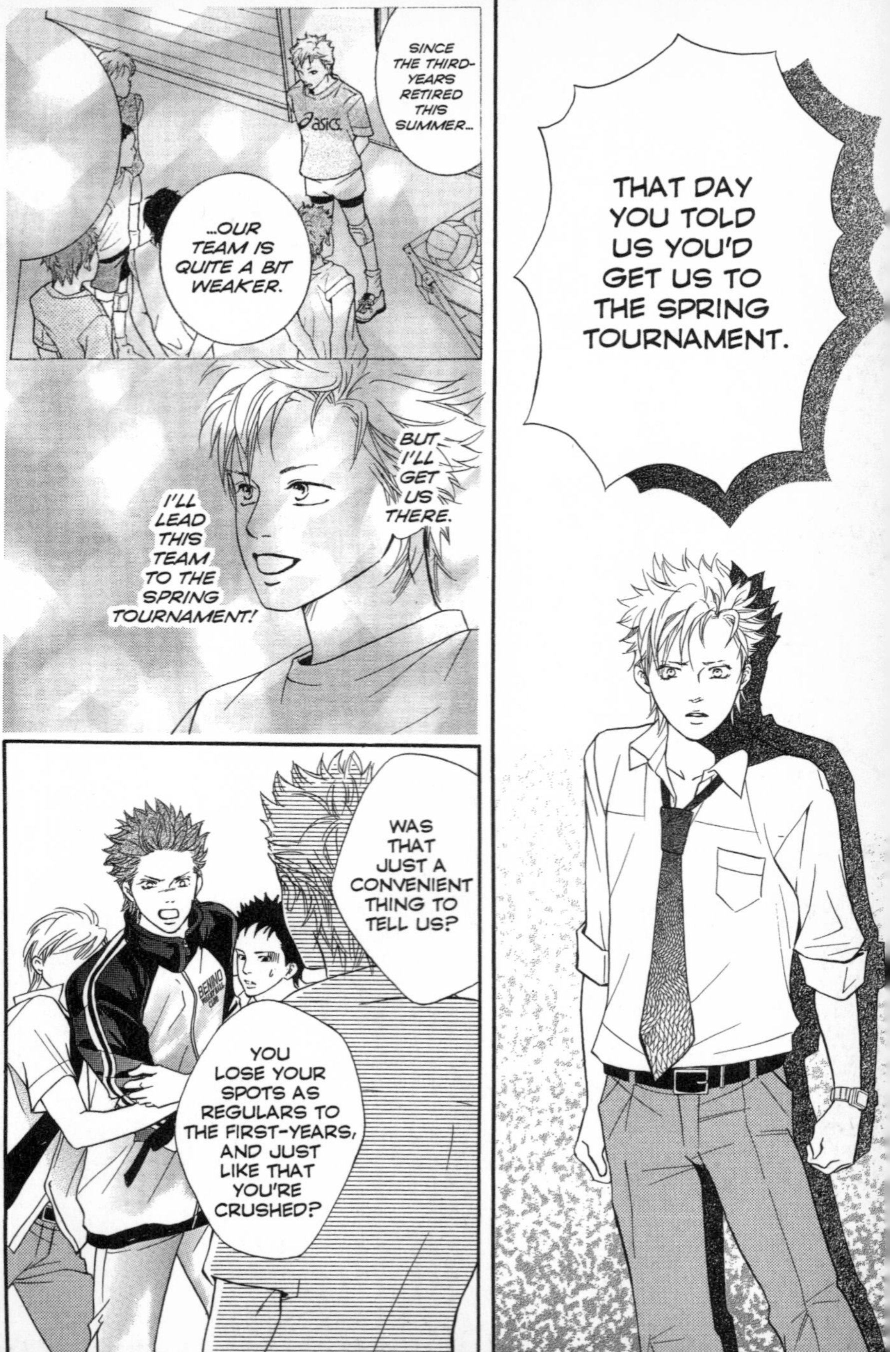
THAT DAY YOU TOLD US YOU'D GET US TO THE SPRING TOURNAMENT.
SINCE THE THIRD-YEARS RETIRED THIS SUMMER...
...OUR TEAM IS QUITE A BIT WEAKER.
BUT I'LL GET US THERE.
I'LL LEAD THIS TEAM TO THE SPRING TOURNAMENT!
WAS THAT JUST A CONVENIENT THING TO TELL US?
YOU LOSE YOUR SPOTS AS REGULARS TO THE FIRST-YEARS, AND JUST LIKE THAT YOU'RE CRUSHED?

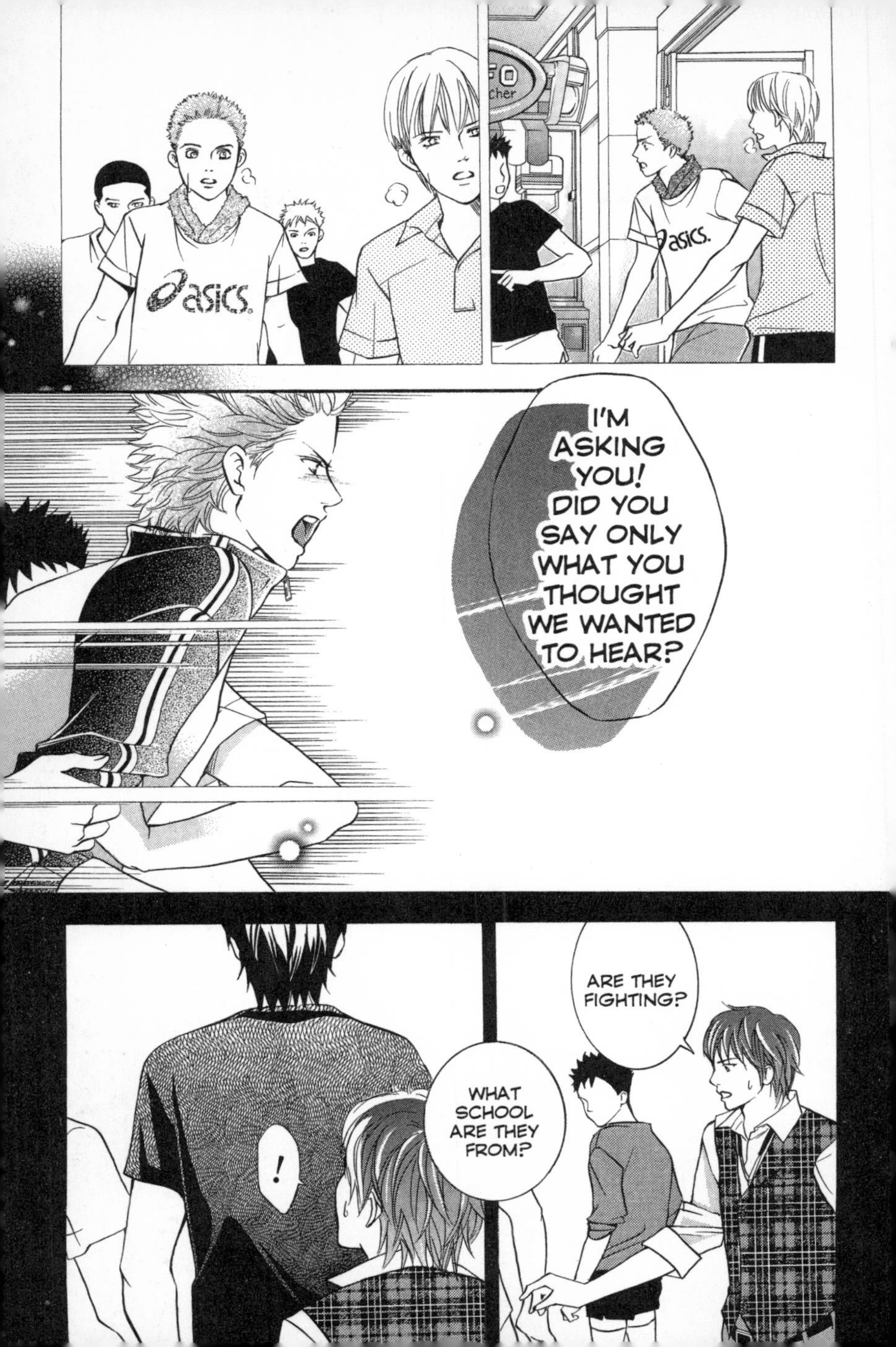
I'M ASKING YOU! DID YOU SAY ONLY WHAT YOU THOUGHT WE WANTED TO HEAR?
ARE THEY FIGHTING?
WHAT SCHOOL ARE THEY FROM?
!

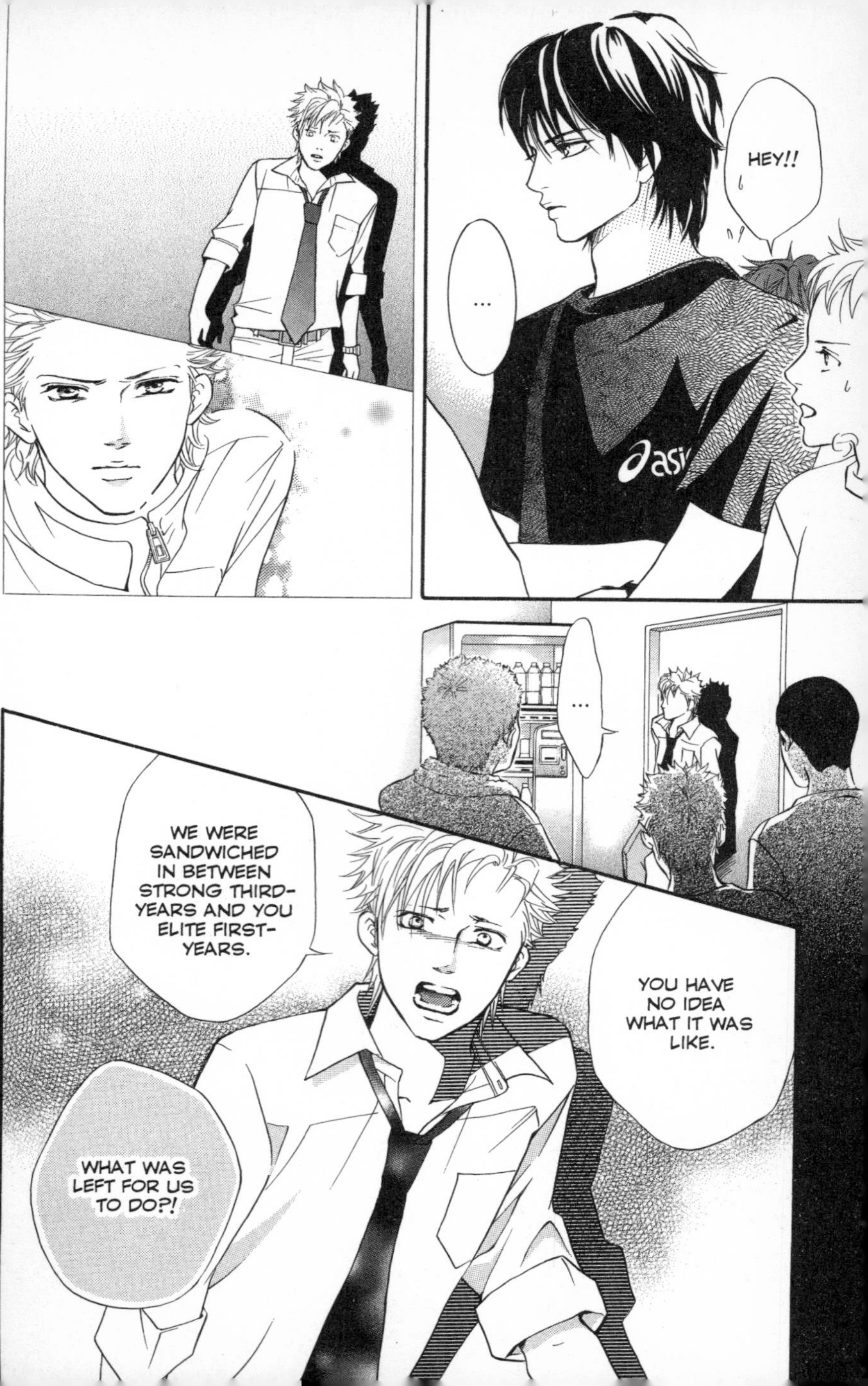
HEY!!
...
...
YOU HAVE NO IDEA WHAT IT WAS LIKE.
WE WERE SANDWICHED IN BETWEEN STRONG THIRD-YEARS AND YOU ELITE FIRST-YEARS.
WHAT WAS LEFT FOR US TO DO?!

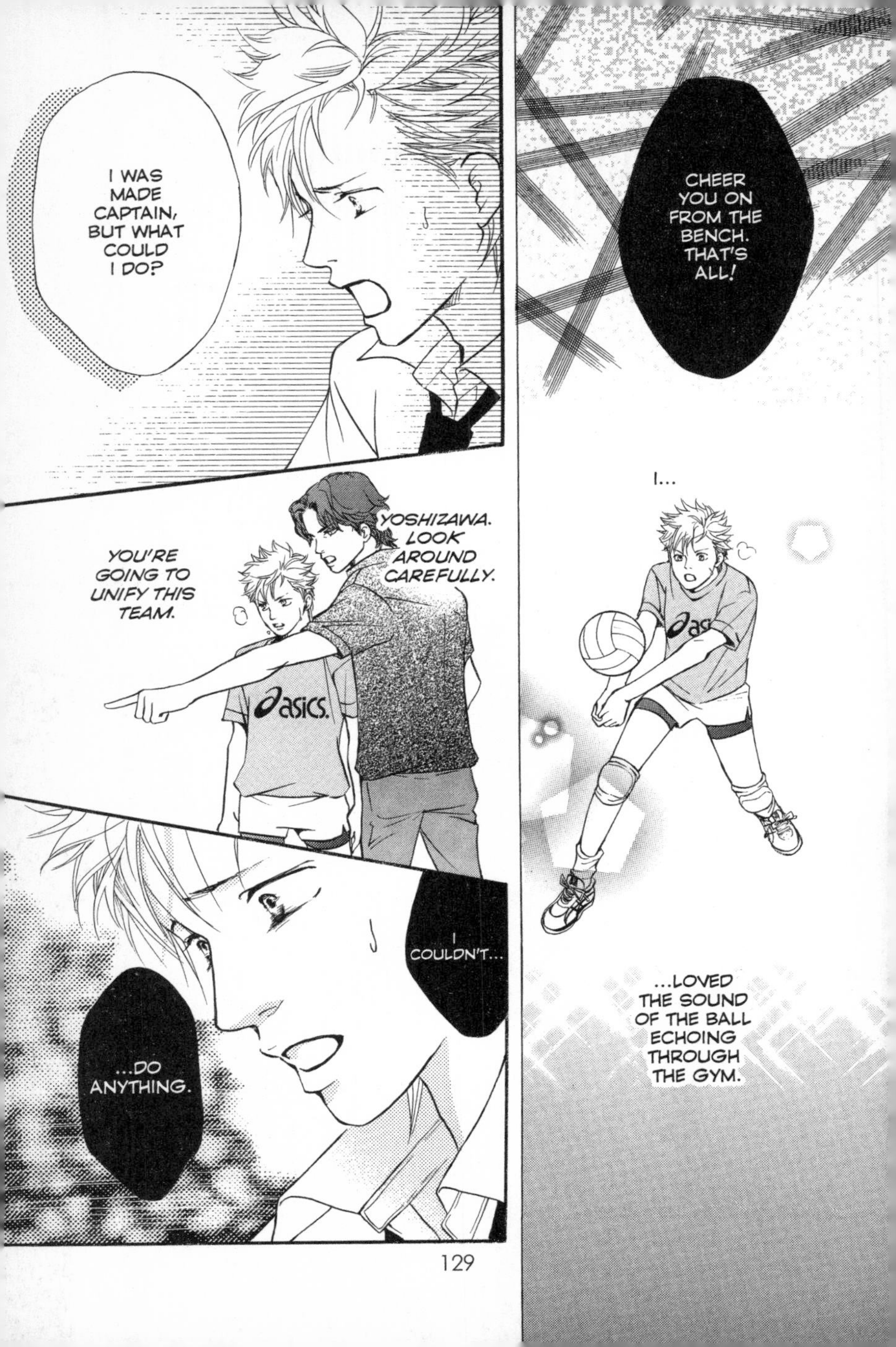
I WAS MADE CAPTAIN, BUT WHAT COULD I DO?
YOSHIZAWA. LOOK AROUND CAREFULLY.
YOU'RE GOING TO UNIFY THIS TEAM.
I COULDN'T...
...DO ANYTHING.
CHEER YOU ON FROM THE BENCH. THAT'S ALL!
I...
...LOVED THE SOUND OF THE BALL ECHOING THROUGH THE GYM.

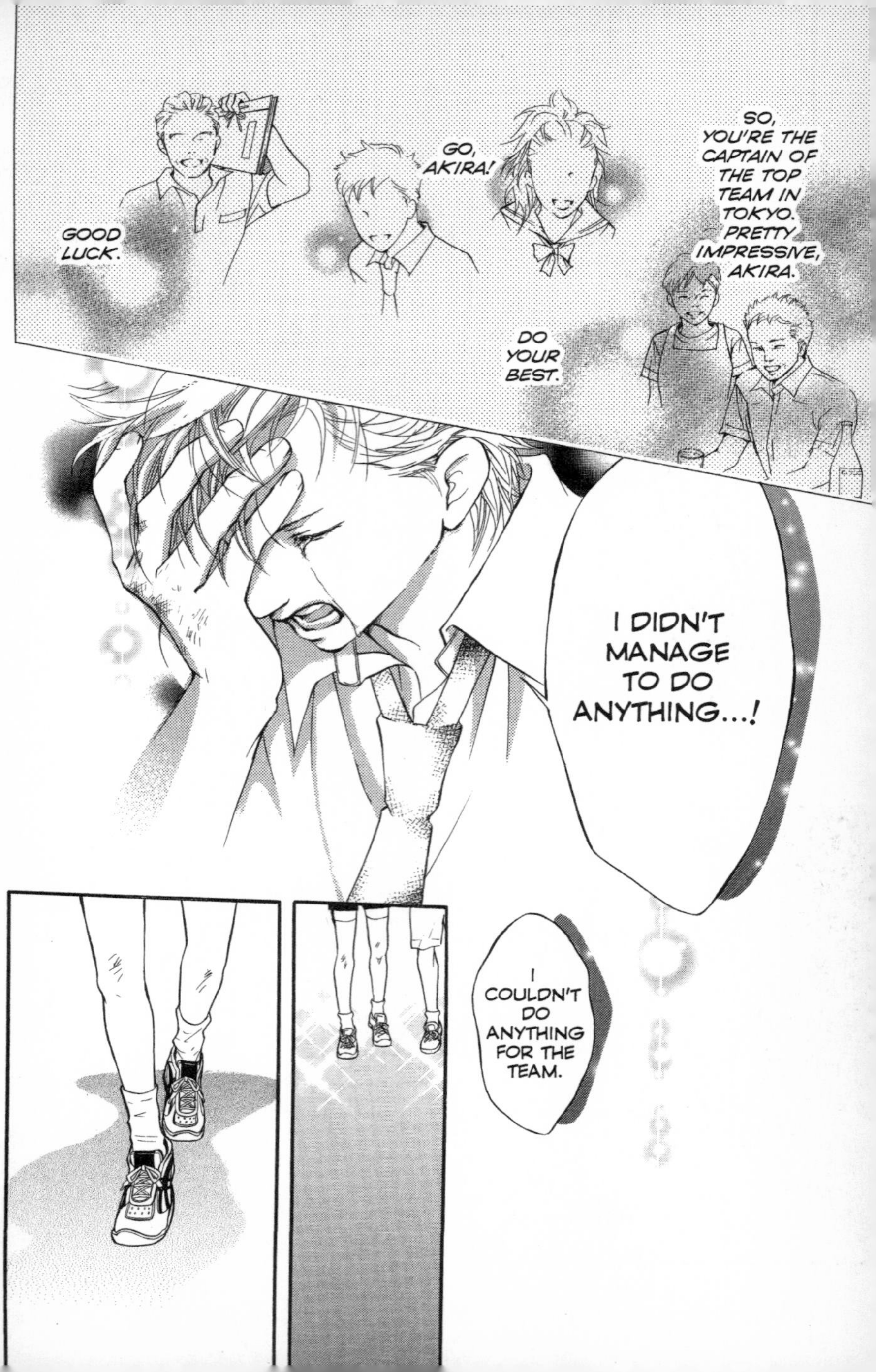
SO, YOU'RE THE CAPTAIN OF THE TOP TEAM IN TOKYO. PRETTY IMPRESSIVE, AKIRA.
GO, AKIRA!
DO YOUR BEST.
GOOD LUCK.
I DIDN'T MANAGE TO DO ANYTHING...!
I COULDN'T DO ANYTHING FOR THE TEAM.

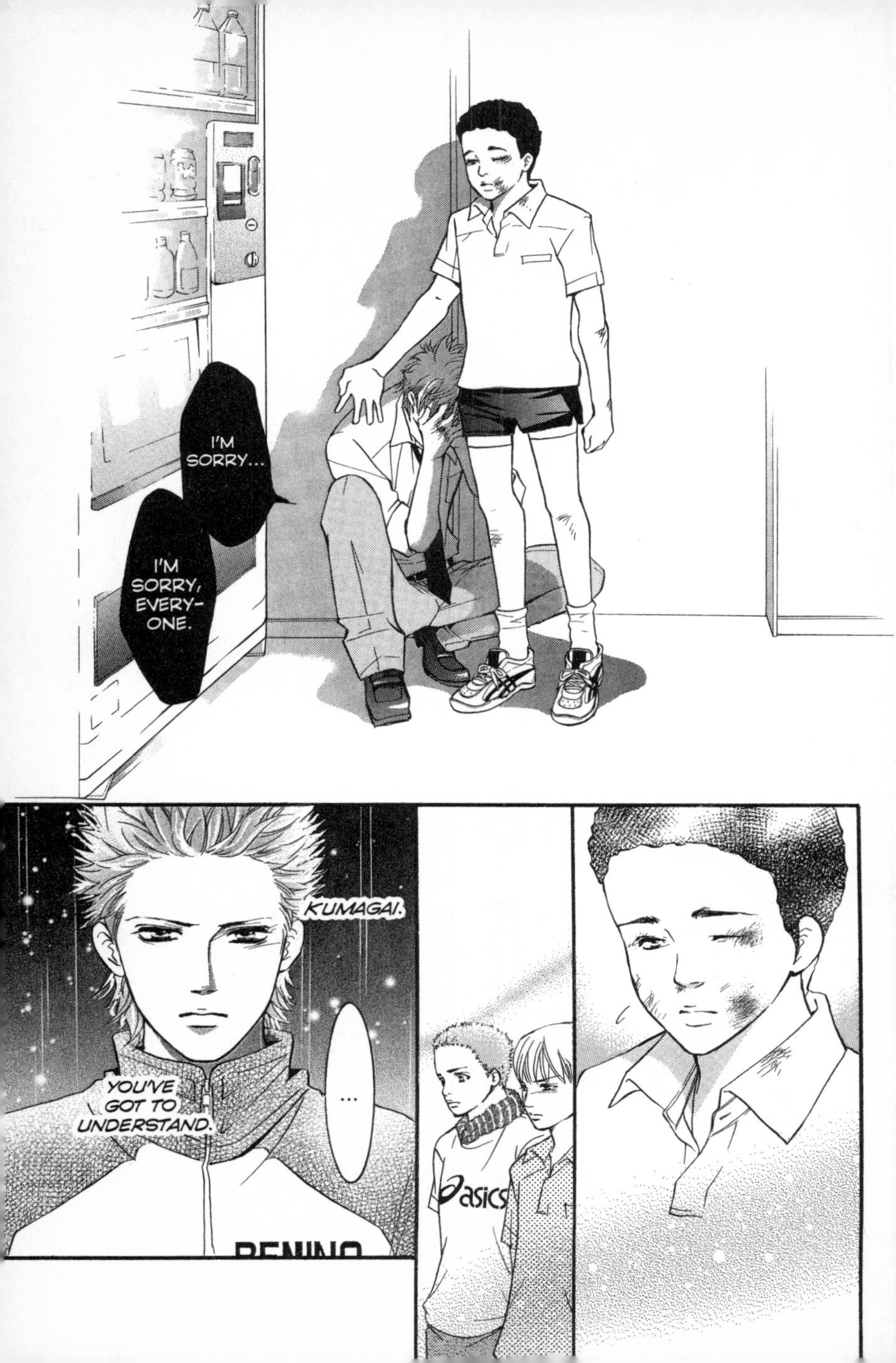
I'M SORRY...
I'M SORRY, EVERY-ONE.
KUMAGAI.
...
YOU'VE GOT TO UNDERSTAND.

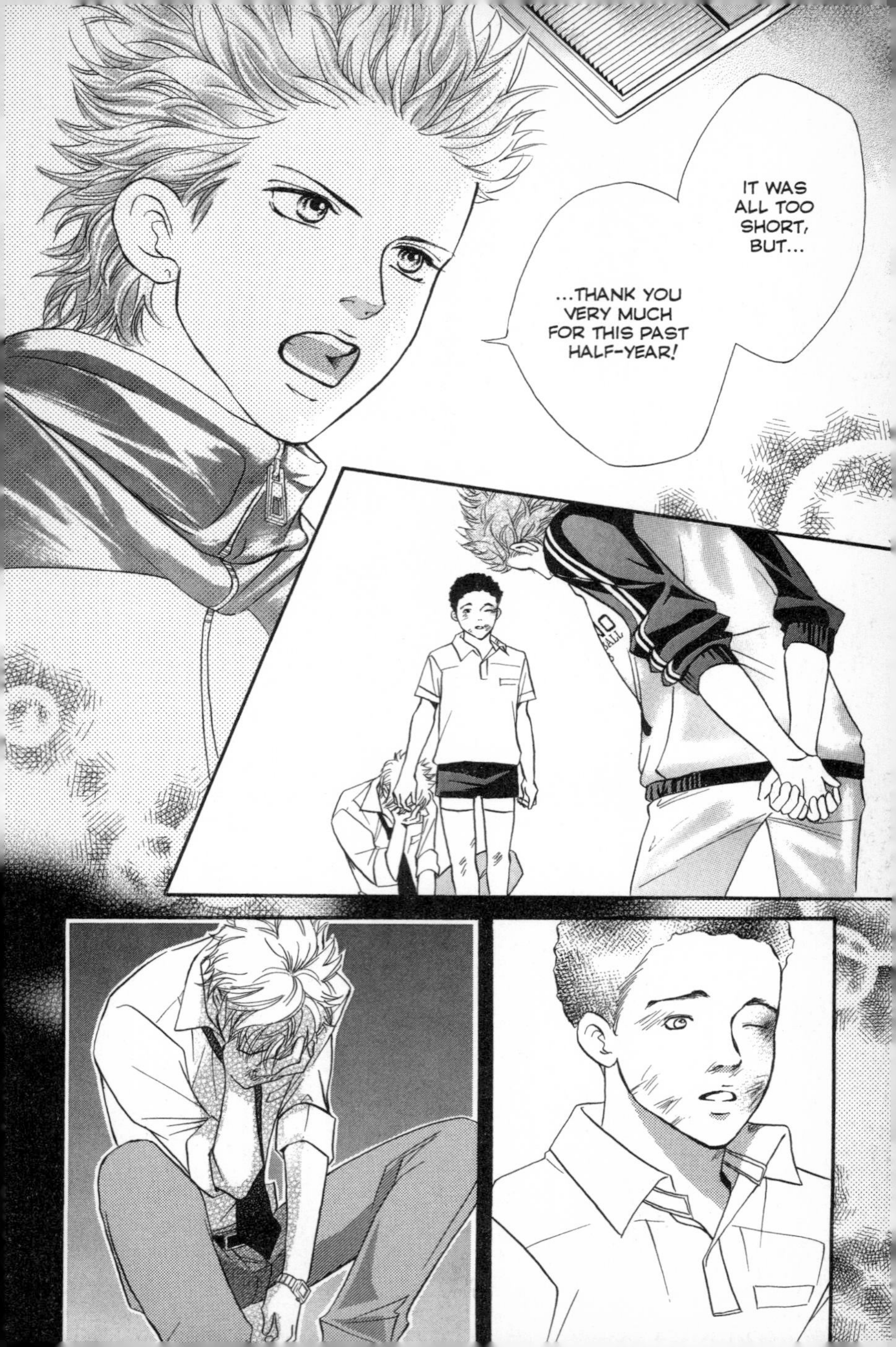

IT WAS ALL TOO SHORT, BUT...
...THANK YOU VERY MUCH FOR THIS PAST HALF-YEAR!

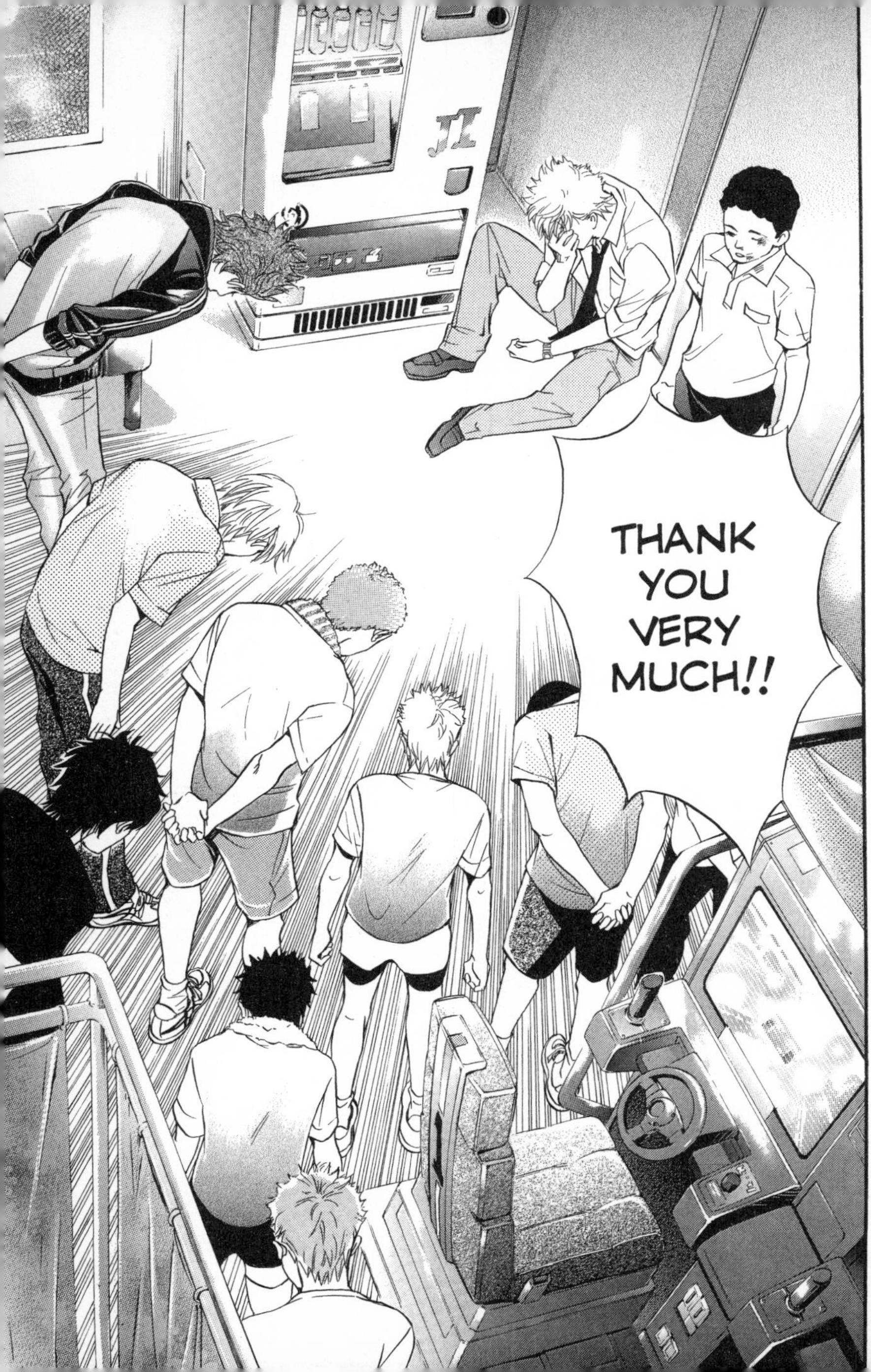
THANK YOU VERY MUCH!!

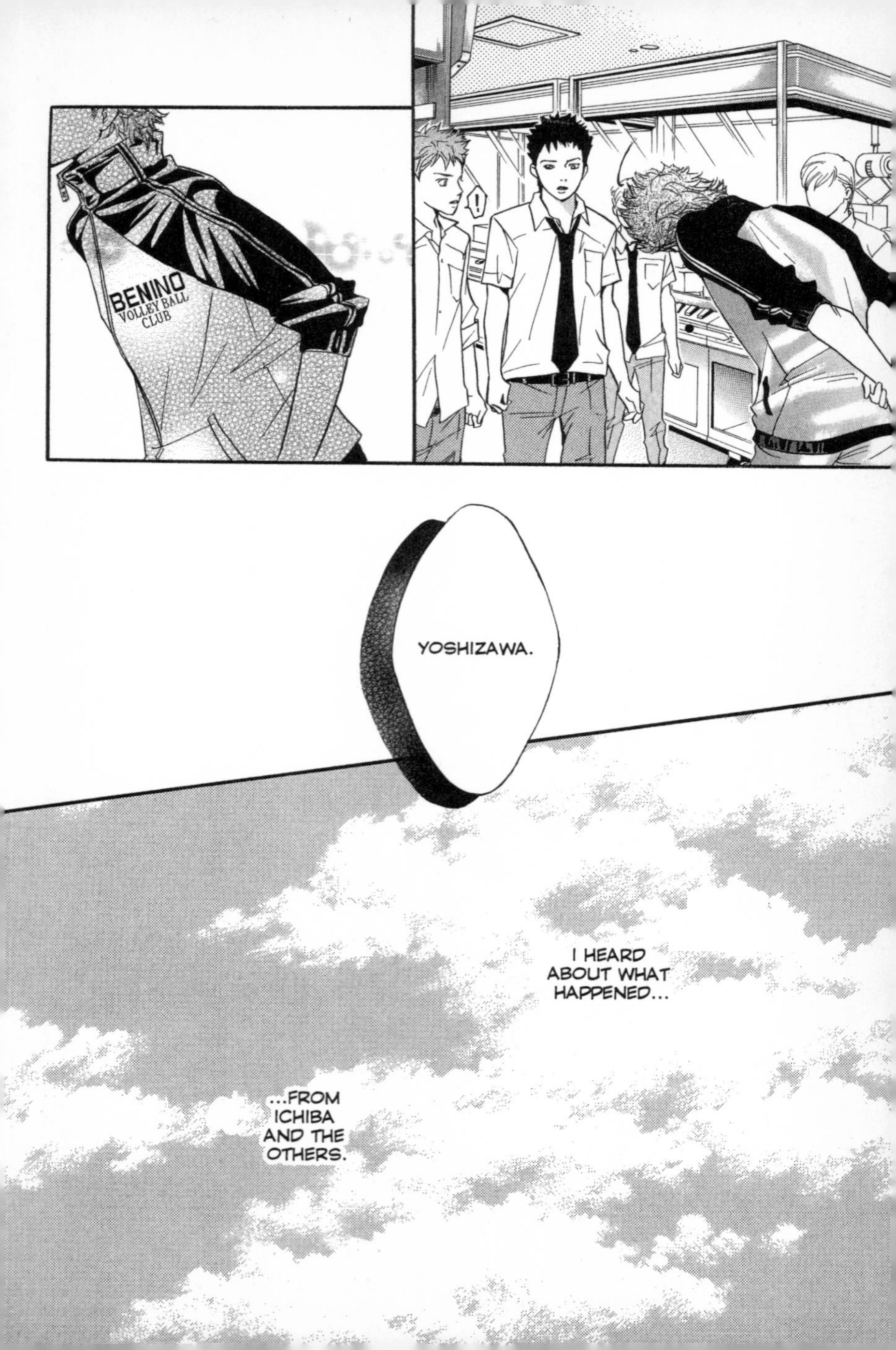
!
BENINO
VOLLEY BALL
CLUB
YOSHIZAWA.
I HEARD ABOUT WHAT HAPPENED...
...FROM ICHIBA AND THE OTHERS.

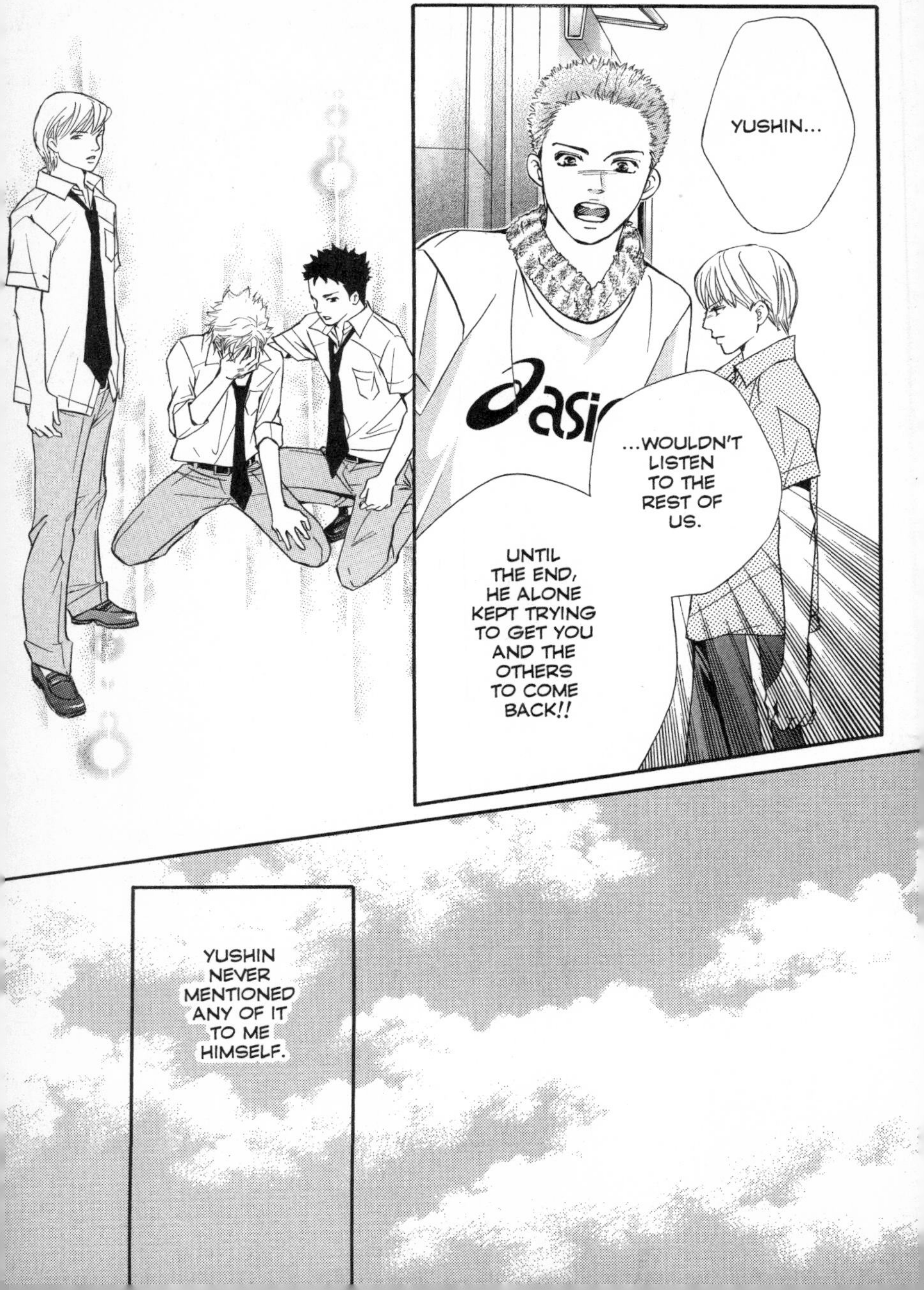
YUSHIN...
...WOULDN'T LISTEN TO THE REST OF US.
UNTIL THE END, HE ALONE KEPT TRYING TO GET YOU AND THE OTHERS TO COME BACK!!
YUSHIN NEVER MENTIONED ANY OF IT TO ME HIMSELF.

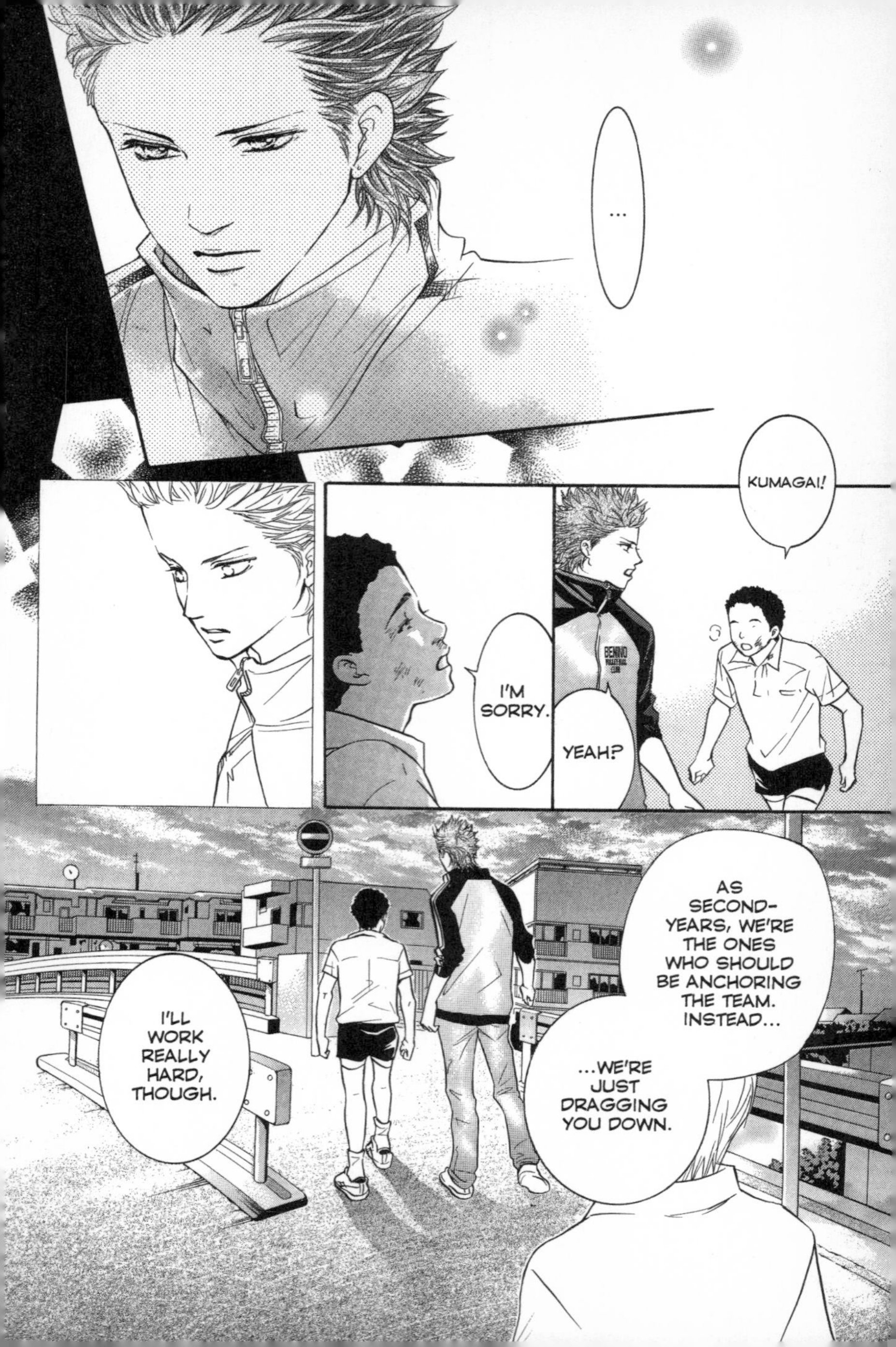
...
KUMAGAI!
YEAH?
I'M SORRY.
AS SECOND-YEARS, WE'RE THE ONES WHO SHOULD BE ANCHORING THE TEAM. INSTEAD...
...WE'RE JUST DRAGGING YOU DOWN.
I'LL WORK REALLY HARD, THOUGH.

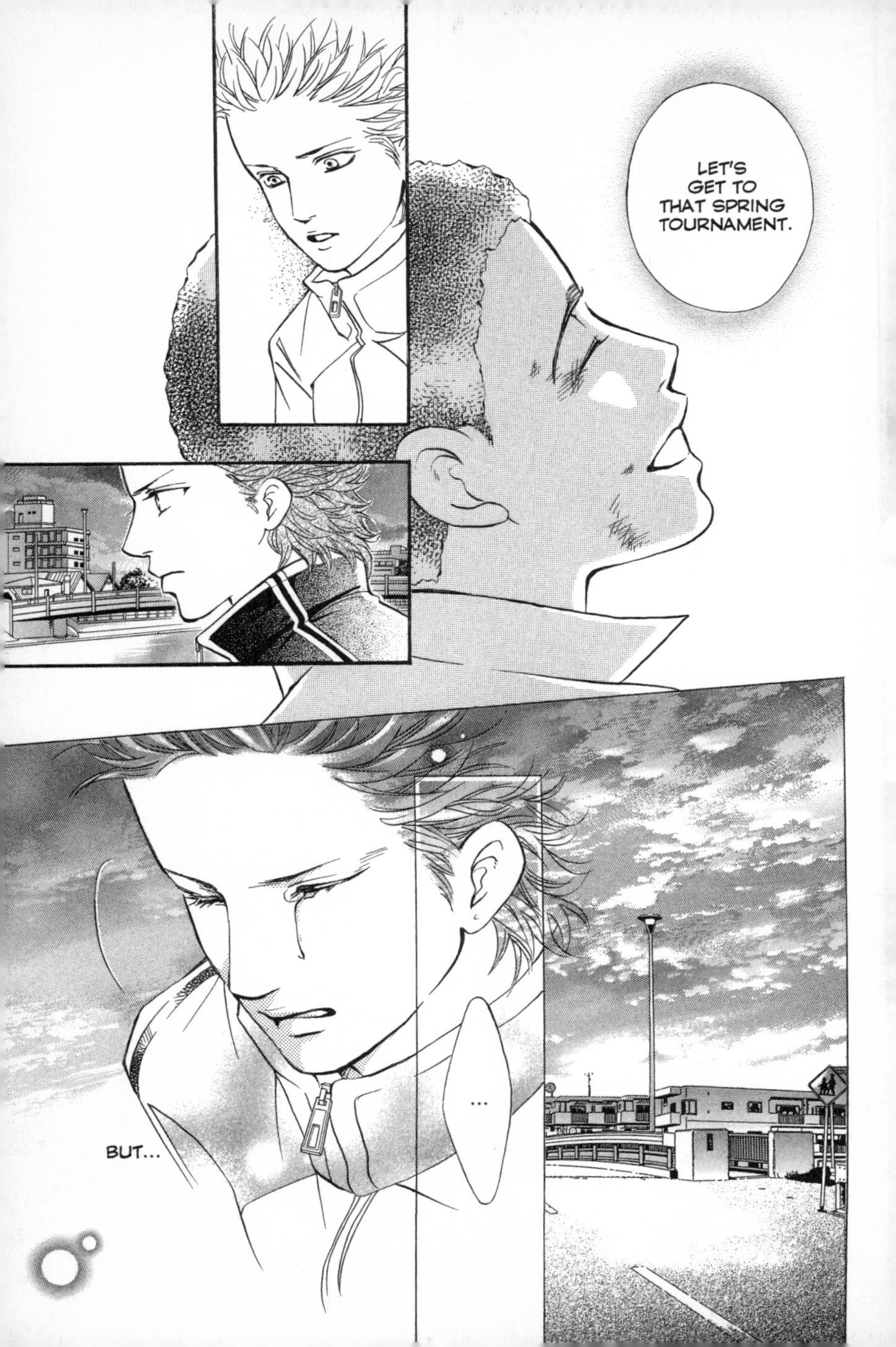
LET'S GET TO THAT SPRING TOURNAMENT.
...
BUT...

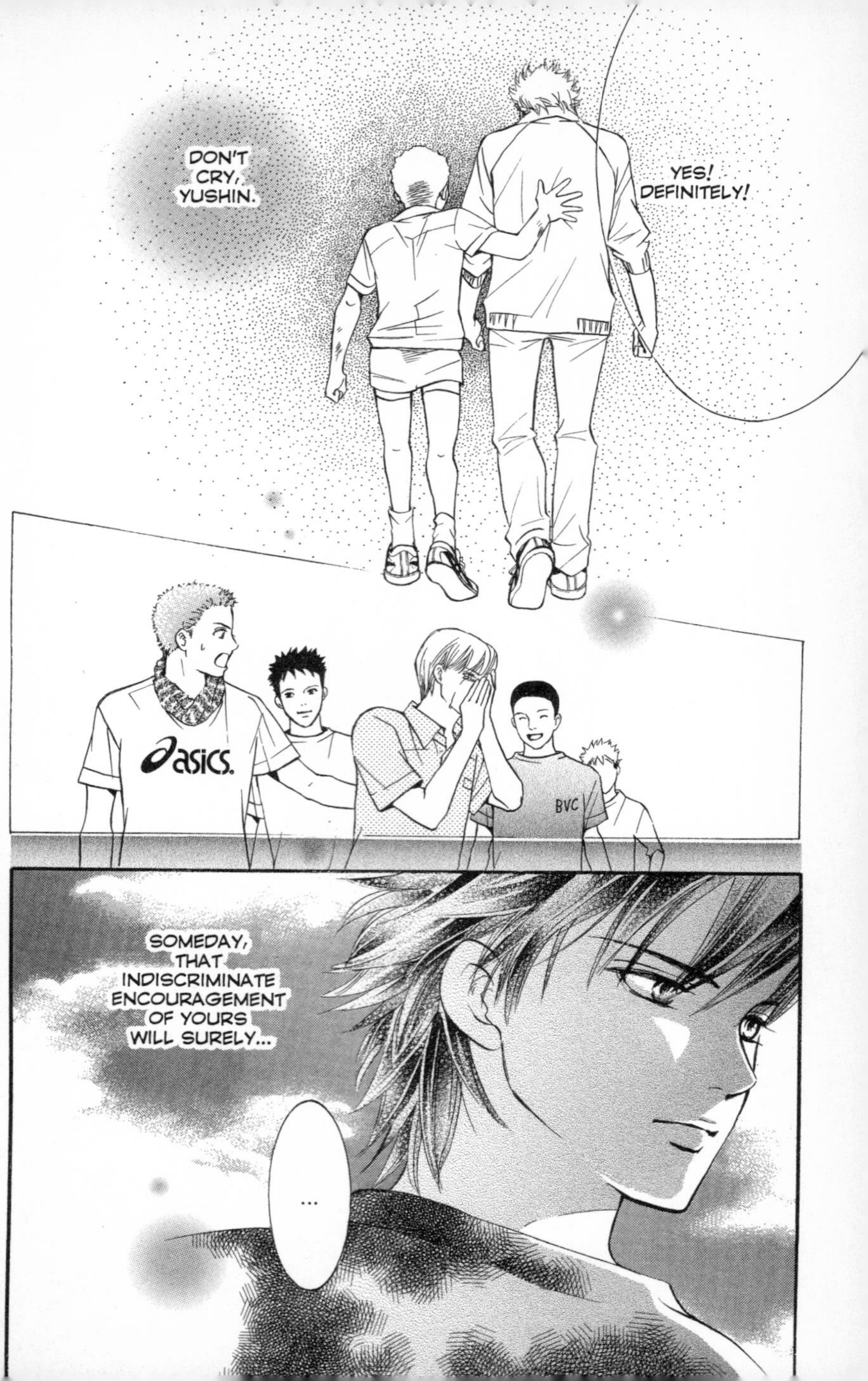
YES! DEFINITELY!
DON'T CRY, YUSHIN.
BVC
asics
SOMEDAY, THAT INDISCRIMINATE ENCOURAGEMENT OF YOURS WILL SURELY...
...

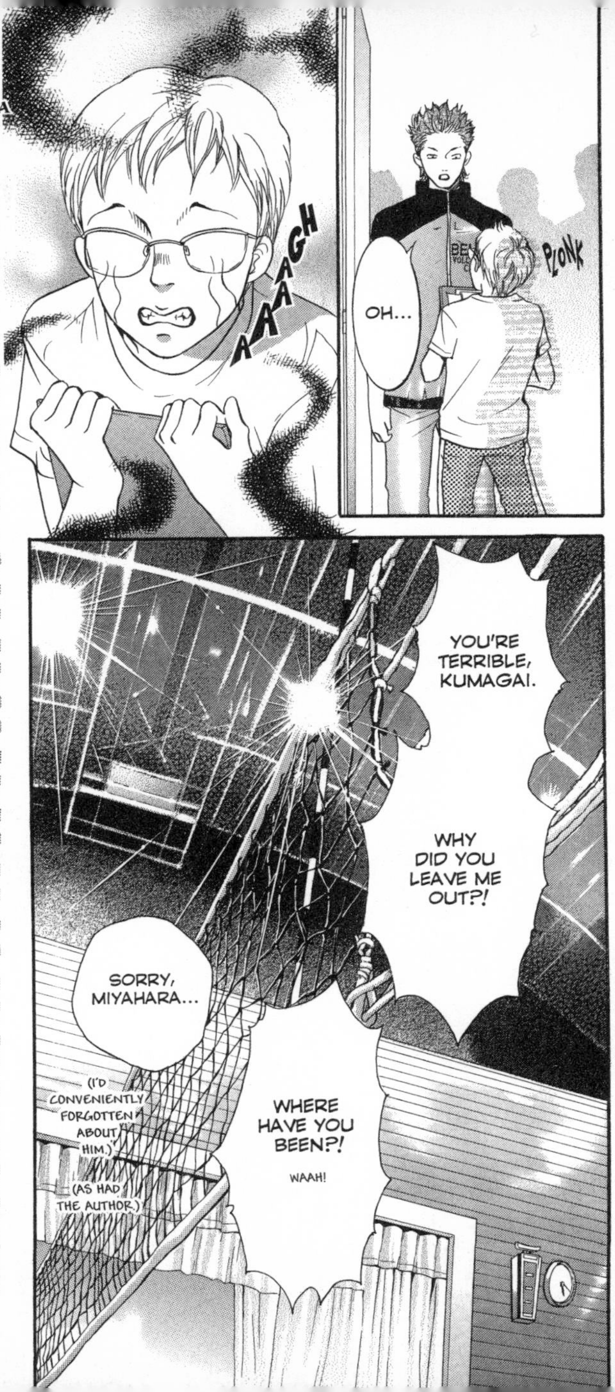
OH...
PLONK
AAAAAGH
YOU'RE TERRIBLE, KUMAGAI.
WHY DID YOU LEAVE ME OUT?!
WHERE HAVE YOU BEEN?!
WAAH!
SORRY, MIYAHARA...
(I'D CONVENIENTLY FORGOTTEN ABOUT HIM.)
(AS HAD THE AUTHOR.)

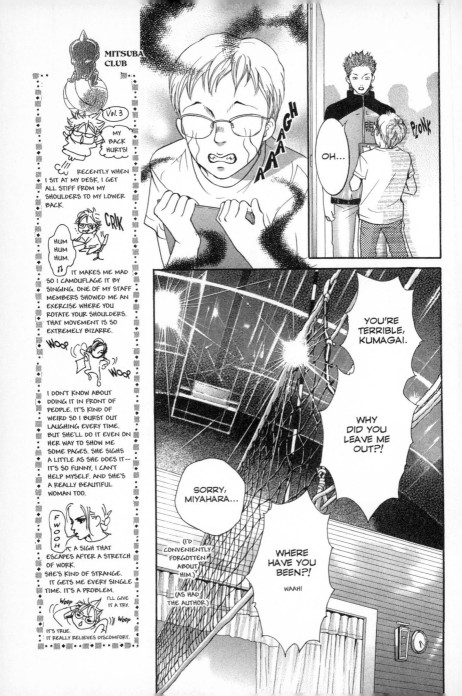

MITSUBA CLUB

Vol. 3

MY BACK HURTS!

RECENTLY WHEN I SIT AT MY DESK, I GET ALL STIFF FROM MY SHOULDERS TO MY LOWER BACK.

CRIK

HUM HUM HUM.

IT MAKES ME MAD SO I CAMOUFLAGE IT BY SINGING. ONE OF MY STAFF MEMBERS SHOWED ME AN EXERCISE WHERE YOU ROTATE YOUR SHOULDERS. THAT MOVEMENT IS SO EXTREMELY BIZARRE.

WOOP WOOP

I DON'T KNOW ABOUT DOING IT IN FRONT OF PEOPLE. IT'S KIND OF WEIRD SO I BURST OUT LAUGHING EVERY TIME. BUT SHE'LL DO IT EVEN ON HER WAY TO SHOW ME SOME PAGES. SHE SIGHS A LITTLE AS SHE DOES IT-- IT'S SO FUNNY, I CAN'T HELP MYSELF. AND SHE'S A REALLY BEAUTIFUL WOMAN TOO.

FWOOOH

A SIGH THAT ESCAPES AFTER A STRETCH OF WORK.

SHE'S KIND OF STRANGE.

IT GETS ME EVERY SINGLE TIME. IT'S A PROBLEM.

I'LL GIVE IT A TRY.

WOOP WOOP

IT'S TRUE. IT REALLY RELIEVES DISCOMFORT.

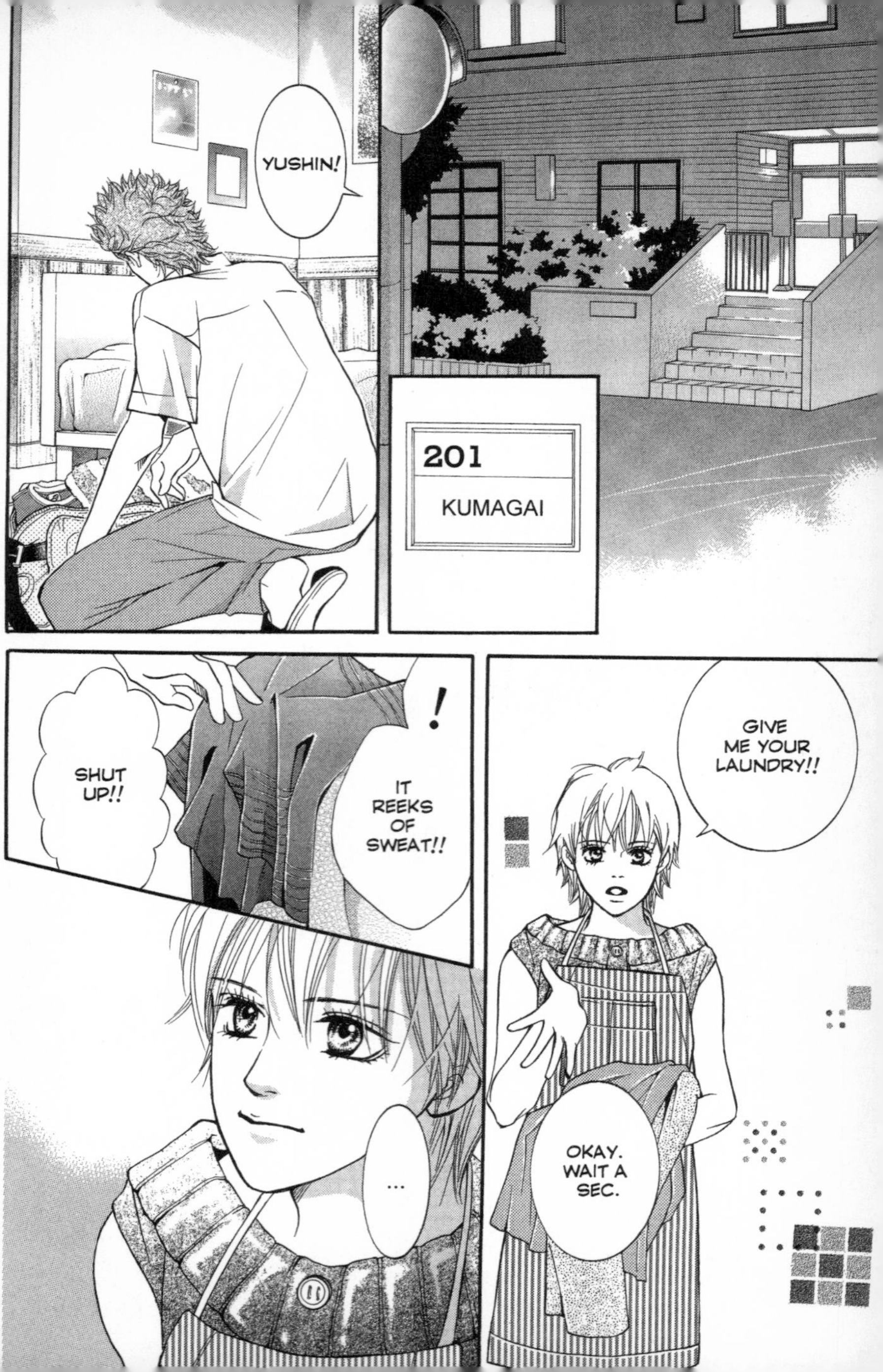
201
KUMAGAI
YUSHIN!
GIVE ME YOUR LAUNDRY!!
OKAY. WAIT A SEC.
!
IT REEKS OF SWEAT!!
SHUT UP!!
...

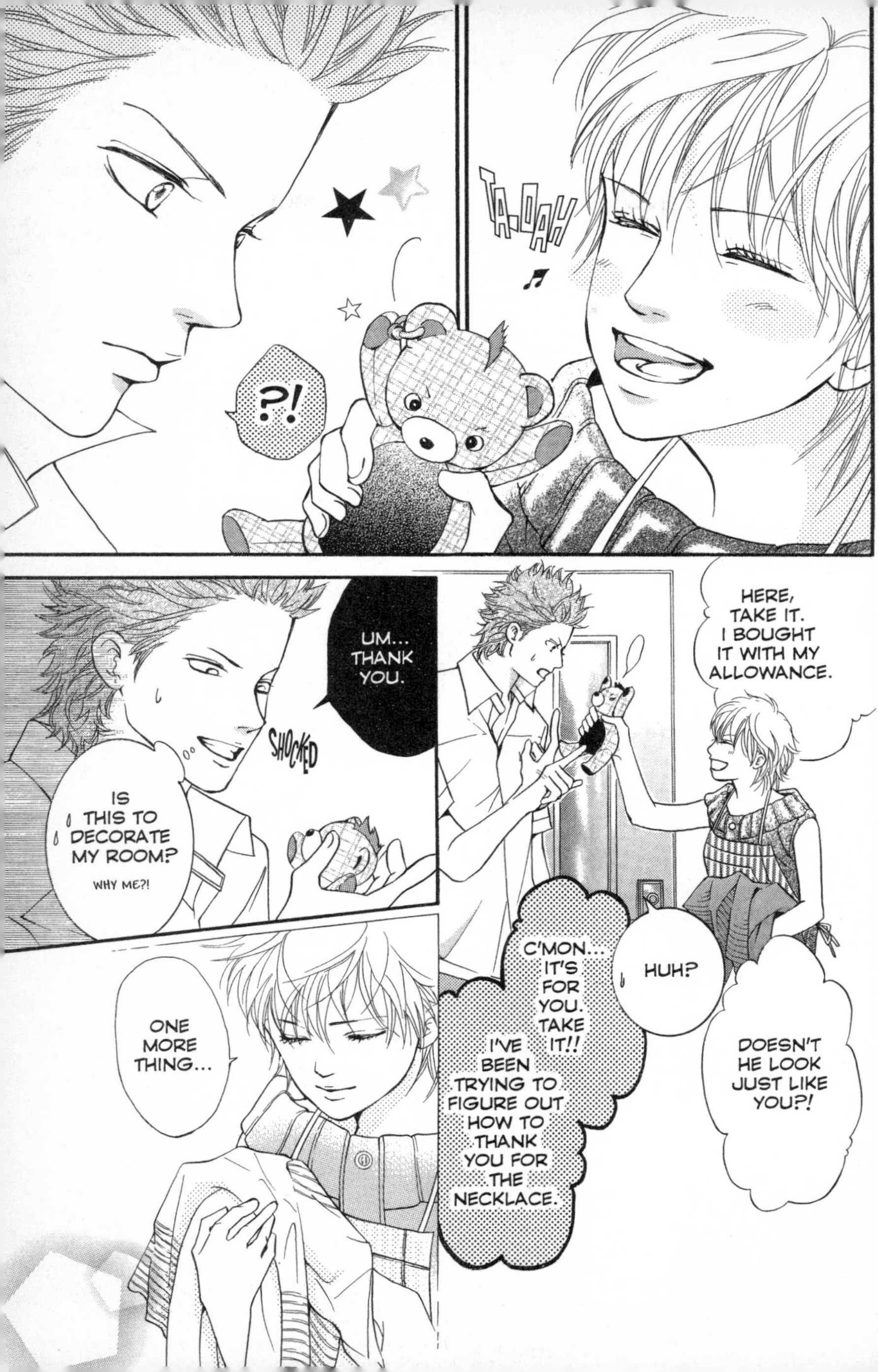
TA-DAH
♪
?!
HERE, TAKE IT. I BOUGHT IT WITH MY ALLOWANCE.
HUH?
C'MON... IT'S FOR YOU. TAKE IT!!
DOESN'T HE LOOK JUST LIKE YOU?!
I'VE BEEN TRYING TO FIGURE OUT HOW TO THANK YOU FOR THE NECKLACE.
UM... THANK YOU.
SHOCKED
IS THIS TO DECORATE MY ROOM?
WHY ME?!
ONE MORE THING...

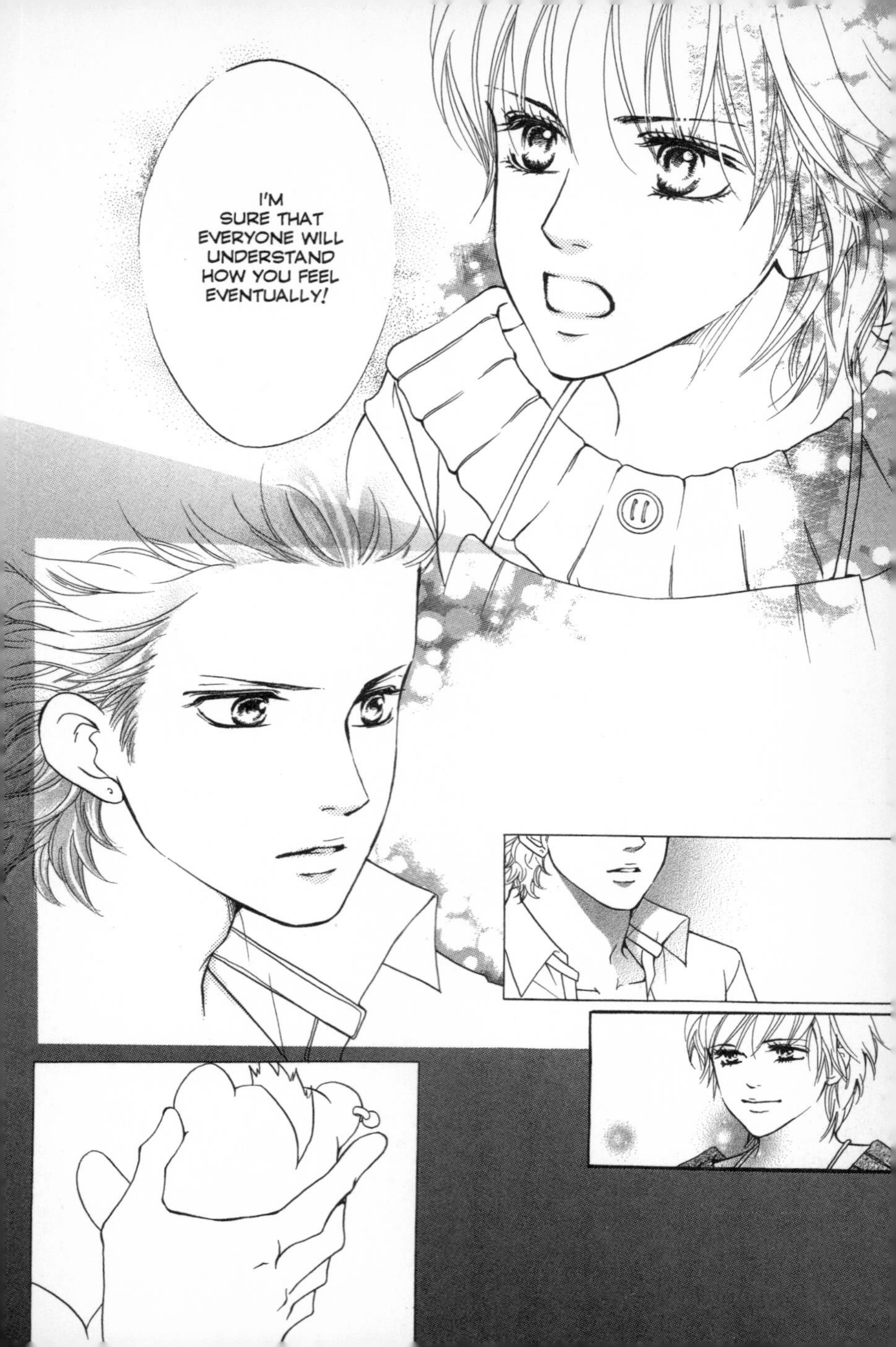
I'M SURE THAT EVERYONE WILL UNDERSTAND HOW YOU FEEL EVENTUALLY!

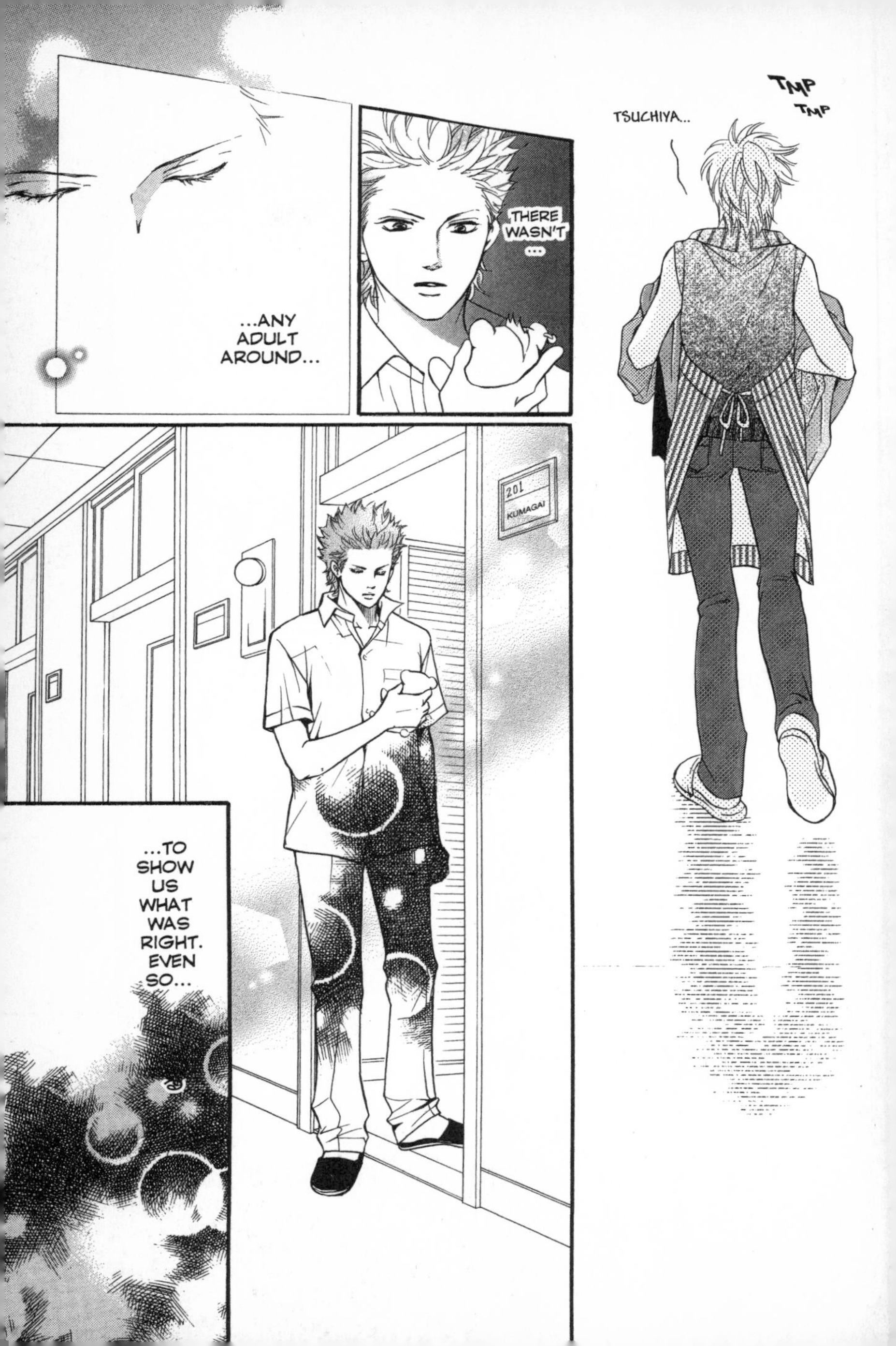
TMP
TMP
TSUCHIYA...
THERE WASN'T ...
...ANY ADULT AROUND...
201
KUMAGAI
...TO SHOW US WHAT WAS RIGHT. EVEN SO...

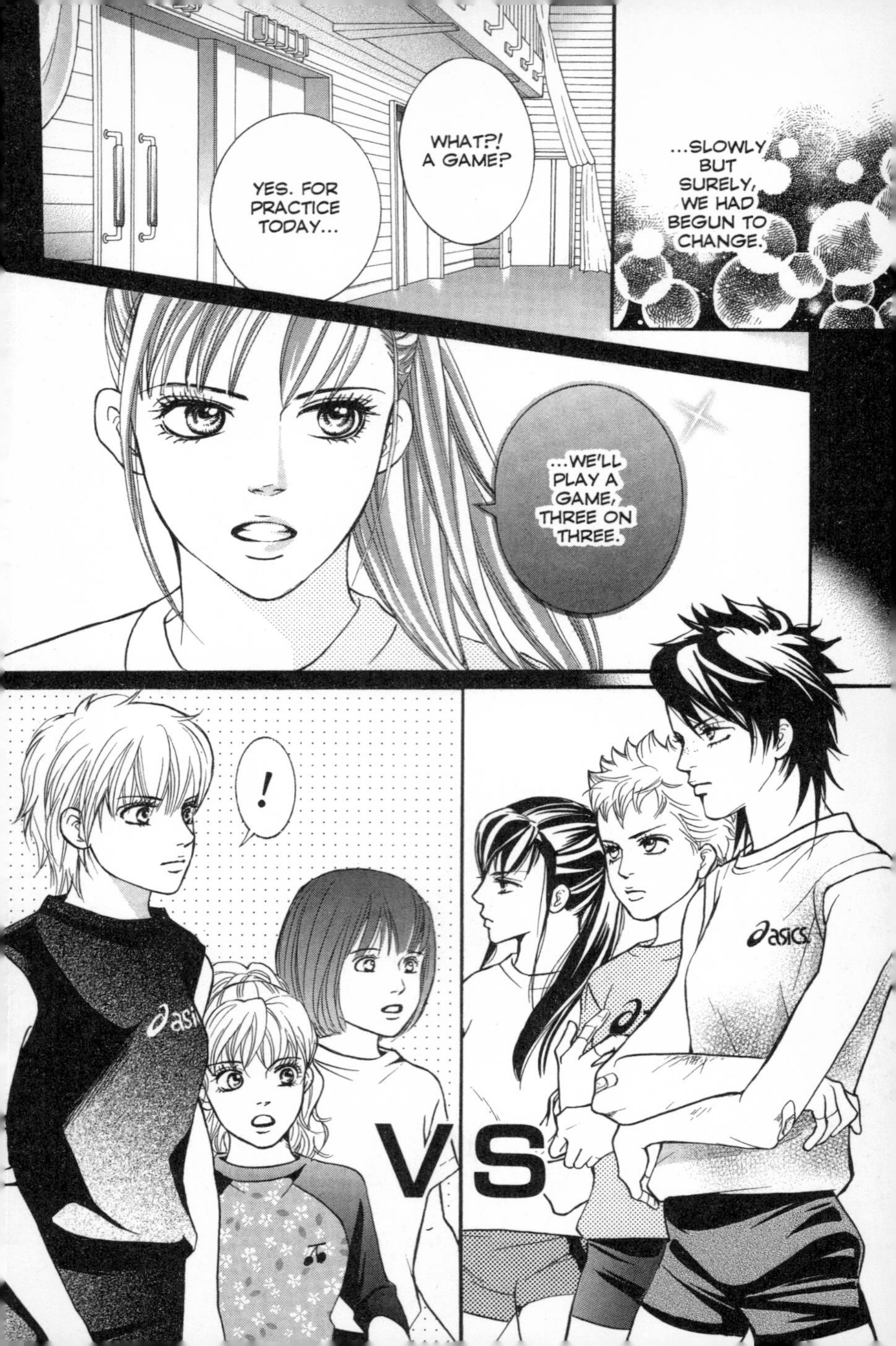
...SLOWLY BUT SURELY, WE HAD BEGUN TO CHANGE.
WHAT?! A GAME?
YES. FOR PRACTICE TODAY...
...WE'LL PLAY A GAME, THREE ON THREE.
VS
!

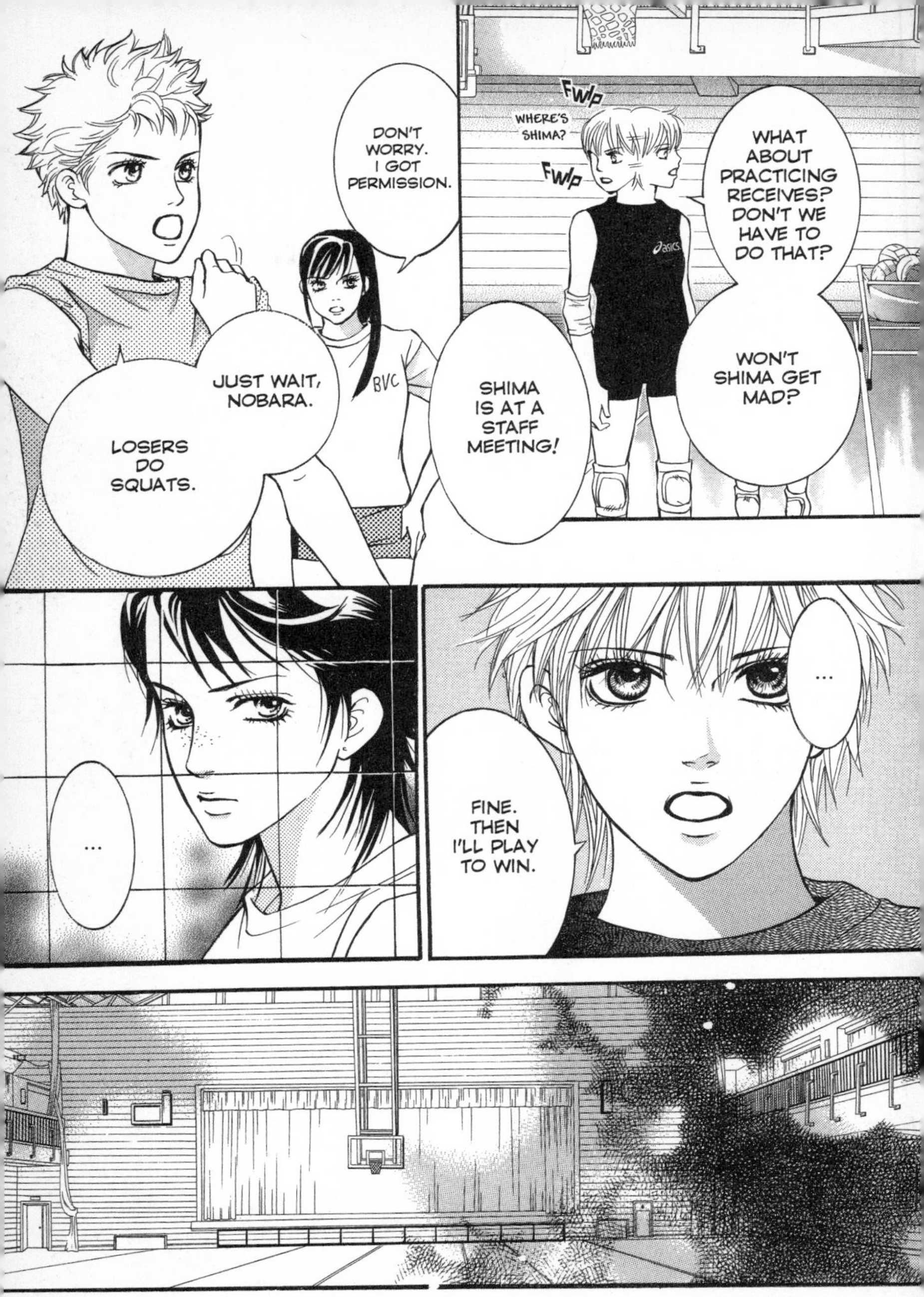
FWIP
WHERE'S SHIMA?
FWIP
WHAT ABOUT PRACTICING RECEIVES? DON'T WE HAVE TO DO THAT?
WON'T SHIMA GET MAD?
SHIMA IS AT A STAFF MEETING!
DON'T WORRY. I GOT PERMISSION.
JUST WAIT, NOBARA.
LOSERS DO SQUATS.
...
FINE. THEN I'LL PLAY TO WIN.
...

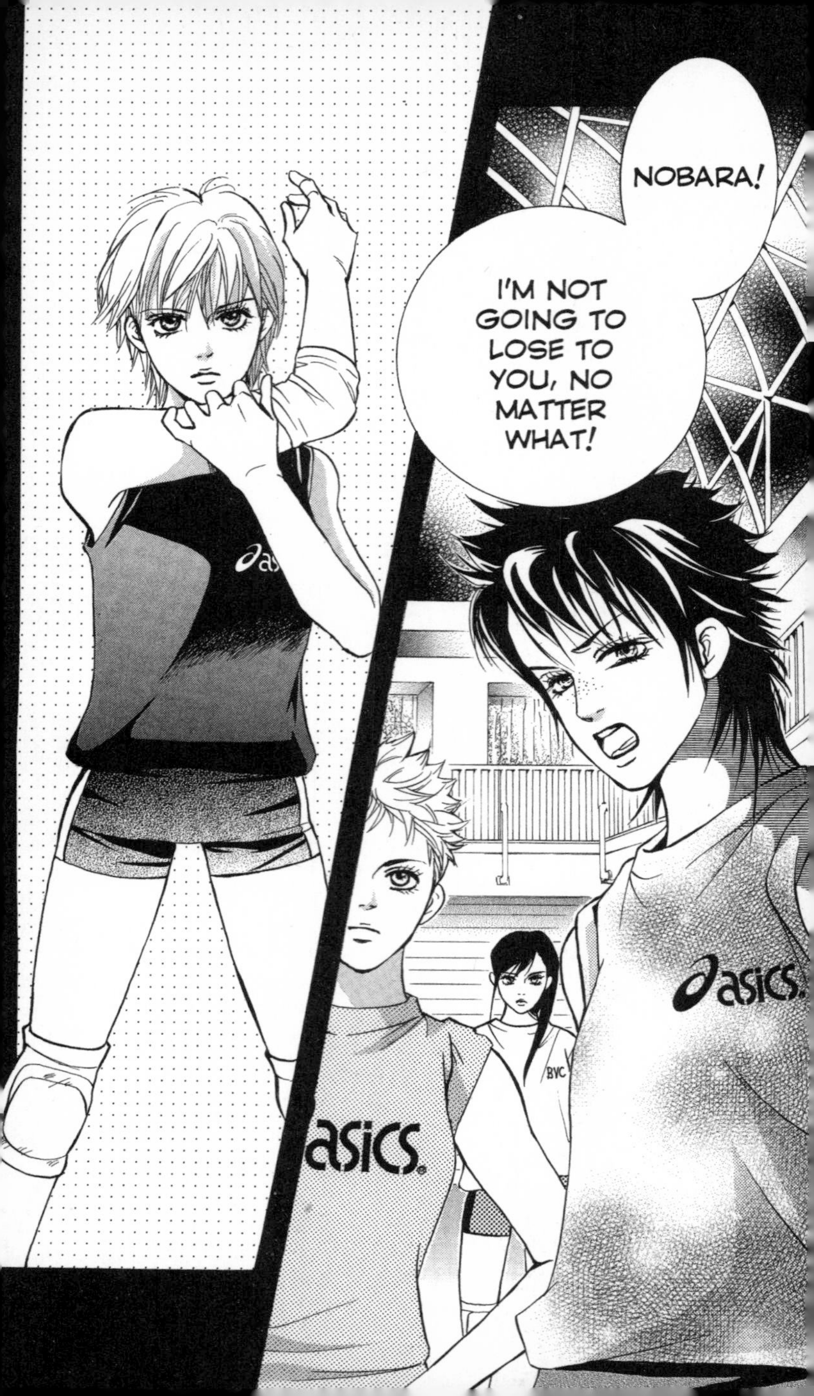
NOBARA!
I'M NOT GOING TO LOSE TO YOU, NO MATTER WHAT!

GAME 3
TOO SOFT, SUMIYOSHI!

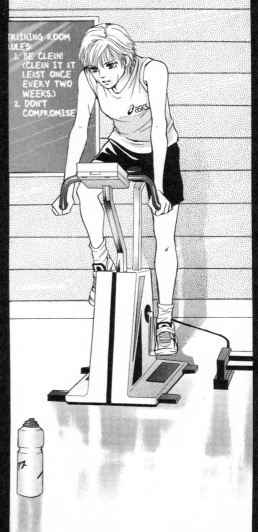

TRAINING ROOM RULES:
1. BE CLEAN! (CLEAN IT AT LEAST ONCE EVERY TWO WEEKS)
2. DON'T COMPROMISE

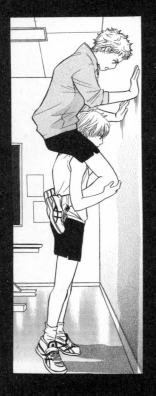

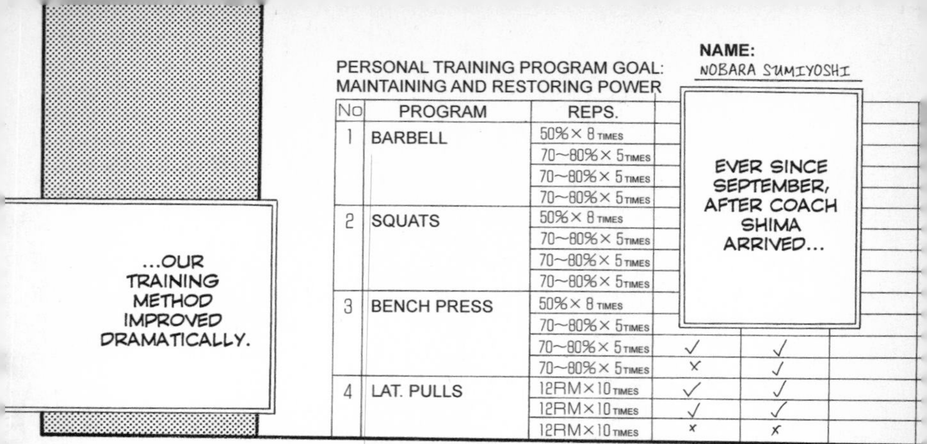
NAME:
NOBARA SUMIYOSHI
EVER SINCE SEPTEMBER, AFTER COACH SHIMA ARRIVED...
PERSONAL TRAINING PROGRAM GOAL: MAINTAINING AND RESTORING POWER
...OUR TRAINING METHOD IMPROVED DRAMATICALLY.

No	PROGRAM	REPS.		
1	BARBELL	50% × 8 TIMES		
		70~80% × 5 TIMES		
		70~80% × 5 TIMES		
		70~80% × 5 TIMES		
2	SQUATS	50% × 8 TIMES		
		70~80% × 5 TIMES		
		70~80% × 5 TIMES		
		70~80% × 5 TIMES		
3	BENCH PRESS	50% × 8 TIMES		
		70~80% × 5 TIMES		
		70~80% × 5 TIMES	✓	✓
		70~80% × 5 TIMES	×	✓
4	LAT. PULLS	12RM × 10 TIMES	✓	✓
		12RM × 10 TIMES	✓	✓
		12RM × 10 TIMES	×	×

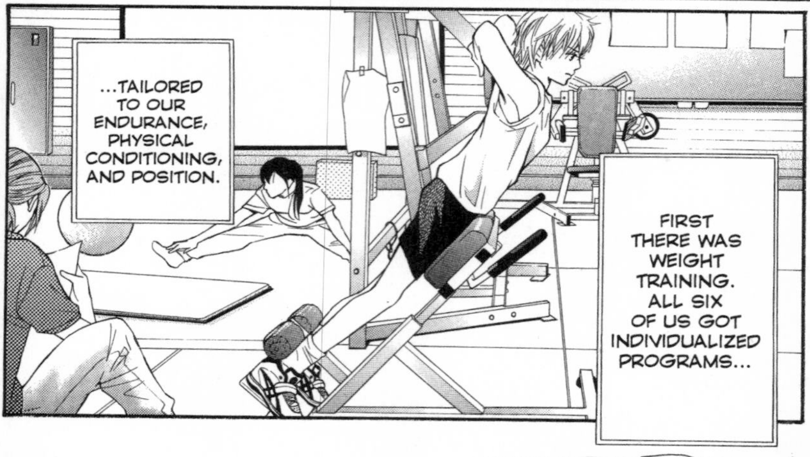
FIRST THERE WAS WEIGHT TRAINING. ALL SIX OF US GOT INDIVIDUALIZED PROGRAMS...
...TAILORED TO OUR ENDURANCE, PHYSICAL CONDITIONING, AND POSITION.

THE MAKING OF *CRIMSON HERO*

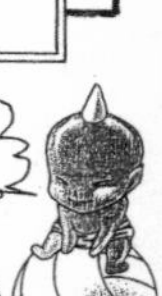

KANAKO HAS A NATURAL PHYSICAL ABILITY, POWERFUL JUMPS, AND A RIVALRY WITH NOBARA. OF COURSE NOBARA HAS TO DO HER BEST, BUT THE SAME IS TRUE FOR KANAKO IN ORDER FOR CRIMSON FIELD TO WIN. THERE HAS TO BE A STRONG CENTER PLAYER--ONLY THEN CAN NOBARA COME ALIVE AS THE LEFT ATTACKER. KANAKO...WHO CAN BE FLATTERED INTO ANYTHING. KANAKO...WHO'LL FORGET ANY UNPLEASANT INCIDENT WITHIN THREE DAYS. KANAKO...WHO WANTED A BOYFRIEND BUT SOMEHOW ENDED UP PASSIONATE ABOUT VOLLEYBALL. I HAVE GREAT EXPECTATIONS FOR HER GROWTH.

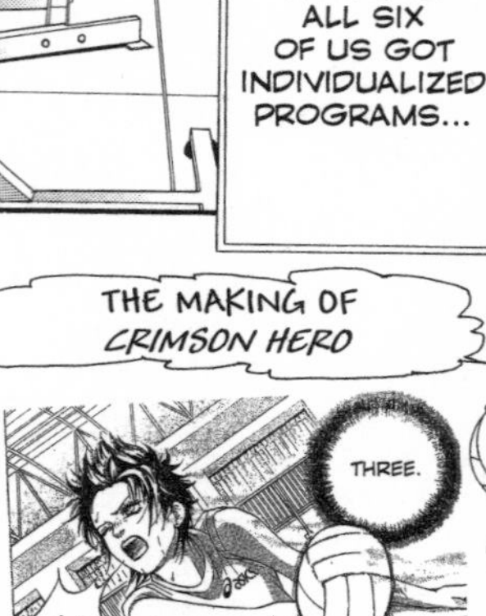
THREE.
4
AAAGH

KANAKO NODA
CENTER

SHE HAS LOTS OF KOGAL FRIENDS. BUT SHE CAN EASILY STRIKE UP CONVERSATIONS WITH QUIET GIRLS IN CLASS, LIKE GOTO.

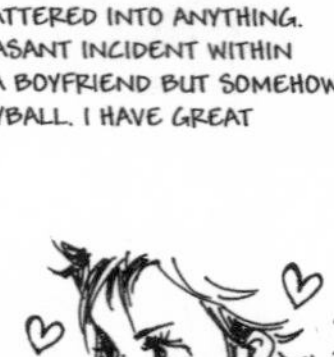

SHE'S TALL SO SHE PUTS A LOT OF EFFORT INTO FINDING CLOTHES THAT SUIT HER. AT NEARLY 6 FEET, I BET SHE ALWAYS STANDS OUT.

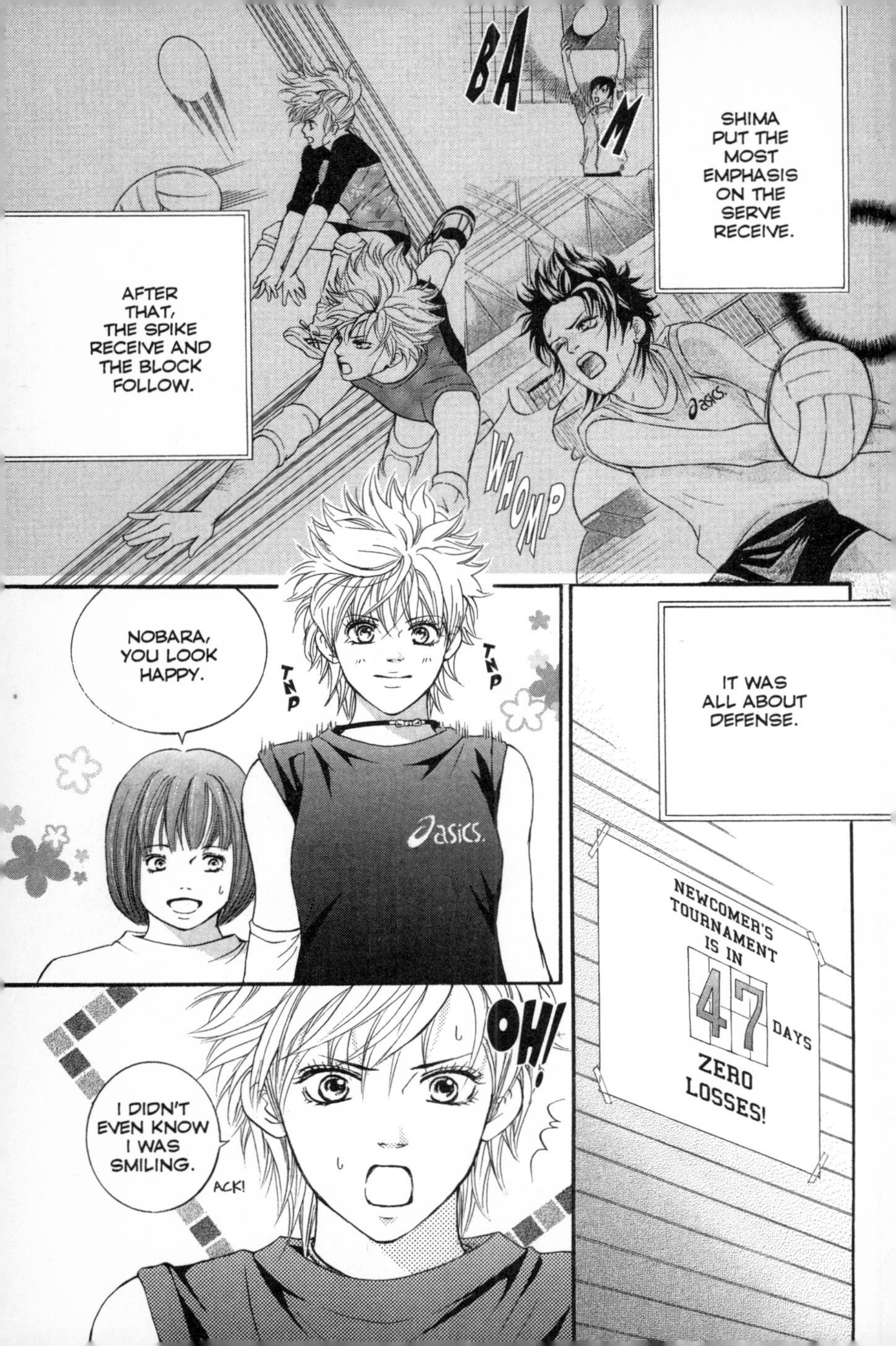
SHIMA PUT THE MOST EMPHASIS ON THE SERVE RECEIVE.
BAM
AFTER THAT, THE SPIKE RECEIVE AND THE BLOCK FOLLOW.
WHOMP
IT WAS ALL ABOUT DEFENSE.
NEWCOMER'S TOURNAMENT IS IN 47 DAYS
ZERO LOSSES!
TNP
TNP
NOBARA, YOU LOOK HAPPY.
OH!
I DIDN'T EVEN KNOW I WAS SMILING.
ACK!

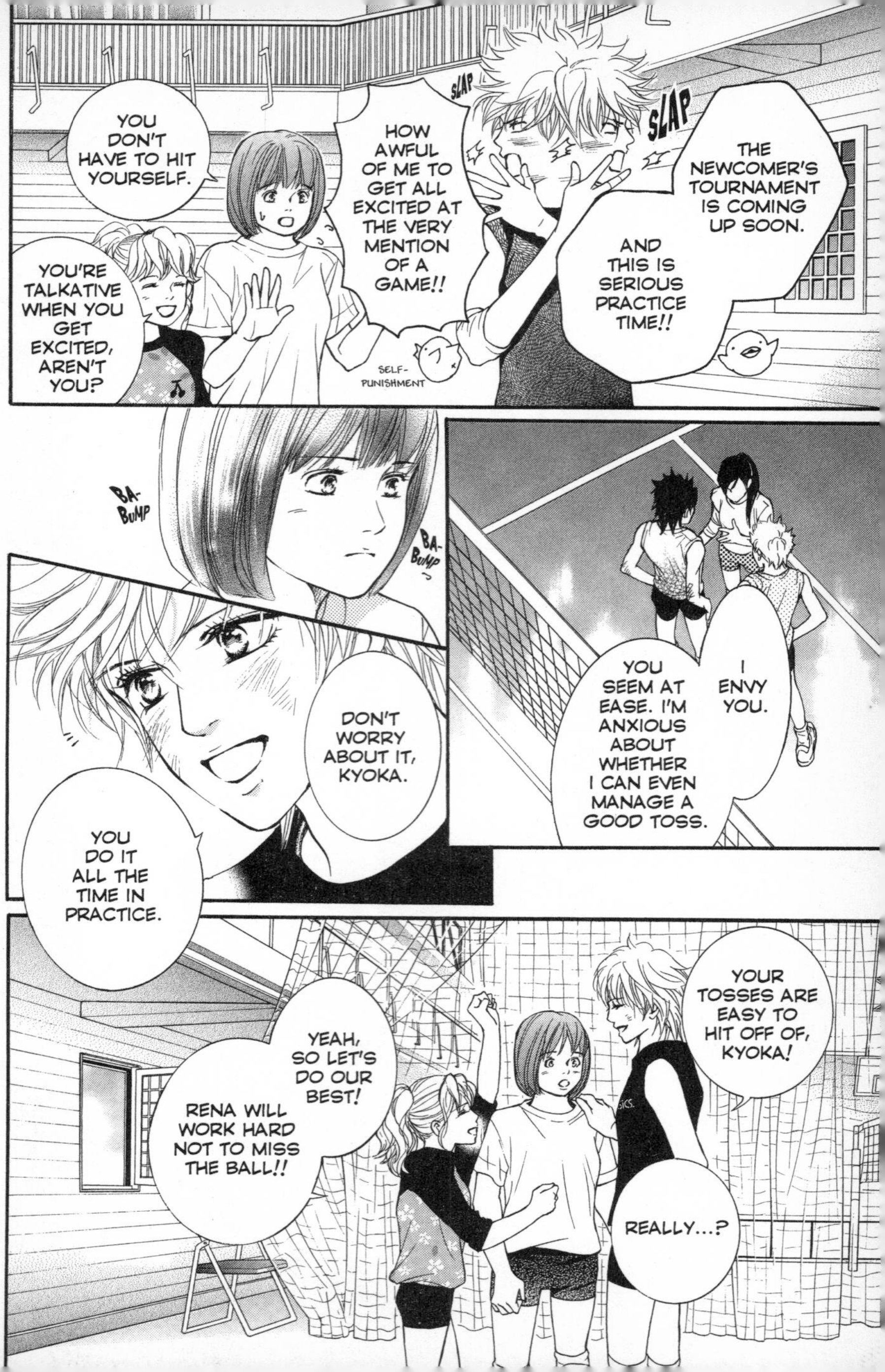
THE NEWCOMER'S TOURNAMENT IS COMING UP SOON.
AND THIS IS SERIOUS PRACTICE TIME!!
SLAP
SLAP
HOW AWFUL OF ME TO GET ALL EXCITED AT THE VERY MENTION OF A GAME!!
SELF-PUNISHMENT
YOU DON'T HAVE TO HIT YOURSELF.
YOU'RE TALKATIVE WHEN YOU GET EXCITED, AREN'T YOU?
I ENVY YOU.
YOU SEEM AT EASE. I'M ANXIOUS ABOUT WHETHER I CAN EVEN MANAGE A GOOD TOSS.
BA-BUMP
BA-BUMP
DON'T WORRY ABOUT IT, KYOKA.
YOU DO IT ALL THE TIME IN PRACTICE.
YOUR TOSSES ARE EASY TO HIT OFF OF, KYOKA!
REALLY...?
YEAH, SO LET'S DO OUR BEST!
RENA WILL WORK HARD NOT TO MISS THE BALL!!

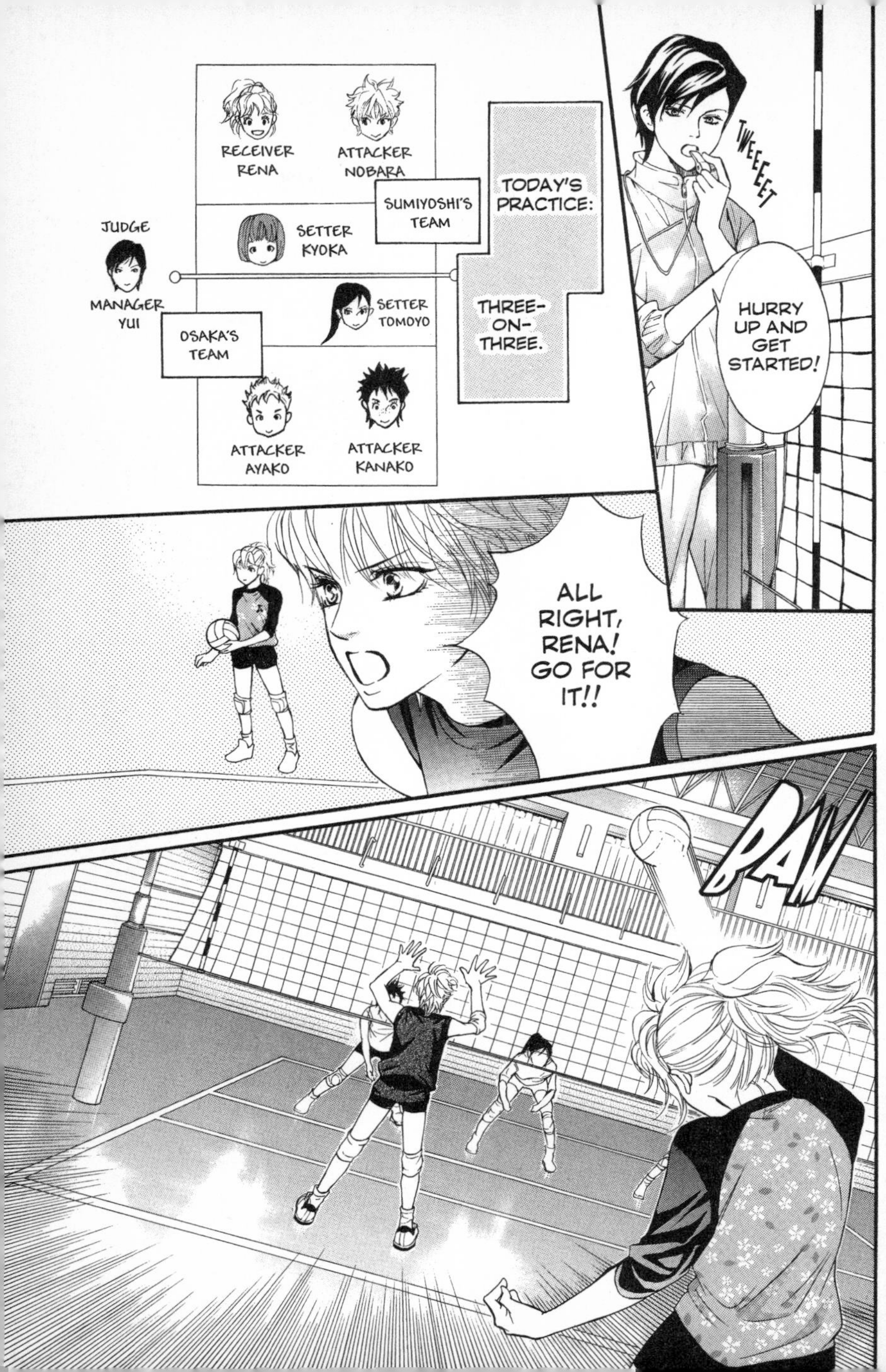
TWEEEEET
HURRY UP AND GET STARTED!
TODAY'S PRACTICE:
THREE-ON-THREE.
SUMIYOSHI'S TEAM
RECEIVER RENA
ATTACKER NOBARA
SETTER KYOKA
JUDGE
MANAGER YUI
OSAKA'S TEAM
SETTER TOMOYO
ATTACKER AYAKO
ATTACKER KANAKO
ALL RIGHT, RENA! GO FOR IT!!
BAM

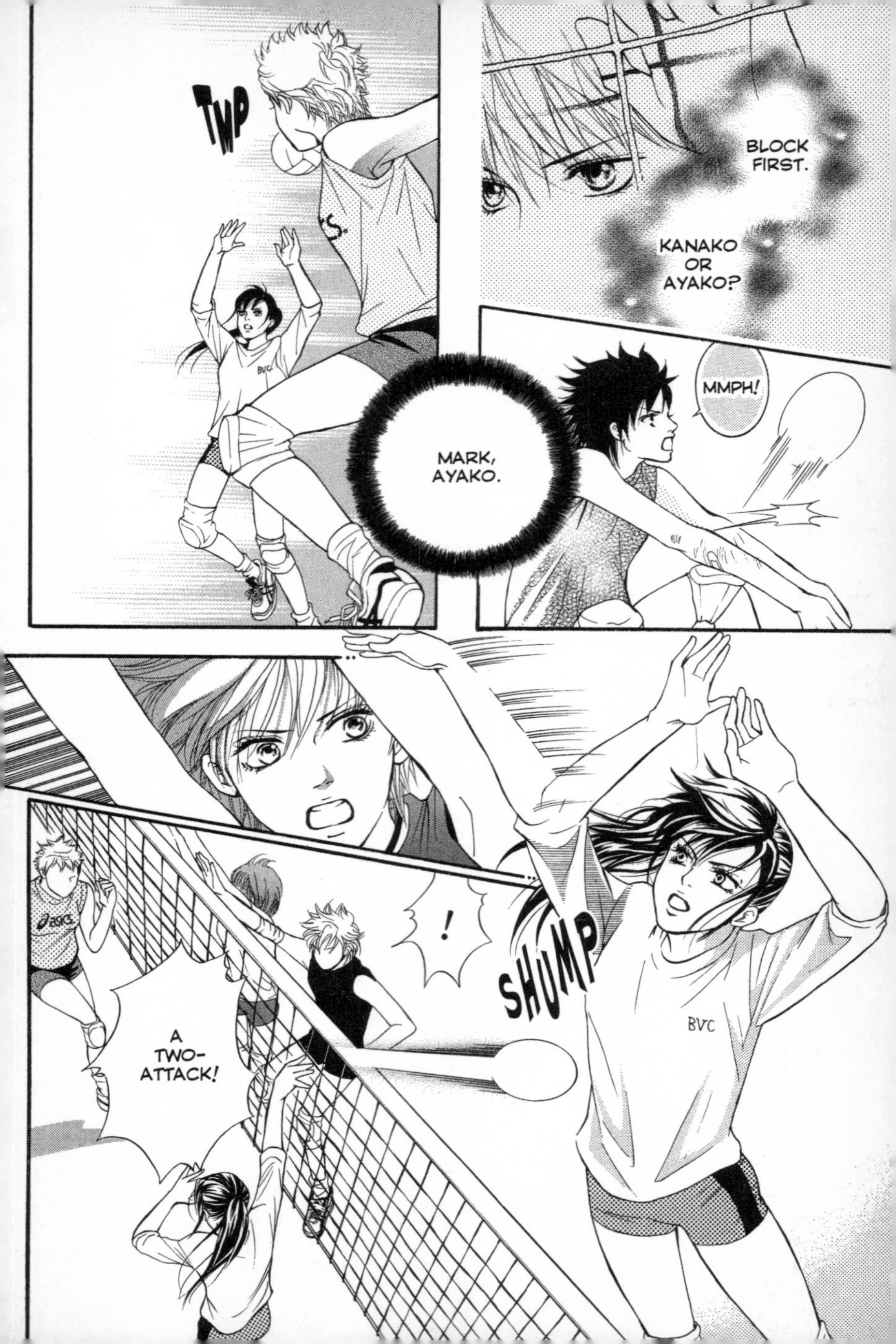

BLOCK FIRST.
KANAKO OR AYAKO?
MMPH!
MARK, AYAKO.
TMP
!
SHUMP
A TWO-ATTACK!

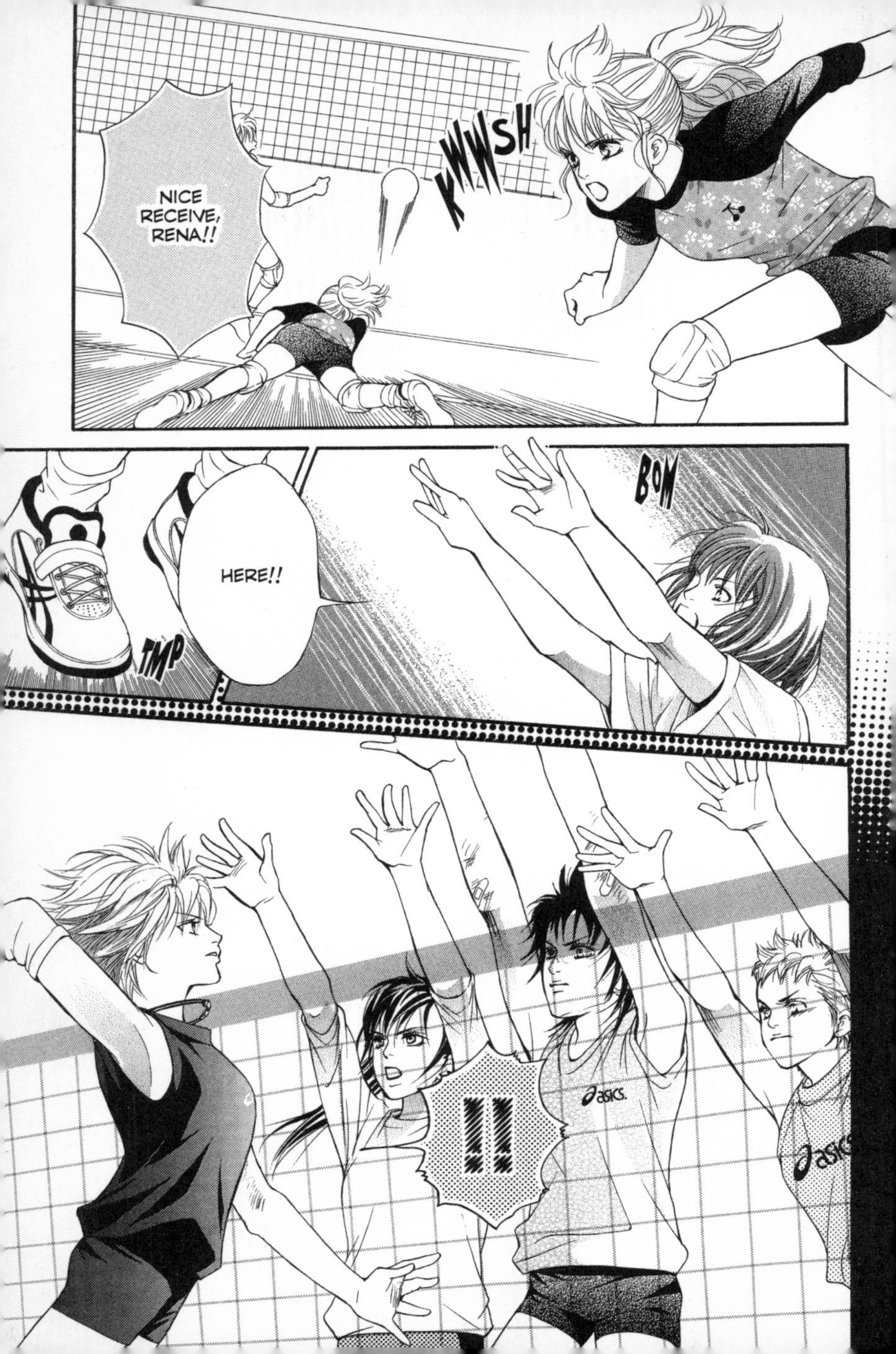
KWWSH
NICE RECEIVE, RENA!!
BOM
HERE!!
TMP
!!

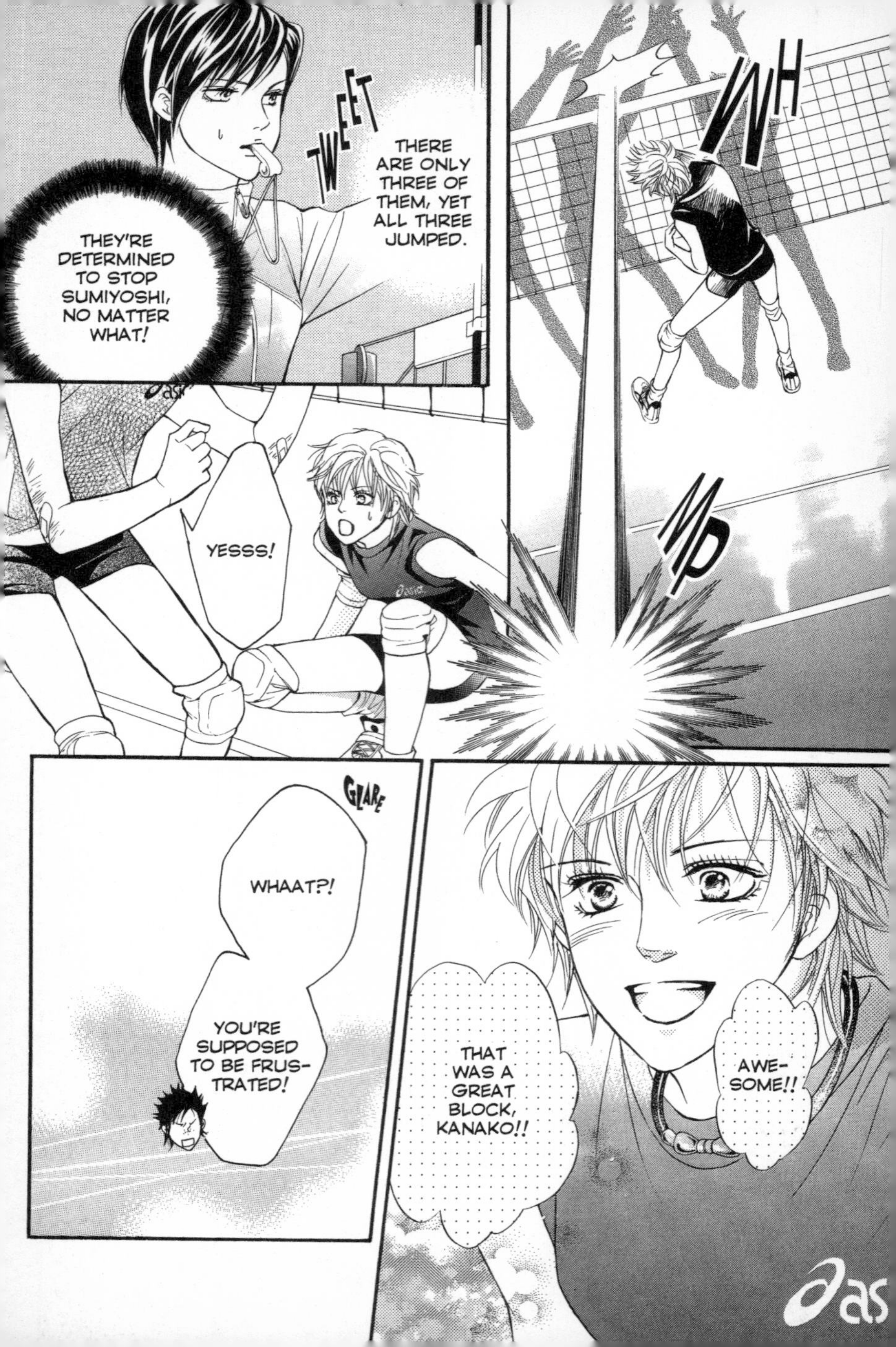

WH
MP
TWEET
THERE ARE ONLY THREE OF THEM, YET ALL THREE JUMPED.
THEY'RE DETERMINED TO STOP SUMIYOSHI, NO MATTER WHAT!
YESSS!
AWE-SOME!!
THAT WAS A GREAT BLOCK, KANAKO!!
GLARE
WHAAT?!
YOU'RE SUPPOSED TO BE FRUS-TRATED!

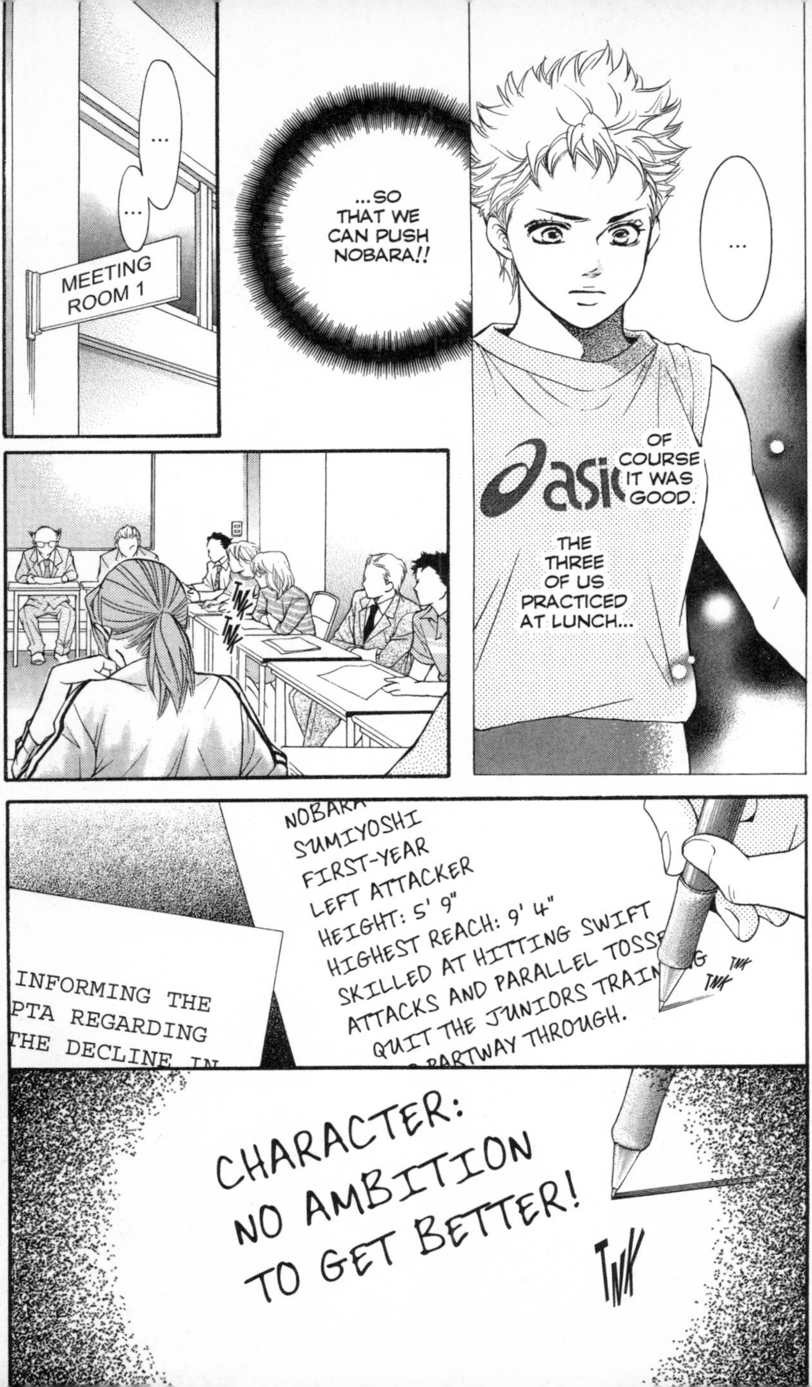
...
OF COURSE IT WAS GOOD.
THE THREE OF US PRACTICED AT LUNCH...
...SO THAT WE CAN PUSH NOBARA!!
...
...
MEETING ROOM 1
TNK
TNK
NOBARA SUMIYOSHI
FIRST-YEAR
LEFT ATTACKER
HEIGHT: 5' 9"
HIGHEST REACH: 9' 4"
SKILLED AT HITTING SWIFT ATTACKS AND PARALLEL TOSSES
QUIT THE JUNIORS TRAINING PARTWAY THROUGH.
TNK
TNK
INFORMING THE PTA REGARDING THE DECLINE IN
CHARACTER: NO AMBITION TO GET BETTER!
TNK

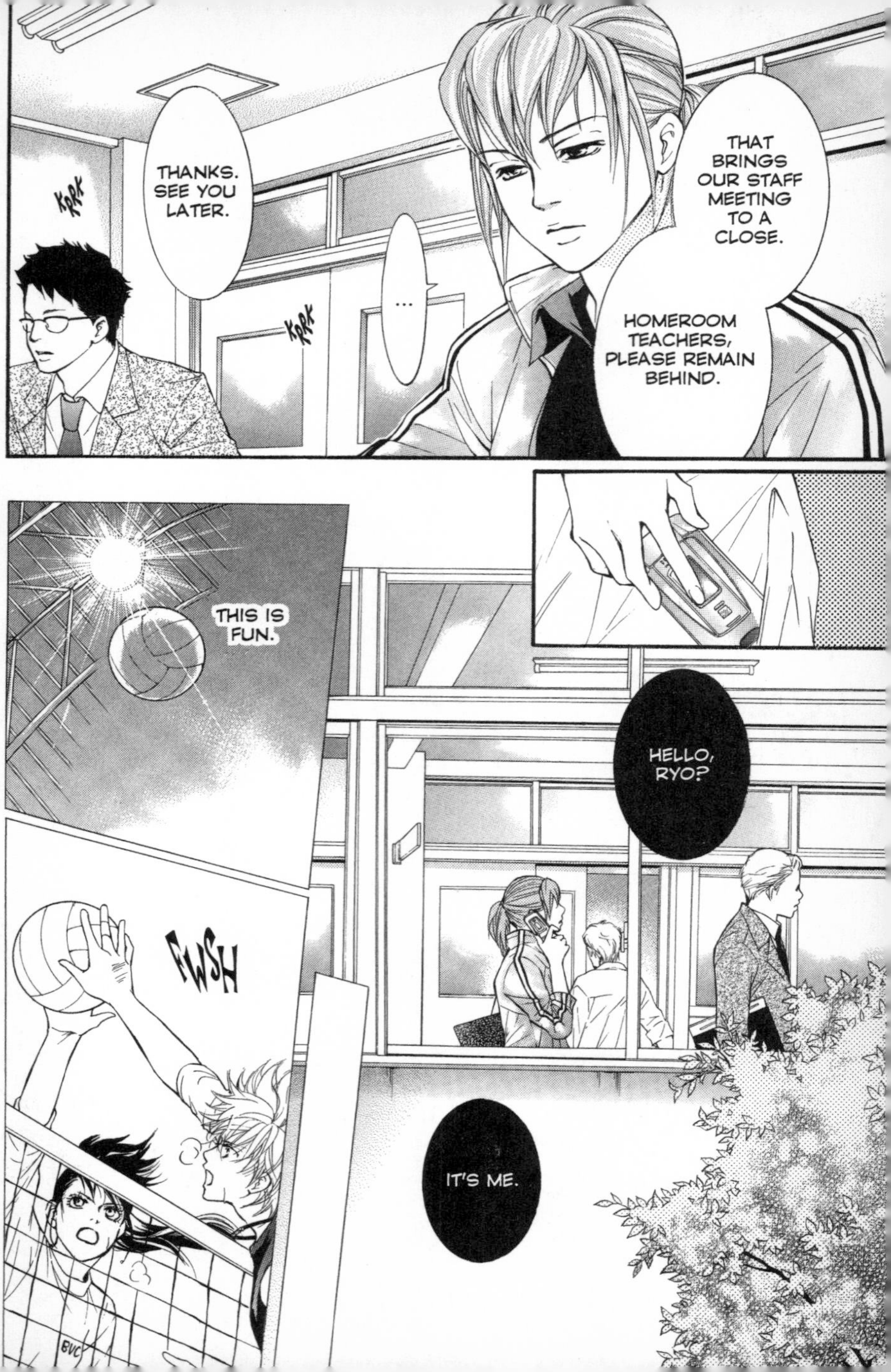
THAT BRINGS OUR STAFF MEETING TO A CLOSE.
HOMEROOM TEACHERS, PLEASE REMAIN BEHIND.
KRRK
...
THANKS. SEE YOU LATER.
KRRK
HELLO, RYO?
IT'S ME.
THIS IS FUN.
FWSH

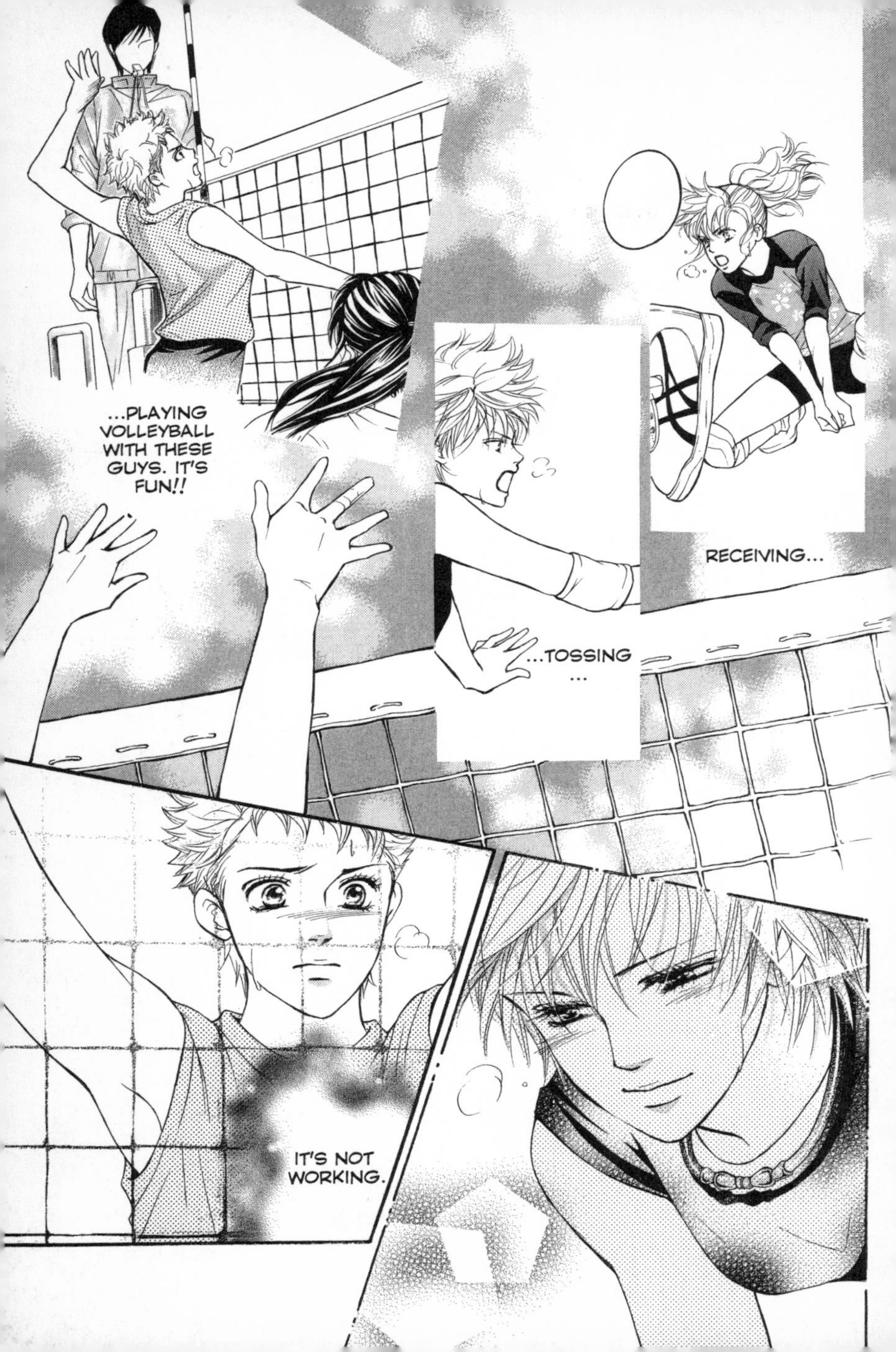
RECEIVING...
...TOSSING ...
...PLAYING VOLLEYBALL WITH THESE GUYS. IT'S FUN!!
IT'S NOT WORKING.

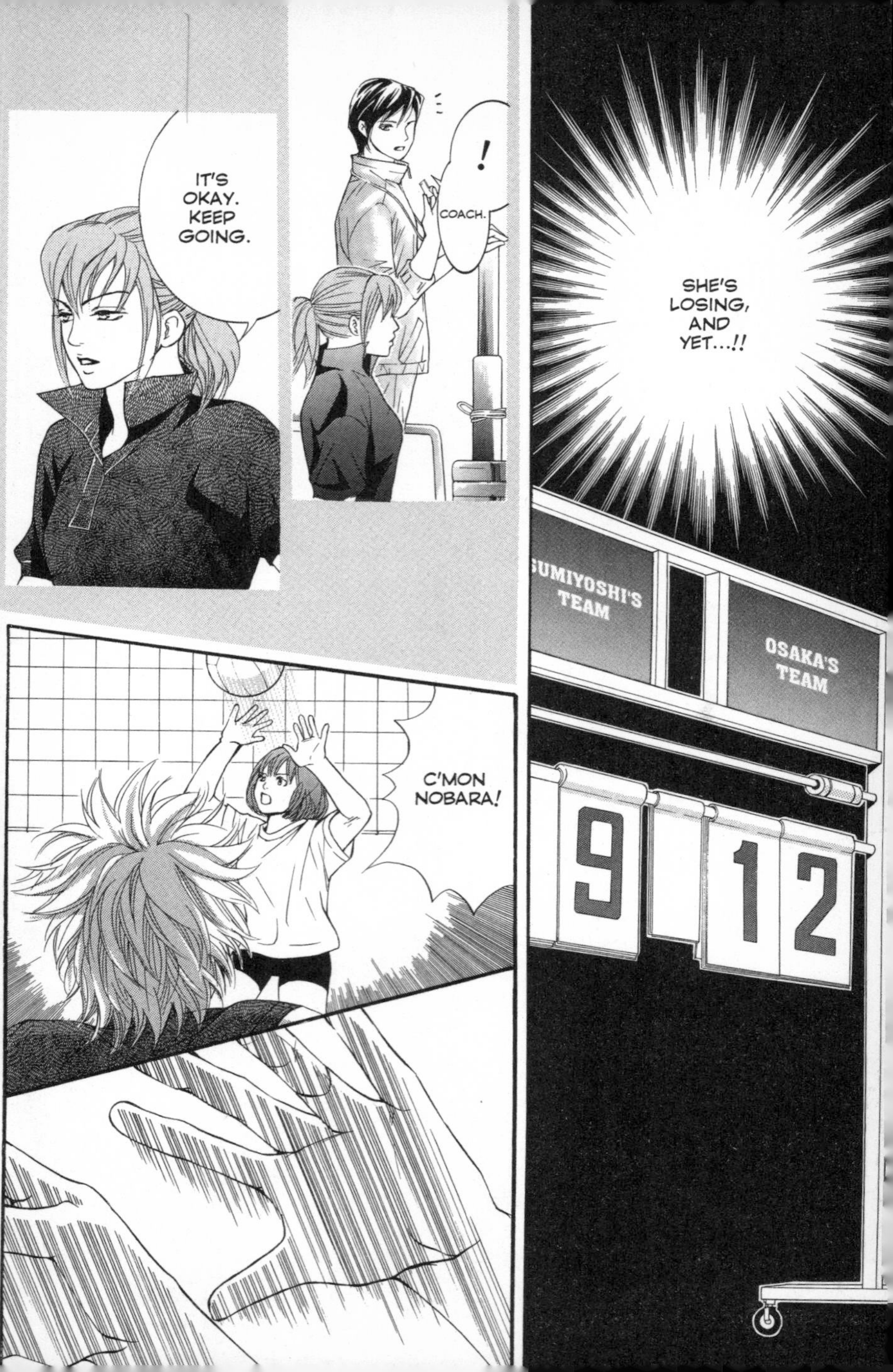
SHE'S LOSING, AND YET...!!
SUMIYOSHI'S TEAM
OSAKA'S TEAM
9
12
!
COACH.
IT'S OKAY. KEEP GOING.
C'MON NOBARA!

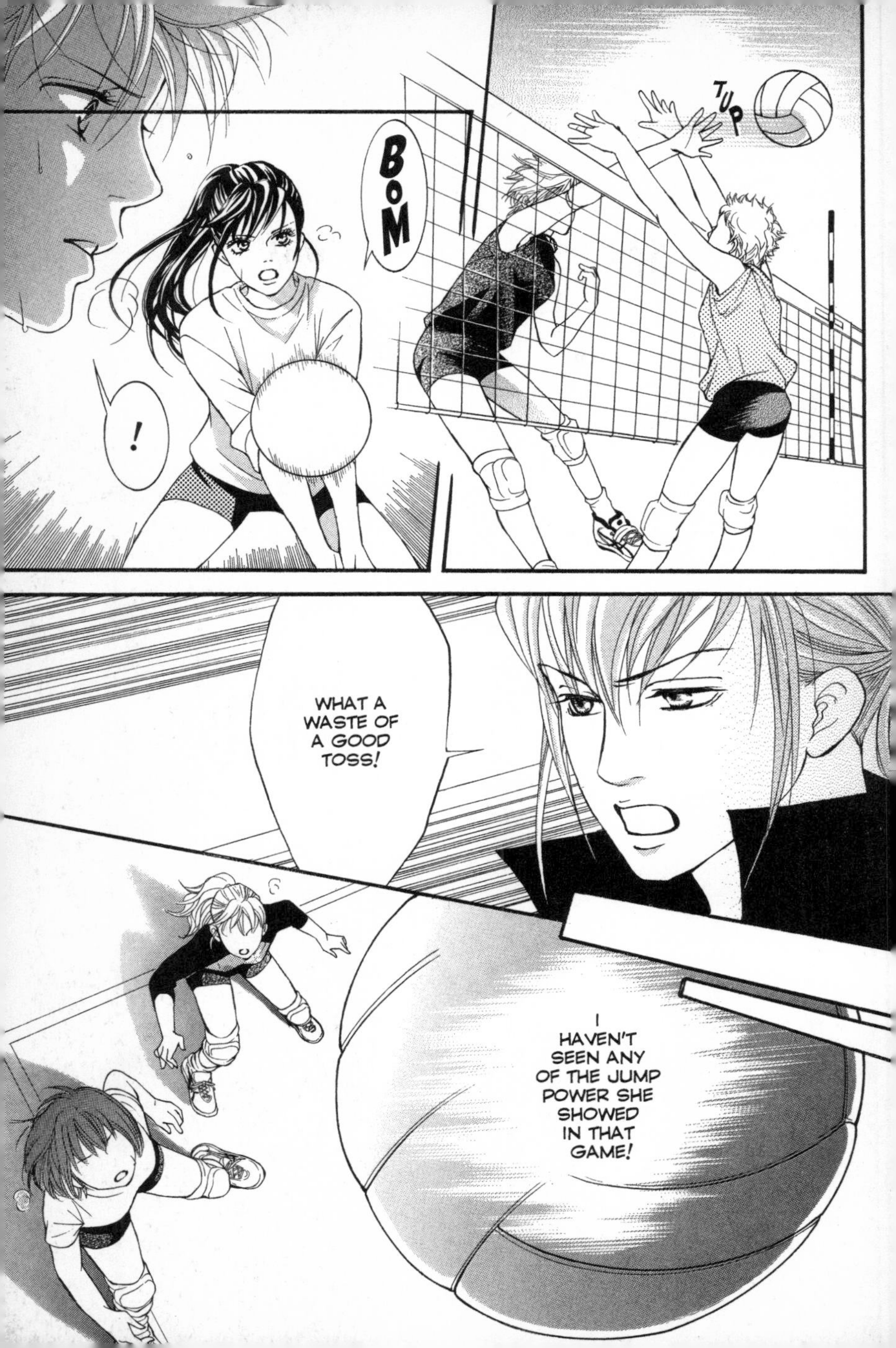
TUP
BOM
!
WHAT A WASTE OF A GOOD TOSS!
I HAVEN'T SEEN ANY OF THE JUMP POWER SHE SHOWED IN THAT GAME!

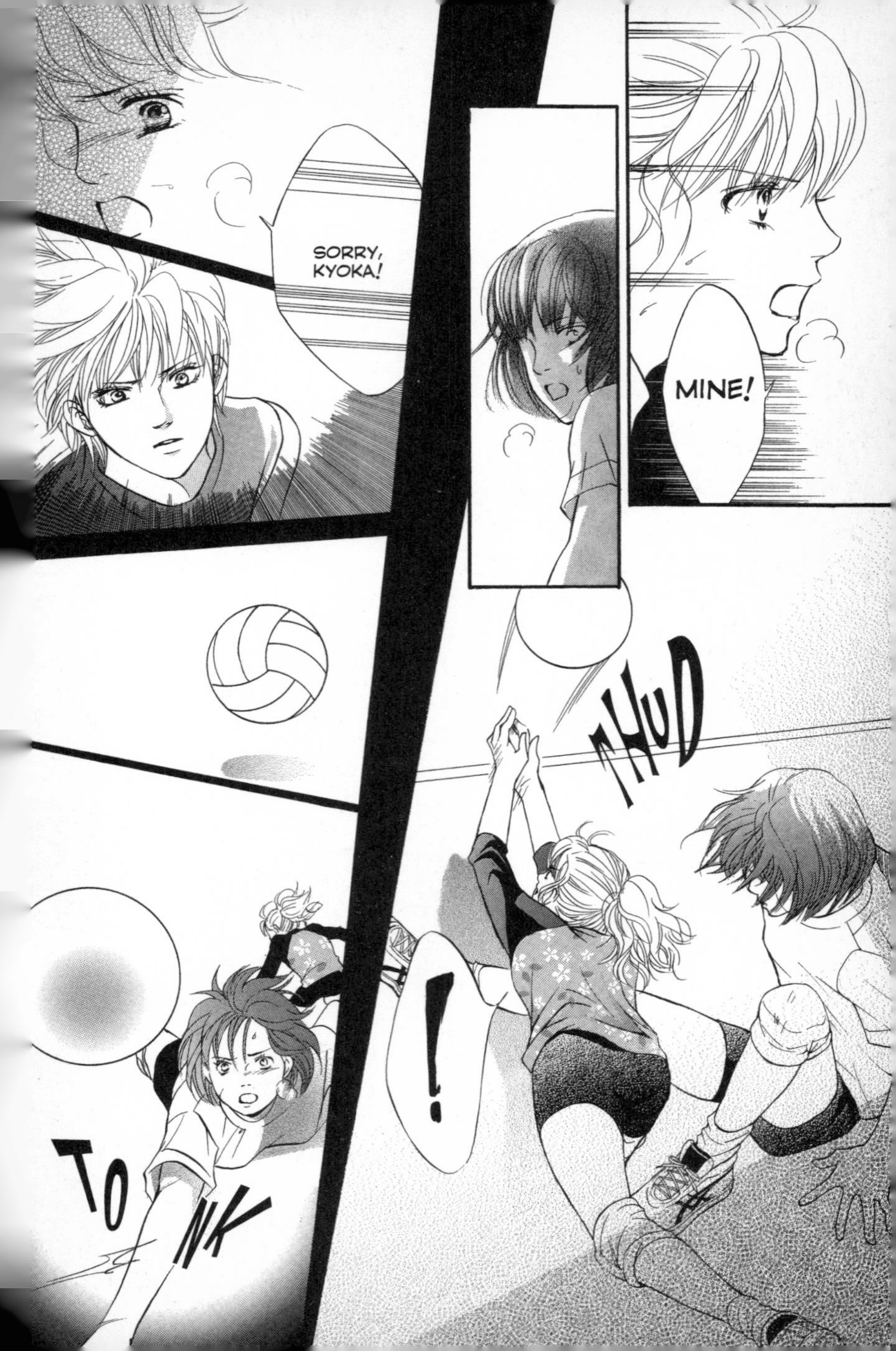
MINE!
SORRY, KYOKA!
THUD
!
TONK

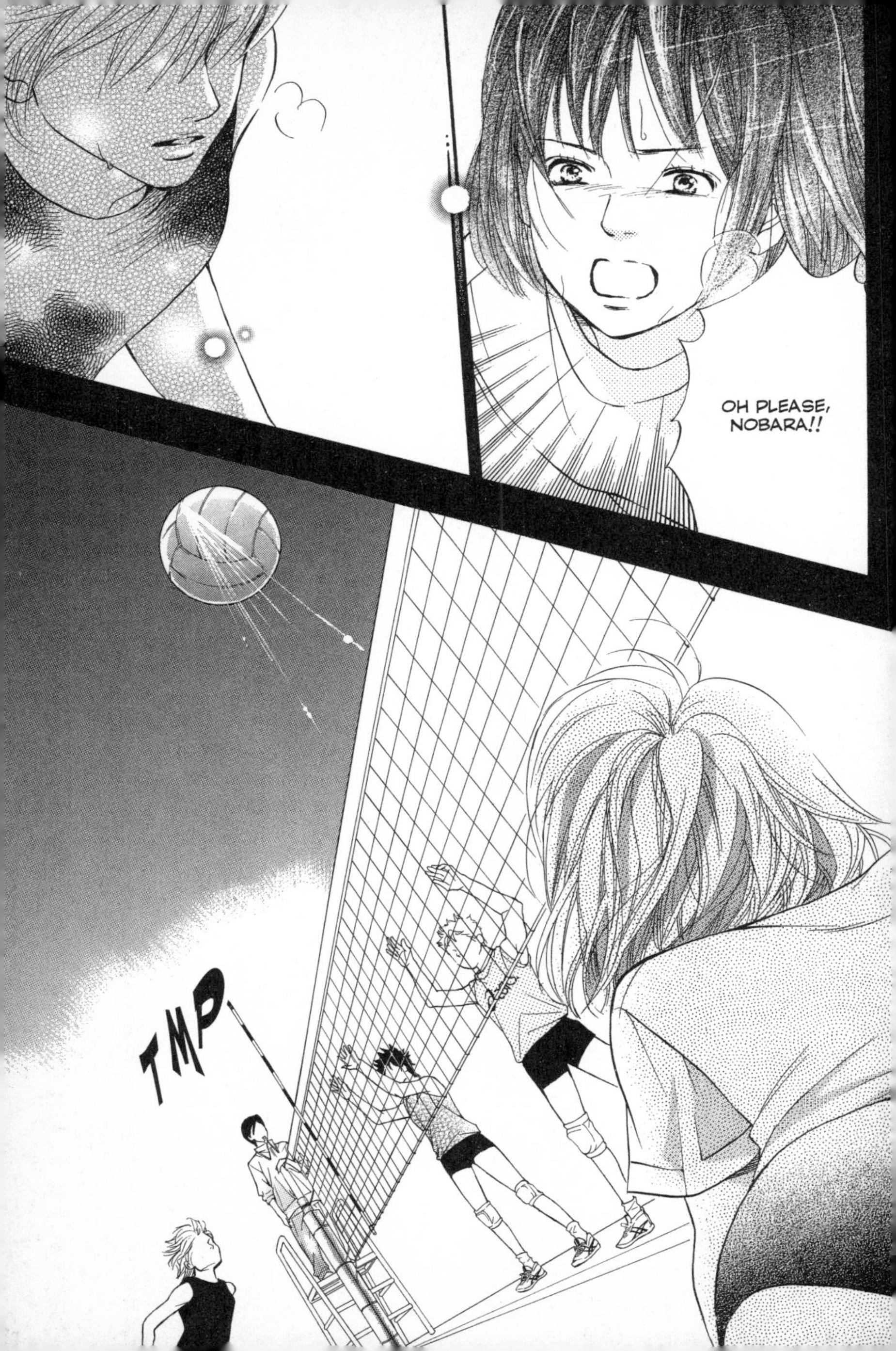
OH PLEASE, NOBARA!!
TMP

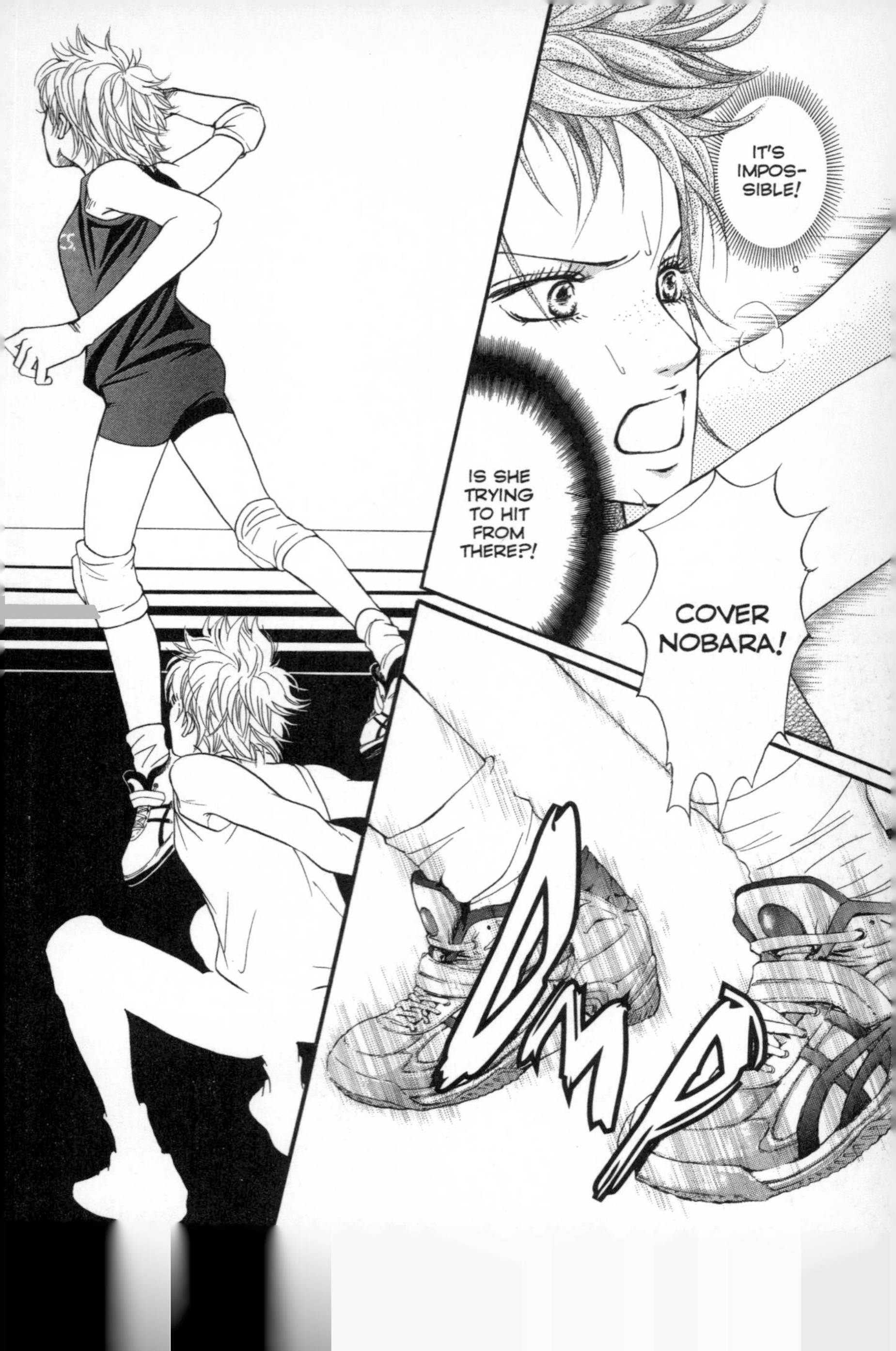
IT'S IMPOS-SIBLE!
IS SHE TRYING TO HIT FROM THERE?!
COVER NOBARA!
DMP

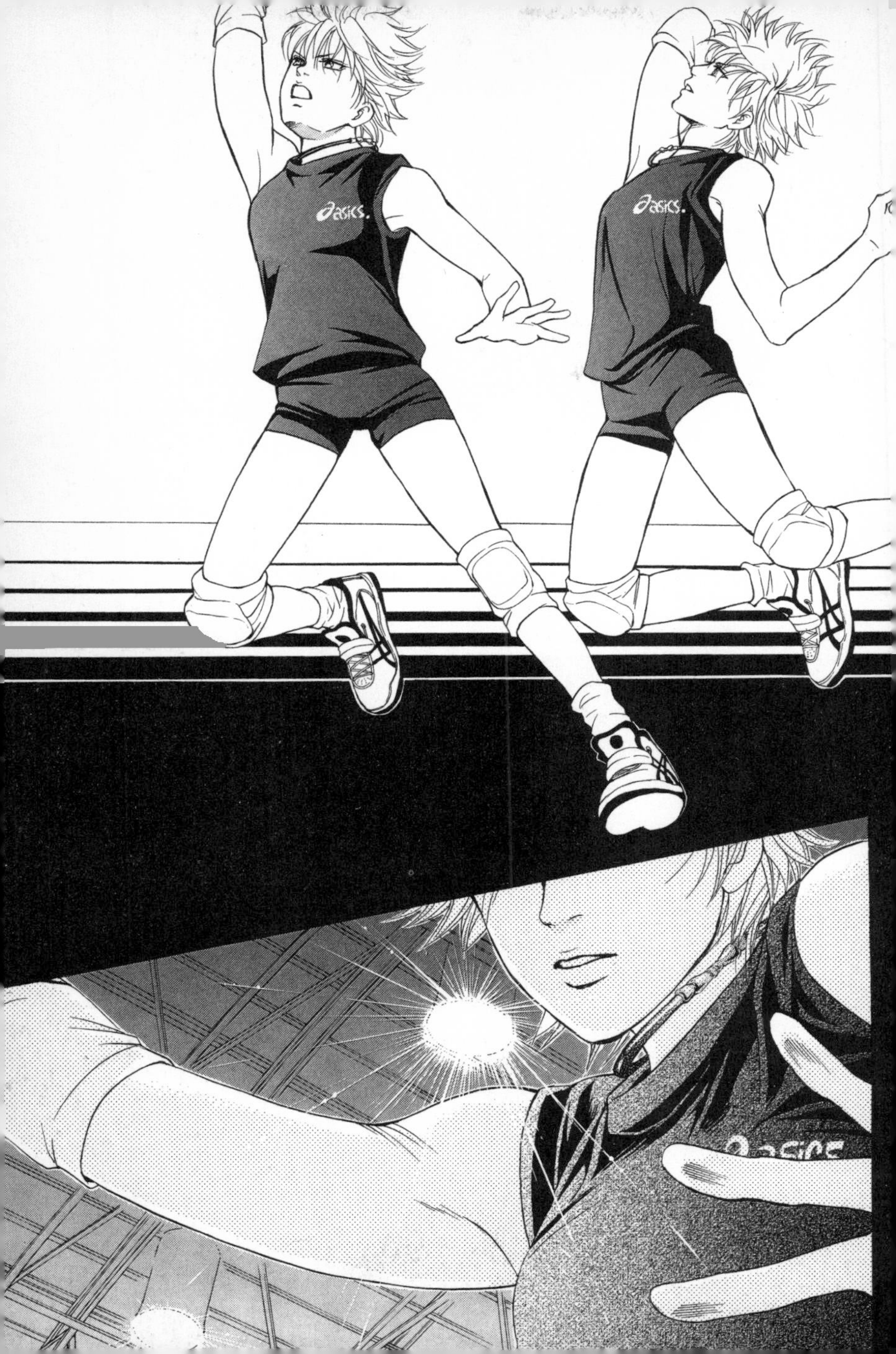
asics.
asics.
asics

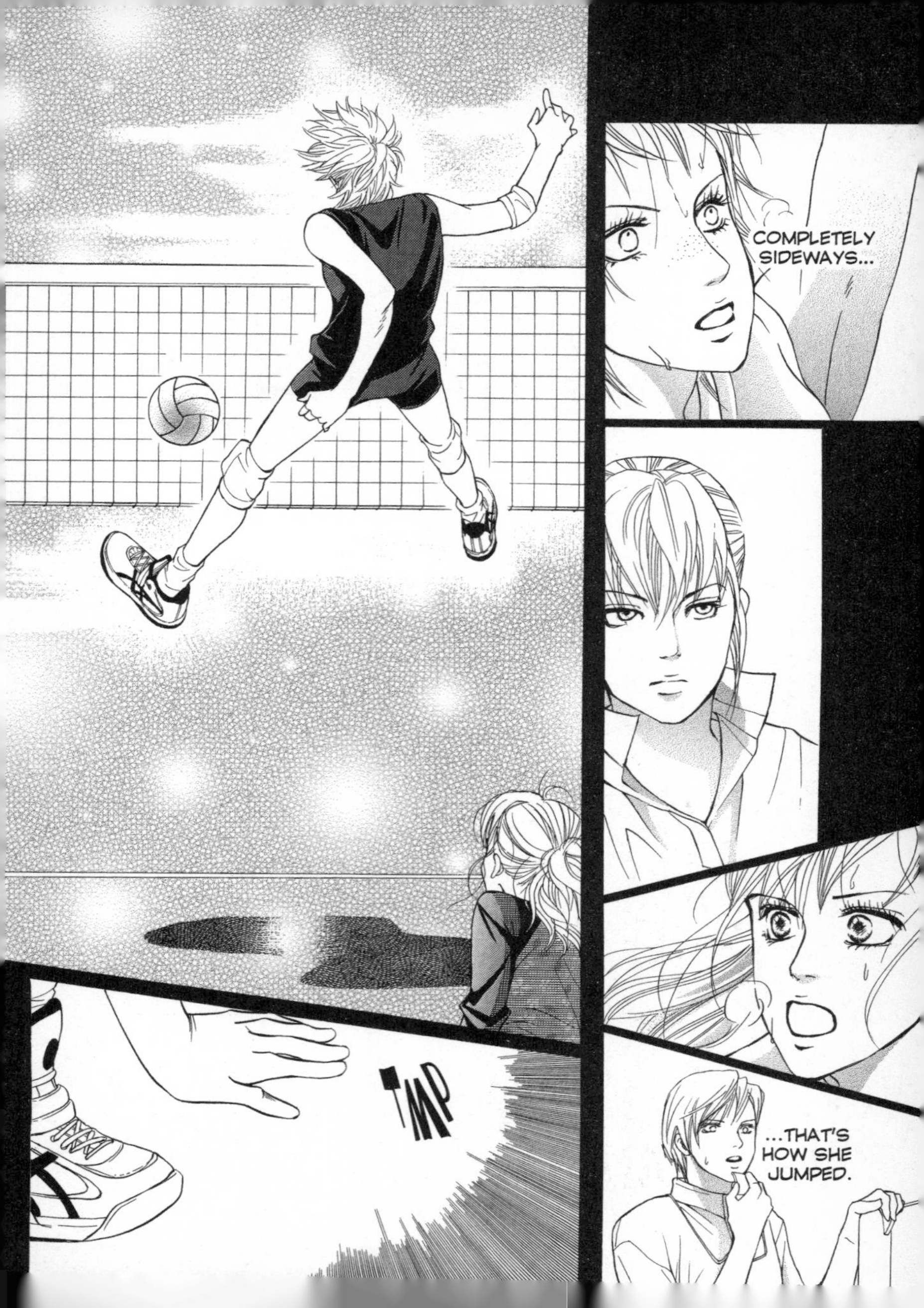
COMPLETELY SIDEWAYS...
...THAT'S HOW SHE JUMPED.
TMP

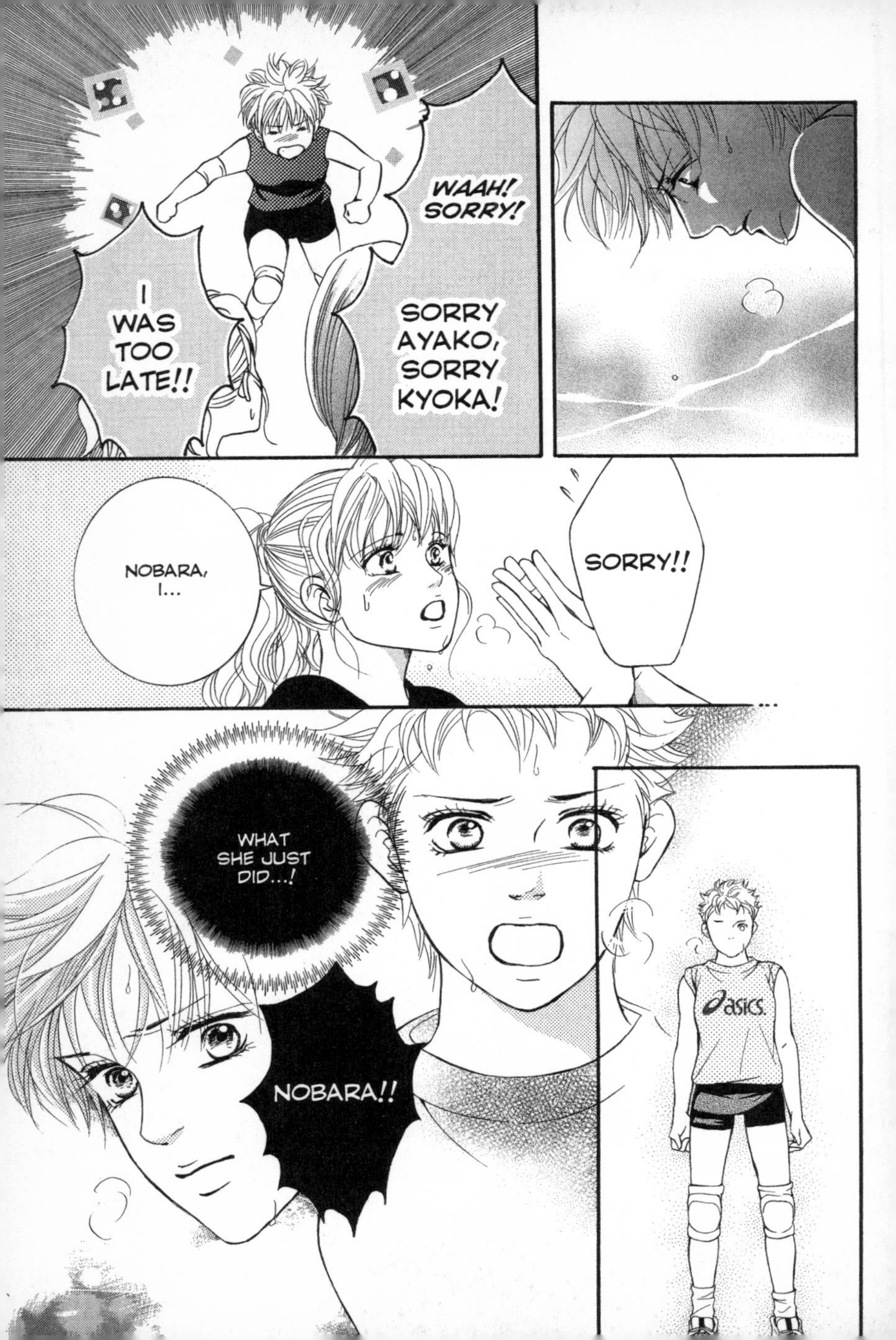
WAAH! SORRY!
SORRY AYAKO, SORRY KYOKA!
I WAS TOO LATE!!
SORRY!!
NOBARA, I...
WHAT SHE JUST DID...!
NOBARA!!

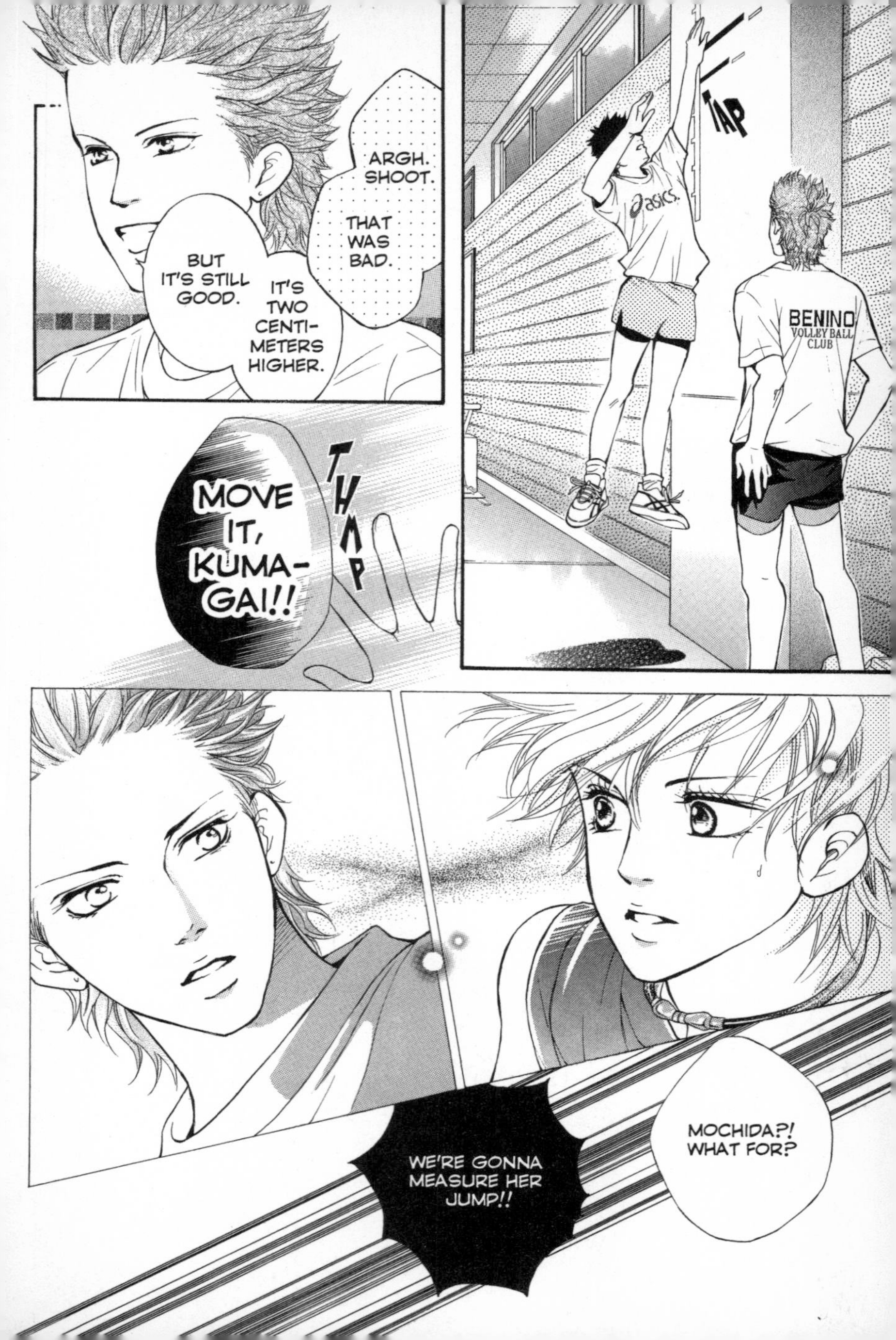
TAP
BENINO
VOLLEY BALL
CLUB
ARGH. SHOOT.
THAT WAS BAD.
IT'S TWO CENTI- METERS HIGHER.
BUT IT'S STILL GOOD.
THUMP
MOVE IT, KUMA- GAI!!
MOCHIDA?! WHAT FOR?
WE'RE GONNA MEASURE HER JUMP!!

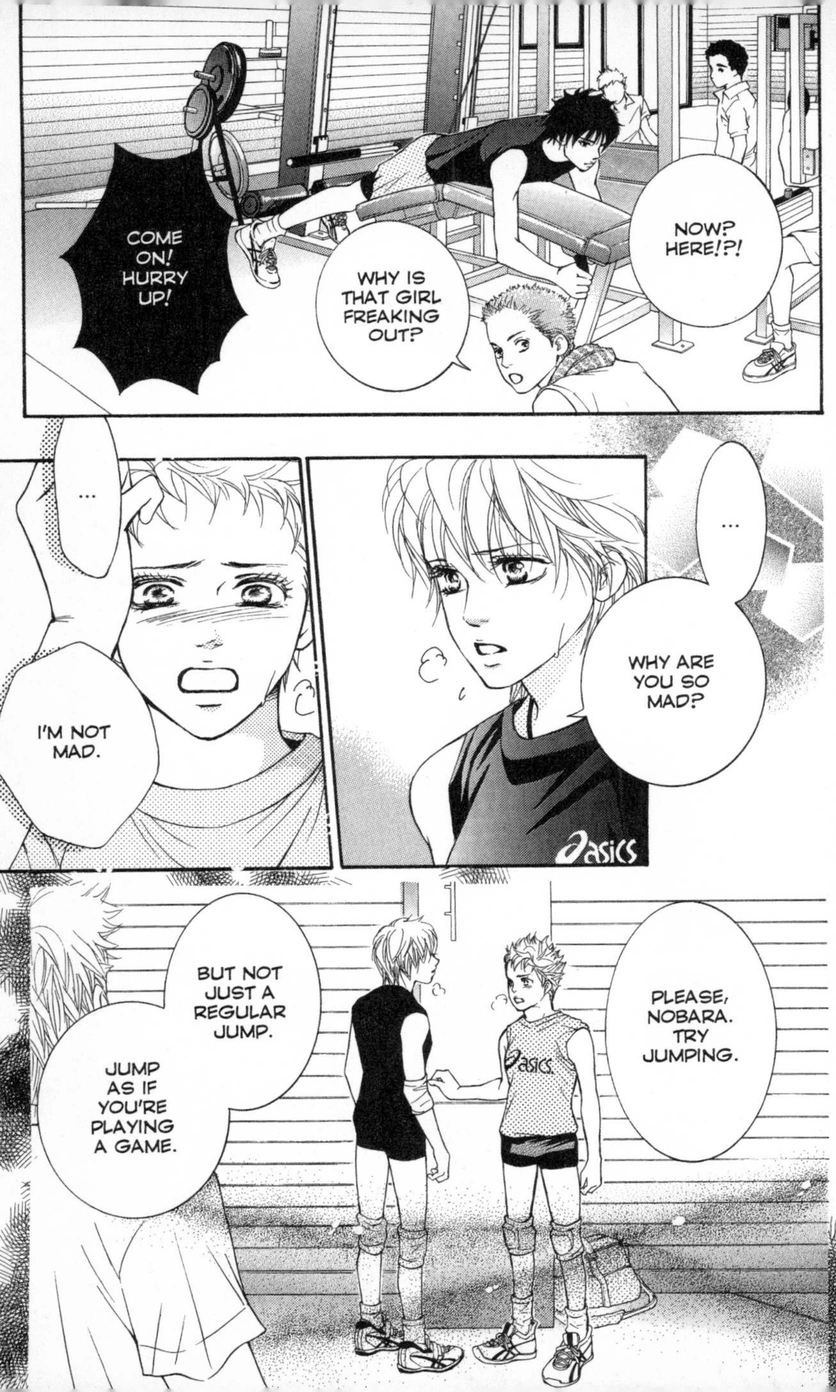
NOW? HERE!?!
WHY IS THAT GIRL FREAKING OUT?
COME ON! HURRY UP!
...
WHY ARE YOU SO MAD?
...
I'M NOT MAD.
PLEASE, NOBARA. TRY JUMPING.
BUT NOT JUST A REGULAR JUMP.
JUMP AS IF YOU'RE PLAYING A GAME.

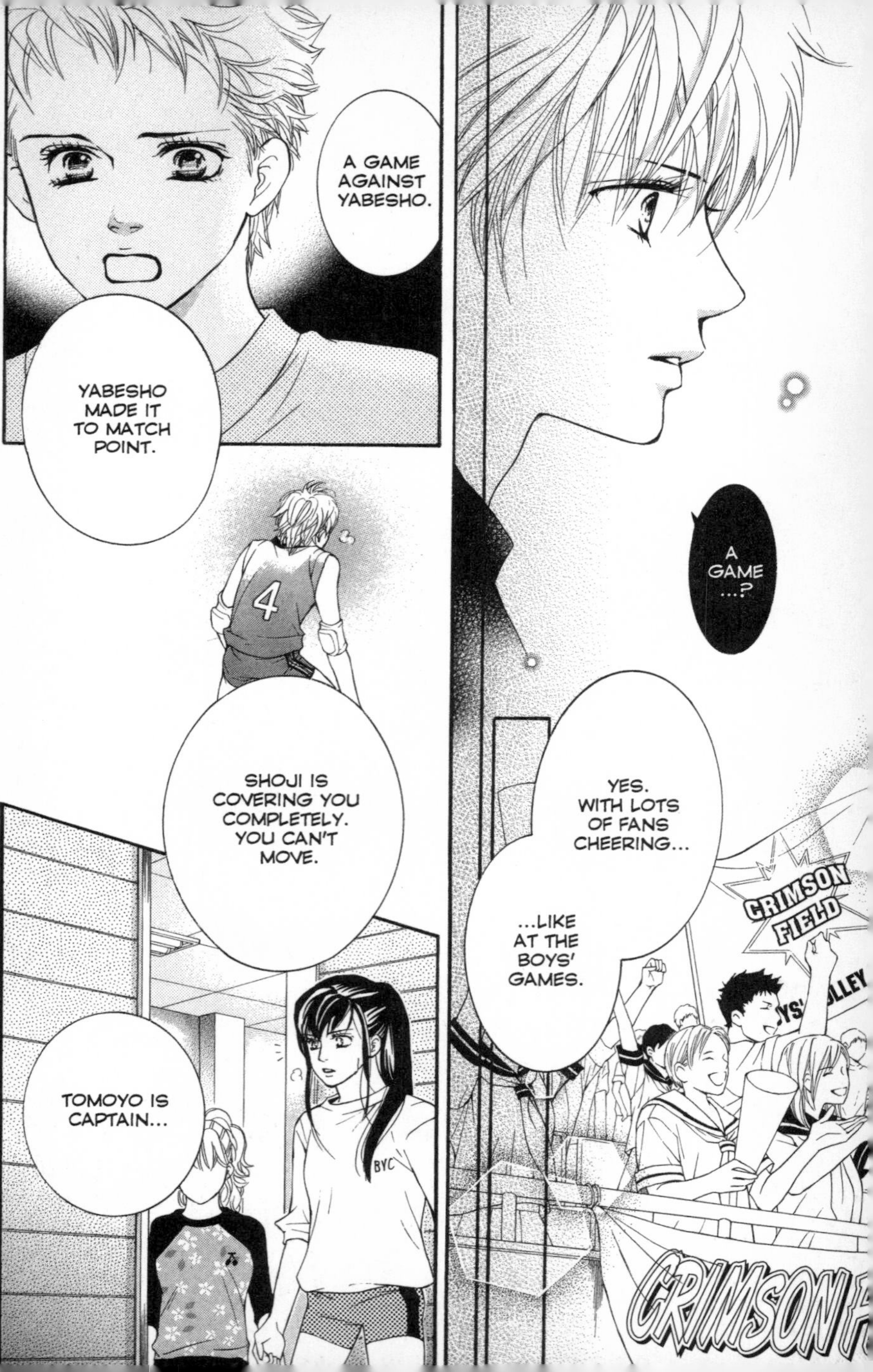
A GAME ...?
YES. WITH LOTS OF FANS CHEERING...
...LIKE AT THE BOYS' GAMES.
CRIMSON FIELD
A GAME AGAINST YABESHO.
YABESHO MADE IT TO MATCH POINT.
SHOJI IS COVERING YOU COMPLETELY. YOU CAN'T MOVE.
TOMOYO IS CAPTAIN...

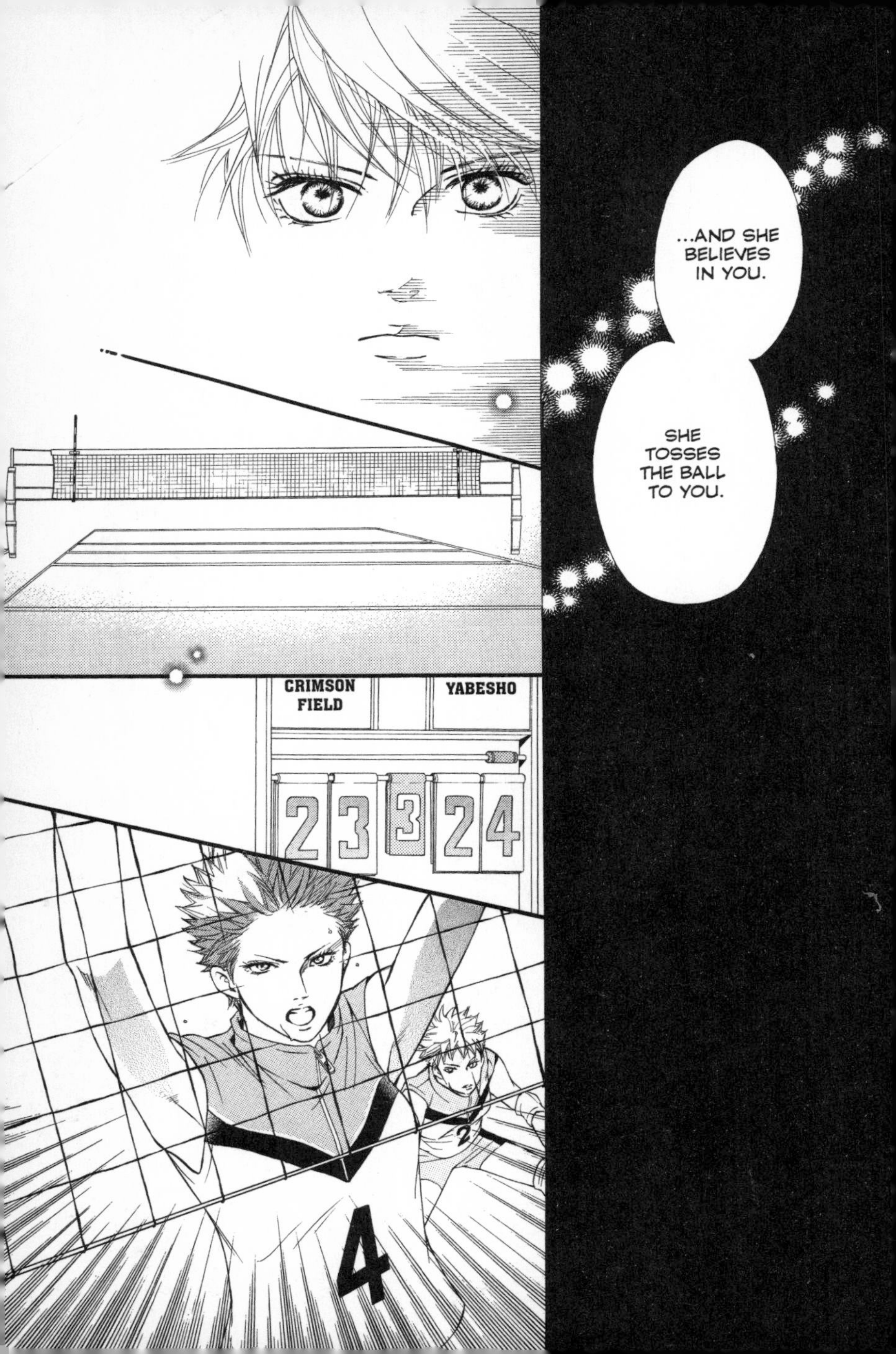
...AND SHE BELIEVES IN YOU.
SHE TOSSES THE BALL TO YOU.
CRIMSON FIELD
YABESHO
23 3 24
4

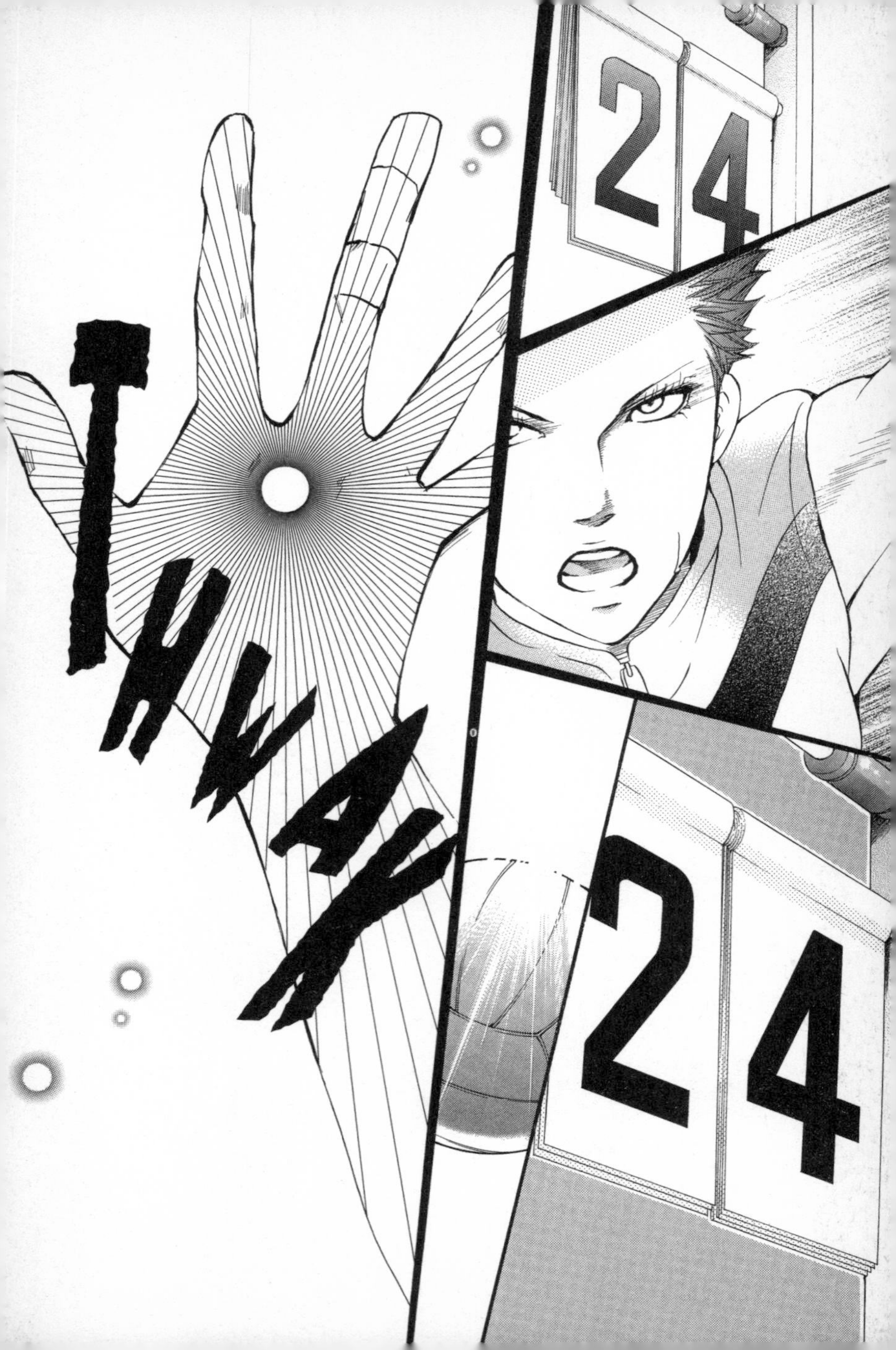

24
THWAK
24

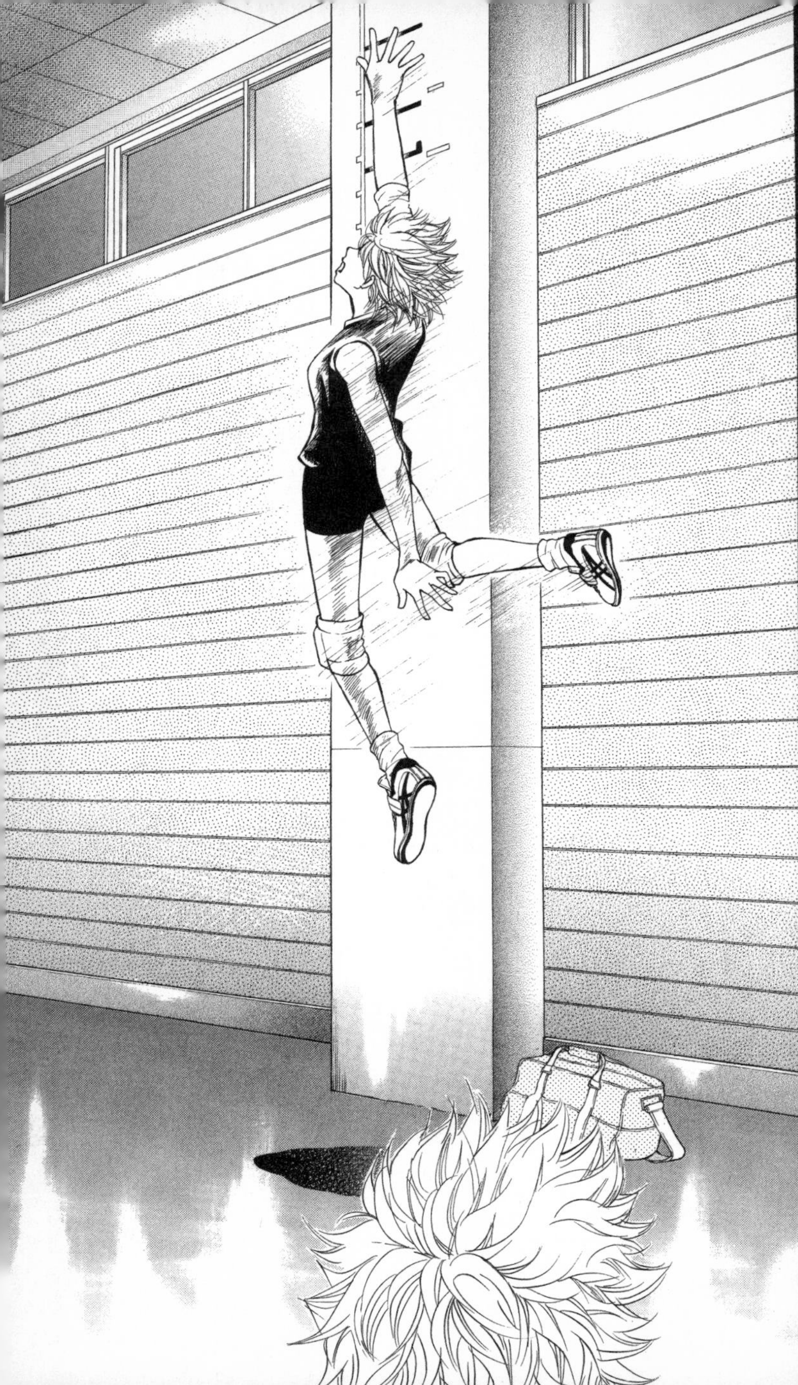

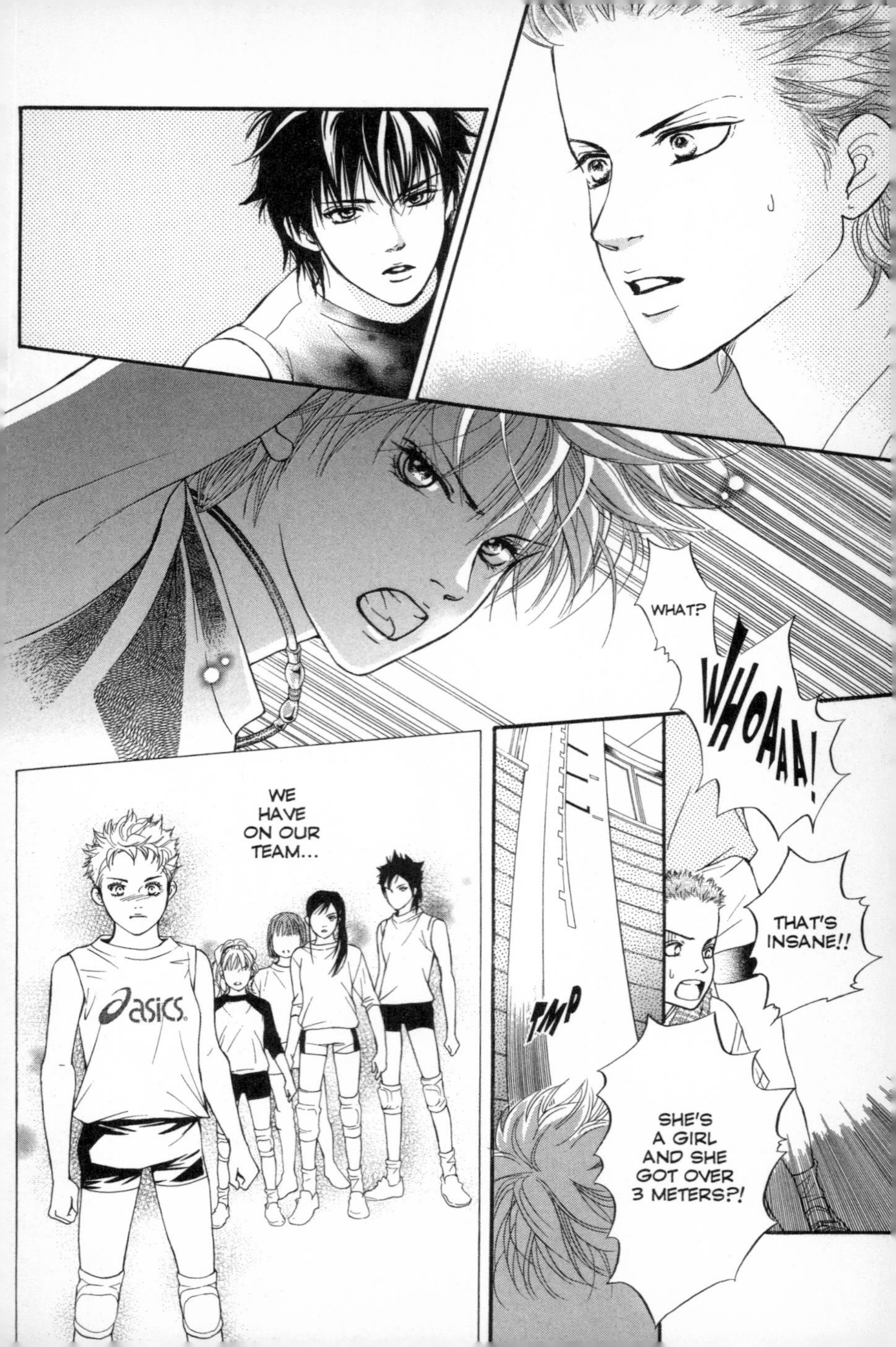
WHAT?
WHOAAA!
THAT'S INSANE!!
TMP
SHE'S A GIRL AND SHE GOT OVER 3 METERS?!
WE HAVE ON OUR TEAM...

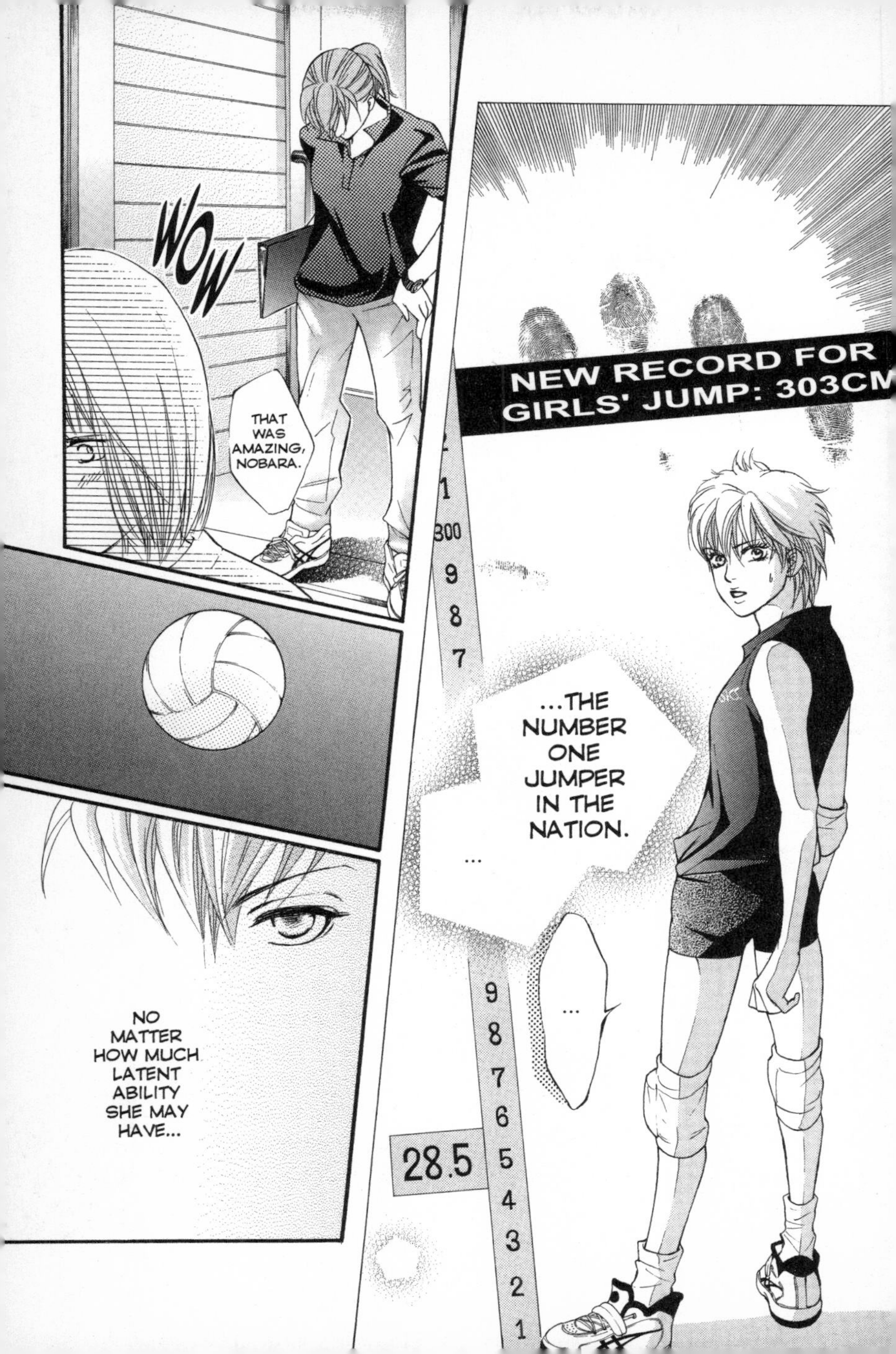
NEW RECORD FOR GIRLS' JUMP: 303CM
1
300
9
8
7
...THE NUMBER ONE JUMPER IN THE NATION.
...
...
9
8
7
6
5
4
3
2
1
28.5
WOW
THAT WAS AMAZING, NOBARA.
NO MATTER HOW MUCH LATENT ABILITY SHE MAY HAVE...

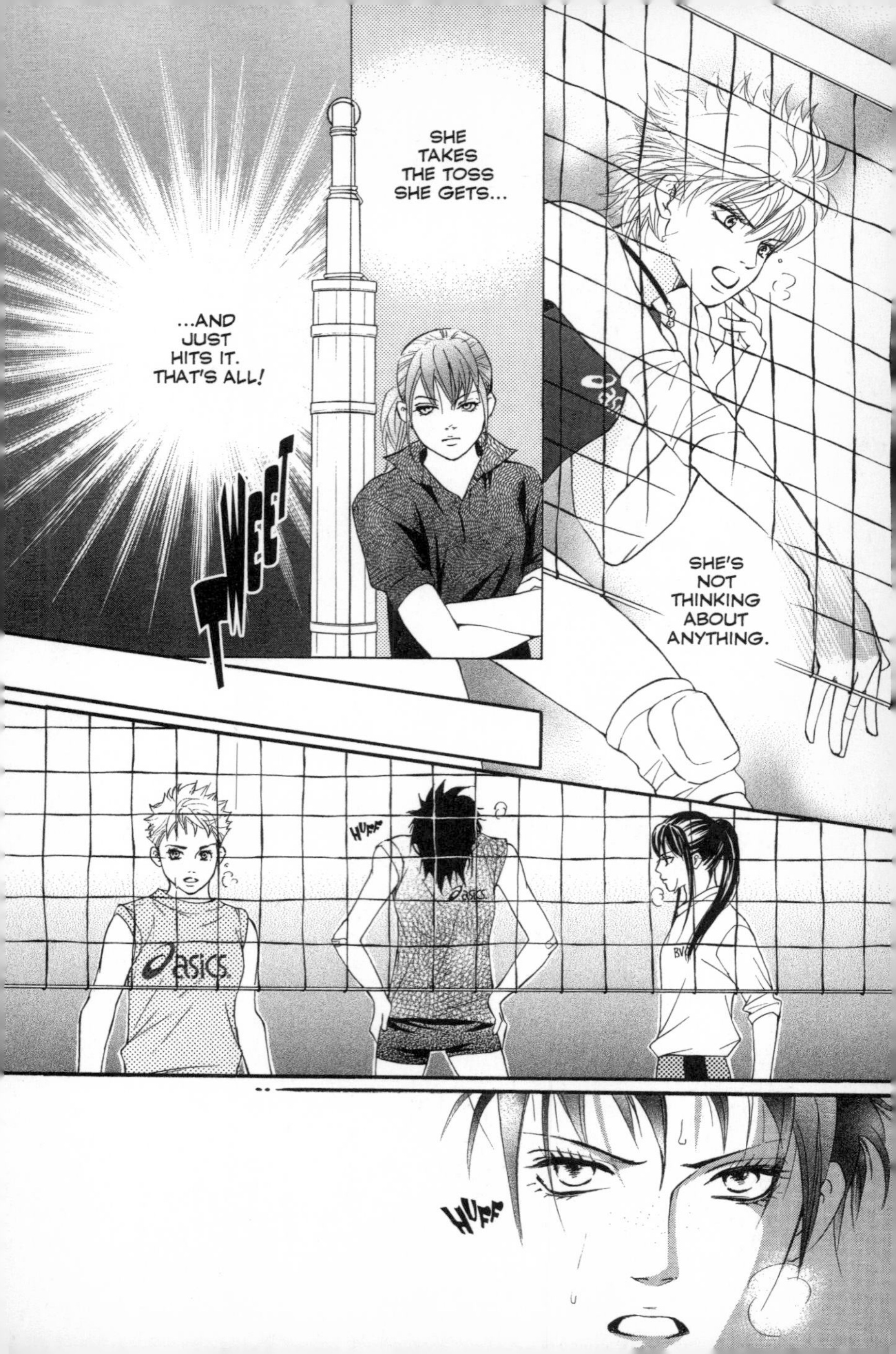
SHE'S NOT THINKING ABOUT ANYTHING.
SHE TAKES THE TOSS SHE GETS...
...AND JUST HITS IT. THAT'S ALL!
TWEET
HUFF
HUFF

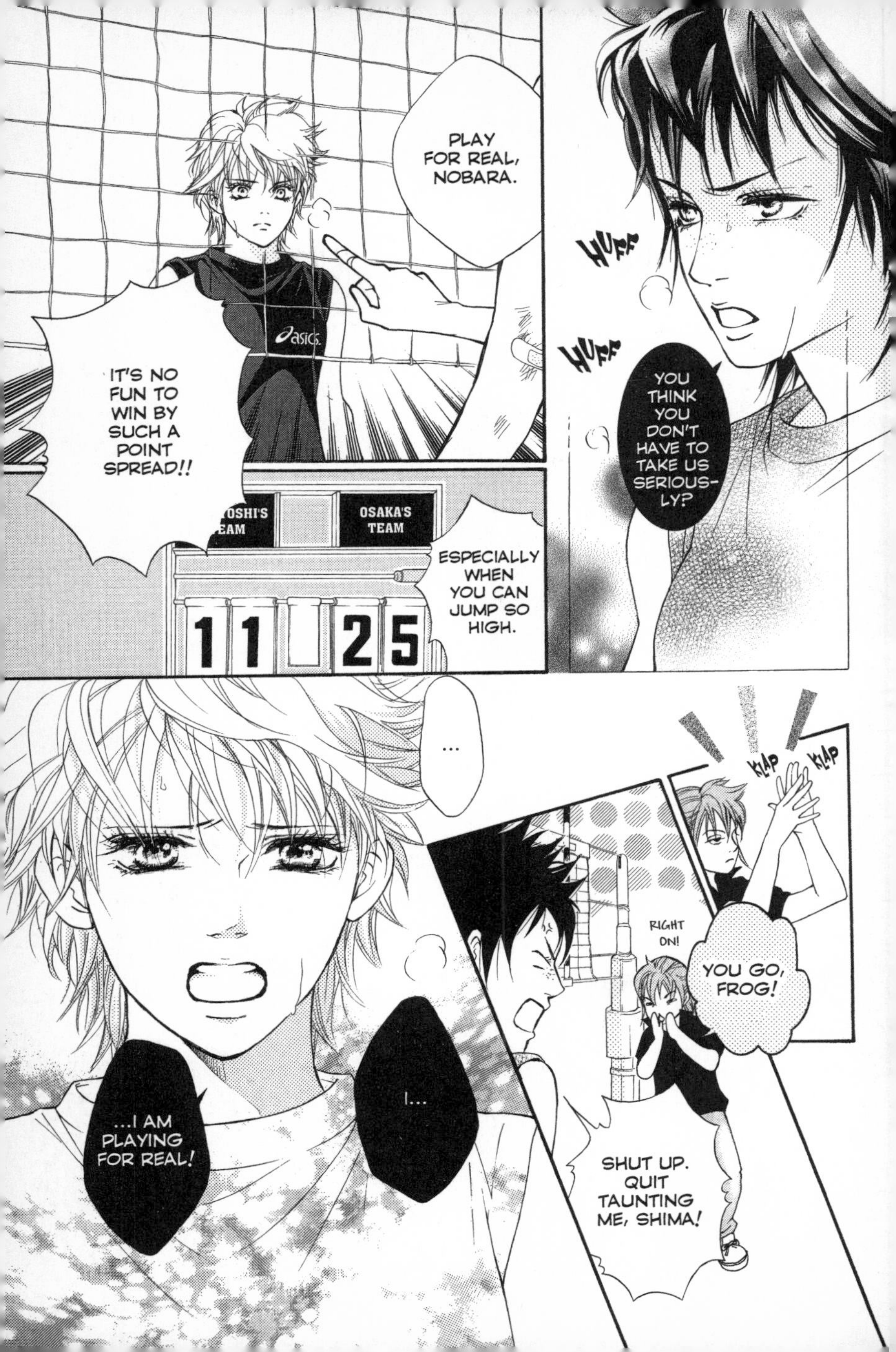
HUFF
HUFF
YOU THINK YOU DON'T HAVE TO TAKE US SERIOUSLY?
PLAY FOR REAL, NOBARA.
IT'S NO FUN TO WIN BY SUCH A POINT SPREAD!!
OSAKA'S TEAM
11 25
ESPECIALLY WHEN YOU CAN JUMP SO HIGH.
KLAP KLAP
YOU GO, FROG!
RIGHT ON!
SHUT UP. QUIT TAUNTING ME, SHIMA!
...
I...
...I AM PLAYING FOR REAL!

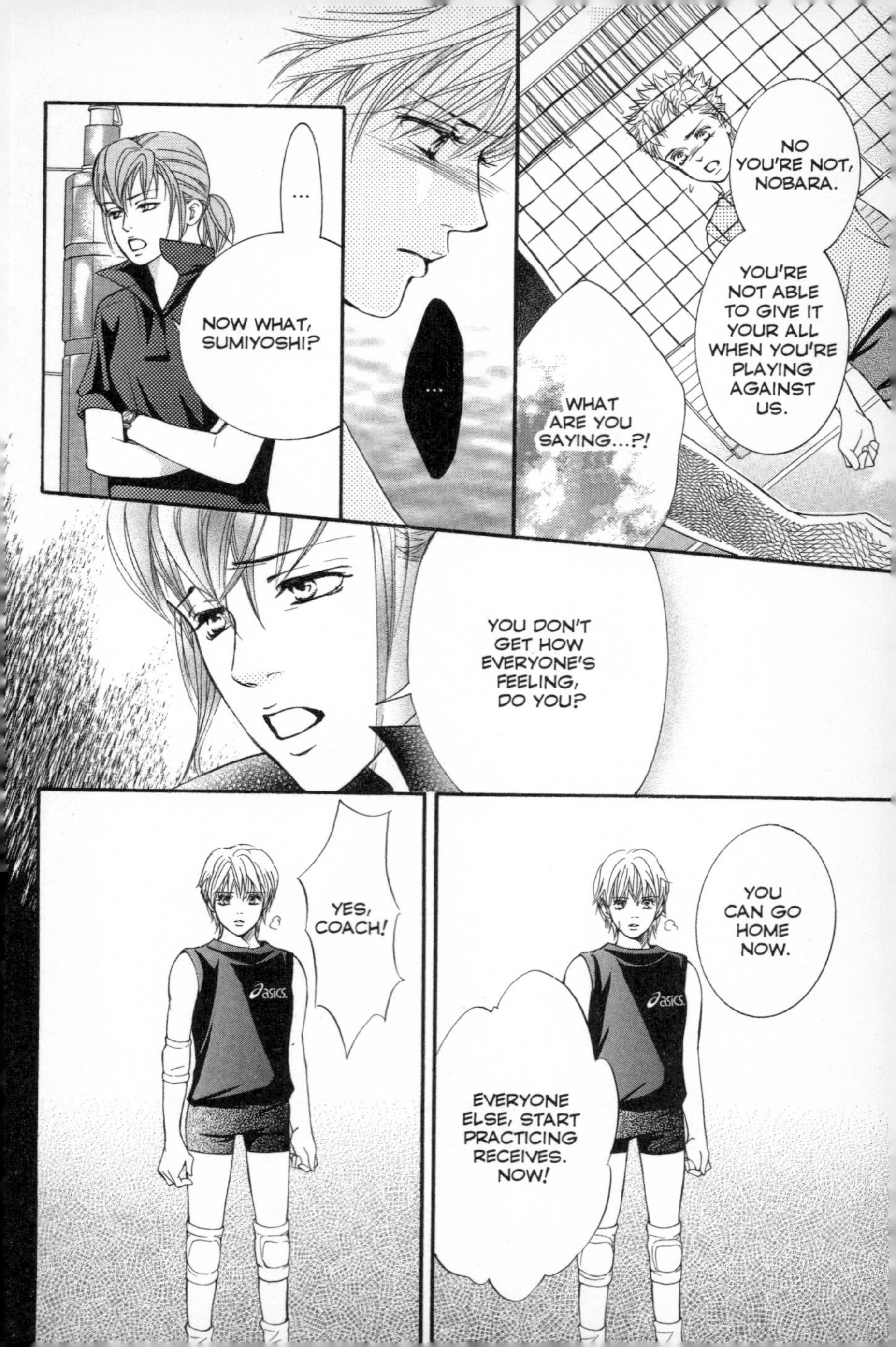
NO YOU'RE NOT, NOBARA.
YOU'RE NOT ABLE TO GIVE IT YOUR ALL WHEN YOU'RE PLAYING AGAINST US.
WHAT ARE YOU SAYING...?!
...
...
NOW WHAT, SUMIYOSHI?
YOU DON'T GET HOW EVERYONE'S FEELING, DO YOU?
YOU CAN GO HOME NOW.
EVERYONE ELSE, START PRACTICING RECEIVES. NOW!
YES, COACH!

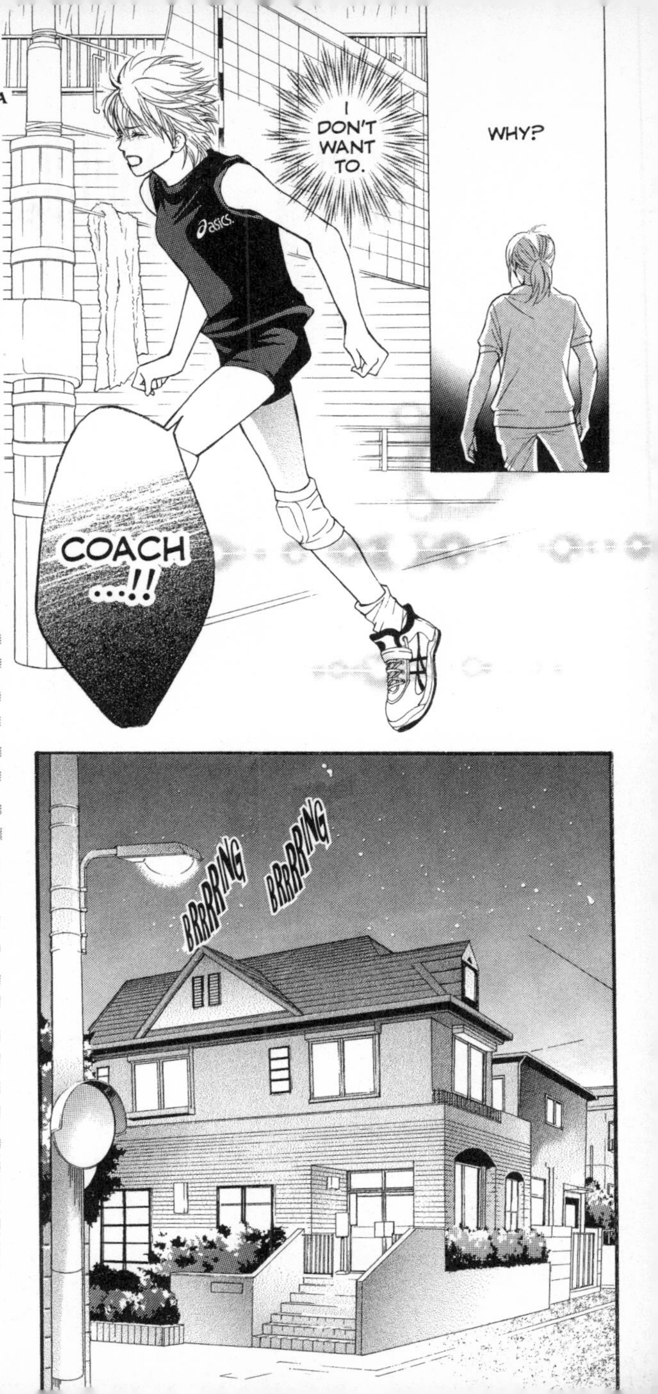
WHY?
I DON'T WANT TO.
COACH ...!!
BRRRRING
BRRRRING

MITSUBA CLUB

Vol.4

ABOUT TWO MONTHS AGO, ONE OF MY STAFF MEMBERS LEFT THE COMPANY TO WORK ON HER OWN MANGA. SHE HAD ASSISTED ME FOR FOUR YEARS, SINCE THE TIME I WAS WORKING ON *AKUMA DE SOUROU*. SHE WAS A GREAT PERSON--HER PRESENCE ALONE COULD EASE A TENSE WORK ENVIRONMENT. THAT'S THE KIND OF PERSON SHE WAS.

WE'VE GONE THROUGH HELL AND HIGH WATER TOGETHER. I WOULDN'T TELL HER THIS DIRECTLY (AW, TELL HER!) BUT SHE WAS AN IMPORTANT PRESENCE IN MY LIFE, LIKE FAMILY. I STILL THINK SO. I WAS AFRAID BOTH SHE AND I WOULD BREAK DOWN IN TEARS IF WE SAID OUR REAL FEELINGS, SO WE HAD A LIGHTHEARTED FAREWELL PARTY. "FAREWELL PARTY"! (I'M SOUNDING MORE AND MORE LIKE A STUDENT AT GRADUATION. DARN IT!)

I'D BEEN SO BUSY THAT I HADN'T VISITED HER APARTMENT IN A WHILE. I FINALLY DID, AND ON THE WAY BACK AT THE TRAIN STATION I KEPT TURNING AND LOOKING AT HER. SHE KEPT SMILING AND WAVING HER HAND THE WHOLE TIME. AS I WAS THINKING, "IT'S COLD SO HURRY UP AND GO HOME," I BECAME QUITE SAD FOR REAL. AND FROM THE BOTTOM OF MY HEART, I REGRETTED THE FACT THAT ON HER LAST DAY OF WORK, THE OFFICE WAS A HELLISH SCENE OF CARNAGE. SORRY. IT WAS YOUR LAST DAY! WE WATCHED SOME K-1 AFTER-WARDS, THOUGH.

SHE IS NOW BACK AT HER FAMILY HOME, WORKING ON HER OWN MANGA.

I AM CONFIDENT THAT SOMEDAY MANY PEOPLE WILL SEE YOUR WORK IN THE PAGES OF A MAGAZINE.

TAKE GOOD CARE OF YOUR HEALTH. I'LL ALWAYS BE ROOTING FOR YOU. AND THANK YOU FOR ALL THOSE YEARS. I WAS HAPPY TO GET TO WORK WITH YOU. I LOVE YOU LOTS.

THERE, I SAID IT!

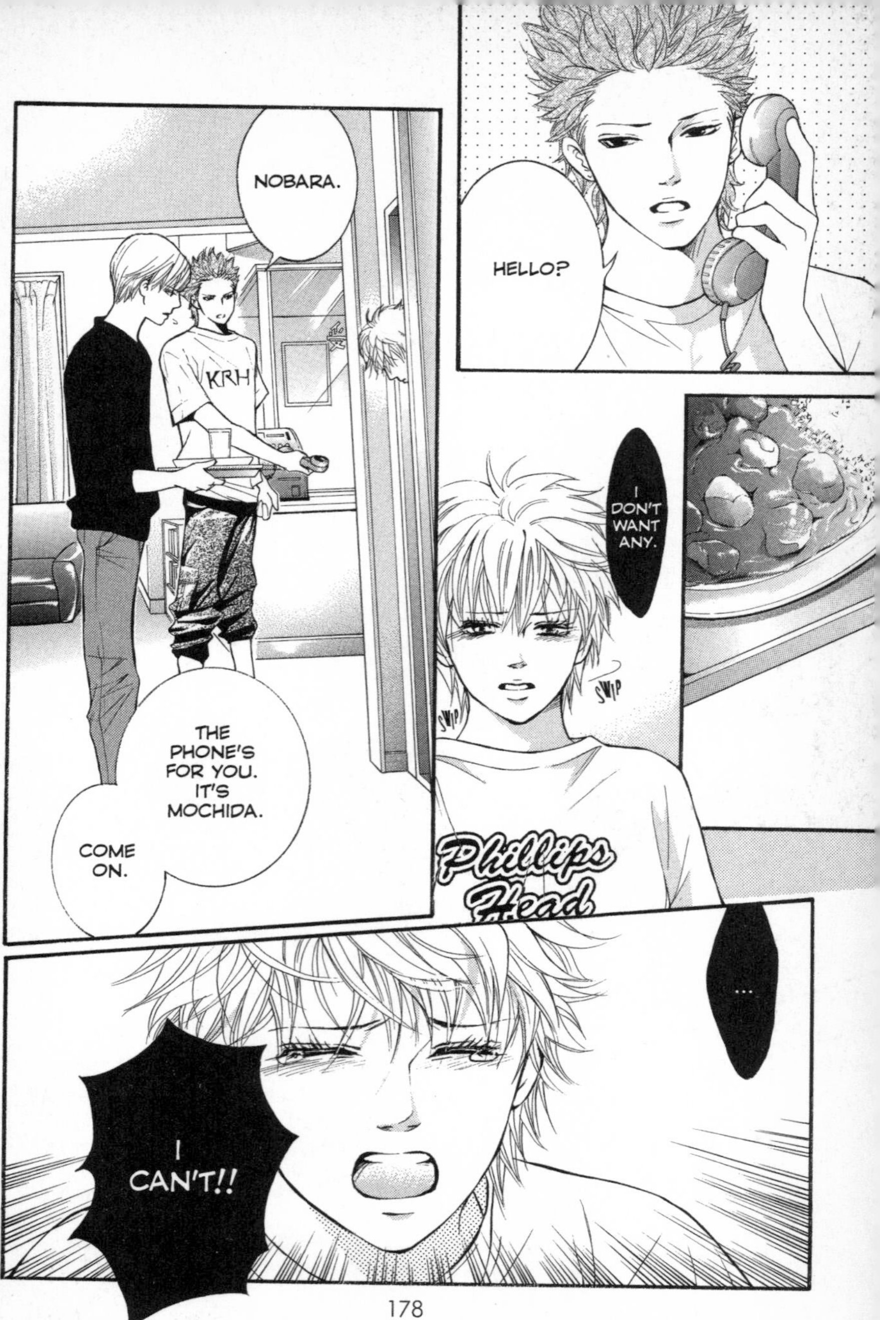
HELLO?
I DON'T WANT ANY.
SWIP
SWIP
Phillips Head
NOBARA.
KRH
THE PHONE'S FOR YOU. IT'S MOCHIDA.
COME ON.
...
I CAN'T!!

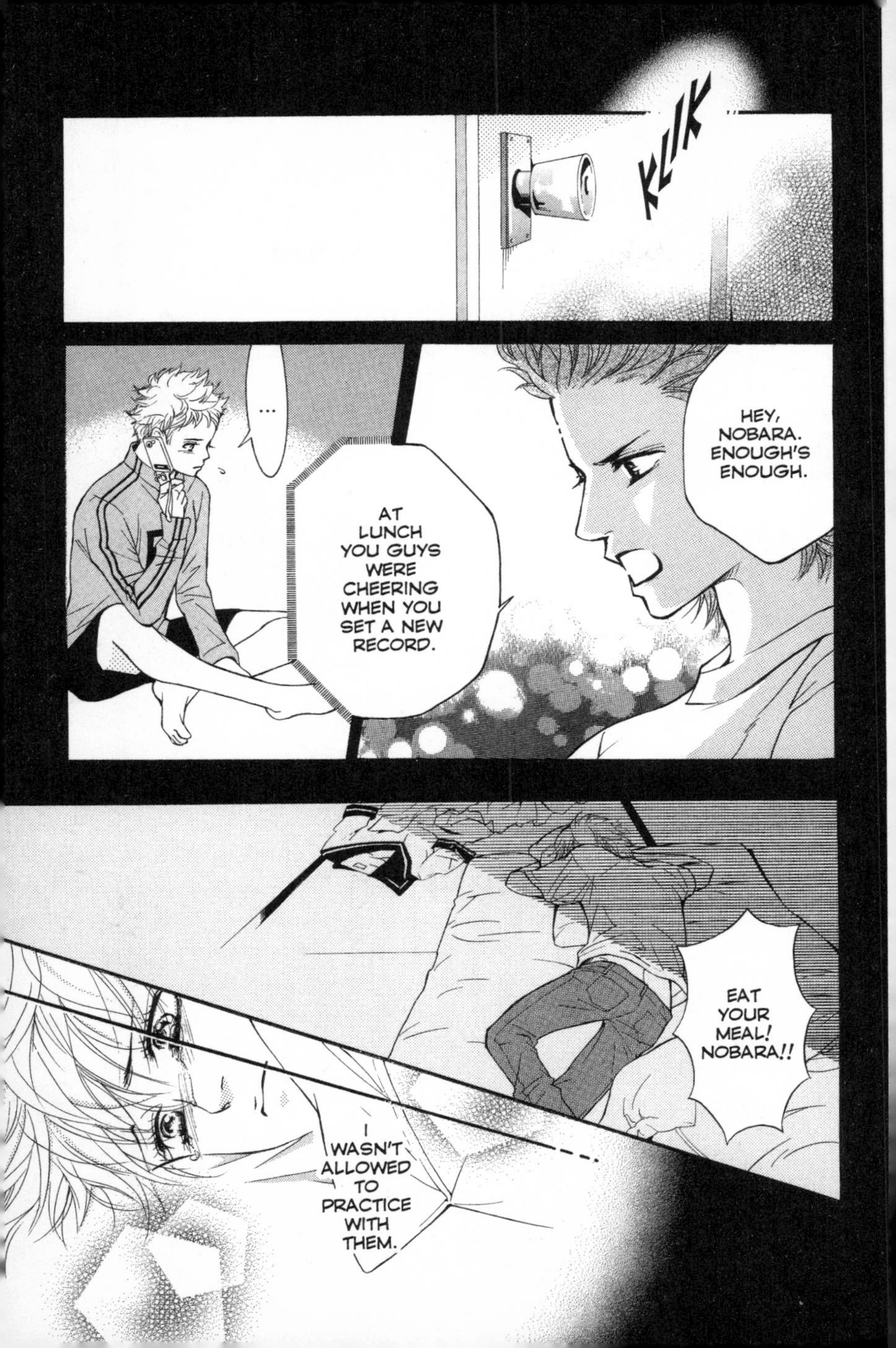
KLIK
HEY, NOBARA. ENOUGH'S ENOUGH.
AT LUNCH YOU GUYS WERE CHEERING WHEN YOU SET A NEW RECORD.
...
EAT YOUR MEAL! NOBARA!!
I WASN'T ALLOWED TO PRACTICE WITH THEM.

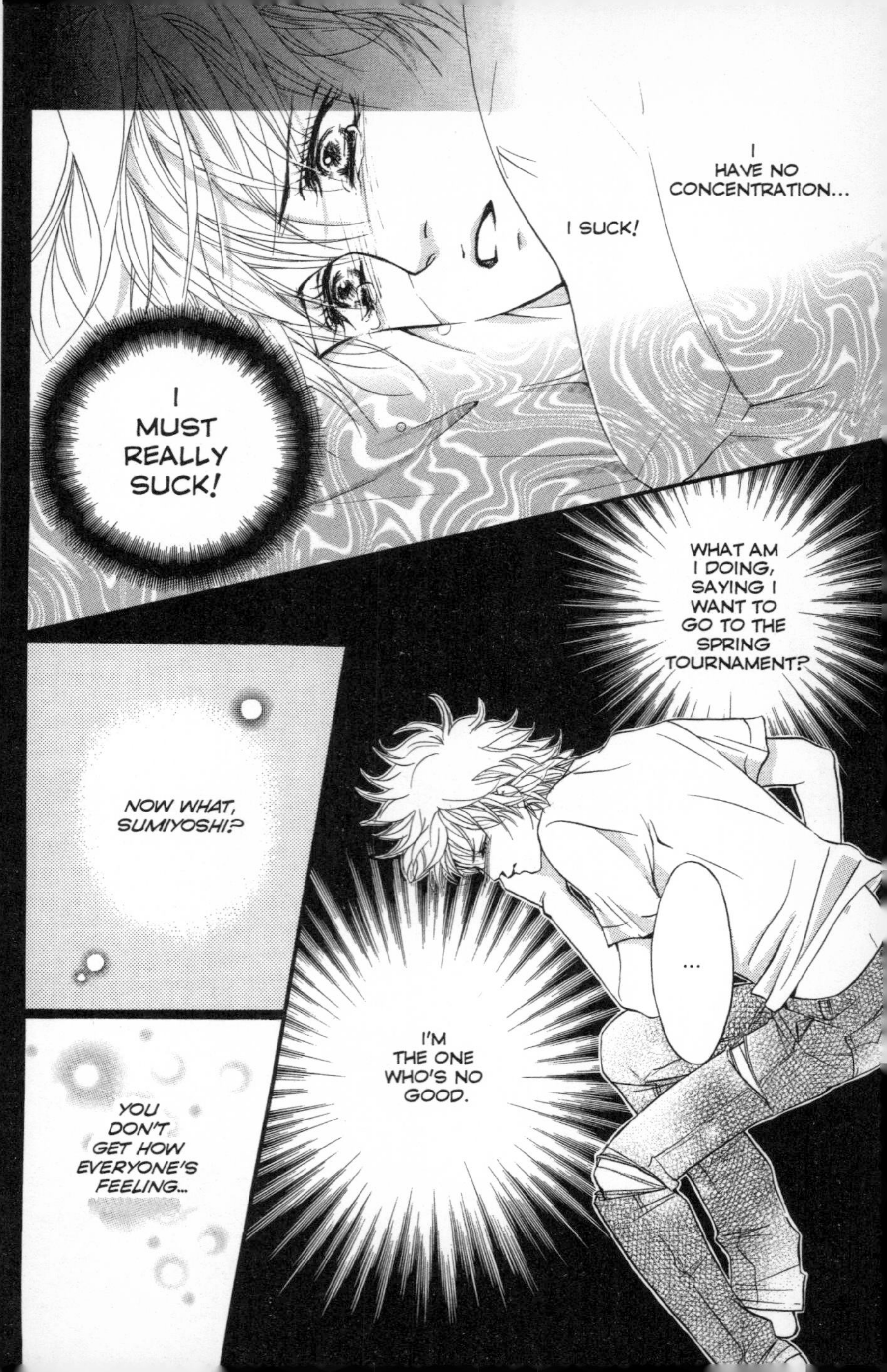
I HAVE NO CONCENTRATION...
I SUCK!
I MUST REALLY SUCK!
WHAT AM I DOING, SAYING I WANT TO GO TO THE SPRING TOURNAMENT?
...
I'M THE ONE WHO'S NO GOOD.
NOW WHAT, SUMIYOSHI?
YOU DON'T GET HOW EVERYONE'S FEELING...

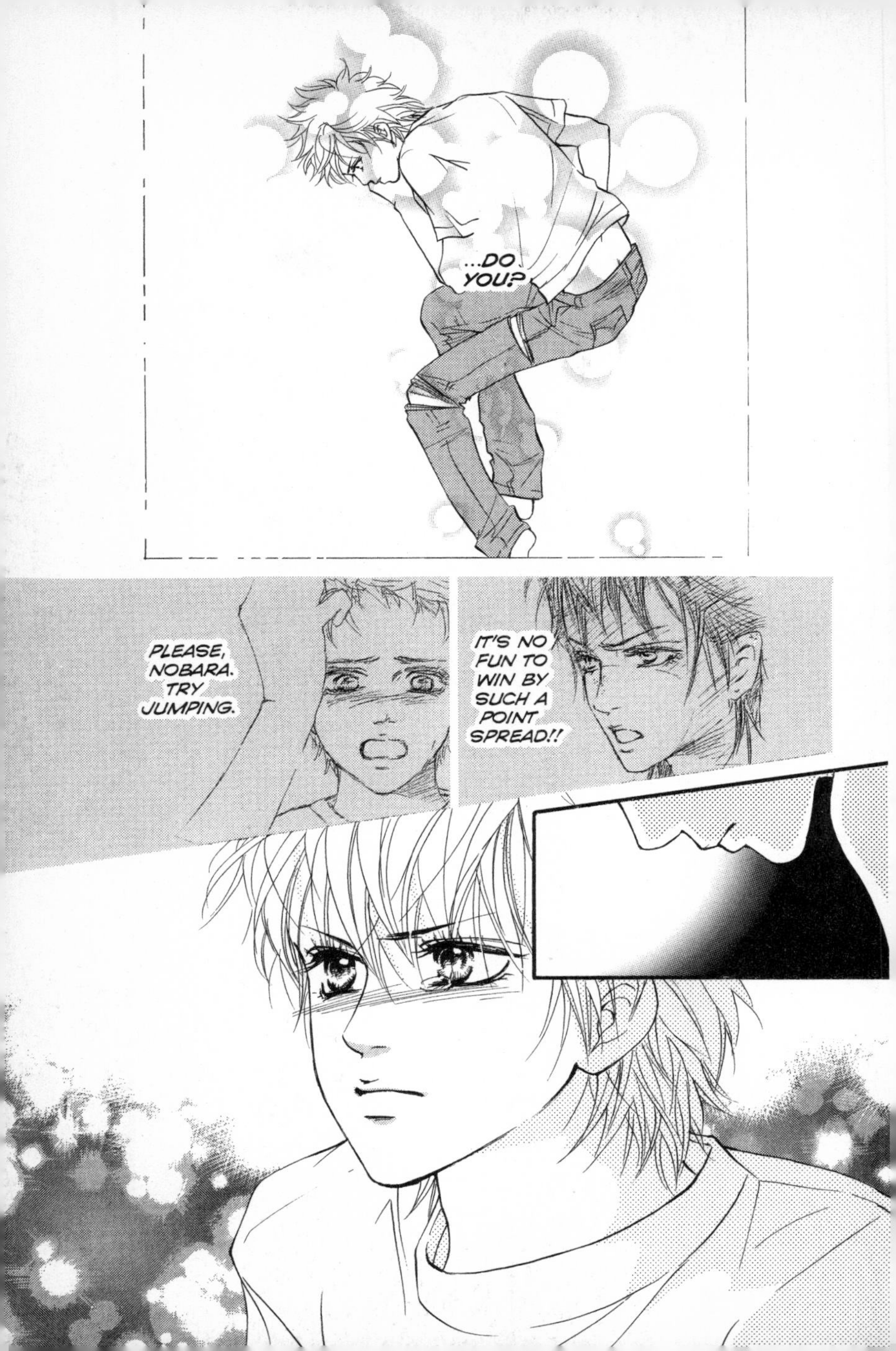
...DO YOU?
IT'S NO FUN TO WIN BY SUCH A POINT SPREAD!!
PLEASE, NOBARA. TRY JUMPING.

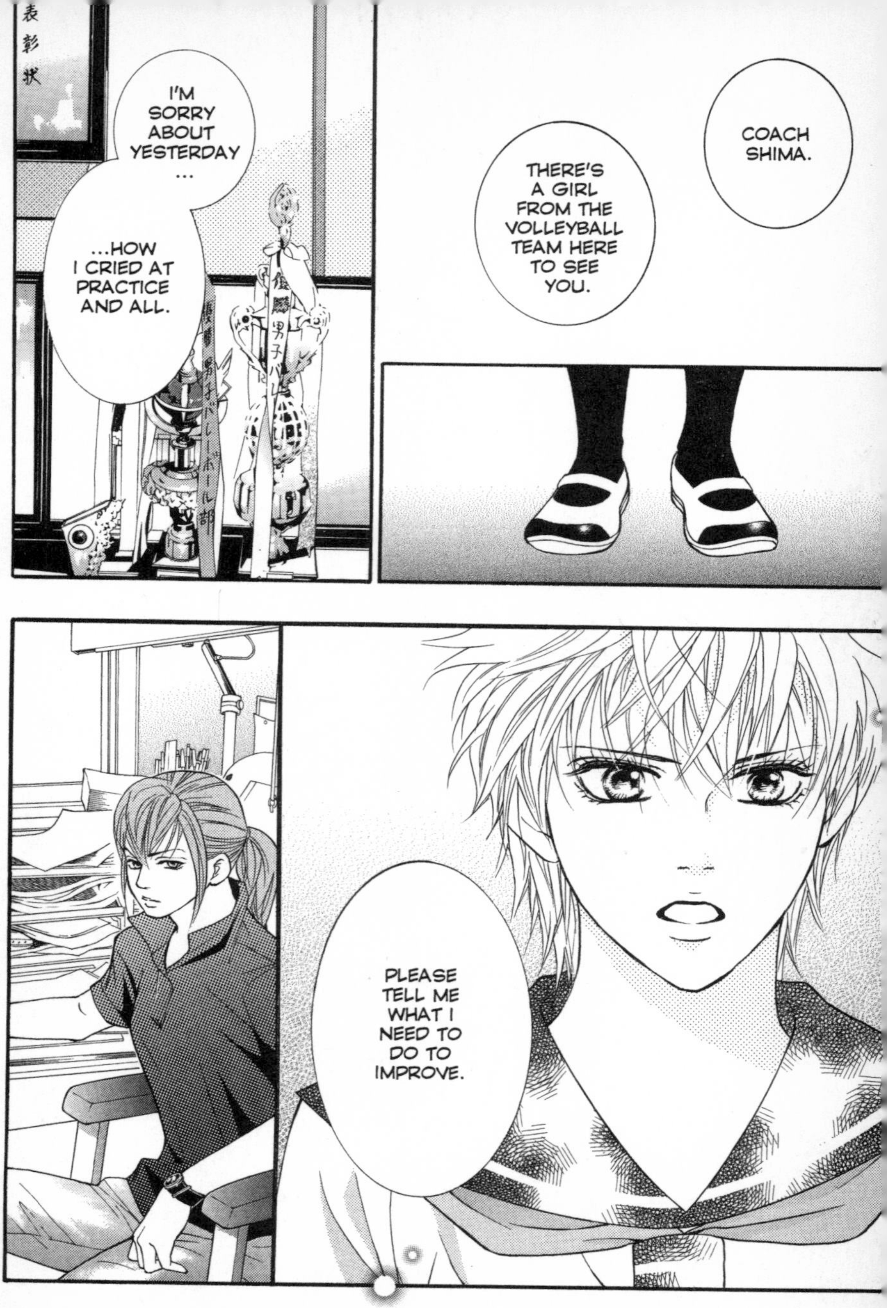
COACH SHIMA.
THERE'S A GIRL FROM THE VOLLEYBALL TEAM HERE TO SEE YOU.
表彰状
I'M SORRY ABOUT YESTERDAY...
...HOW I CRIED AT PRACTICE AND ALL.
PLEASE TELL ME WHAT I NEED TO DO TO IMPROVE.

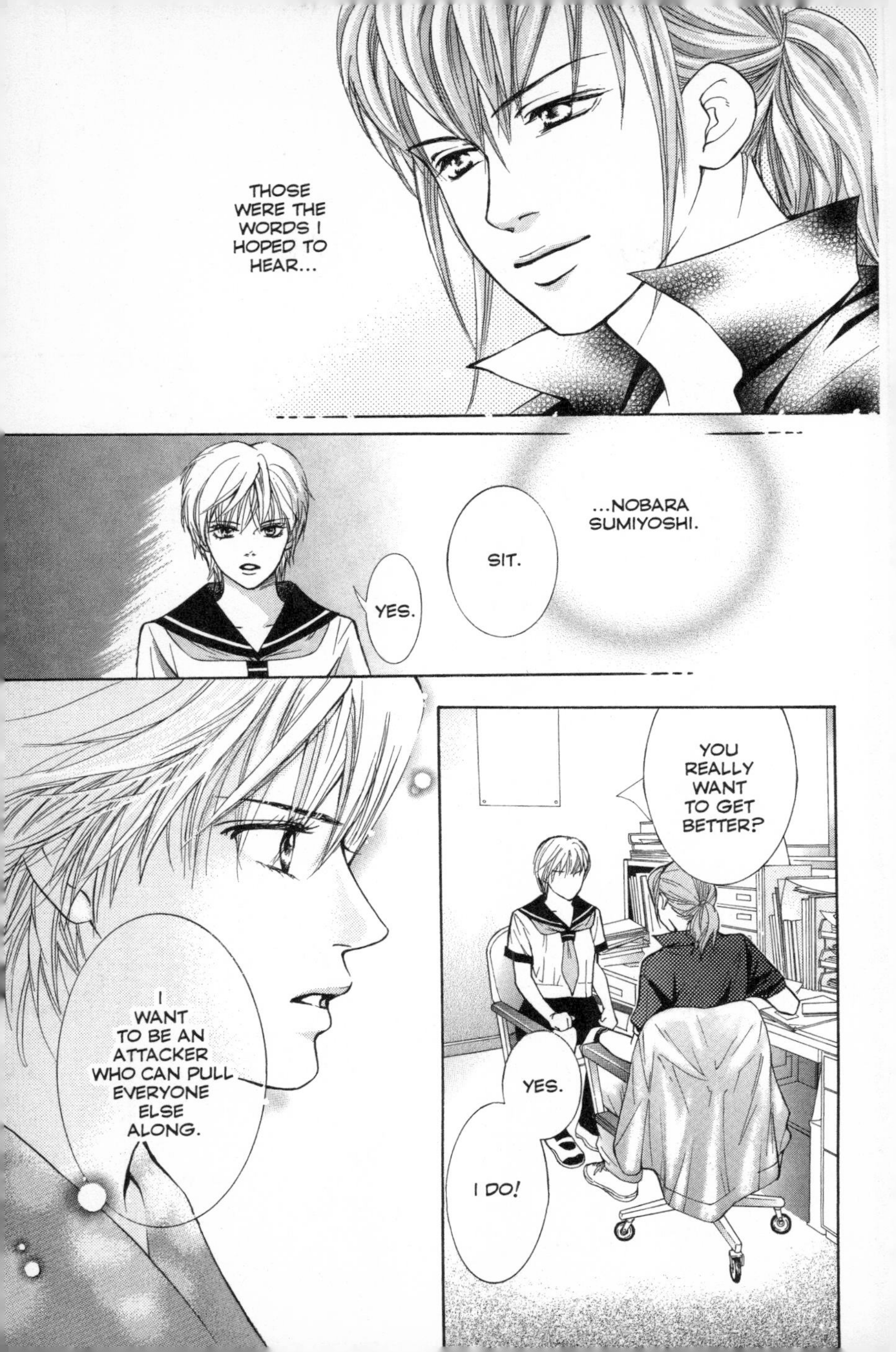
THOSE WERE THE WORDS I HOPED TO HEAR...
...NOBARA SUMIYOSHI.
SIT.
YES.
YOU REALLY WANT TO GET BETTER?
YES.
I DO!
I WANT TO BE AN ATTACKER WHO CAN PULL EVERYONE ELSE ALONG.

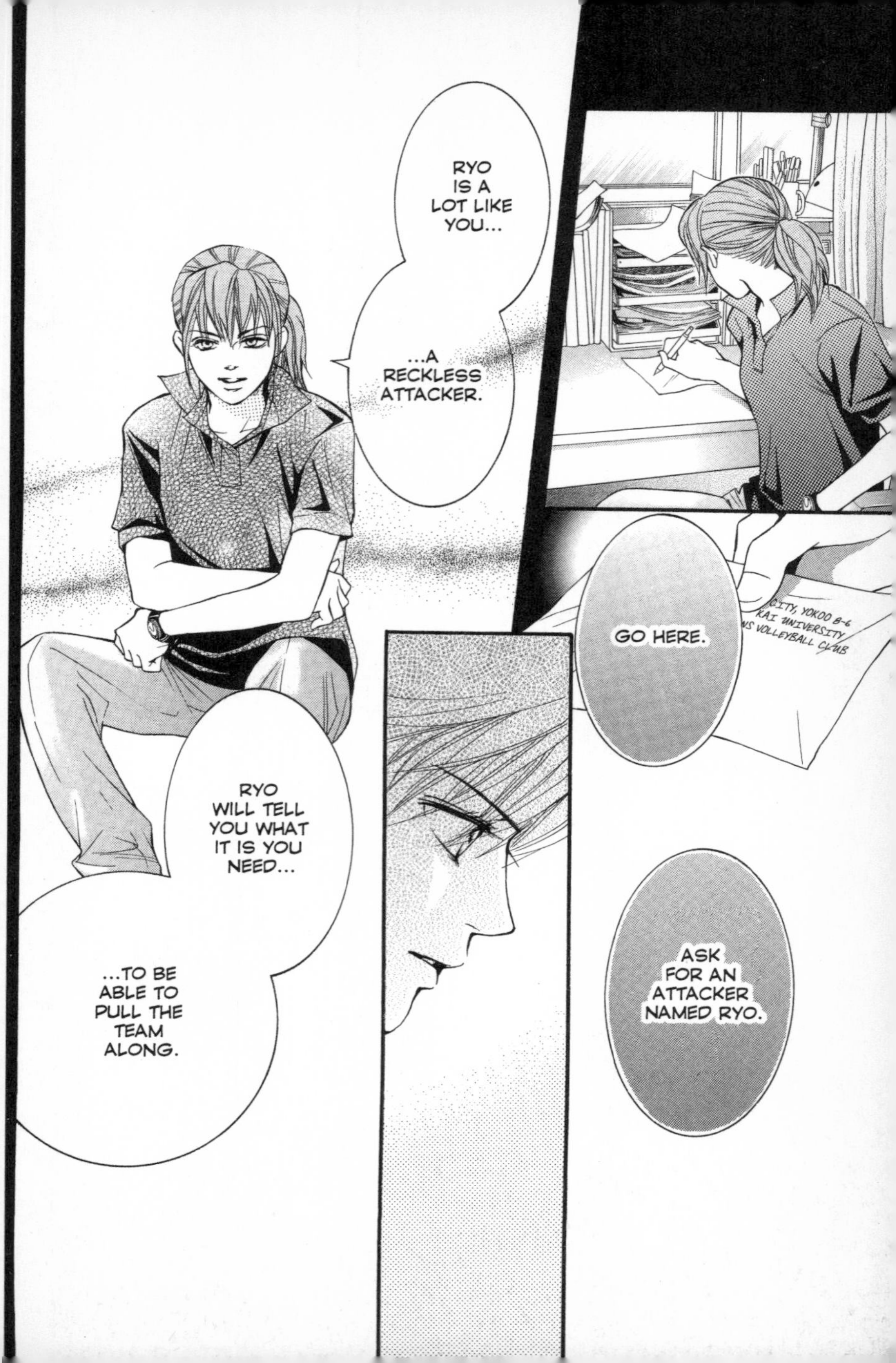
GO HERE.
CITY, YOKOO 8-6
KAI UNIVERSITY
NS VOLLEYBALL CLUB
ASK FOR AN ATTACKER NAMED RYO.
RYO IS A LOT LIKE YOU...
...A RECKLESS ATTACKER.
RYO WILL TELL YOU WHAT IT IS YOU NEED...
...TO BE ABLE TO PULL THE TEAM ALONG.

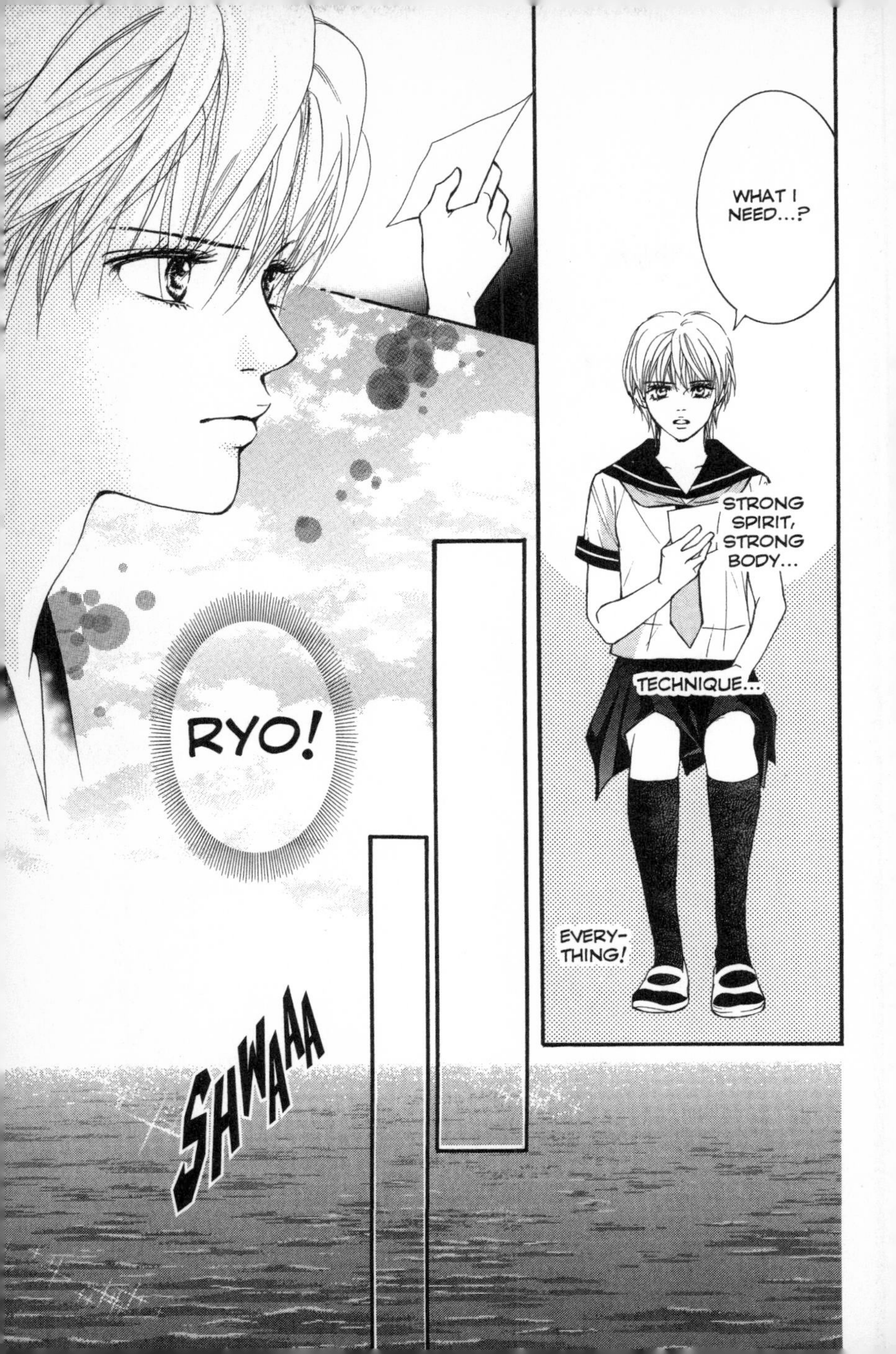
WHAT I NEED...?
STRONG SPIRIT, STRONG BODY...
TECHNIQUE...
EVERY-THING!
RYO!
SHWAAA

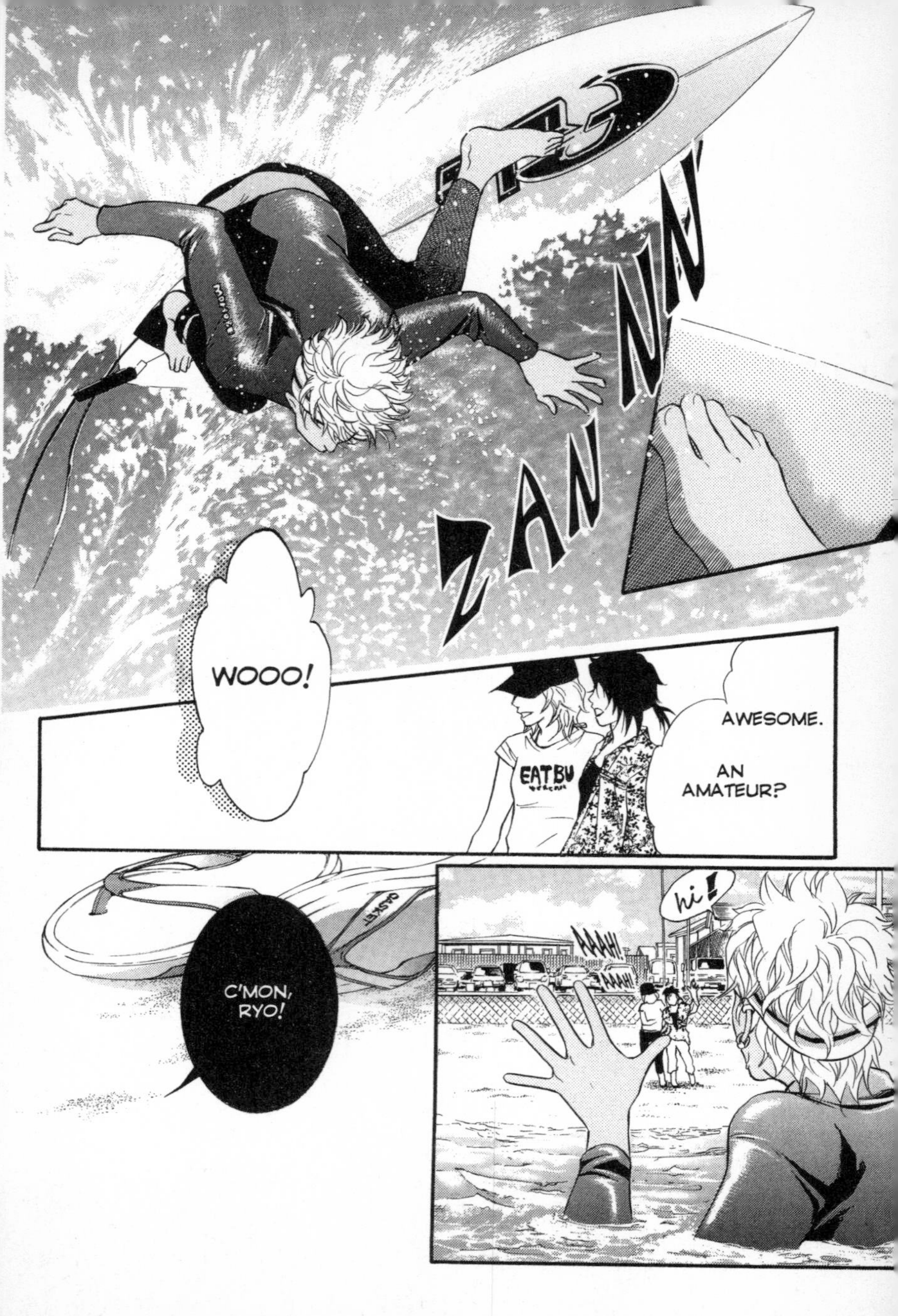
ZAN NAN
WOOO!
AWESOME.
AN AMATEUR?
EATBU
hi!
AAAH!
AAAH!
C'MON, RYO!

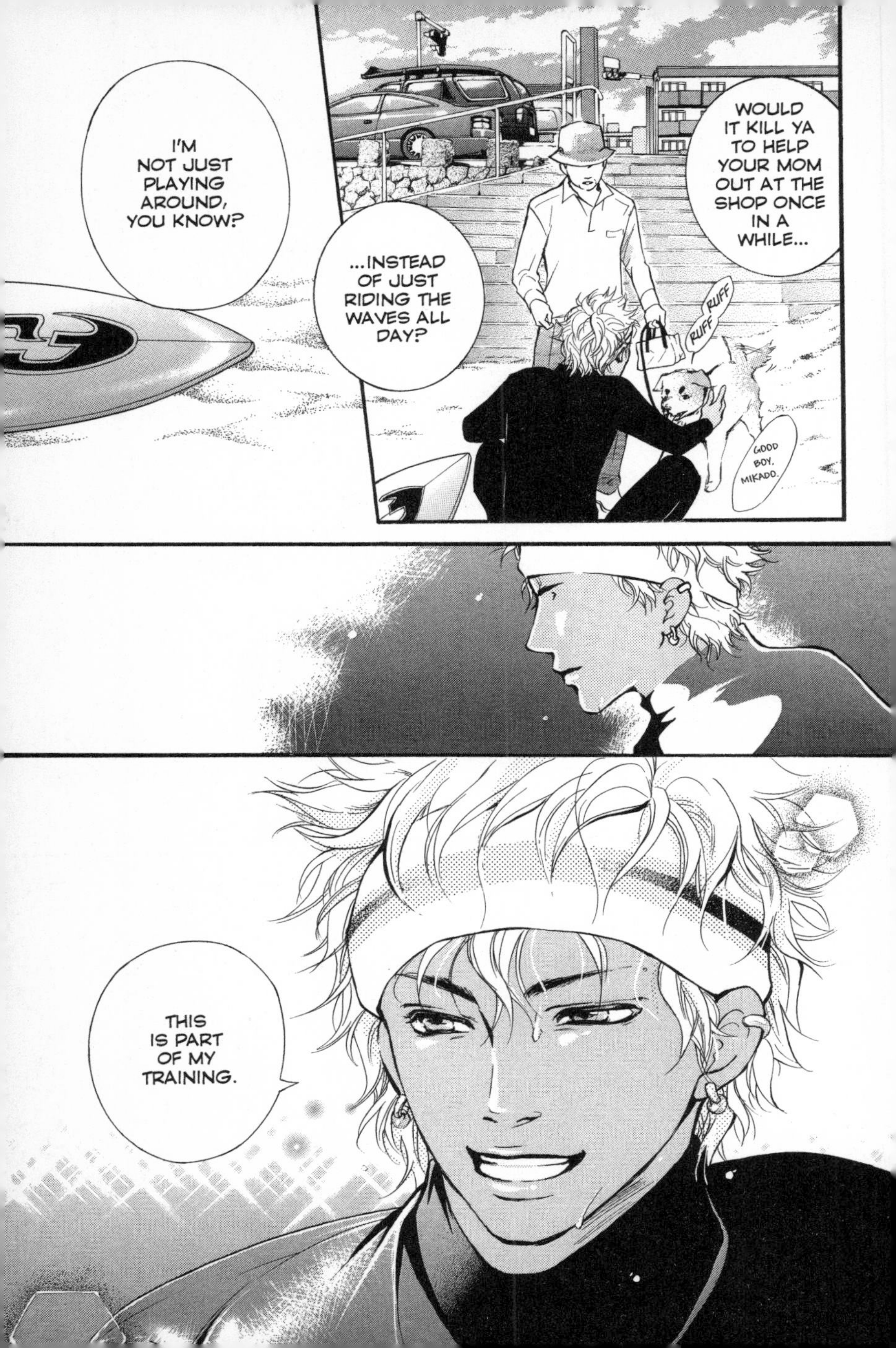
WOULD IT KILL YA TO HELP YOUR MOM OUT AT THE SHOP ONCE IN A WHILE...
...INSTEAD OF JUST RIDING THE WAVES ALL DAY?
RUFF RUFF
GOOD BOY, MIKADO.
I'M NOT JUST PLAYING AROUND, YOU KNOW?
THIS IS PART OF MY TRAINING.

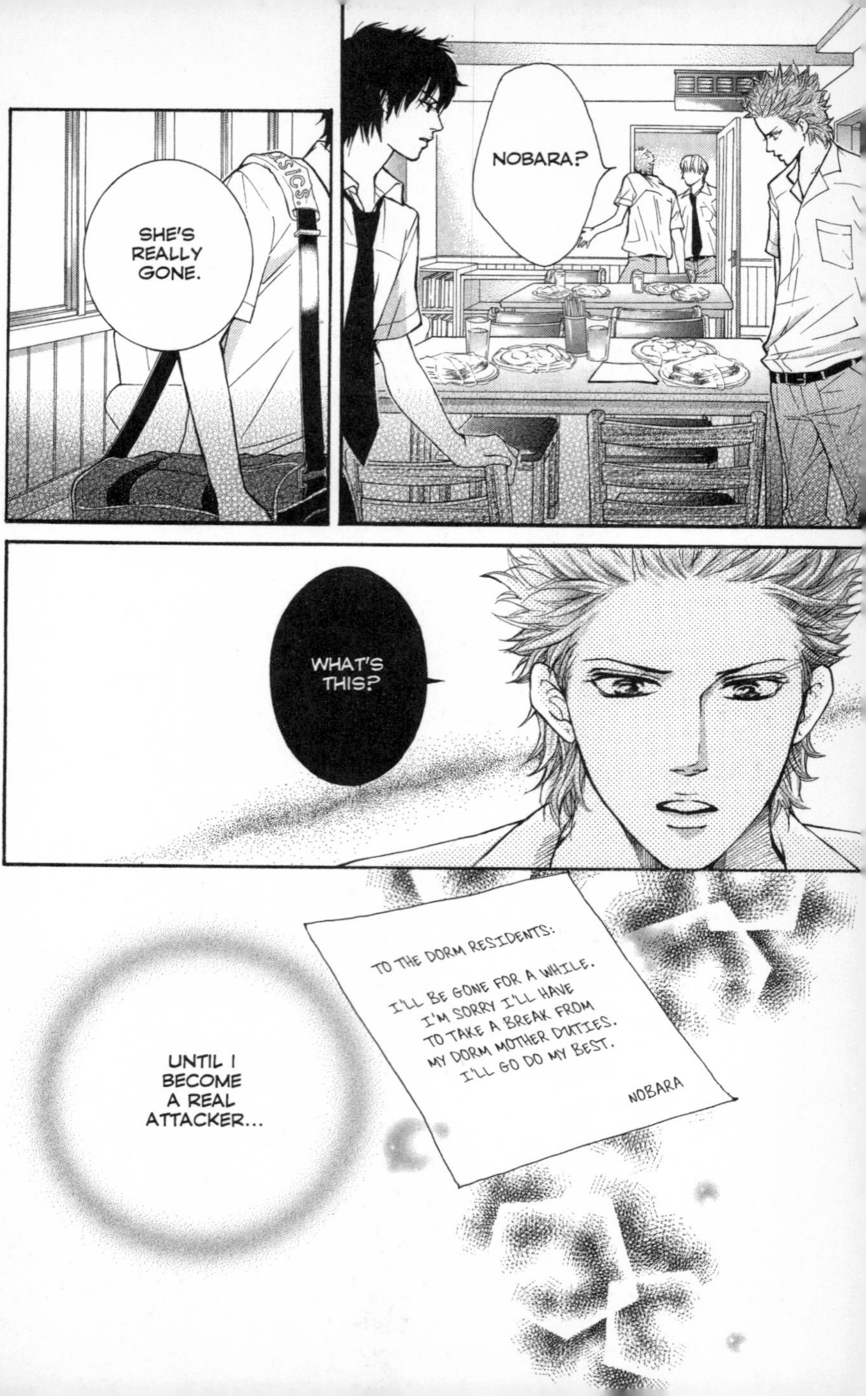
NOBARA?
SHE'S REALLY GONE.
WHAT'S THIS?
TO THE DORM RESIDENTS:
I'LL BE GONE FOR A WHILE.
I'M SORRY I'LL HAVE TO TAKE A BREAK FROM MY DORM MOTHER DUTIES.
I'LL GO DO MY BEST.
NOBARA
UNTIL I BECOME A REAL ATTACKER...

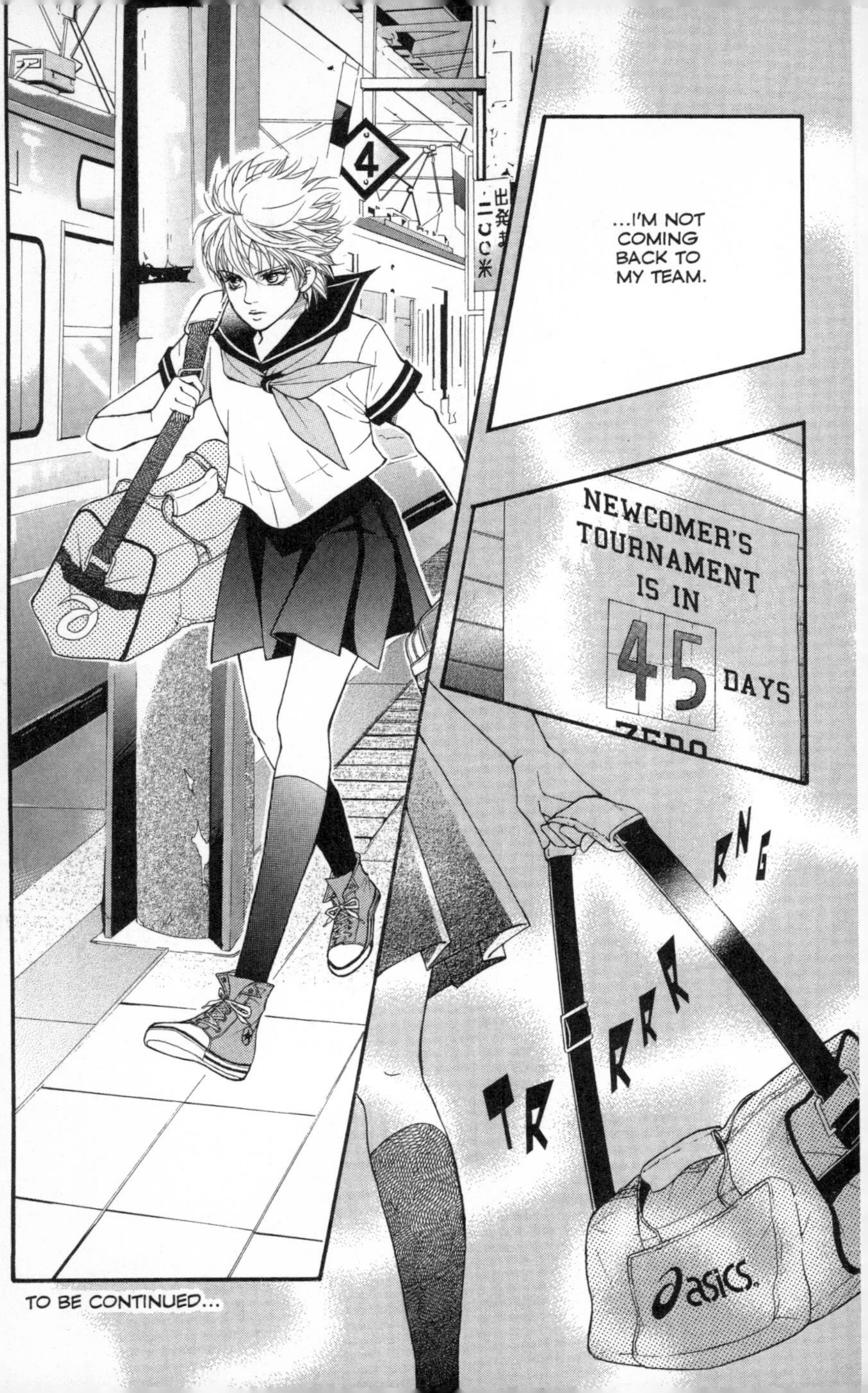
...I'M NOT COMING BACK TO MY TEAM.
NEWCOMER'S TOURNAMENT IS IN 45 DAYS
TRRRR RNG
asics
4

TO BE CONTINUED...

♥I went to a neighborhood shrine and quietly practiced some receives. I started with just trying to pass the ball right back. Yet I couldn't even do that!!! I thought I was doing it exactly as described in the textbook, but the ball kept going in unexpected directions!!! It made me remember how I used to spend gym class praying the serve wouldn't come to me.

—Mitsuba Takanashi, 2006

At age 17, Mitsuba Takanashi debuted her first short story, *Mou Koi Nante Shinai* (Never Fall in Love Again), in 1992 in *Bessatsu Margaret* magazine and now has several major titles under her belt.

Born in the Shimane Prefecture of Japan, Takanashi now lives in Tokyo, where she enjoys taking walks, watching videos, shopping, and going to the hair salon. Takanashi has a soft spot for the Japanese pop acts Yellow Monkey and Hide, and is good at playing ping-pong.

CRIMSON HERO

VOL. 7
The Shojo Beat Manga Edition

This volume contains material that was originally published in English in
Shojo Beat magazine, July–October 2007 issues. Artwork in the magazine may have
been slightly altered from that presented here.

STORY AND ART BY
MITSUBA TAKANASHI

Translation & English Adaptation/Naoko Amemiya
Touch-up Art & Lettering/Mark Griffin
Graphics & Cover Design/Courtney Utt
Editor/Nancy Thistlethwaite

Editor in Chief, Books/Alvin Lu
Editor in Chief, Magazines/Marc Weidenbaum
VP of Publishing Licensing/Rika Inouye
VP of Sales/Gonzalo Ferreyra
Sr. VP of Marketing/Liza Coppola
Publisher/Hyoe Narita

Published by VIZ Media, LLC
P.O. Box 77010
San Francisco, CA 94107

Shojo Beat Manga Edition
10 9 8 7 6 5 4 3 2 1
First printing, December 2007

www.viz.com   store.viz.com

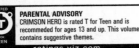

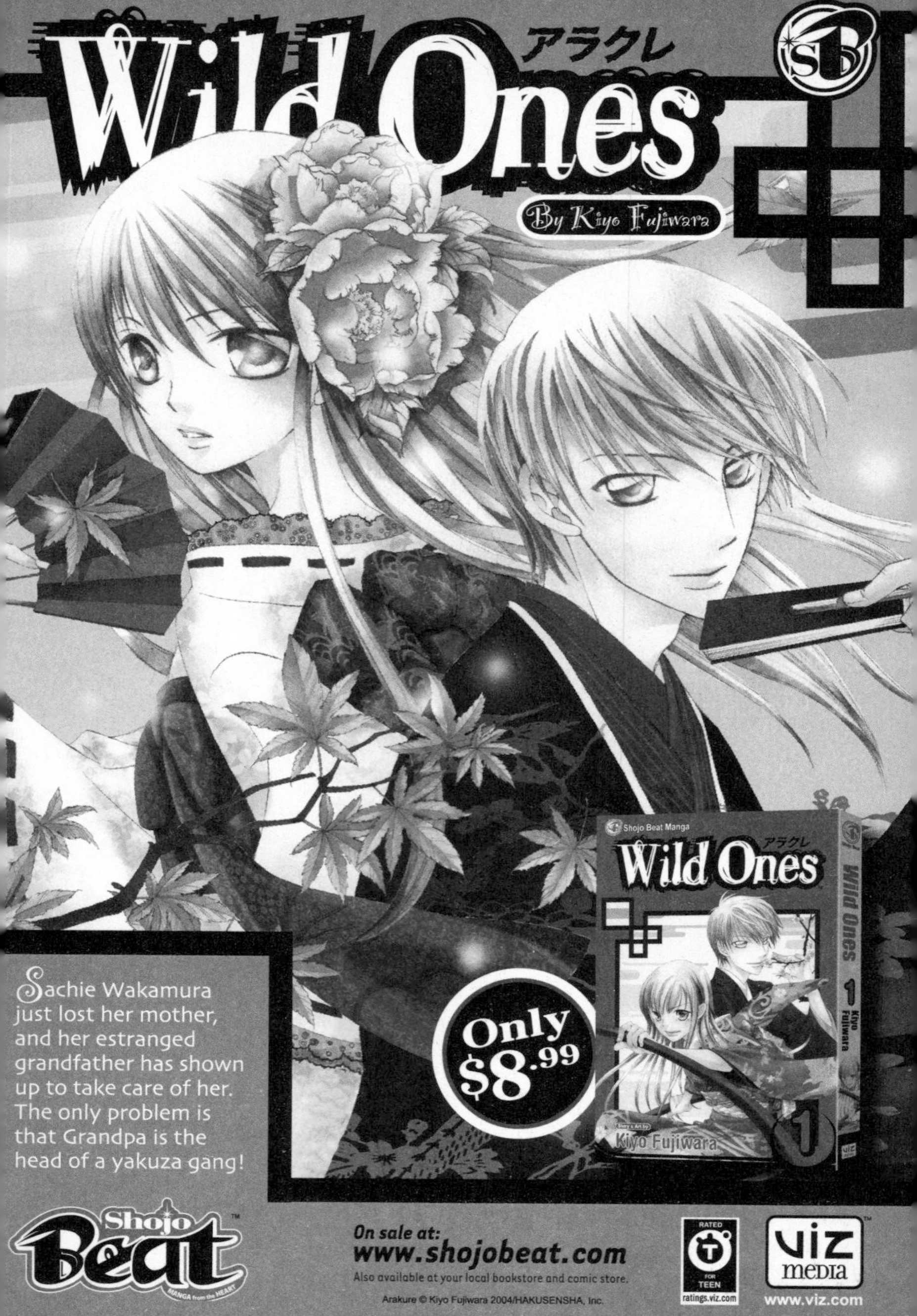
Wild Ones
アラクレ
By Kiyo Fujiwara
Sachie Wakamura just lost her mother, and her estranged grandfather has shown up to take care of her. The only problem is that Grandpa is the head of a yakuza gang!
Only $8.99
Shojo Beat Manga
Wild Ones
Kiyo Fujiwara
Shojo Beat
On sale at:
www.shojobeat.com
Also available at your local bookstore and comic store.
Arakure © Kiyo Fujiwara 2004/HAKUSENSHA, Inc.
RATED T FOR TEEN
ratings.viz.com
VIZ media
www.viz.com

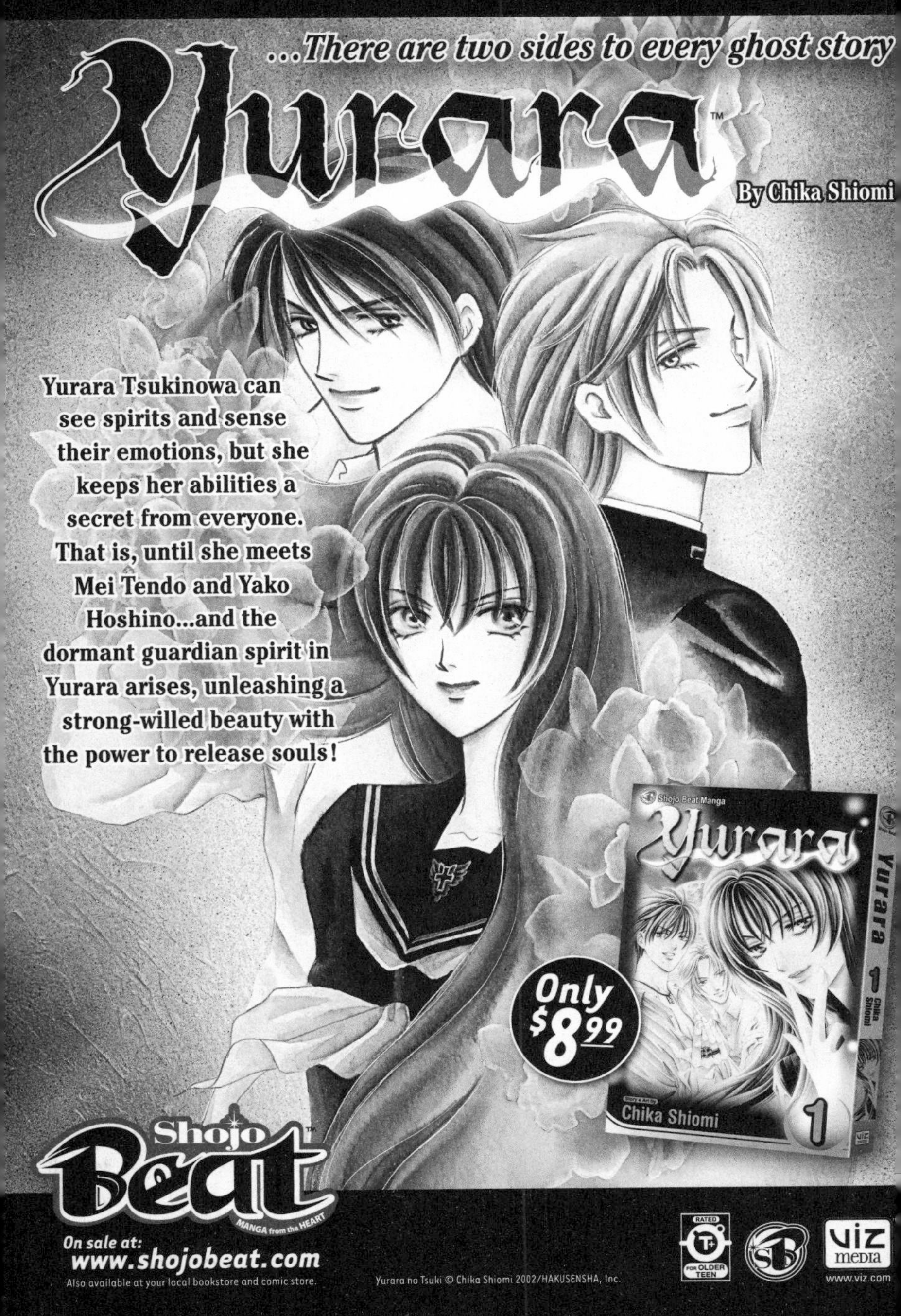
...There are two sides to every ghost story
Yurara™
By Chika Shiomi
Yurara Tsukinowa can see spirits and sense their emotions, but she keeps her abilities a secret from everyone. That is, until she meets Mei Tendo and Yako Hoshino...and the dormant guardian spirit in Yurara arises, unleashing a strong-willed beauty with the power to release souls!
Shojo Beat Manga
Yurara
Chika Shiomi
1
Only $8.99
Shojo Beat™
MANGA from the HEART
On sale at:
www.shojobeat.com
Also available at your local bookstore and comic store.
Yurara no Tsuki © Chika Shiomi 2002/HAKUSENSHA, Inc.
RATED T+ FOR OLDER TEEN
VIZ media
www.viz.com

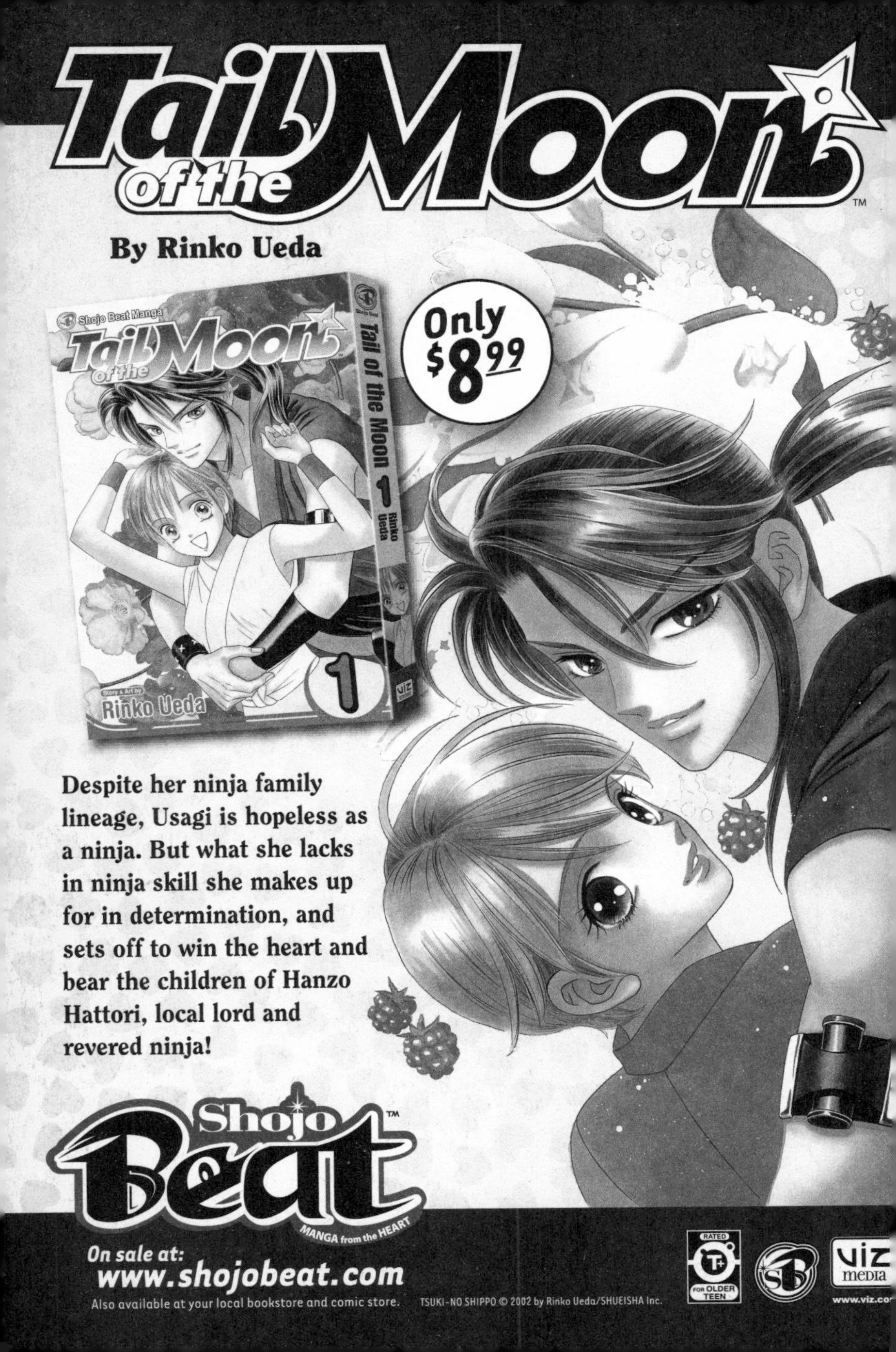

Tail of the Moon™
By Rinko Ueda
Shojo Beat Manga
Tail of the Moon
Tail of the Moon 1 Rinko Ueda
Story & Art by Rinko Ueda
1
Only $8.99
Despite her ninja family lineage, Usagi is hopeless as a ninja. But what she lacks in ninja skill she makes up for in determination, and sets off to win the heart and bear the children of Hanzo Hattori, local lord and revered ninja!
Shojo Beat™
MANGA from the HEART
On sale at:
www.shojobeat.com
Also available at your local bookstore and comic store.
TSUKI-NO SHIPPO © 2002 by Rinko Ueda/SHUEISHA Inc.
RATED T+ FOR OLDER TEEN
VIZ media

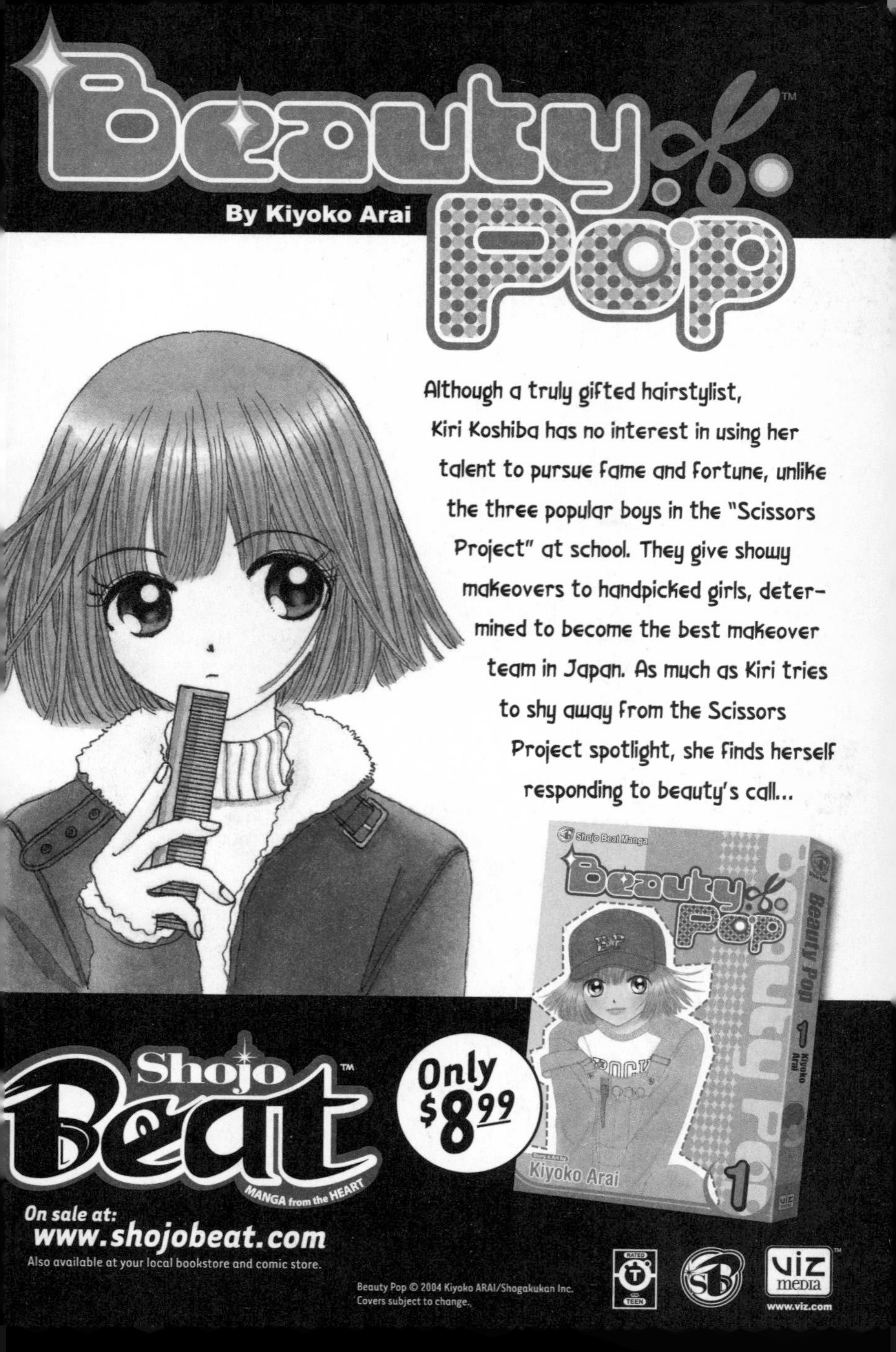
Beauty Pop™
By Kiyoko Arai
Although a truly gifted hairstylist, Kiri Koshiba has no interest in using her talent to pursue fame and fortune, unlike the three popular boys in the "Scissors Project" at school. They give showy makeovers to handpicked girls, determined to become the best makeover team in Japan. As much as Kiri tries to shy away from the Scissors Project spotlight, she finds herself responding to beauty's call...
Shojo Beat Manga
Beauty Pop
Kiyoko Arai
1
Shojo Beat™
MANGA from the HEART
Only $8.99
On sale at:
www.shojobeat.com
Also available at your local bookstore and comic store.
Beauty Pop © 2004 Kiyoko ARAI/Shogakukan Inc.
Covers subject to change.
RATED T TEEN
VIZ media
www.viz.com

Tell us what you think about Shojo Beat Manga!

Our survey is now available online. Go to:

shojobeat.com/mangasurvey

Help us make our product offerings better!

THE REAL DRAMA BEGINS IN...